Beyond Separate Education
Quality Education
for All

Beyond Separate Education
Quality Education
for All

edited by

Dorothy Kerzner Lipsky, Ph.D.
Senior Research Scientist
Office of Sponsored Research
The Graduate School and University Center
City University of New York
and *Assistant to the Superintendent*
Bellmore (NY) Public Schools

and

Alan Gartner, Ph.D.
Professor and Director
Office of Sponsored Research
The Graduate School and University Center
City University of New York

·P·A·U·L·H·
BROOKES
PUBLISHING CO

Baltimore • London • Toronto • Sydney

Paul H. Brookes Publishing Co.
Post Office Box 10624
Baltimore, Maryland 21285-0624

Copyright © 1989 by Paul H. Brookes Publishing Co., Inc.
All rights reserved.
Typeset by The Composing Room of Michigan, Inc., Grand Rapids, Michigan.
Manufactured in the United States of America by
The Maple Press Company, York, Pennsylvania.

Library of Congress Cataloging in Publication Data

Beyond separate education : quality education for all / [edited by]
    Dorothy Kerzner Lipsky and Alan Gartner.
          p.   cm.
      Bibliography: p.
      Includes index.
      1. Special education—United States.   2. Mainstreaming in
    education—United States.   I. Lipsky, Dorothy Kerzner.   II.
    Gartner, Alan.
    LC3981.B48   1989   371.9′046′0973—
    dc19   88-30495
    ISBN 1-55766-017-4

For Daniel,
Our Teacher

Contents

Contributors

Richard Allington, Ph.D.
Professor
State University of New York at Albany
246 Van Wie Point Road
Glenmont, NY 12077

Adrienne Asch, M.S.
New Jersey Bioethics Communication
Post Office Box CN061
Trenton, NJ 08625

Douglas Biklen, Ph.D.
Professor and Director
Division of Special Education and
    Rehabilitation
Syracuse University
805 South Crouse Avenue
Syracuse, NY 13244-2280

Cathleen Corrigan, M.Ed.
Teacher
Edward Smith Elementary School
Broad and Lancaster Streets
Syracuse, NY 13210

Howard Gardner, Ph.D.
Professor of Education
Longfellow Hall
Graduate School of Education
Harvard University
Appian Way
Cambridge, MA 02138

Alan Gartner, Ph.D.
Professor and Director
Office of Sponsored Research
The Graduate School and University
    Center
City University of New York
33 West 42nd Street
New York, NY 10036

Thomas K. Gilhool, LL.B., M.A.
Secretary of Education
Pennsylvania Department of Education
333 Market Street
Harrisburg, PA 17126-0333

Jenifer Goldman, B.A.
Research Assistant
Longfellow Hall
Graduate School of Education
Harvard University
Appian Way
Cambridge, MA 02138

Harlan Hahn, Ph.D.
Professor of Political Science
University of Southern California
717 11th Street
Santa Monica, CA 90402

Lawrence W. Lezotte, Ph.D.
Director
National Center for Effective Schools
Research and Development
2199 Jolly Road
Okemos, MI 48864

M. Stephen Lilly, Ed.D.
Dean
College of Education
Washington State University
Pullman, WA 99164-2114

Dorothy Kerzner Lipsky, Ph.D.
Senior Research Scientist
Office of Sponsored Research
The Graduate School and University
    Center
City University of New York
33 West 42nd Street
New York, NY 10036

Frank J. Macchiarola, J.D., Ph.D.
Professor of Business
Columbia University, and
President and Executive Director
The Academy of Political Science
3431 Bedford Avenue
Brooklyn, NY 11210

Anne McGill-Franzen, Ed.D.
Lecturer
State University of New York at Albany
246 Van Wie Point Road
Glenmont, NY 12077

Deborah Quick, M.S.
Edward Smith Elementary School
Broad and Lancaster Streets
Syracuse, NY 13210

Wayne Sailor, Ph.D.
Department of Special Education
San Francisco State University
612 Font Boulevard
San Francisco, CA 94132

Susan Stainback, Ed.D.
Professor
College of Education
University of Northern Iowa
Cedar Falls, IA 50613

William Stainback, Ed.D.
Professor
College of Education
University of Northern Iowa
Cedar Falls, IA 50613

Margaret C. Wang, Ph.D.
Professor and Director
Temple University Center for Research in
    Human Development and Education
9th Floor, Ritter Hall Annex
13th Street and Cecil B. Moore Avenue
Philadelphia, PA 19122

Foreword

The interest in American education that has emerged during the past decade has been most heartening. It has represented the rediscovery of the importance of children to our society after a period of neglect. Indeed, in the early 1980s, there was a great deal of indifference toward our children and our schools. Support for public education had waned after the spurt of interest that followed the space travel of the Soviet Union's Sputnik. The quality of schools and education was not of much priority, except for parents who had been experiencing disappointment in the education of their children. This was particularly true in urban America; those of us who were working in education felt an isolation and a lack of interest on the part of American society.

It was the publication of *A Nation at Risk* in 1983 that began the process of developing a broader and widespread interest in American public education. That report, which was produced under the initiative of President Reagan's first Secretary of Education, Terrell H. Bell, spoke so candidly about the state of American public education that many people and institutions felt compelled to increase both their interest and involvement in education. Its basic message—that the most critical institution for the future of our nation was so vulnerable—brought about renewed concern about public schooling. The image, portrayed by the Bell Commission, of the decline in the quality of our schools was both dramatic and compelling. Therefore, the interest in education cut across all political points of view and reached well into the various communities of the nation. An abundant number of studies and reports were subsequently issued, many of them by state governments that felt challenged by the Commission's charges. An outgrowth of the Reagan Administration's cutback in domestic spending was the belief that, although the federal government had identified the problems with American education, there was no willingness on the part of the national administration to solve the problems. As a result, the belief that local and community solutions were essential became widespread. The concern was not restricted to government action, nor was it limited to those who had been traditionally identified with education and school reform. Even American corporations began to investigate their role in assisting with the educational recovery. The response of the business community was enlightened, as groups such as the Committee for Economic Development (CED) moved quickly and intelligently to understand the dimensions of the problems with schools and their implications for the future. The CED's studies, which moved from an analysis of education to an understanding of children and their needs, demonstrated the extent to which that organization was willing to address the problem in direct terms, those that would result in increased financial support for schools and children. To a considerable extent, the CED represented the feelings of many in the business community.

The school reform efforts indicate that there was broad interest by many who have long been considered outsiders in education. Interest on the part of the public has also generated a great deal of reaction within the education community. What remains to be determined, however, is the extent to which the reforms that have been forthcoming are educationally sound and lead to success for our children. It is imperative for us to ask whether our educational practices are actually beneficial to the children. We must be careful that proposed and implemented solutions do not make problems worse.

At the outset, I should indicate my strong doubt about the effectiveness of some school reform activities that have taken place. I think that we have approached many of the solutions without first coming to terms with the real problem of public education in the United States. Despite the standards for student success imposed by school districts and states and the introduction of many school reforms at the district or school level, we are still not seeing the kind of success that we must have if the reform of public education in this country is to have real meaning for our children.

Signs of failing schools and school systems that are not responding are all around us. Even after massive expenditures and efforts to encourage students to stay in school, the dropout rate for all youths is increasing again after a brief period when the rate was stemmed. In many urban areas, the rate exceeds 50% of the student body as more youth drop out of school rather than graduate. Nationally, in 1982, only 51.8% of black students graduated by age 19, and for Hispanic Americans, only 40.3% graduated by the age of 19. It appears that a standard 4-year high school program is becoming the exception rather than the rule.

Adding to the problem, there are far too many signs that students who are staying in school and meeting the standards set out by school officials are not being challenged to excel and are satisfied with marginal success. The national performance level of students on objectively measured tests, such as the SATs, and the findings of scholars such as Diane Ravitch, indicate that students are not reaching their potential in education. There are indications that schools are neither places where sufficient numbers of students are having their needs met, nor feeling an obligation to do outstanding work.

The distressing findings about the condition of children who are attending schools have been more than matched by findings about the condition of children within the larger society. The percentage of poor children in American society has grown from 16% in 1970 to 22% in 1987, and shows no signs of abating. Each day in America, 40 teenage girls give birth to their third child. Since 1960, the delinquency rates of youngsters age 10–17 has increased by 130%. By virtually every indicator used to describe the circumstances of children within American society, the numbers indicate distressingly high levels of severe problems.

Nearly 60% of children born in 1983 will live with only one parent before age 18; 90% of these children will live in female-headed families. A majority of these families will have incomes under $10,000 per year. When we compare the condition of the children of America with the rest of the world, the results are even more disturbing. The infant mortality rate in low income communities of America is continuing to increase—and even outstrip—the rate of some third world nations.

Poor economic and health conditions do not stand alone. They affect the educational performance of our children as well as their basic capacity to learn. You cannot establish more hopeful school settings for America's teenagers without first understanding the seriousness of their problems. For example, the rate of suicide among males age 15–19 was 29% higher in 1980 than in 1973. In 1984, murders took the lives of more black males age 15–24 than any other single cause of death. Furthermore, the United States now has the highest rate of teenage drug use of any industrialized nation of the world. More than 61% of all high school seniors in America have used drugs at some time. Thus, the problems in schools are no longer just speaking out in class, chewing gum, or being late. Instead, the problems consist of handgun use in school, teenage pregnancy, and drug abuse. These are problems that cut across class and race lines, and touch the lives of all of our children.

The deterioration in the quality of public education, the extreme conditions of social and economic poverty affecting the lives of children, and the lack of a basic strategy for improving the condition of children have worked to create an enormous problem for America in the coming century. The school reform movement cannot ignore these social and economic conditions.

The challenge then is not in the reform of the structure of public education alone. The solution does not simply rest in correcting the classrooms, schools, or school districts. This is not to ignore that an enormous amount can—and must—be done in those places. Rather, it is that the current reform measures are largely incomplete, and new ones must be forthcoming if our children are going to be successful. It is also to say that unless we are prepared to change the way we understand and deal with youth, our reforms will not be successful. If we begin to think that Band-Aid solutions are the significant ones, we will be fighting minor battles and at the same time losing major ones.

EDUCATIONAL REFORM

It is my purpose to first analyze some of the reforms that have taken place and offer statistics on how well they have done or can do. Second, I will turn to reforms that are still forthcoming with the strong conviction that effective programs can improve the condition of our children. I do it also out of a belief that all children are equal and can learn. The job of our social institutions—and in the case of education, particularly the schools—is to promote that equality and learning.

In terms of what has already taken place in public education reform, I believe that the most important reforms to date have been those that have come from the School Effectiveness work pioneered by Ronald Edmonds. These reforms emerged by taking a strong exception to the work of scholars who emphasized that socioeconomic factors had a devastating impact on the ability of children to succeed in school. Such arguments gave aid and comfort to those who concluded that the situation within public education was virtually hopeless and served as an excuse for some professionals to explain away the schools' failures. It was Edmonds's research—the results of which he was willing to demonstrate in the New York City schools between 1978 and 1982—which showed that children could learn, despite their socioeconomic conditions, if schools were more effective. Edmonds believed that we already knew how to educate children. The real question for Edmonds was whether we would make that choice to educate them. Edmonds's perspective and optimism were, in large part, responsible for a "can do" attitude on the part of many school professionals. Those schools became laboratories where successful school practices were developed.

Edmonds's five factors (see Chapter 2, this volume) were reduced to hard work in the school on the part of administrators, teachers, and students. Edmonds's strategy was actually one of community building, and concentrated on having people share in the process of defining problems and reaching solutions. Those persons who worked with the School Effectiveness programs that were inspired by the Edmonds model found that they were putting in a great deal more work, but that the work was purposeful, and hence, worth doing. While there were certain "requirements" related to assessment and instructional strategies, they did not develop from administrators and, therefore, made a great deal of sense to the classroom teachers. Unlike so many of the innovations of the 1960s and 1970s that stressed the process of involvement and deemphasized the product of that enterprise, Edmonds wanted concrete results that were reflected in test scores. While Edmonds had strong reservations about most of the tests that had been developed—he believed that the most successful tests were based on teacher input and tested what had actually been taught in the classroom—he was willing to fight for objective measures that would serve as gross indicators of success.

What is particularly appealing about the current School Effectiveness movement is that it concentrates its effort on the school, and empowers those who are part of that school community to influence their children's own success. They are able to accept as a basic creed the fact that all students can learn, and so they look upon each student as a challenge that can be met. The data exist to tell them that other schools, with children similar to theirs, have been successful.

Unfortunately, there have been some serious compromises in the integrity of the Edmonds model. In some cases, it has been used as an excuse for administrators to force change. In others, it has been used as an excuse to support efforts simply to strengthen teacher empowerment within the schools. These compromises, when they have interfered with the basic requirement of the Edmonds model, have been distortions rather than improvements. These changes have been essentially wrong.

Changes in the reform movement have also occurred at the local level. In Rochester, New York, for example, the salary structure has been dramatically enhanced (e.g., a teacher's salary can be as much as $70,000 per year) in return for a commitment of greater teacher productivity and success in working with children. In many cases, the effort to get more effective teachers in the schools has used increased teacher salaries as an incentive. The focus, if on salaries alone, will not produce the effective teachers that our youngsters need. While increases in teacher salaries have, in general, been justified, the attempt to tie salaries to increased teacher quality must be accompanied by a plan and by guarantees to make certain that it happens. The test of effectiveness is when the teachers are required to produce, and actually do produce, more substantial results in terms of their success with the youngsters. In essence, there must be a strong sense of reward for achievement. School districts must be willing to say what they want accomplished and then reward the teachers who help to achieve it. There must be improvement in important measures: the amount of time that students and teachers spend together, the improvement in student performance on standardized tests over time, more positive evaluations by students of the commitment of their teachers, and increased teacher and student attendance. These are not all of the possible measures, and, in fact, they may not be the most important ones for a particular community. As Edmonds's work implies, it is the community itself that will help design the most appropriate outcome measures. In any event, the surest sign of progress is that the performance of students and teachers is dealt with honestly and intelligently.

Other reform steps have included state mandates and state regulations enacted to tighten academic standards. These reforms have been widespread and have had mixed results. Very often, they have less than a realistic sense of what can and should be done, and have often been imposed as if the institutional arrangements that are necessary to implement reform were not a factor at all. An example of this type of reform was one introduced several years ago in New York State that required 2 years of foreign language instruction for students in vocational programs in the New York City public schools. Given the need for substantial education in technical areas and limited time available, the relative importance of foreign language study for a student in a career program is, to my mind, certainly debatable. There is, as well, a great deal of hesitancy on the students' part to add foreign languages to the list of skills they must master. But the most critical reason for not imposing the language requirement at this time is the inability of the school system to ensure that the student in the vocational school can be provided the foreign language instruction necessary to meet the requirement. This is due to the fact that there are simply not enough foreign language teachers in service, and those who are licensed to teach foreign languages have not generally been assigned to vocational schools. Thus, the system is not able to deliver sufficient assistance for many students so that they can satisfactorily meet the state's language requirement. Thus, the State Education Department, in establishing a "higher" standard, is actually putting into place one that cannot be met. Even more significantly, with today's students questioning the suitability of schools to meet their needs, what can the justification be for imposing a requirement that hardly meets the students' needs? The new requirements appear to be an educational improvement; in truth, they have strong negative consequences. If a former Schools' Chancellor approaches the reform so critically, and sees it as a form of self-protection for the State Education Department, rather than as a measure intended to assist youngsters, one wonders how the average vocational high school student sees these efforts.

In many places, the school reform movement has been proceeding at a tremendous rate to require that the students produce better results in the classroom. From 1980 to 1987, 45 of the 50 states raised their minimum requirements for high school graduation, 42 of the states did so in mathematics, and 34 states did so in science. In some states, we are seeing signs of success, although it is by no means clear that the success will be long lasting or that it represents a foundation upon which other successes can be built. In California, for instance, from 1983 to 1987, the number of students taking 3 or more years of mathematics is up by 15%, and the number of students taking 3 or more years of science is up 20% over the same period. But what happens if the percentage of students succeeding in schools is diminished by the heightened standards?

From 1983 to 1987, 24 states, most of them in the South, have adopted differing versions of broad reform packages with demands for higher standards for students and/or staff. Thirty-eight of the states have taken steps to alter the ways in which teachers are recruited, tested, assigned, retained, promoted, or compensated. This interest and attention has been strengthened by financial support to the schools as well. There has been a great infusion of funding, particularly at the state level, which has resulted in a growth of education since 1980 by 26%.

The results of increased attention to standards have, in many cases, reflected the initiative of governors who have been committed to the development of more effective schooling within their states. Their efforts have included the involvement of business, the overhauling of state education departments, the infusion of new funds, and the increase in public attention to the matters of education. These governors have served on regional and national task forces and have worked with their colleagues in making education an important part of the agenda of state government. Many of these governors are no longer in their positions, but they have left a significant legacy for their colleagues. Such leaders include Governors M. White (D-TX), B. Babbitt (D AZ), L. Alexander (R-TN), T. Kean (R-NJ), and R. Riley (D-SC). While much of the innovation has come from school systems in the South, where the need was the greatest, it has included all parts of the nation and has been led by both Democrats and Republicans.

It is clear to me that many of the trends toward school reform will continue. There is sufficient feeling within the school community that effective schools, and even effective school districts, that concentrate on the needs of youngsters and expect to be effective, can and will succeed. There is also an eagerness at the state level to accept the challenge of educating and caring for youngsters. The Chief State School Officers, who are now leading state education departments nationally, are developing a "can do" philosophy that will challenge bureaucracies and produce educational results on behalf of children. For example, State Superintendents T. Gilhool (PA), D. Hornbeck (MD), B. Castor (FL), G. Tirozzi (CT), and S. Cooperman (NJ) are determined to bring improvement in schooling to their states and have already met with some success.

The overall strategies and trends in several of the states are clear enough. We can expect to see: the promotion of collaboration with outside groups and interests, especially universities and the private sector; increased pressure for student performance to be improved; stronger links to jobs programs and economic development agendas; and greater efforts to reach the students who are not succeeding in their studies (e.g., the at-risk students). The Chief State School Officers see the reform agenda as being in their hands, and they are increasingly putting pressure on school districts within their states to adopt strategies to reach more at-risk youngsters. While this is still not a universal phenomenon, it is clear that more of the state chiefs are becoming convinced of the need to put education reform in effect.

EDUCATING STUDENTS WITH SPECIAL NEEDS

While it is clear that the nation's agenda has included education, we are not yet properly attentive to the needs of students who are not succeeding or those who are often outside of our attention. Indeed, the literature of school reform is regrettably silent about students who are labeled handicapped. As we have moved to evaluate and place in educational programs enormous numbers of students with disabilities, there has been little attention paid to the quality of the educational programs of these youngsters once they have been placed. For example, when I visited schools, I was often encouraged by administrators to avoid special education classes. In such schools, while administrators were eager to show how they were engaged in effective educational programs, it was as if students with disabilities did not exist. Placing the education of youngsters with handicapping conditions on the agenda of school reform is an undertaking of considerable importance and difficulty, since the desire to limit our responsibility to these students is enormous. Former Secretary of Education Bell, in remarking on the progress of our efforts at school improvement, has said that the reform of education in America has helped, "70% of the students, but not affected the 30% at-risk."

Those who have been excluded from participation in the benefits of citizenship demand to be placed in positions of equality. They want to vote, exercise property rights, or be admitted to a place of public accommodation. Such was the long fought struggle for the education of children with handicapping conditions. It was PL 94-142, the Education for All Handicapped Children Act, 1975, that granted those youngsters access to education, and because of that important grant of civil rights, American elementary and secondary schooling has been significantly altered, and improved.

The passage of PL 94-142 has meant that the forces that are urging positive change for children with handicapping conditions have had to reflect upon the meaning of that victory. In fact, there are disagreements among those who want to do the very best for children. The disagreements come about as they struggle to define what it is that represents "best practice." Many have sought the extension of PL 94-142 to provide increased benefits and services for children with an expansion of the definition of "handicapping condition," so that large numbers of children in need qualify for special services by virtue of their handicap. Many have embraced these services as separate education and have urged that real reform be the provision of services. For many advocates, and not only advocates in education, the measure of our care and commitment as a society is the funding that we provide in order to meet the needs of those in distress.

As compelling as it is to urge that more resources be committed to public education, it has become increasingly clear that more funding is not the answer. Make no mistake: while funding certainly is a part of the answer, it is not the whole answer. The answer lies in improving the quality of education for all children, and in having youngsters with handicapping conditions participate in the benefits that come from that improvement. Indeed, the purpose of this book is to promote the cause of education of students with disabilities within the context of education reform for all children. The authors are strongly committed to the cause of children. They are not satisfied with the progress that has been made because they know that so much more can be done if we, as a society, make the effort to improve the education condition. Therefore, they advocate on behalf of all children.

In addressing strategies that can work on behalf of children, there are several important issues. Here, I will detail seven. The first of these is that our solutions must be based upon confidence in the ability of all children to be successful. That confidence must motivate and inspire any of the reforms that are introduced. Such a belief in all of the children will ensure that we do not exclude from our educational reform efforts students with special needs. Our models for excellence must be inclusive and ensure that all students have a place in them.

A second feature of school reform is that it must be credible for educators, students, and their parents. Far too many students today regard school as a place where hostile things happen and where they are not well treated or understood. Too many students have not been dealt with in a decent manner, nor have they been encouraged to overcome their deficiencies. Instead, they are often ridiculed and made to feel incapable and insignificant. They do not want to attend school because it is already clear to them that they are not wanted. An immediate step must be the infusion of resources into activities that have strong and positive relationships with youngsters, most especially, extracurricular activities and guidance services. The effort must be made to make the issue of schooling a matter of personal attention.

A third feature for school reform must include the introduction of parents and volunteers into the school setting. For years, the role of parents in the process of public education was minimal. The parent's responsibility was basically viewed, by the professional, as one of bringing the student to school. While parents have formal roles to play in the implementation of PL 94-142 and in the mandates of some school districts that require

Parent-Teacher or Parent Associations in each school, parents have not been fully included in education. The role for parents cannot be fully prescribed here, but the primary reform that can occur is that which welcomes and encourages parents, one in which their participation is considered to be a positive event for the school community and one where the school makes those arrangements necessary to encourage increased parental involvement.

The introduction of volunteers who wish to be part of the education of our children should also be encouraged. Community groups and organizations, representatives of business and labor organizations, and organizations of senior citizens and retired persons should be made to feel welcomed in the school and should be made part of the support community that provides assistance to youngsters. When the people who are part of these groups feel that the schools welcome them and that they can be of benefit to children, then the schools and the community will benefit from this participation. In the 1990s, the school reform movement will be considered more successful if we accept the participation of parents and volunteers in the activities of the schools. Strengthening the schools requires the assistance and participation of the surrounding community.

Fourth, school reform should include a reconceptualization of the role of education. All too often, we think that education is restricted to what takes place within the school. In actuality, student learning occurs in many places that should also be integrated into the educational process. One of the most important of these activities involves youth employment and jobs for school-age youngsters after school and during summer vacations. Research indicates that combining work with school there is an increase in learning and improved employment opportunities after graduation. Successful cooperative education programs that are now in existence in many school districts across the country reflect these results. At the present time, our schools are not teaching youngsters how to prepare for adult life, and all too often, student competencies do not include the barest essentials about the world of work. The values of the work experience and the preparation for work are lessons that the students want, and more importantly, need.

But it is not the private sector alone that should have some essential contact with the school system. The government also must begin to pay more attention to the school as the locus for services to children. For example, we have seen positive results for youngsters in the development of universal feeding programs at breakfast and lunch. There is need for more essential health and mental health services to be delivered at the school. These include social service agencies and community recreation programs that must be coordinated with school programs to address the needs of "latch key" children. There are major battles yet to be waged within the bureaucracies that serve children in order to make the services that are provided more effective within the schools.

Fifth, school reform must define "higher expectations." Students are often criticized for not being willing or able to do acceptable work. The reason is not that students are unable to respond to an appropriate challenge, but rather that school personnel refuse to put that challenge forward and to see it through. The answer lies in providing challenges that have meaning. This is clear enough in terms of reading, writing, and mathematics at the elementary school level, however, it becomes more difficult when it gets to the high school level. Students often are required to take classes and meet required course distributions that have been in place for so long that the reason for taking them has been lost in time. These classes and the requirements must be reviewed, and not with a view toward an abstract notion of higher standards. Those standards must have a strong justification in terms of what students in the 1990s need. If that is done, students, parents, and teachers can be expected to believe that the requirements are both purposeful and beneficial.

Sixth, the reform agenda must include the need to build a "community." The aspect of the School Effectiveness Program that was most intriguing to me was the interaction within the school community. While Edmonds was quite convincing about the factors that were the key to a successful school, the sense of community that was engendered by school activities had the most appeal for me. Also, when I see schools at the high school level that are performing well for the students, it is always clear that the students and staff feel a sense of ownership in the school. Signs of the school as a community include: when teachers were pleased to stay after class, when students had to be literally thrown out of the building so that they could get home for supper, when every corner of the building was used by clubs and organizations, when classes were conducted in association with other classes, when the exam periods in the school were taken so seriously that the activities in school took on a different characteristic, when team sports were enjoyed by participants and many spectators, or when the students looked forward to the school newspaper. School reform must capture the sense of community that results in a good learning experience for the students.

Finally, the element of caring must be a part of school reform. The school reform movement needs people who are willing to try to make a difference with their lives. School reform needs teachers who enjoy teaching, who are committed to advocacy on behalf of children, and who demonstrate their feeling for students by being willing to hold the students and themselves accountable. Teaching, like parenting, is not a simple job, and today, more than ever in America's history, we need teachers who not only understand the difficulties of teaching, but who are also committed to being successful at it.

This volume represents the work of school reformers who have supported the present educational initiatives and who realize that much more must be done. They do so because they have been involved with the teaching and learning of children, both in general and special education, and believe that all children are entitled to quality education.

Frank J. Macchiarola, J.D., Ph.D.
Professor of Business,
Columbia University
and President and Executive Director,
The Academy of Political Science

Acknowledgments

Common to our work has been a belief in the capacity of all children and a striving toward improved institutional arrangements to enable all students to flourish. This book is part of that ongoing effort, not yet finished.

Any book owes debts to many persons. At the New York City Public Schools, Frank J. Macchiarola gave us the opportunity and challenge in his instructions to us, "to do right by the children." And our colleagues there, most especially the late Ethel Mingo, Arlene Pedone, and Waldemar Rojas, were encouraging and supporting partners. Ralph Edwards, at the *Harvard Educational Review,* gave us an opportunity to present our ideas beyond special education toward a refashioned mainstream, and Melissa Behm at Brookes Publishing understood our vision and deftly assisted in making this book a reality.

The book is not ours alone; it is also the work of the contributors. Each of them is both a researcher and a doer, and we are grateful for their participation, their willingness to see this as a priority amidst a busy schedule, and for the quality of their work.

In contributing royalties from the sale of this book to The Association for Persons with Severe Handicaps (TASH), we affirm our belief that beyond the words must come actions.

Acknowledgments

Introduction

There are two education debates occurring in America today. One, launched by the publication of *A Nation at Risk* in 1983, concerns education in general. Largely excluded from attention in this debate are students who are labeled handicapped. They have been the subject of a separate debate as to the future of what is called "special education." It is the authors' intent here to bring together those two debates in order to examine the education of all of America's children. In doing so, they focus on the students who are labeled handicapped for two reasons—both to rectify their exclusion from the broader debate, and to ensure that the reforms necessary to meet their needs encompass those of students called typical.

The issue is how to create exemplary programs for all students. To do so, the authors believe, requires a basic challenge to the conception and design of education programs in general, including the division between what is called regular and special education.

Throughout the history of the common school, there has been tension between inclusion and exclusion. On the one hand, there has been a progressive inclusion of an ever broader range of students—girls, children of color, children of noncitizens, those whose parents were not property owners, and most recently, children who are labeled handicapped, including those who are the most severely impaired. Since the beginning of the 20th century, outright exclusion has been limited by the compulsory attendance laws, the child labor laws of the 1920s and 1930s, *Brown* and subsequent school desegregation decisions, The Education for All Handicapped Children Act in 1975, and the *Lau* decision concerning the Limited English Proficient.

Simultaneously, there have been what Tropea (1988) calls "backstage efforts" to maintain order. Currently, this includes increasing numbers of children not enrolled, especially children who are homeless and from immigrant families (*New Voices*, 1988); those who, faced with new higher standards without necessary additional assistance, "drop out" or are "pushed out"; and most pertinent to our concerns here, the establishment of special services: separate curricula, separate programs, separate classes. In New York City, for example, with an overall school population of nearly one million pupils, there are more than 100,000 students in special education programs, over 310,000 students in the federal and state remedial programs, and nearly 73,000 in the mislabeled bilingual education—in sum, nearly half a million students. And in the extremes of such segregation, several years ago, the city schools, in response to attacks on gay and lesbian students, set up a separate program for these students, rather than directly confronting such homophobia.

The ostensible purpose of these programs is student benefit, and, generally, they talk about returning students, newly strengthened, to the regular program. In reality, this rarely happens (Gartner & Lipsky, 1987). Indeed, recent studies have shown that these programs are designed in ways that are incongruent with the regular education program—in terms of curriculum, teaching strategies, and scheduling (Allington & Johnston, 1986; Jenkins, 1987; see also Chapter 5, this volume). Thus, it is no surprise that for many students, referral to these programs is a one-way ticket. For those placed in special education programs, there is the added benefit for schools that the pupils' test scores are not usually included in the "report cards" now used to monitor school system performance. This device mirrors the practice used in the 1910s when concern about students called "laggards" led the schools to establish ungraded special classes whose pupils were not considered in the calculation of school performance.

Indeed, much of current special education practices finds its precursor in the early years of the 20th century. Reporting on the practices of the Philadelphia, Baltimore, and Detroit school systems in the 1910s, Tropea (1988) describes their classifications of students as "irregular attendants and neglected children," "unmanageable in the regular schools," "incorrigible, backward and otherwise defective," "a type who could not be effectively taught in the regular classes," and "children of immigrants" (p. 2). All this mirrored in a 1983 summary of national data:

> at least half of the learning disabled population could be more accurately described as slow learners, as children with second-language backgrounds, as children who are naughty in class, as those who are absent more often or move from school to school, or average learners in above average school systems. (Shepard, Smith, & Vojir, 1983, p. 82)

We have then a situation where large numbers of students are failed by the schools and are excluded or expelled. When included, they are separated or segregated; and even when successful enough to graduate, they are often ill-prepared as future learners, workers, or citizens. In urban districts, this may include as many as two-thirds or more of the youth (*An Imperiled Generation*, 1988); in the country, this number approaches one-half the youth.

There is an alternative to all this. It involves fundamental changes in school system goals, in the conceptualization of education, and in school practices. Rather than viewing its role as improving the performance of a few, school systems both need to acknowledge the belief that all students can learn, and to accept the responsibility to assure that this happens. In Kuhn's (1962) formulation, a new paradigm is required as to the nature of intelligence, the roles and characteristics of learners, and the organization of instruction.

Rather than viewing education along a single dimension, as measured in today's so-called intelligence and achievement tests, there is the concept of multiple forms of intelligence (Gardner, 1983). In Chapter 7 of this volume, Goldman and Gardner present a description of seven types of intelligence and their consequence for school organizations.

There is a need to break away from conceptions of learning that are based largely upon research about boys alone. Building upon Gilligan's (1982) pioneering studies, there is now a strong basis for recognizing differences in women's ways of knowing (Belenky, Clinchy, Goldberger, & Tarule, 1986). Instruction that is premised on single ways of comprehension eschews a more relativistic understanding that all knowledge is constructed. Similarly, school organization that emphasizes competitiveness penalizes those whose "ethic of caring" stresses respect for others' views over absolutes of right and wrong (Goldberg, 1988, p. 1). The author of recent studies about women's ways of knowing points out that such discoveries "may concern not just women but others on the margin as well" (Lyons, 1988, p. 32)—including children of the poor, children of color, and children who are labeled handicapped.

Along with a new understanding of intelligence and of differences in ways people learn must come new conceptions of the role of the learner. Too often seen simply as the outcome of teaching, learning is an activity of students; that is, the student is the producer of his or her own learning. Whatever the roles of other resources—teachers, texts, or other curricula materials—it is the student who must learn for him- or herself in the end. Not as an empty vessel to be filled, but as an active learner. To be effective in this role, to be, if you will, a productive worker in one's own learning, students need to be respected and to have a sense of self-respect. Rather than being disdained and negatively stereotyped, all students, including those with impairments, need to be seen as "capable of achievement and worthy of respect" (Lipsky & Gartner, 1987, p. 69).

In the current practice of special education there is a lack of expectation that students having received services in special education will return to general education, that is, to the mainstream. This is indicated even at the national level. While the federal Office of Special Education Programs (OSEP) requires states to provide a massive amount of data about their special education programs, no data are required on this topic at a national level. Explaining this, Patricia J. Guard, Deputy Director, OSEP, wrote:

> Thank you for your letter in which you ask about data concerning children who had been certified as handicapped and have returned to regular education.
> While these are certainly very interesting data you request, these data are not required in State Plans nor has the Office of Special Education Programs collected them in any other survey. (Guard, 1986)

The decision not to collect "interesting data" can conceivably be made for various reasons. For instance, policy makers may believe that the data are not important, or that the results may be feared, or that the collection process is not worth the potential benefit. There is no doubt that collecting decertification data might be difficult and most likely show an embarrassingly low level of return to general education. The authors believe, however, that the major reason such data are not collected has to do with beliefs and attitudes, both implicit and explicit, generally held about the purposes of special education and its students (see Chapter 1, this volume, for further discussion of this topic).

School organization and practices must be designed to enhance the role of the student. Current practices do the opposite. For example, rather than building upon the unique role of the student as the active producer of learning, they are institutionally based upon: arbitrary enrollment dates based upon a child's birthday, not level of development; fixed school calendars as an inheritance of a 19th century agricultural economy; school days set by teacher and custodian contracts; school periods in arbitrary blocks of time regardless of subject matter, instructional strategies, or student needs; a 1 teacher to 30 pupil model that encourages (if not requires) whole class lecturing despite its demonstrated ineffectiveness for most students (Brophy, 1986). Fortunately, there are alternatives that meet the needs of students, as well as those of other key players, parents, and teachers. They recognize that individual learners have different needs, learn in a variety of ways, and at various rates. Furthermore, they do not result in designs that have the consequence (if not the intent) of failing or segregating some students in order to benefit others.

Programs of cooperative learning have demonstrated the capacity to enable students of varying skills to work and learn together, and to do so in a way that builds teamwork, now so valued in increasing worker productivity. In cooperative learning designs, students learn from each other. In peer tutoring programs, there is the recognition that one can learn by teaching; that is, in tutoring it is the tutor who can benefit most. And this is especially true in both general education for students with special learning needs (Gartner, Kohler, & Riessman, 1971), as well as those who are labeled handicapped (Jenkins, 1987; Osguthorpe & Scruggs, 1986).

For students who are labeled handicapped, there is growing recognition that, at most, they differ in degree, not kind, from other students. Increasingly, efforts are underway to educate them with other students. In some instances, this involves educating groups of "at-risk" students, those now labeled as mild and moderately handicapped, along with students in remedial programs (Epps & Tindal, 1987; Idol, West, & Lloyd, 1988; Wang, 1988; Will, 1986). More fundamentally, new fully integrated models have been put forth (Biklen, 1985; Gartner & Lipsky, 1987; Skrtic, 1987; Stainback & Stainback, 1984). While the particular designs vary, including several presented in this volume, they have two major factors in common. First, the models feature acceptance of responsibility by teachers for a diverse group of students, and, second, they feature the development of classroom organization and instructional strategies that see opportunities, not impediments in the integration of students with disabilities into the mainstream classroom.

The response to individual differences need not involve the exclusion of some, the expulsion of others, the separation and segregation of yet others, and the "dumbing down" of the curriculum. We can organize schools so that all succeed (Edmonds, 1979a, 1979b; Goodlad & Oakes, 1988).

Writing more than half a century ago, Lippman said, "If a child fails in school and then fails in life, the schools cannot sit back and say:

> You see how accurately I predicted this. Unless we are to admit that education is essentially impotent, we have to throw back the child's failure at the school, and describe it as a failure not by the child but by the schools. (Block & Dworkin, 1976, p. 17)

And, Edmonds (1979b), calling on his landmark research on effective schools, made clear that what was missing is will, not knowledge.

> We can, whenever and wherever we choose, successfully teach all children whose schooling is of interest to us. We already know more than we need in order to do this. Whether we do it must finally depend on how we feel about the fact that we haven't done it so far. (p. 29)

Good educational practices are not simply something nice to achieve: they are an imperative. A group of educational litigators, one of whom is now the Secretary of Education for the Commonwealth of Pennsylvania, made the point succinctly. "Play school is out. . . . [T]he law requires that practice in the schools measure up to what has been demonstrated by the profession to be possible. What is done must be calculated to be effective" (Laski, Gilhool, & Gold, 1983, p. 8).

In the chapters that follow, descriptions of such educational practices are presented. The authors, whose views on particular practices vary, share a belief in the capacity and entitlement of all children and in the societal responsibilities—expressed through the schools—for their effective education.

We invited Frank J. Macchiarola to write the foreword because in his tenure as Chancellor of the New York City Public Schools, from 1978–1983, he affirmed belief in all of the children and in the obligation of the system to ensure their achievement. Here, he helps frame the book in the context of the broader school reform movement.

In Chapter 1, the authors' present the background to the passage in 1975 of PL 94-142, the Education for All Handicapped Children Act, and the process of its implementation during the past dozen years. Our assessment acknowledges its achievements and concludes that as currently being implemented, the law is in need of fundamental restructuring.

In Chapter 2, Lezotte summarizes the history and findings of the effective schools research, providing the basis for applying its lessons to include students who are presently labeled handicapped.

In Chapter 3, Stainback and Stainback use the framework of the "Regular Education Initiative" as a basis for both critiquing its limitations and describing the adaptations needed in regular education instructional practices and organization to increase its capacity to serve a wider range of students.

Sailor, in Chapter 4, takes the commitment to educate all students in the regular school to mean the inclusion of those persons with severe disabilities, what he calls the "zero rejection population." This model includes services for these students in a comprehensive local school and in the community. He develops a five-stage design, involving variations in focus and location of instructional activities across student age.

Allington and McGill-Franzen, in Chapter 5, examine the school experiences of students assigned to remedial or special education programs, and find little that systematically differentiates either the students in these programs or the programs' services. Despite this, they note that the schools offer two distinct sets of services with little overlap in planning or personnel, little increase in the quantity of high quality reading instruction provided, and little congruence between each of these separate pull-out programs and the basic program in which these students spend the bulk of their time. To counter these failures of school organization, the chapter authors propose two models to increase effective instructional opportunities for all low-achieving students. The first program would join content specialist teachers in partnership with groups of regular teachers. The second program would eliminate the role of specialist teachers, moving all teachers into the classroom, thereby reducing class size by nearly one-half.

In Chapter 6, Wang turns from school organization and teacher assignment designs to classroom practices for students. Using the general rubric of adaptive instruction, she describes the process of identifying student learning characteristics that are relevant for instructional planning and the various forms or adaptations to the curriculum that can be used to meet characteristics of individual learners.

Chapter 7 discusses both assessment and instruction. Goldman and Gardner begin first by questioning the theoretical basis of the present conceptions of intelligence. They offer, instead, Gardner's alternative view of intelligence—the concept of multiple intelligences, of which they present seven. Following a description of these seven intelligences, the chapter authors describe forms of assessment and types of instruction derived from a multiple intelligences perspective. They propose that the conceptualization of multiple intelligences suggests the need for an individual education for all students. Goldman and Gardner recommend a revised and enhanced role for teachers and two new adult roles, those of a student-curriculum broker and a school-community broker, to enhance the individual proclivities of all students.

Lilly, in Chapter 8, is concerned with teacher preparation. He believes that the maladaptive view of students that characterizes the separation of special education from education in general in the schools is reflected and replicated in teacher preparation programs. As such, he formulates a new construct for teacher preparation from the new design of education for students who are labeled handicapped, the new concepts of school reform, and the new proposals for teacher education in general. The result he proposes is an end to separate special education teacher preparation.

Chapter 9 discusses how the stigmatizing consequences of labeling students are applied to parents. Lipsky reviews the literature and goes on to point out that many factors must be considered in developing programs of parental involvement. Such factors include: class, race, family composition, cultural response to disability, and the age of family members. In doing so, she calls for a partnership between parents and professionals: one built neither on the subordination of the former to the latter, which is implicit in many parent education programs, nor on an identity of knowledge or roles. Rather, she called for a partnership built on the complementarity and equality in the interests of the child.

In Chapter 10, Asch gives voice to the students, a constituency little heard from in the discussion of special education. Blending insights from her own experiences with interview and research data, Asch describes the academic and social limits of the current education of students with disabilities. Her chapter crafts a careful balance between the commitment to include all students in an integrated system and the need to recognize individual differences.

Biklen, Corrigan, and Quick, in Chapter 11, look to the meaning of integration for the nonlabeled children. They discuss their research that indicates that the behaviors learned by special and general education students in integrated classes can be applied to their relationships outside of the school environment. They indicate ways in which teachers' behavior can be modeled for students, as well as ways in which teachers can foster the effective interaction of all students. They emphasize the need to help all students to present themselves in the best possible light and that necessary adaptations be treated as normative and thus implemented in an unobtrusive manner.

Toward the refashioning of education of students who are labeled handicapped, Hahn, the author of Chapter 12, calls attention to the competing definitions of disability. Disability can be defined as the function-limitations model, derived from a medical basis, that undergirds most current special education practice and rehabilitation programs, and the new minority-group model derived from a sociopolitical analysis, most clearly expressed in section 504 of the Rehabilitation Act. This section identifies disability as a source of discrimination and seeks to outlaw such practices. Hahn goes on to contrast the sharply different educational approaches consequent upon these alternative conceptualizations— the former striving to remediate functional deficits (but inevitably falling short in a nonadaptive environment), while the latter seeking to build a positive sense of identity among persons with disabilities, based upon their distinctive experiences and capabilities.

In Chapter 13, Gilhool combines legal analysis concerning full integration of students with disabilities and their right to an effective education with a description of the "states-of-the-art" of educational practice. He concludes with a proposal and description of an effective school act for all students.

In the closing chapter, views of disability and their expression in the current model of special education are examined. Looking first at current educational reform efforts that, for the most part, ignore students who are labeled handicapped, the authors then turn to reforms within special education. These reforms are addressed from three perspectives, including those which: 1) bridge the gap between special and general education, 2) blend together (or blur the margin between) aspects of the two systems, and 3) end the dual systems in favor of a unified system, a refashioned mainstream. This chapter concludes by suggesting several public policy initiatives and by identifying forces for change.

The authors of each chapter have individual views; the editors selected them for the excellence of their work, not a forced homogeneity. There are, however, a shared set of values and views that are believed to lead toward both excellence and equity in education. These include:

The belief that students are more alike than different

The belief that all students have individual needs

The need to fashion educational programs, in schools and communities, adapted both to these shared and individual needs

The need to do this in ways that are respectful of student differences, individual capacity, unique strengths of persons with disabilities, and the roles of parents

The recognition that there are methods of school organization, instructional strategies, and use of personnel, that provide the bases effectively to educate all students in integrated settings

The realization that the refashioned school will not only produce better education for all students, it both needs and will produce expanded and enhanced professional roles for school personnel

REFERENCES

Allington, R.L., & Johnson, P. (1986). The coordination among regular classroom reading programs and targeted support programs. In B.I. Williams, P.A. Richmond, & B.J. Mason (Eds.), *Designs for compensatory education: Conference proceedings and papers* (pp. 3–40). Washington, DC: Research and Evaluation Associates, Inc.

Am imperiled generation: Saving urban schools. (1988). Princeton, NJ: The Carnegie Foundation for the Advancement of Teaching.

Belenky, M.F., Clinchy, B.M., Goldberger, N.R., & Tarule, J.M. (1986). *Women's ways of knowing: The development of self, voice, and mind.* New York: Basic Books.

Biklen, D. (1985). *Achieving the complete school: Strategies for effective mainstreaming.* New York: Teacher's College Press.

Block, N.J., & Dworkin, G. (Eds.). (1976). *The I.Q. controversy.* New York: Random House.

Brophy, J.B. (1986). Research linking teacher behavior to student achievement: Potential implications for instruction of Chapter I students. In B.I. Williams, P.A. Richmond, & B.J. Mason (Eds.), *Designs for compensatory education: Conference proceedings and papers* (pp. 121–179). Washington, DC: Research and Education Associates, Inc.

Edmonds, R. (1979a). Effective schools for the urban poor. *Educational Leadership*, 15–27.

Edmonds, R. (1979b). Some schools work and more can. *Social Policy, 9*(5), 25–29.

Epps, S., & Tindal, G. (1987). The effectiveness of differential programming in serving students with mild handicaps: Placement options and instructional programming. In M.C. Wang, M.C. Reynolds, & H.J. Walberg (Eds.), *Handbook of special education: Research and practice: Vol. 1: Learner characteristics and adaptive education* (pp. 213–252). New York: Pergamon Press.

Gardner, H. (1983). *Frames of mind: The theory of multiple intelligences*. New York: Basic Books.

Gartner, A., Kohler, M.C., & Riessman, F. (1971). *Children teaching children: Learning through teaching*. New York: Harper & Row.

Gartner, A., & Lipsky, D.K. (1987). Beyond special education: Toward a quality system for all students. *Harvard Educational Review, 57*(4), 367–395.

Gilligan, C. (1982). *In a different voice: Psychological theory and women's development*. Cambridge: Harvard University Press.

Goldberg, K. (1988). Among girls "ethic of caring" may stifle classroom competitiveness, study shows. *Education Week, 1*, 24.

Goodlad, J.I., & Oakes, J. (1988). We must offer equal access to knowledge. *Educational Leadership, 45*(5), 16–22.

Idol, L., West, J.F., & Lloyd, S.R. (1988). Organizing and implementing specialized reading programs: A collaborative approach involving classroom, remedial, and special education teachers. *Remedial and Special Education, 9*(2), 54–61.

Jenkins, J.R. (1987). Similarities in the achievement levels of learning disabled and remedial students. *Counterpoint, 7*, 16.

Kuhn, T.K. (Ed.) (1962). *The structure of scientific revolutions*. Chicago: University of Chicago Press.

Laski, F.J., Gilhool, T.K., & Gold, S.F. (1983, June). *A Legal Duty to Provide Effective Schooling*. Paper presented at the Adaptive Instruction Conference, Harrisburg, PA.

Lyons, N. (1988). Learning from new research about women. *Education Week, 7*(19), 32.

New voices: Immigrant students in U.S. public schools. (1988). Boston: National Coalition of Advocates for Students.

Osguthorpe, R.T., & Scruggs, T.E. (1986). Special education students as tutors: A review and analysis. *Remedial and Special Education, 7*(4), 15–26.

Shepard, L.A., Smith, M.L., & Vojir, C.P. (1983). Characteristics of pupils identified as learning disabled. *American Educational Research Journal, 20*, 309–331.

Skrtic, T. (1987). *Prenuptial agreements necessary for wedding special and general education*. Paper presented to the American Educational and Research Association, Washington, DC.

Stainback, W., & Stainback, S. (1984). A rationale for the merger of special and regular education. *Exceptional Children, 51*(2), 102–111.

Tropea, J.L. (1988). *Urban schools' backstage order and children at risk: An historical perspective*. A paper presented for The Rockefeller Archive Center Conference on Children At Risk, Mt. Kisco, NY.

Wang, M.C. (1988). Weighing the 'regular education initiative'. *Education Week, 7*(32), 28, 36.

Will, M. (1986). *Educating students with learning problems—a shared responsibility*. Washington, DC: U.S. Department of Education.

part I

Background and Current Situation

chapter **1**

The Current Situation

Dorothy Kerzner Lipsky and Alan Gartner

It has been more than a decade since the enactment of PL 94-142, the Education for All Handicapped Children Act. Those students who began school at the time the act was first implemented have yet to exhaust their entitlement under it, that is, a free and appropriate public education until 21 years of age. In assessing its implementation, it is important to remember both the recency of its passage and the magnitude of its achievement.

PL 94-142: BACKGROUND AND PROVISIONS

Throughout the decade of the 1960s and into the 1970s, in testimony before committees of the Congress, in court suits, and in state capitols, parents and other advocates on behalf of children with disabilities described a harsh reality. For their children there was exclusion from public schools. Or, if they were not excluded, when included, they found limited services and segregated and second-class settings. Additionally, parents found that fees were charged for what was provided free to other students, and, in some cases, there was discriminatory treatment of racial minorities and those whose native language was not English.

Laws in individual states chipped away at these conditions, and between 1966 and 1974, a series of federal laws built system capacity. As in race relations, it was the federal courts that provided the key impetus. *Brown v. Board of Education* (1954) provided an example to those championing the rights of students with disabilities by: 1) affirming the importance of education to the "life and minds" of children, 2) establishing the inequality of separate education, and 3) providing a model for change. Ironically, in presenting South Carolina's case before the U.S. Supreme Court, John Davis warned that acceptance of the plaintiffs' arguments in the race area would lead to the obligation to integrate children with handicaps.

3

In *Pennsylvania Association of Retarded Citizens* (PARC) *v. Commonwealth of Pennsylvania,* the federal district court in 1971 overturned a state law that had relieved the Commonwealth from educating those children it found "uneducable" or "untrainable." And in the District of Columbia, in *Mills v. Board of Education* (1972), the federal district court the following year ruled that limited funds could not be the basis for excluding students with handicaps from receiving services.

An increasingly disorderly crazy quilt of state laws and growing pressure from parent advocates, ably abetted from within the government through officials of the new Bureau of Education for the Handicapped, led next to the 1974 Amendments to the Elementary and Secondary Education Act (PL 93-380). These contained most of the provisions of what was to become a year later PL 94-142. What they lacked was an explicit timetable and firm requirements placed upon the states.

In the spring of 1974, Representative John Brademas (D-Ind.) introduced H.R. 7217, and 6 months later, Senator Jennings Randolph (D-WV) introduced S.6. The House bill passed on June 18, 1975, the Senate bill passed on July 29th, the conference report was adopted by each of the bodies in mid-November, and President Gerald Ford, after some hesitation as to the cost, signed the bill on November 29, 1975.

The law's title, the Education for All Handicapped Children Act, is a clear reflection of the *PARC* decision. Specifically, it states that school systems could no longer pick and choose, according to some standard of educability, which children to educate. The law provides for *all* handicapped children.

PRINCIPLES OF PL 94-142

In examining the law, nine basic principles can be derived (Walker, 1987). These principles and the history behind them are discussed in the following section.

Principle 1. Establish the Right of Access to Public Education Programs

Prior to enactment of PL 94-142 and state mandatory statutes, disabled children had no guarantee that they would be accepted by public school agencies. Exclusionary clauses, refusal to provide services, the charging of fees for services in a system otherwise guaranteeing a free public education, and denial of entry to integrated programs were documented during the hearing process and in casework carried out by individual congressional offices. Congress concluded that the mandatory provisions of the federal law were justified under its responsibilities to guarantee equal protection of the laws under the Fourteenth Amendment of the Constitution.

Principle 2. Require Individualization of Services to Alter Automatic Assumptions about Disability

The special educational needs of disabled children, particularly those with the more severe handicaps, were not being met in schools. Congress was clearly concerned that existing programs were based on categories of handicaps and not on individual needs, that services were not available in regular classrooms or in integrated school environments, that parents and family members experienced difficulties in obtaining "appropriate" educational services for their children, and that minority and culturally different children were identified and placed in special education classes at rates substantially higher than their numbers in the general population would warrant.

Principle 3. Establish the Assumption that Disabled Children Need not be Removed from Regular Classes

Congress was interested in the normalization of services for disabled children. This was prompted by the belief that the presence of a disability did not necessarily require separation and removal from the regular classrooms, from the neighborhood school environment, or from regular academic classes. While children with severe intellectual or emotional impairments might require separate classes and highly specialized services, the emphasis of service delivery should be on the needs of the child, not on traditional or convenient patterns of services.

Principle 4. Broaden the Scope of Services Provided by Schools

Consistent with the principle of integration of children with disabilities in public schools was the necessity of expanding services available to support their academic programs. The provision of related services necessary for a child to benefit from the integrated environment was to be part of the school program, as were general health services, extracurricular activities, and other developmental support services provided to nondisabled children. PL 94-142 reinforced a general move away from the medical model for children with disabilities by acknowledging that medical diagnoses were not valuable in determining educational needs. However, the law also stipulated that some related (medical) services were to be provided if they met the educational mission.

Principle 5. Establish a Process for Determining the Scope of Services

Definitions of categories of services were delineated according to current service patterns; these were designed with the assumption that these would be a sufficient guide for service delivery for children in the least restrictive environment. "Appropriate services" referred to those services sufficient to meet the student's diagnosed needs through the individualized program, with parents, teachers, and school systems being equal in the decision-making process. Safeguards through a negotiating and appeals process would allow parents the ability to challenge the school system's experts, to seek other experts and counsel, to agree on a program of services, to appeal further, or to go to court. Provisions establishing procedural protections in identification, assessment, and placement likewise guided the definition of disability. Congress was satisfied to describe the normalization principles it was concerned about, to provide examples of the services it intended to authorize, and to allow states and local agencies some discretion in an area of decision making that was likely to change.

Principle 6.   Establish General Guidelines for Identification of Disability

Congress was not willing to leave definition and identification of disabilities wholly to the good intentions of educators. In an area where there was some difference of opinion about the size and characteristics of the learning disabilities population, Congress placed a 2% (of total school population) cap on the number of children eligible to be counted, pending a study by the Commissioner of Education. Further, the law placed an overall 12% cap on the portion of the school population eligible to be identified and counted as disabled for the purposes of funding.

Principle 7.   Establish Principles for Primary State and Local Responsibility

Congress was assisting states and localities to provide education through federal financial assistance, although state and local educational agencies retained a primary role in providing an appropriate education for all disabled children. Congress acknowledged that current resources were not sufficient, during the deep recession of 1974–1975, and that it intended real action in return for financial assistance. Stringent programmatic conditions of eligibility had to be met prior to submission of a state plan, and assistance was tied to children being served.

Principle 8.   Clarify Lines of Authority for Educational Services

To resolve the overlapping lines of responsibility for services, Congress established a clear line of authority through the educational system in each state. This was done to ensure that educational services could be guaranteed to disabled children on the same basis as they were guaranteed to nondisabled children. The state educational agency and, through it, each local educational agency, became responsible for ensuring appropriate education and related services. While multiple agencies and funding sources might assist in service provision, the state remained the final responsible unit for ensuring a free public education for all handicapped children, regardless of where the child received services.

Principle 9. Move Beyond Staffing and Training of Personnel

While PL 94-142 addressed the issue of personnel training and required a comprehensive system of personnel development, it rejected the capacity-building models of the 1960s and the question of whether staff were sufficiently knowledgeable or trained to educate children with disabilities. While inservice and preservice training would be required, they were not viewed as insurmountable barriers to the principal problem of establishing the rights of disabled children to a public education.

Congress did not focus at length on the relationship between special education and general education in the public schools, nor on the methodologies or curricular content of special education. Similarly, it did not address what steps would be sufficient to meet the diverse learning needs of students with disabilities. Such decisions were to be professional judgments left to educators, within the parameters of procedural safeguards, and would include access to the courts. This would ensure that the needs of children were individually examined and that conflicts in professional and parental judgments had a legal forum.

Concerns about children with severe disabilities focused on the separation of these children from their peers in the mainstream—that is, out-of-school and out-of-district placements, in separate schools, centers, hospitals, and institutions. The law reflects a strong presumption that public authorities would follow the prescriptive goals of normalization and services in the mainstream for all children with disabilities, once responsibility within the public education sector was established. Federal policy was based on the assumption that children with disabilities, while perhaps having different and specialized needs, were able to participate in public schools without confronting professional turf, stigma, and differential resource allocation problems. Having established detailed governance relationships and procedural protections to guide each step of the educational process, federal policy left definitional issues concerning who is eligible, what they are eligible for, and in what setting, largely up to state and local judgment. This would be checked by the strengthened roles of parents and advocates who could invoke due process procedures and appeals, if necessary (Walker, 1987).

The actual implementation of the law was staggered over the next half-dozen years. There was to be a gradual increase in federal financial support, from 5%–40% by 1982. (This figure has never been reached. The most recent level was 8.5% federal support.) An increasing percentage of the federal funds was to be passed through by the states to local districts. While all children birth to 21 years of age in need of services were to be identified, there was a state option concerning service provision for those under 5 years of age. (Amendments passed in 1986 [PL 99-457] provide incentives to serve students from birth to 5 years of age.)

PL 94-142: A DECADE OF IMPLEMENTATION

In many ways, the implementation of PL 94-142 is one of the finest achievements of American public education. Students previously excluded from public education are now being served, additional resources have been committed, and far-reaching changes have taken place. For example:

Over 650,000 more students are being served now than were when the law was enacted. During the 1986–1987 school year, 4.42 million students, from birth through 21 years of age, were served. After several years of stability, this represents a 1.2% increase over the 1985–1986 school year. In total, this is approximately 11% of the overall public school enrollment (*Tenth Annual Report,* 1988, Table 1, p. 4, Figure 1, p.5)

Funds devoted to special education have increased substantially, from $100 million in FY 1976 to $1.6 billion in FY 1985.

While there are some exceptions, such as students in prisons, from migrant families, and in some institutional settings, for the most part location of the student does not seem to be a factor in the availability of services. The overall responsibility of state education agencies (SEAs) has been achieved, perhaps more so in special education than in other areas of SEA-LEA (local education agency) joint responsibility. With New Mexico's submission of a state plan in August, 1984, all 50 states are presently participating under PL 94-142.

What Are the Achievements and Deficits in the Implementation of the Law?

Achievements include: 1) access, 2) a general recognition and acceptance of entitlement to education of students labeled as handicapped, and due process procedural rights for them and their parents, and 3) some limited progress on "mainstreaming," especially in nonacademic areas. Far less progress has been made in determining who should receive special education services. Additionally, less progress has been made in the quality of education provided, whether measured by knowledge and skills acquired, graduation rates, return to general education, or post–high school achievement. The operation of parallel programs and systems for students called normal and for others labeled as handicapped is both cause and consequence of these limits.

> If the law has been massively successful in assigning responsibility for students and setting up mechanisms to assure that schools carry out those responsibilities, it has been less successful in removing barriers between general and special education. PL 94-142 and other public policies of the time did not anticipate the need to take special steps to eliminate turf, professional, attitudinal, and knowledge barriers within public education. It did not anticipate that the artifice of delivery systems in schools might drive the maintenance of separate services and keep students from the mainstream, that the resource base for special education and other remedial services

would be constrained by economic forces, or that special education might continue to be dead-end programs in many school districts. Nor could it anticipate how deeply ingrained were our assumptions about the differences between students with learning problems and those without, and the substantial power of high (or, unfortunately, low) expectations in learning. (Walker, 1987, p. 109)

Based on a comprehensive review of the literature, Ysseldyke (1987) succinctly summarizes the disparity between the state of the art and the state of practice:

1. There is currently no defensible psychometric methodology for reliably differentiating students into categories. Yet, school personnel in all but two states are required by [state] law to use indices of pupil performance on psychometric measures to classify and place students.
2. There is no evidence to support the contention that specific categories of students learn differently. Yet, students are instructed in categorical groups on the notion that these groups of students learn differently.
3. With the exception of sensorily impaired students, categorically grouped students do not demonstrate a set of universal and specific characteristics—or, for that matter, even a single universal and specific characteristic. There is no logic to current practice.
4. The current system used by public schools to classify exceptional children does not meet the criteria of reliability, coverage, logical consistency, utility, and acceptance to users. (Ysseldyke, 1987, p. 265)

What Are the Factors that Produced the Current Situation?

While the drafters of PL 94-142 may have been naive, particularly about the "artifice of delivery systems," the law itself does not require the largely separate and unequal special education service system that has developed. Despite the emphasis in the law on identification, certification, and classification, the evaluation process prescribed does not demand separate categorical programs. Indeed, it requires no categorical programs at all. What it does require for each student is an appropriate placement in the least restrictive environment (LRE). In considering the placement for an individual student, standards of both appropriateness and LRE requirements must be met. And while several possible placements may be appropriate for a student, the one chosen should be that which is in the least restrictive environment. A 1983 Sixth Circuit Court of Appeals decision, *Roncker v. Walter,* addressed the two factors directly:

Where a segregated facility is considered superior, the court should determine whether the services which make that placement superior could feasibly be provided in a non-segregated setting. If they can, the placement in the segregated school would be inappropriate under the Act. (*Roncker v. Walker,* 700 F.2d, 1058, *cert. denied,* 104 S.Ct.196)

While PL 94-142 itself does not require the type of special education service system that has evolved, it is fair to say that what has developed by and large is in keeping with its direction. Also, it has clearly encouraged the state legislation and regulations that maintain separation.

Partly as a result of a narrow reading of the stricture that federal aid *supplement* and not *supplant* local efforts, school practices in remedial education, so-called bilingual education, and special education have favored separate, "pull-out," programs (see Chapter 5, this volume). For the most part, as PL 94-142 was implemented in school systems, general and special educators designed separate programs. Teacher training programs in general and in special education (see Chapter 8, this volume), the absence of alternative models and paradigms of integration, made unlikely any other outcome. Additionally, given the reduction in support for remedial education programs in this period, school systems had limited resources with which to support options within general education. McGill-Franzen (1987) points out that the increase in the number of students identified as learning disabled neatly matches the decline in Chapter I participants over the past decade.

Not only did the reduction of support for remedial education encourage the growth of special education, but the funding patterns of special education promoted growth and internal segregation. While some see the additional funding for students placed in special education programs as promoting "bounty hunting," the few studies of special education finance offer no conclusive evidence. What they do support is the general cost of special education at about twice that for other students (Kakalik, Furry, Thomas, & Carney, 1981; Raphael, Singer, & Walker, 1985; Singer & Butler, 1987; Wright, Cooperstein, Renniker, & Padilla, 1982). Such funding patterns provide continuing encouragement of separate placements.

> Funding formulas that create incentives for more restrictive and separate class placement or that support particular configurations of services based on special education teacher allocations maintain an inflexible program structure and fail to allow models that encourage students to remain in general classrooms with resource room or individualized help. One need only examine the variation in statistics between general classroom placements at the state level and the state funding formulas to know that states that provide financial incentives for separate placements, or which traditionally have had dual systems of services, place students disproportionately in more restrictive placements. States such as New York, Illinois, Florida, Maryland, the District of Columbia, Pennsylvania, New Hampshire, and New Jersey have much higher rates of separate classroom placements for certain disability groups for these reasons. (*Note.* From Lisa J. Walker, "Procedural Rights in the Wrong System: Special Education is Not Enough," in *Images of the Disabled, Disabling Images,* Alan Gartner and Tom Joe, Eds. [Praeger Publishers, New York, a division of Greenwood Press, 1987], Chapter 6, pp. 110, 111. Copyright © 1987 by Praeger Publishers. Reprinted with permission.)

While funding affects programs, it is not the source of the current problem. The source of the problem lies in societal assumptions about disability.

> P.L. 94-142 was a product of its time. Developing out of *PARC* and *Mills,* cases dealing with exclusion from education and training services on the basis of disability, the law passed when the rights of a disabled person to participate in the

community were just beginning to be voiced. It came when institutionalization was being questioned, but the history of services and the knowledge of disability, as public policy matters, were limited. It came at the beginning of the civil rights movement of disabled adults before many articulate disabled veterans and disabled young adults had been integrated into society, able and willing to fight for their rights. It came as a new generation of parents with disabled children confronted the school system for the first time and were not willing to take "no" as an answer for their children.

The language of the law also reflects the knowledge and assumptions of that time. Its intent was the establishment of public policy to protect disabled children and youth from exclusion from and discrimination in the public school setting. Disabled students were to be dealt with as individuals—their needs were to be assessed individually—but also as a group who were presumed to need special and individualized services different from what were presumed to be needed for students without disabilities. This services model and the mechanisms for identifying the students who could be best served by this model were assumed to be, if not a science, an art which sensitive professionals, in consultation with parents, would deliver once the discriminatory barriers to services were removed.

While underscoring that it intended to remove the medical treatment model as the basis on which public policy should be set, P.L. 94-142 established the right of students with handicapping conditions to be treated equally and on an individual basis in determining their school needs. But without adjusting the organization of services within schools, changing attitudes toward disability, altering the substantial state and local funding streams that make it difficult to treat disabled students as part of the mainstream, nor collapsing the categorical definitions that define the population as being different, P.L. 94-142 may have served to reinforce a hybrid structure—one with elaborate protections to assure the rights of disabled students, but carried out by a separate delivery system of special education services, which remains in many instances outside the normal scope of school business. (*Note.* From Lisa J. Walker, "Procedural Rights in the Wrong System: Special Education is Not Enough," in *Images of the Disabled, Disabling Images,* Alan Gartner and Tom Joe, Eds. [Praeger Publishers, New York, a division of Greenwood Press, 1987], Chapter 6, pp. 107, 108. Copyright © 1987 by Praeger Publishers. Reprinted with permission.)

REFERRAL AND ASSESSMENT

No area in special education has been the subject of more concern than the procedures for the referral and assessment of students. Together, these activities raise issues as to: 1) professional judgment, particularly regarding the identification of students labeled as learning disabled, and 2) discrimination, as seen in the differential treatment of children of color and those whose proficiency in English is limited.

Aside from those students with obvious physical handicaps who are identified before entering a classroom, referral occurs "when student behavior and academic progress varies from the school norm." (Walker, 1987, p. 105). The assumption in such cases is that there is something wrong with the student. In particular, referral is more likely to occur in cases where the student is a member of a minority group or from a family whose socioeconomic status varies from the district's norm. Further,

> decisions about special education classification are not only functions of child characteristics but rather involve powerful organizational influences. The number of programs, availability of space, incentives for identification, range and kind of competing programs and services, number of professionals, and federal, state, and community pressures all affect classification decisions. (Keogh, 1988)

Referral rates vary widely. This is apparent from examining two different sets of data from 28 large cities. As a percentage of total student enrollment, referral rates range from 6%–11%. The figures for assessment vary even more widely. For the same 28 cities, the percentage of students who are referred and then placed in special education ranges from 7.8%–91.8% (*Special Education,* 1986, Tables 8 and 9).

The most extensive study of the evaluation process reports that results are barely more accurate than a flip of the coin, with the evaluation process often providing a psychological justification for the referral (Ysseldyke, Thurlow, et al., 1983).

Among the major practical problems in the assessment process are: 1) the disregard of results in decision making (White & Calhoun, 1987), 2) evaluators' incompetence and biases (Davis & Shepard, 1983; Ysseldyke & Algozzine, 1983, 1984; Ysseldyke, Algozzine, Regan, & Potter, 1980; Ysseldyke, Algozzine, Richey, & Graden, 1982), and 3) the inadequacy and inappropriateness of the instruments used (Wang, Reynolds, & Walberg, 1986). As to this last, a basic standard for the use of norm-referenced tests is the inclusion of subjects similar to those being tested among the normed population. A careful study of the manuals of the most commonly used norm-referenced tests, both general IQ and achievement, reports that they "provided no evidence that their tests are valid for use with handicapped students" (Fuchs, Fuchs, Benowitz, & Barringer, 1987, p. 267). Stating the obvious and appropriate conclusion, the authors declare: "Tests without validation data on handicapped people simply should not be used with this group to determine diagnoses, classifications, placements, and evaluations of academic progress" (page 269). Nonetheless, it is just such tests that are used for these purposes.

When tests are used in such inappropriate ways, there seems little reason to challenge Hobbs's assessment that the classification system of students with disabilities is "a major barrier to the efficient and effective delivery of services to them and their families and thereby impedes efforts to help them" (1980, p. 274). Beyond the faults in test use, Biklen (1988) points to the way testing transforms persons with disabilities in need of services into patients or clients rather than being seen as socially valued persons, "albeit one(s) needing and receiving some treatment" (p. 128).

In practice, the major assessment problems involve students labeled as learning disabled. While the overall special education student population grew

20% in the decade between 1976–1977 and 1986–1987, those labeled as learning disabled grew 119%. They now constitute 44% of all special education students (Hume, 1988a). Among the 50 states, their percentage varies from 30%–67%, and from 0%–73% among 30 large cities (Binkard, 1986; *Special Education*, 1986).

PROBLEMS CONCERNING THE LABELING OF STUDENTS AS LEARNING DISABLED

The problem is not only the excessive numbers of students classified as learning disabled; there are even more troubling issues as to the accuracy of the label:

More than 80% of the student population could be classified as learning disabled by one or more definitions presently in use (Ysseldyke, 1987).

Based upon the records of those already certified as learning disabled and those not, experienced evaluators could not tell the difference (Davis & Shepard, 1983).

Students identified as learning disabled cannot be shown to differ from other low achievers with regard to a wide variety of school-related characteristics (Algozzine & Ysseldyke, 1983; Bartoli & Botel, 1988; Ysseldyke, Thurlow, Christenson, & Weiss, 1987).

A study of special education in Colorado concluded: "The single most important finding is that more than half the children do not meet statistical or valid clinical criteria for the identification of perceptual or communicative disorders" (Shepard & Smith, 1981).

The meaning of such inappropriate assessment standards was described by Chicago parents whose child was diagnosed as learning disabled (Granger & Granger, 1986). Because the boy was not reading in school, and ignoring the fact that he read at home, the school's diagnostician determined that the boy should be placed in special education.

> The trap of Special Education was now open and waiting for the little boy. It is a beguiling trap. Children of Special Education are children of Small Expectations, not great ones. Little is expected and little is demanded. Gradually, these children— no matter their IQ level—learn to be cozy in the category of being "special." They learn to be less than they are. (pp. 26, 27)

While these parents rejected the "safety" of the LD (learning disabled) label, for many parents the LD label provides solace for the underachievement of their children (Carrier, 1986).

There is little in school practice to justify labeling nearly 2 million students as learning disabled; similarly, an analysis of the professional literature suggests it is unwarranted. Coles (1987) both challenges the data as to the consequences of differences in brain activity and sets their meaning in context:

> Learning difficulties, and any neurological dysfunctions associated with them, develop not from within the individual but from the individual's interaction within social relationships. Brain functioning is both a product of and a contributor to the individual's interactions, it is not a predetermined condition. (p. 78)

While Coles's critique addresses the limitations inherent in the learning disabilities formulation, Gardner's concept of multiple intelligences expands the horizon (see chapter 7, this volume).

Simultaneous with the growth in the number of students labeled as learning disabled, there has been a decline (by some 300,000 between 1976–1977 and 1985–1986) in those labeled as retarded. This shift in the retarded population is nothing new. As a result of shifting definitions, expressed in IQ cutoff scores, the number of persons labeled as retarded was 6 million prior to 1959, 30 million based on a 1959 definition, and 5 million according to a 1973 revised definition (Stephens, 1988, p. 69; for the American Association on Mental Deficiency definitions, see Grossman, 1983).

In what can be called a form of classification plea bargaining, the Department of Education explained the reduction in the number of students labeled as retarded as follows:

> These decreases in the number of children classified as mentally retarded are the result of an increasing sensitivity to the negative features of the label itself and to the reaction on the part of local school systems to allegations of racial and ethnic bias as a result of the use of discriminatory or culturally biased testing procedures. (*Seventh Annual Report,* 1985, p. 4)

While there may be "increasing sensitivity," the overrepresentation of students of color in this category continues. During the 1986–1987 school year, the U.S. Department of Education, Office of Civil Rights, reported that while minority students constituted 30% of all public school students, they accounted for 42% of all students classified as educable mentally retarded (EMR), 40% of those classified as trainable mentally retarded (TMR), and 35% of those classified as seriously emotionally disturbed (SED). The disproportion is greatest among black students; they constituted 16% of the overall student body but 35% of the EMR students, 27% of the TMR students, and 27% of the SED students (Hume, 1988b, p. 5). While there is basis for a causal relationship between poverty and impairment, and given the correlation in the United States between race and poverty, between race and impairments, this explanation of the overrepresentation fails. The explanation fails when one considers the absence of such disproportion among students labeled as physically handicapped. Disproportions are also true between boys and girls. While boys represent 51% of all public school students, they make up 58% of the students labeled as retarded, 78% of those labeled as SED, 63% of the speech impaired, and 71% of those with specific learning disabilities (Hume, 1988c).

PLACEMENT, LEAST RESTRICTIVE
ENVIRONMENT, AND "MAINSTREAMING"

While referral and assessment procedures vary widely, and students certified as handicapped and in need of special education services are "placed" in special education programs based upon such discrepant outcomes, PL 94-142 is clear concerning least restrictive environment criteria. "Removal from the regular education environment" is to occur "only when the nature and severity of the handicap is such that education in regular classes with the use of supplementary aids cannot be achieved satisfactorily" (1975, Sec. 612 [5] [B]).

Despite this clear language, there is continuing dispute as to its meaning and wide variation in implementation. Responding to complaints of operators of private facilities, U.S. Department of Education Assistant Secretary Madeleine Will altered her earlier standard that "has been interpreted as virtually requiring all handicapped children be educated in a regular classroom setting" (Will Writes NAPSEC, 1988, p. 3).

Indeed, the reality is far from the standard set by the law. During the 1985–1986 school year, barely a quarter of the students served in special education programs received services in general education classes at least 80% of the school day. Further, 41% were pulled out of regular classes from 21%–60% of the day, and the remaining 24% were served in separate classes or programs for more than 60% of the school day (Hume, 1988a).

From 1976–1977, when data on the implementation of PL 94-142 first were collected, 67% of the students were served in regular classes, full-time or with resource room services, 25% in special classes, and 9% in separate schools or other environments (Walker, 1987). A decade later, with an increase of some half a million students served in special education programs, the placement figures for the 1985–1986 school year are uncannily alike: 67% in general classes (full- or part-time), 24% in special classes, and 9% in separate schools or other environments (*Tenth Annual Report*, 1988, p. 30).

These overall figures mask a great deal of variation—between states, among categories of handicapping conditions, and over time.

> While five states place 60 or greater percent of their students with handicaps full time in regular classes, another eight place fewer than 10 percent full time in regular classes.
> At the opposite extreme, while seven states place 45 percent or more of their students with handicaps in separate classes or separate settings, five other states place fewer than 15 percent in such settings. (*Ninth Annual Report*, 1987, Table EC1, p. E-45).

Shifting the focus to the 11 states with a million or more school population and a hundred thousand or more students with handicaps, representing 55% and

Table 1. Certification and placement: 11 largest states

	Percent of students labeled as handicapped	Percent of students in regular classes full-time	Percent of students in special classes, special schools, or other separate settings
11 state average	11.14	26.7	31.6
State(s) with highest percent	14.88	58.7	56.9
State(s) with lowest percent	8.89	0.7	18.8

Note. From the *Ninth Annual Report to Congress on the Implementation of the Education of the Handicapped Act,* (Table EC1). Washington, DC: U.S. Department of Education.

53%, respectively, of the national totals in 1984–1985, wide variation again is found.

While the national average of students labeled as handicapped was 11.14%, among these 11 states the range was from one-fifth less than that (8.8% in California) to one-third greater (14.8% in New Jersey). Turning to placements, the national average for the least restrictive placements, in regular classes full-time, was 26.7%; among these 11 states the range was from one-fortieth of that (0.7% in Georgia) to more than double (58.7% in Michigan). And looking at students in special classes, special schools, or other separate settings (e.g., the most restrictive settings), the national average was 31.6%, and the range among these 11 states was from barely half that (18.8% in North Carolina) to nearly twice that number (56.9% in New York).

Turning to categories of handicapping conditions, there have been sharp changes over time, as well as continuing wide variability among all 50 states. The national average among students for all handicapping conditions served full- or part-time in regular classes was 67% in 1985–1986. The range was from 90%–36%, from more than a quarter greater than the average to less than half of it. For those students labeled as learning disabled, the national average was 77% placed in regular classes; the range was from 97%–35%, from nearly all such students to barely one-third of them. For those students labeled as speech impaired, the national average was 92% placed in regular classes, and for several states it was 99% served there; in one state it dropped to only 61%. For those students labeled as mentally retarded, the national average was 28% placed in regular classes; the range was from 87% –5%, from more than 2½ times to one-sixth the size of the national average. And for those students labeled as emotionally disturbed, the national average was 43% placed in regular classes; the range was from 76%–3%, from nearly twice the national average to a twentieth of it (*Tenth Annual Report,* 1988, Table BC 1, p. B-44).

This variability continues. A recent paper issued by the Office of Special Education Programs reports:

> The District of Columbia is 25 times more likely than Oregon to place a student labelled as handicapped in a separate school or residential facility.
>
> Some states are five or six times more likely than others to educate a disabled student in a separate classroom, school, or other facility.
>
> Compared to the five most integrated states, other states are, on the average nearly six times as likely to place a student in a separate school or residential facility. (Danielson & Bellamy, 1988)

The report's authors, the director of the Office of Special Education Programs and its special studies chief, note that: "The statute is clear in creating a presumption that services be provided in the regular education environment to the extent appropriate for each student" (Danielson & Bellamy, p. 10). Nonetheless, they say their findings are not a measure of compliance with the law, which, in a strained reading at best, they declare dictates placement procedures, not the resulting patterns of placement. This is particularly surprising in light of the department's recent report to the Congress on the implementation of PL 94-142 (*Ninth Annual Report*, 1987). Based on reviews of 25 states, this report declared that: "Virtually every State had significant problems in meeting its LRE responsibilities" (p. 166). Further: "Evidence suggests that States have not established procedures to ensure that the removal of handicapped children from the regular education environment is justified" (p. 166). Indeed, the report to Congress concludes: "Reviews of some individual student records in these [25] States also revealed a substantial lack of evidence that LRE is even considered before a placement is made. On the contrary, some placements seem to be made on the basis of the handicapping condition or for administrative convenience" (*Ninth Annual Report*, 1987, p. 178).

Separation of Students Versus Mainstreaming

Separation in itself is not the only problem. Separation reduces the likelihood that students will return to general education. An intermediate step is what has come to be called "mainstreaming," a term that does not appear in the text of the law. Mainstreaming refers to the provision of opportunities for students labeled as handicapped who are in special education settings to spend a portion of their time in general education.

A unique analysis of "mainstreaming" in the Pittsburgh schools gives dramatic evidence of its actual limitations (Sansone & Zigmond, 1986). The district classifies approximately 6% of its students as mildly to moderately disabled, serving them in 38 of the district's 56 elementary schools. Based on an examination of their academic schedules, "the percent of [special] students assigned to regular classes ranged from 3 to 7 percent. This means that over 90 percent of the mildly handicapped elementary students . . . were *never* assigned to regular education academic classes'' (Sansone & Zigmond, 1986, p. 455). Participation is limited in three ways: 1) scheduling students for fewer than the full number of periods in the week, 2) having students attend several different general education classes for the same subject, and 3) assigning students to inappropriate (by age or level) general education classes. Thus, fewer than one-tenth of mildly handicapped students participated in the mainstream, and of this small number, less than half participated in the mainstream class on a full basis (Sansone & Zigmond, 1986, p. 456). Given such program limitations, it is no surprise that only 1.4% of the students return to general education (*Special Education,* 1986, Table 13, p. 33).

Pittsburgh's figure of only 1.4% of special education students returning to general education is about average for the country's large cities (*Special Education,* 1986). As we note in the Introduction, there are no national data collected, and the large city data are flawed because they are based upon self-reports, they lack common definitions, and, at least for some cities, the actual situation is overstated. Similarly, a report that is touted as challenging the assertion that placement in special education is a "one way street" has several limits (Walker et al., 1988). Included among these limitations are the following:

1. The study is based on a review of records, not actual student experiences.
2. Student placements are described by categorical labels not by the nature (or degree of restrictiveness) of their placement.
3. The study sample is limited to three cities and was only conducted over a 2-year period.
4. The study doesn't state clearly as to what alternative placements decertified students are moved.

Furthermore, Walker's report states that 17% of the students no longer receive special education services. Interpretation of this high figure is confounded by the fact that more than half of the students were labeled as speech impaired or learning disabled, and most were receiving only related services. In other words, it is those receiving the least intensive special education services who are most likely to be decertified. A disturbing finding is the high percentage—12%—of the special education students whose classification were changed during the 2 years. One-quarter of those originally labeled as physically/multiply handicapped, one-fifth of those originally labeled speech impaired, and one-seventh of those originally labeled emotionally/behaviorally disabled were reclassified (Walker et al., 1988, Tables 2, 6). This raises serious questions, not addressed by the authors of the study, both as to the adequacy of the initial evaluations and the bases of the reclassification. They do note movement back and forth between special education and remedial programs.

PROGRAM OUTCOMES

Systematic and comprehensive data on special education program outcomes are scarce. We have already noted the absence of data concerning students returning to general education. Similarly, there are no national data on special education students' graduation rates, on their rates of learning (they are generally excused from the standardized tests), on their preparation for postsecondary schooling, or on their employment. Again, we believe this reflects a set of attitudes and expectations concerning students labeled as handicapped. Such attitudes suggest they are not expected to achieve, and that it is enough that they receive services. Or, alternatively, the attitude may be that the benefits are assumed, but are rarely assessed.

The basic premise of special education is that students with deficits will benefit from a unique body of knowledge and from smaller classes staffed by specially trained teachers using special materials. But there is no compelling body of evidence demonstrating that segregated special education programs have significant benefits for students. On the contrary, there is substantial and growing evidence that suggests the opposite is true. Reviews and meta-analyses of what have come to be called special education "efficacy studies" consistently report little or no effects for students of all levels of severity placed in special education settings (Carlberg & Kavale, 1980; Cegelka & Tyler, 1970; Epps & Tindal, 1987; Glass, 1983; Kavale & Glass, 1982; Leinhardt & Pallay, 1982; Madden & Slavin, 1982, 1983; Semmel, Gottlieb, & Robinson, 1979; Ysseldyke, 1987). Even the authors of a petulant attack on challenges to present special education practices offer little to defend them (Kauffman, Lloyd, & McKinney, 1988). In 50 recent studies comparing the academic performance of mainstreamed and segregated students with mild handicapping conditions, the mean academic performance of the integrated group was in the 80th percentile, while the segregated students scored in the 50th percentile (Weiner, 1985).

A review of programs for academically handicapped students found no consistent benefits of full-time special education programs. Rather, it found full- or part-time regular class placements more beneficial for students' achievement, self-esteem, behavior, and emotional adjustment (Madden & Slavin, 1982). A study in one state found that 40% 50% of students labeled as learning disabled did not realize the expected benefits from special education (Bloomer, 1982).

Reporting on data for the 1986–1987 school year, the Department of Education estimates that the dropout rate among students in special education is at least 10% greater than for nonhandicapped students. Among students over age 16 labeled as handicapped, 26% of those who left school dropped out, compared to 16%–18% among the general education student population. The real dropout rate may be higher; an additional 11.5% of these students left school for "unspecified reasons," many of whom are likely to have dropped out. Interestingly, the highest dropout rate was among the least impaired category, learning disabled, where the rate was an astonishing 47% of all those over age 16 (*Tenth Annual Report*, 1988, Table 18, p. 47).

In summarizing impediments to achieving national policy in the education of students with mild handicaps, a recent study rejects the prevalent "pull-out" strategy as ineffective, and concludes, "This split-scheduling approach . . . is neither administratively nor instructionally supportable when measured against legal requirements, effective schools research or fiscal consideration" (Hagerty & Abramson, 1987, p. 316).

A careful review of the literature on effective instruction strongly indicates that most special education programs run counter to the basic effectiveness tenets in teaching behaviors, organization of instruction, and instructional support (Bickel & Bickel, 1986). Another study points out that:

> [T]here appear to be at least three discrepancies between the suggestions for best practice and the observation of actual teaching practice for mildly handicapped students: (a) there is almost no instruction presented to these students that might be classified as involving high level cognitive skills, (b) there is a small amount of time spent in activities that could be considered direct instruction with active learner response and teacher feedback, and (c) students receive a low frequency of contingent teacher attention. (Morsink, Soar, Soar, & Thomas, 1986, p. 38)

While many of these shortcomings are present in general education classes, the needs of students appropriately classified as handicapped make the absence of the desired practices even more consequential.

At the classroom level, the time special education students spend on academic tasks is not greater than that for general education students: about 45 minutes of engaged time per day (Ysseldyke, 1983). Most often, there is little qualitatively different in special education instruction in the areas of additional time on task, curriculum adaptation, diverse teaching strategies, adaptive equipment, or advanced technology. Despite their small size, classrooms remain "teacher-centric."

SUMMARY

In sum, there is little in the current design of special education that makes a difference for students labeled as handicapped. This is true for the present, while they are in school, and for the future, after they leave school. A study of those who left school (those who graduated as well as those who "aged-out") in 10 Washington school districts during the 1984–1985 school year portrays these dismal outcomes (Edgar, 1987). Of the dropouts, 61% were neither employed nor in school ("No Activity" in the study's term); this was true of 36% of the graduate and age-out students (Edgar, 1987). The study by Ysseldyke, Thurlow, et al. (1987) showed few differences in time allocated to instruction of students with varying labels of handicap, and demonstrated that special education instruction supplanted rather than supplemented general education services. They concluded:

> In order to make a difference for handicapped students, to move them ahead toward a caught-up status, we will have to explore programming alternatives that have greater flexibility and that can address areas of instructional need, at the first step, in terms of time allocations. (p. 54)

The limited expectation for student learning in special education programs is reflected in the following results of a study of special education in large cities:

Only 7 of 31 cities evaluate "student achievement/outcomes"
Only 3 of 31 cities conduct "longitudinal student outcomes studies"
Only 9 of the 24 special education directors whose districts do not conduct such evaluations believe "student achievement/outcome studies" are needed (*Special Education,* 1986, Table 21, p. 45).

Thus, combining the numbers of special education directors whose districts conduct such evaluations and those who do not, but who say they are needed, 15 of the 31 directors of large-city special education programs neither collect student outcome data nor believe that such evaluations are needed. While the failure to evaluate outcomes does not in itself indicate limited expectations, at the least it does indicate a lack of concern with outcomes, which we believe comes from limited expectations of student capacity.

REFERENCES

Algozzine, B., & Ysseldyke, J.E. (1983). Learning disabilities as a subset of school failure: The over-sophistication of a concept. *Exceptional Children, 50,* 242–246.
Bartoli, J., & Botel, M. (1988). *Reading/Learning disability: An ecological approach.* New York: Teachers College Press.
Bickel, W.E., & Bickel, D.D. (1986). Effective schools, classrooms, and instruction: Implications for special education. *Exceptional Children, 52*(6), 489–500.
Biklen, D. (1988). The myth of clinical judgment. *Journal of Social Issues, 44*(1), 127–140.
Binkard, B. (1986). State classifications of handicapped students: A national comparative data report. *Counterpoint, 12,* 6–14.
Bloomer, R. (1982). *Mainstreaming in Vermont: A study of the identification process.* Livonia, NY: Brador Publications.
Brown v. Board of Education, 347 US 483 (1954).
Carlberg, C., & Kavale, K. (1980). The efficacy of special versus regular class placement for exceptional children: A meta-analysis. *Journal of Special Education, 14,* 295–309.
Carrier, J.G. (1986). *Learning disability: Social class and the construction of inequality in American education.* Westport, CT: Greenwood Press.
Cegelka, W.J., & Tyler, J. (1970). The efficacy of special class placement for mentally retarded in proper perspective. *Training School Bulletin, 66,* 33–66.

Coles, J. (1987). *The learning mystique: A critical look at "learning disabilities."* New York: Pantheon.

Davis, W.A., & Shepard, L.A. (1983). Specialists' use of test and clinical judgment in the diagnosis of learning disabilities. *Learning Disabilities Quarterly, 19,* 128–138.

Edgar, E. (1987). Secondary programs in special education: Are many of them justifiable? *Exceptional Children, 53*(6), 555–561.

Epps, S., & Tindal, G. (1987). The effectiveness of differential programming in serving students with mild handicaps: Placement options and instructional programming. In M.C. Wang, M.C. Reynolds, & H.J. Walberg (Eds.), *Handbook of special education: Research and practice: Vol. 1. Learner characteristics and adaptive education* (pp. 213–248). New York: Pergamon Press.

Fuchs, D., Fuchs, L.S., Benowitz, S., & Barringer, K. (1987). Norm-referenced tests: Are they valid for uses with handicapped students? *Exceptional Children, 54*(3), 263–271.

Glass, G.V. (1983). Effectiveness of special education. *Policy Studies Review, 2,* 65–78.

Granger, L., & Granger, B. (1986). *The Magic Feather.* New York: E. P. Dutton.

Grossman, H.J. (Ed.). (1983). *Terminology and classification in mental retardation.* Washington, DC: American Association on Mental Deficiency.

Hagerty, G.J., & Abramson, M. (1987). Impediments to implementing national policy change for mildly handicapped students. *Exceptional Children, 53*(4), 315–324.

Hobbs, N. (1980). An ecologically oriented service-based system for classification of handicapped children. In E. Salzmeyer, J. Antrobus, & J. Glick (Eds.), *The ecosystem of the "risk" child* (pp. 271–290). New York: Academic Press.

Hume, M. (1988a, March 4). Another year increases the demands on special education, report shows. *Education Daily,* pp. 7–8.

Hume, M. (1988b, March 15). Despite progress, states have problems to overcome in special education. *Education Daily,* pp. 1–3.

Hume, M. (1988c, February 17). OCR data shows minorities overrepresented among disability groups. *Education Daily,* pp. 5–6.

Kauffman, J.M., Lloyd, J.W., & McKinney, J.D. (Eds.). (1988). [Special Issue]. *Journal of Learning Disabilities, 21*(1).

Kavale, K.A., & Glass, G.V. (1982). The efficacy of special education interventions and practices: A compendium of meta-analysis findings. *Focus on Exceptional Children, 15*(4), 1–14.

Keogh, B.K. (1988). Learning disabilities: Diversity in search of order. In M.C. Wang, M.C. Reynolds, & H.J. Walberg (Eds.), *Handbook of special education: Research and practice: Vol. 2. Mildly handicapped conditions* (pp. 225–252). New York: Pergamon Press.

Leinhardt, G., & Pallay, A. (1982). Restrictive educational settings: Exile or haven? *Review of Educational Research, 52,* 557–578.

Madden, N.A., & Slavin, R.E. (1982). *Count me in: Academic achievement and social outcomes of mainstreaming students with mild academic handicaps.* Baltimore: The Johns Hopkins University Press.

Madden, N.A., & Slavin, R.E. (1983). Mainstreaming students with mild handicaps: Academic achievement and social outcomes. *Review of Educational Research, 53,* 519–569.

Mills v. Board of Education, 348 F. supp. 866. (D.C. 1972).

Morsink, C.V., Soar, R.S., Soar, R. M., & Thomas, R. (1986). Research on teaching: Opening the door to special education classrooms. *Exceptional Children, 53*(1), 32–40.

Ninth annual report to Congress on the implementation of the Education of the Handicapped Act. (1987). Washington, DC: U.S. Department of Education.

Pennsylvania Association of Retarded Citizens (PARC) v. Commonwealth of Pennsylvania, 334 F. Supp. 1257 (E.D. Penn. 1971).

PL 93-380, Amendments to the Elementary and Secondary Act (1974).

PL 94-142, The Education for All Handicapped Children Act, 1975, Sec. 612(5), B.

Roncker v. Walter, 700 F. 2d 1058, cert. denied, 104 S. Ct. 196 (1983).

Sansone, J., & Zigmond, N. (1986). Evaluating mainstreaming through an analysis of students' schedules. *Exceptional Children, 52,* 452–458.

Semmel, M., Gottlieb, J., & Robinson, N. (1979). Mainstreaming: Perspectives on educating handicapped students in the public schools. In D. Berliner (Ed.), *Review of research in education: Vol. 7.* (pp. 223–279). Washington, DC: American Educational Research Association.

Seventh annual report to Congress on the implementation of the Education of the Handicapped Act. (1985). Washington, DC: U.S. Department of Education.

Shepard, L.A., & Smith, L.A. (1981). *Evaluation of the Identification of Perceptual Communicative Disorders in Colorado.* Boulder: University of Colorado.

Special education: Views from America's cities. (1986). Washington, DC: The Council of Great City Schools.

Stephens, T.M. (1988). *Educating the handicapped: Yesterday, today, and tomorrow.* Unpublished manuscript.

Tenth annual report to Congress on the implementation of the Education of the Handicapped Act. (1988). Washington, DC: U.S. Department of Education.

Viadero, D. (1988, March 2). Study documents jumps in special education enrollments. *Education Week,* 17.

Walker, D.K., Singer, J.D., Palfrey, J.S., Orza, M., Wenger, M., & Butler, J.A. (1988). Who leaves and who stays in special education: A 2-year follow-up study. *Exceptional Children, 54*(5), 393–402.

Walker, L.J. (1987). Procedural rights in the wrong system: Special education is not enough. In A. Gartner & T. Joe (Eds.), *Images of the disabled/Disabling images* (pp. 97–116). New York: Praeger.

Wang, M.C., Reynolds, M.C., & Walberg, H.J. (1986). Rethinking special education, *Educational Leadership, 44,* 18–23.

Wang, M.C., & Walberg, H.J. (1988). Four fallacies of segregationism. *Exceptional Children, 55*(2), 128–137.

Weiner, R. (1985). *P.L. 94-142: Impact on the Schools.* Washington, DC: Capitol Publications.

White, R., & Calhoun, M.L. (1987). From referral to placement: Teachers' perceptions of their responsibilities. *Exceptional Children, 53*(5), 460–469.

Will writes NAPSEC to clarify OSEP guidance on LRE. Letter from Madeleine Will to David Holmes, November 30, 1987. (1988, spring). *CASE Newsletter, 29*(3 4), 1,3.

Ysseldyke, J.E. (1983). Current practices in making psychoeducational decisions about learning disabled students. *Journal of Learning Disabilities, 16,* 226–233.

Ysseldyke, J.E. (1987). Classification of handicapped students. In M.C. Wang, M.C. Reynolds, & H.J. Walberg (Eds.), *Handbook of special education: Research and practice, Vol. 1: Learner characteristics and adaptive education* (pp. 253–271). New York: Pergamon Press.

Ysseldyke, J.E., & Algozzine, B. (1983). LD or not LD: That's not the question. *Journal of Learning Disabilities, 16,* 29–31.

Ysseldyke, J.E., & Algozzine, B. (1984). *Introduction to special education.* Boston: Houghton Mifflin.

Ysseldyke, J.E., Algozzine, B., Shinn, M.R., & McGue, M. (1982). Similarities and differences between low achievers and students classified as learning disabled. *Journal of Special Education, 16,* 73–85.

Ysseldyke, J.E., Thurlow, M.L., Christenson, S.L., & Weiss, J. (1987). Time allocated to instruction of mentally retarded, learning disabled, emotionally disturbed, and non-handicapped elementary students. *Journal of Special Education, 21*(3), 49–55.

Ysseldyke, J.E., Algozzine, B., Richey, L., & Graden, J.L. (1982). Declaring students eligible for learning disabilities services. Why bother with the data? *Learning Disabilities Quarterly, 5,* 37–44.

Ysseldyke, J.E., Thurlow, M.L., Graden, J.L., Wesson, C., Algozzine, B., & Deno, S.L. (1983). Generalizations from five years of research on assessment and decision-making. *Exceptional Educational Quarterly, 4,* 79–93.

Ysseldyke, J.E., Algozzine, B., Regan, R., & Potter, M. (1980). Technical adequacy of tests used by professionals in simulated decision-making. *Psychology in the Schools, 17,* 202–209.

chapter 2

School Improvement Based on the Effective Schools Research

Lawrence W. Lezotte

For most of human history men and women have believed that only an elite is worthy and capable of education and that the great mass of people should be trained as hewers of wood and drawers of water, if they are to be trained at all. It was only at the end of the eighteenth century and the beginning of the nineteenth that popular leaders began to dream of universal school systems that would give everyone a chance to partake of the arts and sciences. Not surprisingly, they had their most immediate successes with the children who were easiest to teach—those who through early nurture in the family and other institutions had been prepared for whatever it was that the school had to offer.

Now in the twentieth century, we have turned to the more difficult task, the education of those at the margins—those who have physical, mental, or emotional handicaps, those who have long been held at a distance by political or social means, and those who for a variety of reasons are less ready for what the schools have to offer and hence are more difficult to teach. (Cremin, 1976, p. 85–86)

We can, whenever and wherever we choose, successfully teach all the children whose schooling is of interest to us. We already know more than we need in order to do this. Whether we do it or not must finally depend on how we feel about the fact that we haven't done it so far. (Edmonds, 1978, p. 35)

In his book *Making the Future Work,* the recognized futurist and author John Diebold makes the following statement: "Enduring change tends to occur when necessity coincides with vision" (1984). In the future, historians of education may well record that the decade of the 1980s was a time when necessity for school improvement and the evolving vision of effective schools came together to produce enduring change in the public schools of the United States. Whether one begins with the historical vision of Lawrence Cremin or the somewhat more revolutionary vision of Ron Edmonds, the necessity and vision are one: to successfully teach *all* the children.

25

School improvement based on the Effective Schools Research (ESR) data represents a struggle that has now spanned more than 20 years. The struggle of this vision of school improvement has successfully overcome numerous barriers and has demonstrated, with accelerating frequency, that we can successfully teach all of the children whose schooling is of interest to us.

In this paper, a brief interpretation of the effective schools movement is presented. The overview is organized around five relatively distinct periods. The first period discusses the problems of definition and the subsequent search for the effective school. This is followed by a second period during which a series of case studies designed to capture the organizational culture of the effective school are completed. The third period represents a critical transition from that of describing the effective school to that of creating more effective schools, one school at a time. The fourth period represents another important adaptation in the effective schools movement. This period characterizes how the larger organizational context of the local school district has come to play an important role in school improvement, and how it can enhance or impede improvement one school at a time. Finally, there is some discussion of the current federal and state policies and programs that are being implemented to ensure the availability of more effective schools for more children.

It is the author's hope that this paper successfully communicates the evolving nature of school improvement, and generates within the reader a renewed sense of optimism regarding our ability to successfully teach all children, including those students presently labeled as handicapped.

SEARCH FOR EFFECTIVE SCHOOLS

The story of the effective schools movement began on July 3, 1966, with the publication by James Coleman of the Equal Educational Opportunities Study (EEOS). On that day, Coleman and his colleagues reported findings that were to become widely accepted. Unfortunately, this public acceptance still constitutes a formidable obstacle to the advancement of educational equity and to the general improvement of student achievement through the instrument of the school. Perhaps the portion of the Coleman findings that best summarizes this issue is the following:

> Schools bring little influence to bear on a child's achievement that is independent of his background and general social context . . . this very lack of an independent effect means that the inequality imposed on children by their home, neighborhood and peer environment are carried along to become the inequalities with which they confront adult life at the end of school. For equality of educational opportunity must imply a strong effect of schools that is independent of the child's immediate social environment, and that strong independence is not present in American schools. (Coleman et al., 1966, p. 325)

Coleman and his colleagues clarified the public policy issue by bringing into sharp contrast the question of whether student achievement derives more from the homes from which children have come or the schools to which they are sent. The issue has been and will likely continue to be fundamental to the discourse on student achievement for a long time to come. It is basic in that it serves to question the sensibleness of increasing public investments in public schools if, in fact, schools do not, and seemingly cannot, make a difference.

Fortunately, several researchers did not accept the "Coleman hypothesis." These researchers, initially working independently of one another, began to formulate a research strategy that would, if successful, begin to challenge the hypothesis. The strategy was for the researchers to go into the "real world" of public schools and see if they could identify individual schools that represented clear exceptions to Coleman's theory. The set of first generation studies generated by these researchers became the foundation for the research base of the effective schools movement. Among the studies frequently cited are: *Inner City Children Can Be Taught to Read: Four Successful Schools* (Weber, 1971); *Elementary School Climate and School Achievement* (Brookover et al., 1978); *Search for Effective Schools: The Identification and Analysis of City Schools that Are Instructionally Effective for Poor Children* (Edmonds & Fredcriksen, 1979).

Those interested in an in-depth synthesis of the early research and public policy debate would find the Edmonds paper, "A Discussion of the Literature and Issues Related to Effective Schooling" (1978), a most important place to begin. Subsequent to the Edmonds paper, four additional syntheses of the effective schools research have been published. These papers are mentioned because they are easily accessible and, when taken in the order of their publication, do a good job of "tracking" the effective schools research, associated policy issues, and the research criticisms. In 1983, a research brief by Glen Robinson, *Effective Schools: A Summary of Research,* was published. Also in 1983, the *Educational Researcher* published an article by Donald MacKenzie: "Research for School Improvement: An Appraisal of Some Recent Trends." In 1985, the now often-quoted article by Stewart Purkey and Marshal Smith, "School Reform: The District Policy Implications of the Effective Schools Literature," was published in the *Elementary School Journal*. Finally, one of the recent summaries of research on effective schools was incorporated in a chapter in the *Third Handbook of Research on Teaching,* published in 1986. The chapter written by Thomas Good and Jere Brophy was entitled: "School Effects."

While it is always dangerous to depend totally on studies conducted by other researchers, these four different summaries do an excellent job of setting forth the research and policy base for what has come to be called the effective schools movement.

Beginning with Coleman et al. (1966) and reviewing the various summaries, one may observe several important issues and conclusions that seem to be associated with this research base. To begin, the validity of Coleman's theory remains largely intact. If, on the one hand, one judges student achievement by means of a "broad gauged," standardized, norm-referenced measure designed to find differences among the test population, then differences in measured student performance tend to be more directly associated with home and family background factors. If, on the other hand, one measures student achievement by assessing student mastery of basic school skills taught as a part of the curriculum, then the differences in school to school effects become more marked, and a stronger case is made for the school effect. The conclusion to be drawn is that the issues of measurement have been, and probably always will be, at or near the center of the debate on effective schools.

Because of the centrality of the measurement questions, any discussion of school improvement must begin with the question: "What would we be willing to accept as observable measurable evidence of school effectiveness or school improvement?" If there is no consensus on these questions, it is doubtful that school improvement would result. Phrased in a more colloquial way: "If you don't know where you are going, any road—or perhaps no road—will get you there."

To assist schools with the discussion of acceptable evidence of school improvement, the following definition of an effective school is offered. Conceptually, an effective school can be defined as one that can, in outcome terms reflective of its teaching for learning mission, demonstrate the joint presence of quality (acceptably high levels of achievement) and equity (no differences in the distribution of that achievement among the major subsets of the student population).

The case study literature that has come to be associated with the effective schools research has proven the generalization of Coleman and colleagues to be wrong in the following sense. The case study literature clearly demonstrates, in numerous settings, that there are schools that are able to attain remarkably high levels of pupil mastery of basic school skills even though these schools are serving large proportions of economically poor and disadvantaged students, minority and nonminority. The criticisms of the effective schools research have been many and pointed, but the one fact that seems to stand up against all the criticisms is the fact that some individual schools are able to achieve these extraordinary results. As long as such places exist, the effective schools debate is not a discussion of theory, but a discussion of commitment and political will.

DESCRIPTIONS OF EFFECTIVE SCHOOLS

During the second major period of the effective schools movement, the researchers' attention turned toward the internal operations of these "effective schools." Ironically, the search for effective schools captured the interest of social scientists and policymakers but not necessarily of educational practitioners. School leaders, teachers, and local boards of education began to take a more active interest in the effective schools research as the descriptions of the effective schools made their way into the literature and language of the educational community.

During this period in the effective schools movement, researchers sought to answer the following general question: "In what ways do effective schools differ from their less effective counterparts?" The research methodology that was used generally consisted of the following:

1. Effective schools, based on measured outcomes, were identified and paired with similar schools in all respects except for the more favorable student outcome profile.
2. Field researchers were sent into these "pairs of schools" to conduct interviews, observations, and surveys designed to develop as rich a description of the life of these schools as possible.
3. The data were then analyzed with the following question in mind: "What are the distinctive characteristics of the effective schools that seem to set them apart from their less effective counterparts?"

What emerged from the field research were descriptions of certain characteristics that seemed to describe how these schools were able to maintain the "exceptional status." Listed below are the five factors that Edmonds described in his earlier research.

1. The principal's leadership and attention to the quality of instruction
2. A pervasive and broadly understood instructional focus
3. An orderly, safe climate conducive to teaching and learning
4. Teacher behaviors that convey the expectation that all students are expected to obtain at least minimum mastery
5. The use of measures of pupil achievement as the basis for program evaluation

Since that original listing, many other studies have cross-validated the original findings. Some of the more recent studies have added additional factors, and others have sought to make the original Edmonds factors more explicit and more operational. New studies have also looked closely at elementary schools, as did Edmonds in his original research. Other recent studies have taken the characteristics or factor theory of the effective school to the secondary levels as well. In addition, the researchers have now documented the existence of the correlates in settings other than those that were characterized as serving primarily economically poor and minority student populations. Finally, the research has been expanded to include studies from cross cultural settings, with England represented most frequently.

What are the major conclusions that seem to emerge from this expanding array of studies of the organization and operation of effective schools? First, the more effective schools do share a describable list of institutional and organizational variables that seem to coexist with school effectiveness when it is defined by measured student mastery of the intended curriculum. Second, these core factors seem to be robust in that they have endured across the various studies. Third, the effective school can and generally does stand alone, even among its counterparts in the same local school district. The major implication is that the institutional and organizational mechanisms that coexist with effectiveness are attainable by the single school and one school at a time. This suggests that effective schooling is within the grasp of the teachers and administrators that define the teaching community of the single school.

With the publication of these descriptions of the effective school, practitioners and community members began to take a more active interest. It became clear that more schools could organize themselves to achieve these extraordinary results. The important question began to refocus itself: How could the knowledge about these effective schools become the basis for the purposeful transformation, through planned change programs, for even more schools?

CREATING MORE EFFECTIVE SCHOOLS: ONE SCHOOL AT A TIME

When school practitioners began to discover that the effective school could be characterized by a relatively short list of alterable school variables, some educators began to see new possibilities for their schools. The reasoning seemed to proceed along the following line: if individual schools had the authority to make their school effective, as suggested by the original effective schools descriptions, then individual schools ought to accept the responsibility for doing so. The problem was that the original research provided little guidance as to how the effective schools got to be effective. In the more common language of the 1980s, the effective schools research provided a vision of a more desirable place for schools to be, but gave little insight as to how best to make the journey to that place.

As a result, three problems began to emerge. First, in many cases, central offices and local boards of education, not knowing a better way, tried to mandate that their local schools become effective, and the sooner the better. This led to the conclusion by many teachers and building level administrators that the effective schools process was just another "top-down" model of school development.

Second, many principals were told that they were responsible for making their schools effective, that it was a matter of administrative responsibility. This led to a number of problems. Principals often erroneously concluded that they were expected to make their schools effective by themselves, and it created anxiety and a great deal of resistance from these principals. There were several reasons for the resistance. Principals felt they were not trained to be agents of change; their evaluations had generally been based on the efficient management of school processes rather than on results. Additionally, principals could not understand how these students could learn if many, if not most, of the lower achieving students came from deprived home and family backgrounds.

Third, teachers began to see the effective schools process as an administrative mechanism that implied that teachers were not already doing their best, given the existing working conditions. To many teachers, creating a "more effective school" meant simply "working harder."

Considering these apparently insurmountable problems and the resistance they engendered in the major "stakeholders" to more effective schools, why was the movement not stopped in its tracks? The survival of the effective schools movement, even against these significant obstacles, seemed to depend on the implementation strategies used by schools. In the paragraphs that follow, I will focus on the processes used by Edmonds and myself as we responded to the numerous invitations to work with schools. Our experience was repeated by many other facilitators of effective schools research with some variations in the processes themselves.

When we began to address the problems of implementation, we believed that if we were going to ask schools to change their practices based on the research findings, research should be used as a guide to the implementation processes as well. We reviewed three interrelated bodies of research for the purpose of identifying the lessons to be learned. The three areas of research we reviewed were grounded in our notion of school change. First, since school change could be regarded as "people change," we examined the research on effective staff development. Second, since school change could be considered organizational change, we looked at the literature on effective organizational development, especially as applied to the school. Third, whether school change is to be viewed as people change or systems change, we were clearly approaching it as planned change. Thus, we reviewed the literature on planned change. Fortunately, the lessons to be learned from the various research data added up to the same general conclusions. Among the guiding principles, we concluded the following about creating more effective schools:

1. Preserve the single school as the strategic unit for the planned change.
2. Principals, though essential as leaders of change, could not do it alone and, thus, teachers and others must be an integral part of the school improvement process.
3. School improvement, like any change, is best approached as a process, not an event. Such a process approach is more likely to create a permanent change in the operating culture of the school that will accommodate this new function called continuous school improvement.

4. The research would be useful in facilitating the change process but it would have to include suggestions for practices, policies, and procedures that could be implemented as a part of the process.

5. Finally, like the original effective schools, these improving schools must feel as if they have a choice in the matter and, equally as important, they must feel as if they have control over the processes of change.

With these guiding principles we set out to create school plans that would take the school from its current level of functioning toward the vision of effectiveness as represented in the research. Literally hundreds of schools launched their effective schools processes. Some did it with help from the outside, some chose to proceed on their own. Some followed the guidelines of the lessons we had learned even without knowing the research, per se, and others chose to try to implement change and ignore what the research on successful change has reported. As a result of this diversity in approaches, we can say that effective schools research worked for some and not for others. Fortunately, the research has worked often enough that there is a large and growing number of schools that can proudly claim that they have the results to prove that more of their students are learning. They feel empowered to commit their professional energies to the proposition that even more students can and will learn in their school in the future.

Two major conclusions can be drawn from the lessons learned from this period of the effective schools movement. First, while research does not have all of the answers, the literature on successful change clearly establishes that some strategies of planned change do indeed work better than others. Second, the process of school improvement based on the effective schools research takes time, involvement, and commitment. Whenever one tries to short cut any one of these essential prerequisites, the results are soon diminished. Clearly, when effective schools processes are followed appropriately, school improvement is effected. However, when effective schools processes are not implemented properly, more effective schools for more students are not produced.

DISTRICT-WIDE PROGRAMS
BASED ON EFFECTIVE SCHOOLS RESEARCH

The early efforts to implement programs of school improvement based on the effective schools research clearly supported the individual school as the strategic unit for change. Effective schools research emphasizes that if school improvement is going to occur, it will take place one school at a time.

Experience with the school-by-school model has taught a number of valuable lessons which, taken together, serve to reinforce the district-wide concept associated with this phase of the effective schools movement. Two forces seem to have combined to reinforce the current emphasis on the overall district planning model. First, political necessity associated with the general educational reform movement of the 1980s meant that local school districts needed a comprehensive program of school improvement if they were going to satisfy their various constituencies. After all, it did not seem to serve the interests of the local board and superintendents if, when asked about their commitment to school improvement, they could only respond by saying that they were doing what they were told by state mandates, although some of their individual schools were engaged in an effective schools process at the building level. From this frame of reference, the effective schools model represented a viable, manageable, and therefore, attractive, district response to the call locally for a program of school improvement.

The second force evolved independently of these larger political considerations. Individuals working with the effective schools model at the school level realized that individual schools exist as part of the larger legal, political, and organizational setting of the local school district. While it became clear that one could successfully effect school improvement at the individual school level and ignore this layered context, it also became clear that this would be difficult to do. However, when an individual school's faculty set out on their own to plan and implement their program, they often found themselves being challenged by their colleagues, or at least being impeded by district level policies, patterns, and practices.

These two forces were joined and a new, stronger formulation of the effective schools process resulted. This new formulation still places great emphasis on school level change, but it now emphasizes the larger organizational context and its role in supporting and enhancing the individual school's efforts. This new formulation builds upon the notion of a district plan that supports school change. In this plan, the policies, programs, and procedures generally thought to be beyond the control of a single school are aligned to support the effort. Those who believe in the collaborative approach at the school level strongly advocate that the district plan be written by a collaborative group of teachers, building and district administrators, and even community and parent representatives. This begins to model the collaborative process at the district level. Once the plan has been written, it would then go to the local board of education where, one hopes, the plan would be approved without significant modifications. This act, then, establishes the plan as a matter of official policy and as the guiding force for school improvement in the district and in each of its individual schools.

There are two types of challenges that are faced in the district planning process. The first challenge is that the plan must address the necessary changes in district level policies and programs to ensure that school level change can occur. The second challenge is that the plan must not go so far as to mandate what each school must do as its improvement plan. The first set of issues, when handled successfully by the district planning group, gives guidance, direction, and the human and financial resources to the school level improvement process. However, if this plan goes too far, the sense of ownership and involvement leading to the needed commitment that is essential at the school level gets lost.

The current emphasis on the district model serves several valuable functions. It acknowledges that when it comes to sustained school improvement, there are no unimportant adults in the system. Additionally, it acknowledges the critical role of the superintendent and the members of the board of education in providing leadership and vision for school improvement. As a matter of fact, this phase of the effective schools process makes it clear that without sustained leadership from the superintendent, it is unlikely that the effective schools movement will become all that it could be. Also, this model recognizes the need to more tightly couple and ensure alignment between the school site and the district office. Finally, it communicates to school level personnel that they are central to school effectiveness and all other personnel should stand ready to do whatever they can to be of assistance.

Early efforts at implementing effective schools produced an expanded list of individual schools that benefitted from these efforts. The increasing emphasis on the district level programs are also beginning to show encouraging signs that districts can move if their efforts reflect the appropriate degrees of coordination and institutional commitment. More time is needed to further refine the district-wide process. But as each preceding phase builds upon what has gone before, the fundamental belief that all students can and will learn will be reinforced.

BEYOND THE LOCAL SCHOOL DISTRICT

The story of the effective schools movement would be incomplete without at least a brief mention of what has been happening at levels of organization beyond the individual school district. Efforts to support school-by-school improvements based on the effective schools research have been a major organizational goal for intermediate educational agencies, state departments of education, regional accreditation groups, and the federal government. Recently, there have been international meetings on effective schools research and practices. It is clear that each of these various efforts adds strength to the effective schools movement.

It would be impossible to present a comprehensive discussion of all the methods each of these different agencies utilizes to assist with local school development. However, a brief discussion of several of these strategies will serve to illustrate the range.

The intermediate agencies, such as county school boards, intermediate districts, and boards of cooperative educational services, tend to provide assistance in three ways. First, they employ and train individuals who are knowledgeable about the effective schools research and deploy them to provide training and technical assistance to the component districts and individual schools. Second, they sponsor conferences and workshops for their constituent districts, bringing in nationally recognized speakers on effective schools to help support local planning efforts. Third, the intermediate districts often have funding mechanisms favorable to the local school districts. These mechanisms, such as matching funds, help the local and the smaller districts to receive the help they need.

Nearly all the state departments of education have been actively involved in school reform. Some of these efforts have specifically targeted the effective schools as the preferred process for school planning and school improvement. In some states, the departments have used mandates to ensure that the effective schools process is put in place. In other states, a wide range of programs such as incentive grants programs, state sponsored conferences, and school recognition programs have been implemented for the purpose of stimulating the more effective schools processes specifically. Evaluations of the various state sponsored programs designed to promote more effective schools are only now beginning to be undertaken. More time will be required before it can be determined which particular strategies and procedures have proven to be most effective in creating the stimulus for positive school change.

The various regional accreditation agencies have begun to redefine the accreditation standards that component schools must meet. Many of the new standards take the schools toward an effective schools process. This change on their part has been especially useful in stimulating secondary school involvement in an ongoing process of planning for school improvement. Until these changes began to occur, senior high school administrators were reluctant to get involved in the effective schools process because it appeared that they would have to engage in two processes where previously one seemed to serve their needs. Now the accreditation process and the effective schools process are becoming one. In the author's opinion, there is every reason to be hopeful. However, stimulating secondary school change will continue to be a challenge to those advocating effective schools. The reason for this is that secondary school personnel are not clear about their primary mission. Also, they are much less ready to speak to their accomplishments in terms of student mastery of the intended curriculum. Nevertheless, those secondary schools that have begun the effective schools process provide optimistic signs to other secondary schools and to the accreditation groups to whom they feel accountable.

One of the most recent developments that holds great promise for the further expansion of the effective schools movement is the 1988 Elementary and Secondary Education Reauthorization Bill. Chapter II programs provide funds to allow local districts to use a portion of their special monies to support the planning and implementation of their school improvement programs based specifically on the effective schools research. Since these provisions are only beginning to be tested in the field, it is far too early to determine their success in stimulating the further implementation of effective schools in districts receiving those special funds. Clearly, this law and these provisions bear watching in the years ahead.

Finally, the effective schools movement has become an international movement in the true sense of the term. In January, 1988, the first International Congress on School Effectiveness (ICSC) was held in London, England. The meeting was attended by nearly 200 educators, both researchers and practitioners, from more than 30 countries. A similar follow-up meeting is planned for 1989. The international dimension begins to give a global perspective to the notion that we can organize schools that truly teach all children, including those children presently labeled as handicapped.

SUMMARY

The five phases of the evolution of the effective schools movement, as presented, obviously did not occur in as neat a fashion as the presentation may have implied. However, each does represent an important facet of the overall effort. Each phase has added a new dimension to the effective schools movement. Each dimension is made richer by the presence of the others, for it is indeed true that in the effective schools movement, the whole is truly greater than the sum of its parts.

The effective school in the United States can be described in two words: "organized enthusiasm." The story of the effective schools movement is one of expanding organization and evolving enthusiasm from local, to district, to state, to national, and even international levels. It seems clear that quality and equity for all our schools is a vision within our grasp. To reach this vision is not so much a technical matter; whether schools are developed that truly teach all the children is a matter of political will. As Ron Edmonds said: "We already know more than we need to teach all the children whose schooling is of interest to us." Whether we do it or not is a matter of choice. Can our republic survive if we continue to waste one of our most precious resources—if we continue to underserve our nation's poor children?

REFERENCES

Brookover, W.B., et al. (1978). Elementary school social climate and school achievement. *American Educational Research Journal, 15*(2), 301–318.

Coleman, J.S., Campbell, E.Q., Hobson, C.J., McPartland, J., Mood, A.M., Weinfeld, F.D., & York, R.L., (1966). *Equality of educational opportunity*. Washington, DC: U.S. Government Printing Office.

Cremin, L.A. (1976). *Public Education*. New York: Basic Books.

Diebold, J. (1984). *Making the future work: Unleashing our powers of innovation for the decades ahead*. New York: Simon & Schuster.

Edmonds, R. (1978, July 10–14). *A discussion of the literature and issues related to effective schooling*. Paper prepared for the National Conference on Urban Education, St. Louis, MO.

Edmonds, R. (1982). Programs of school improvement: An overview. *Educational Leadership, 40*(3), 4–11.

Edmonds, R.R., & Frederiksen, J.R. (1979). *Search for effective schools: The identification and analysis of city schools that are instructionally effective for poor children.* ED 179 396.

Good, T., & Brophy, J. (1986). The social and institutional context of teaching: School effects. *Third handbook of research on teaching.* New York: American Educational Research Association.

Mackenzie, D.E. (1983). Research for school improvement: An appraisal of some recent trends. *Educational Researcher, 5*(17).

Purkey, S., & Smith, M. (1985). School reform: The district policy implications of the effective schools literature. *The Elementary School Journal, 85*(3).

Robinson, G. (1983). *Effective schools: A summary of research.* Arlington, VA: Educational Research Service, Inc.

Weber, G. (1971). *Inner city children can be taught to read: Four successful schools.* Occasional Paper No. 18. Washington, DC: Council for Basic Education.

part **II**

Classrooms and Schools

chapter 3

Integration of Students with Mild and Moderate Handicaps

Susan Stainback and William Stainback

Reynolds and Birch (1982) have pointed out that "the whole history of education for exceptional students can be told in terms of one steady trend that can be described as progressive inclusion" (p. 27). Great strides in this movement have been made relatively recently (Biklen, 1985; Forest, 1986; 1987a; Gartner & Lipsky, 1987; Graden, Casey, & Bonstrom, 1985; Madden & Slavin, 1983; Stainback & Stainback, 1985a; Wang & Birch, 1984b). It has been reflected in the past several decades by the emergence of concepts such as deinstitutionalization, normalization, integration, mainstreaming, zero rejection, delabeling, and merger.

We appear to be at a point in history wherein we are no longer satisfied with just discussing the mainstreaming or integration of some students into regular education. Rather, we have begun to analyze how we might go about integrating or merging special and regular education personnel, programs, and resources to design a unified, comprehensive regular education system capable of meeting the unique needs of all students in the mainstream of regular education (Forest, 1987a; Gartner & Lipsky, 1987; Lipsky & Gartner, 1987; Stainback & Stainback, 1984, 1985b, 1988a). Reviews of educational trends during the past decade have indicated that movement is in the direction of unifying or merging special and regular education (see Gartner & Lipsky, 1987; Stainback, Stainback, & Forest, in press).

There are a number of changes occurring at the present time that will propel us toward further eliminating the special and regular education dichotomy. For example, in the not too distant past, nearly everyone agreed that mainstreaming meant the integration of students labeled mildly handicapped into the mainstream of regular education. Thus, our task was to strengthen regular education to meet these students' needs. However, this is changing. The situation is becoming much more complex. A growing number of researchers, parents, and educators are beginning to advocate that *all* students be integrated into the mainstream of regular education, including those who have traditionally been labeled severely and profoundly handicapped (see Chapter 4, this volume, see also: Forest, 1987a; Gartner & Lipsky, 1987; Jacobs, 1986; Ruttiman & Forest, 1986; Stainback & Stainback, 1987; Strully, 1986). They essentially believe that it is time to stop developing criteria for who does or does not belong in the mainstream, and turn the spotlight instead toward increasing the capabilities of the regular school environment, the mainstream, to meet the unique needs of *all* students.

As this movement intensifies and progresses, it will be essential to remain cognizant that regular education is not at the present time structured or equipped to successfully meet the unique needs of all students. To gear up, special and regular educators will need to join together as one group with the purpose of organizing a strong and comprehensive regular system of education that can meet the needs of all students.

Our primary purpose in this chapter is to outline and discuss the regular education initiative and several of the adaptations needed in regular education to accommodate students traditionally labeled as mildly and/or moderately handicapped. The reader interested in methods of educating students labeled as severely, profoundly and/or multiply handicapped in regular classes is referred to Chapter 4 (this volume), and to Stainback, Stainback, and Forest (in press).

THE REGULAR EDUCATION INITIATIVE

The regular education initiative is an effort by the federal government to review, improve, and coordinate instruction for students with disabilities within general education classrooms. As stated by Madeleine Will, Assistant Secretary of Special Education and Rehabilitative Services, in her November, 1986 Report to the Secretary of Education:

> The Office of Special Education and Rehabilitative Services is committed to increasing the educational success of children with learning problems. OSERS challenges States to renew their commitment to serve these children effectively. The heart of this commitment is the search for ways to serve as many of these children as possible in the regular classroom by encouraging special education and other special programs to form a partnership with regular education. The objective of the partnership for special education and the other special programs is to use their knowledge and expertise to support regular education in educating children with learning problems. (p. 20)

The regular education initiative has made it easier to educate students classified as having mild and moderate disabilities in regular education. By developing the initiative, the Office of Special Education and Rehabilitative Services (OSERS) has supported experimental programs designed to educate students with mild and moderate disabilities in regular education classes. Through "waivers," special education, Chapter I, and other remedial and compensatory education, personnel are able to work in regular classrooms with general educators to help make instructional practices more supportive, adaptive, flexible, and individualized for all students. This contrasts with the earlier practice of working in isolation with students classified as handicapped or disadvantaged. This is designed to alleviate the problem of special personnel having to restrict their assistance to categories of students in isolated situations. Additionally, it lets them work side by side with regular educators to help make regular classes adaptive and individualized for all students. (The consequences of the limits of current practices are described in Chapter 5, this volume.)

While the regular education initiative has many positive attributes, it also has some negative ones. It focuses on students with mild and moderate disabilities and does not address the need to include in regular classrooms and regular education those students labeled severely and profoundly handicapped. It also primarily encourages collaboration between special and regular education as distinct groups. This contrasts with the concept of unifying special and regular education programs into a single, coordinated body focused on the same goal (see Stainback & Stainback, 1987). In addition, the regular education initiative requires that educational services and programs for students assigned a handicapped label be evaluated for appropriateness. Such evaluations are not conducted for nonhandicapped students. This results in inequality, since accountability procedures are built in for some students but not for others. The initiative also requires "special" education personnel, who want to work in regular education to apply for a "waiver" so that they will not have to work with specific categories of students in isolated ways. This makes it troublesome for special education personnel to work side by side with regular education personnel in order to implement flexible, supportive, and adaptive learning environments in regular education, since they must first apply for a waiver or risk losing funding. It would be more congruent with the philosophy and intent behind the least restrictive environment mandate in PL 94-142 if those who want to work only with labeled students in isolated situations were required to apply for the waiver. That is, it should be made easier to educate students in regular classes rather than more difficult. Despite these and other problems, however, the regular education initiative has the potential to significantly enhance the ability of educators to educate students classified as having mild and moderate disabilities in regular education classes

ADAPTATIONS NEEDED IN REGULAR EDUCATION

Teacher and Student Assistance

To meet diverse student needs in regular classes, teachers need assistance in ways of adapting instruction to individual needs. The use of *teacher assistance teams* (TAT) is one way to provide support to teachers in regular education classes. A team might include two or more people, such as students, parents, administrators, classroom teachers, school psychologists, speech and hearing specialists, and/or learning and behavior experts. The team comes together to brainstorm, problem solve, and exchange philosophies, ideas, methods, techniques, and activities directed toward assisting the teacher. The regular classroom teacher is typically the leader or pivotal point of the team. The responsibility of the team is to reduce the frustrations the teacher experiences when he or she is unsure of what to do to assist a child. The team makes as many helpful suggestions as possible and, in some cases, becomes involved in assisting in the implementation of the suggestions.

It should be stressed that the TAT is *not* intended to function as a special education referral system and is *not* a multidisciplinary assessment and placement committee. It is a teacher support system to help classroom teachers serve students in the regular education classroom (Hayek, 1987).

Special educators can serve as *support personnel* to assist classroom teachers with suggestions or provide an extra "pair of hands" to help adapt and individualize instruction to meet the unique needs of all class members. In addition, support personnel can offer students direct support or instruction in the mainstream for such things as understanding and communicating with peers and teachers, completing assignments, and/or developing positive social and friendship behaviors. It should be noted that when support personnel were first used in regular classrooms, they were assigned to work only with students classified as having disabilities or handicaps. They often followed or shadowed these students around in regular education classes. This tended to draw attention to the students with disabilities and set them apart from their peers. Thus, in recent years, support personnel have served a broader role. They often help regular class teachers adapt instruction to meet the needs of a variety of different students and/or directly assist any individual students, labeled or not, who are having difficulty in educational tasks or in gaining peer acceptance.

Peer Tutoring and Buddy Systems   Peer tutoring and buddy systems can be used to encourage students to help one another with various learning tasks. This can be done by teachers and other school personnel guiding and reinforcing students to help each other. Greater student success is often achieved in heterogeneous classrooms by students learning to share with each other and teach each other through various special friends projects, buddy systems, and tutoring programs (Lancioni, 1982; McHale, Olley, Marcus, & Simeonsson, 1981). An added advantage of encouraging this is that students are afforded an opportunity to learn about and practice the interdependent nature of a humane society, a community in which people share with and assist one another, and to accept responsibility for the achievement of goals by others as well as themselves.

Adaptive Instructional Practices

Cooperative Learning Activities (Johnson & Johnson, 1981) In a classroom, cooperative learning activities can provide appropriate learning experiences for students with diverse educational needs. Cooperative learning can be used to bring students of various achievement and intellectual levels together in a positive way, while at the same time allowing each student to work at his or her own individual level and pace (Slavin, Madden, & Leavey, 1984). Such activities encourage positive interaction among students; if the group's goal is to be reached, all students must coordinate their efforts to achieve the goal. (Further discussions of cooperative learning programs are found in Chapters 6 and 14, this volume.)

Individualized Programming Programming designed to accommodate for specific educational characteristics on an individual student basis can also be helpful. Such programming is criterion based. Instructional objectives, pacing, and materials are selected according to their appropriateness to the individual student rather than norm-referenced or selected in accordance with the expected average for the student's peer group.

Adaptive Learning Environments Another procedure that can be used to meet the unique needs of students in regular classes is the implementation of adaptive learning environments such as the one described by Wang and Birch (1984b). Such an environment:

> contains 12 critical design dimensions which in combination, support (a) identification of learning problems through a diagnostic-prescriptive monitoring system integrally related to the program's instructional component; (b) delabeling of mainstreamed "special" students and description of learning needs in instructional, rather than categorical terms; (c) individually designed educational plans that accommodate each student's learning strengths and needs; and (d) teaching of self-management skills that enable students to take increased responsibility for their learning. (p. 33)

(In Chapter 6, this volume, Margaret Wang expands upon these features of adaptive learning.)

In summary, it has been found through experience and research that diverse student needs can be met in regular education classes when teachers are provided assistance and ways of adapting instructional practices to individual differences (Madden & Slavin, 1983; Stainback, Stainback, & Forest, in press).

Evaluation Practices

To meet diverse student needs in regular classes, adaptations are needed in the ways students are provided recognition for educational achievements. In most instances, educational recognition is provided those students who excel in performance in relation to their classmates or to other school members. That is, most educational recognition is based on "norm-referenced assessments," such as getting the highest score or writing the best poem. Such recognition is based on competition and comparison with a peer group. In a system that includes students with varying skills, abilities, and interests, use of such student recognition is often demoralizing, inappropriate, and inherently unfair. Due to the diversity in characteristics among students, each student has at her or his disposal a different set of intellectual and other resources to draw upon for the competition. These underlying differences in resources can make competition with peers for recognition futile for some students, regardless of the effort expended, while other students require minimal effort to be the recipient of recognition. As a result, the norm-referenced educational recognition procedures commonly used in schools today can result in lack of motivation and even negative attitudes toward learning and achievement by many students.

In order to strengthen regular education to meet the needs of all students, assessment for positive attention and recognition should be criterion-based. In criterion-based assessments, students are compared with and encouraged to excel beyond their present highest skill achievements. This contrasts with norm-referenced comparisons and assessments that compare the individual's achievements with the achievements of others who have a different set of resources from which to draw.

Also requiring modification is the current system for reporting student progress or achievement. Most often, such reporting takes the form of letter ratings determined by teachers that are based either on a norm-referenced rating of comparison with class peers or on local, state, or national expected averages. In either case, determination of achieved skills is often not possible since the standards upon which the grades were based can vary greatly from one state, school, class, or even from student to student.

An alternative curriculum-based achievement reporting system could alleviate the nebulous meaning of a letter grade. Using a curriculum-based reporting system, educators could provide a print-out for every student that lists briefly and concisely the highest level of skills mastered by the student in the different curricular areas. Gains made from semester-to-semester and year-to-year could be easily discernable on a per-student basis. Similarly, potential employers or educational agency staff could determine whether a particular student has achieved the skills required to do a job, or to fill a position. They could also determine whether the student has gained the skills necessary for entrance into a course, program, or school and, if not, they could readily determine what skills are missing. Such reporting could be more clear and consistent across students, and more useful in evaluating a student's skills and/or achievements. Such curriculum-based reporting could strengthen regular education programs in meeting the instructional needs of all students by stressing and communicating specific educational skills gained by each student. The reporting system developed in Project Zero moves in this direction (see Chapter 7, this volume).

In short, if regular education is to be strengthened to accommodate a wide diversity of students, it will be important to modify the ways in which students are evaluated and grades are reported. If educators adhere to a norm-referenced approach to setting standards and evaluating progress, there will be students for whom the standards are either too high or too low. Inevitably, failure will result for some students while others will not be challenged, and there will be calls to establish special programs for these students.

School Structure

In order to meet diverse student needs, adaptations are also needed in the basic overall structure of many regular education systems. One change involves the return of special education personnel, services, and resources to the regular education system. Special education was conceived as a means to accommodate for the needs of students who were considered "different" or "special." However, through research and experience, there has been a gradual recognition that *every* student is different and special (Lipsky & Gartner, 1987; Stainback & Stainback, 1984). Thus, those aspects of education that have been developed and are available to deal with differences among students need to be utilized as integral and natural parts of regular education. This should not only help those students labeled as handicapped but should also assist in making the mainstream of regular education more responsive to the instructional needs of all students.

Another structural modification that would enhance flexibility in regular education programs would be to move away from the traditional lock step, graded organizational structure that presently operates in the public schools (Stainback, Stainback, Courtnage, & Jaben, 1985). For example, the current organizational structure is based on the following assumptions:

1. All students of the same chronological age are ready to be taught the same objectives.
2. All students require the same amount of time (i.e., an academic year) to master the predesignated objectives.
3. All students can master the predesignated objectives for the grade level across all curricular areas during the same year.

Both experience and research, however, refute each of these assumptions (Fenstermacher, 1983). Furthermore, when the assumptions are considered collectively, only a very small number of students could in all likelihood meet the criteria of these assumptions.

Because of the assumptions upon which it is based, the lock step graded system impedes rather than facilitates the individualization of educational programming. Contrary to the assumptions underlying the graded system, students are unique, exhibiting a wide diversity of learning needs. "To attempt to encompass these enormous differences within the educational expectations and specifications of a grade, borders on futility if not irresponsibility" (Goodlad, 1970, p. 25).

Rather than continuing in this graded structure, school systems should be modified to more accurately reflect the learning characteristics of students. Such systems should be based on the following assumptions:

1. Students vary from one another in regard to the age at which they are ready to learn specified objectives.
2. Students vary from one another in regard to the rate at which they learn given objectives.
3. The rate at which each student progresses through objectives varies from one curricular area to another.

Because the above assumptions are more reflective of characteristics among students, such assumptions should underlie the basic organizational structure of the schools. Proposed educational structures that are more closely aligned with the assumptions noted above include "nongraded" (Goodlad, 1984) and "individually guided education" (Nussel, Inglis, & Wiersme, 1976). More flexible systems include modifications such as: 1) nongraded grouping arrangements, 2) variable pacing and time requirements for learning, and 3) evaluation and programming based on individual student characteristics and achievement levels (criterion-referenced) rather than group averages (norm-referenced). There are a growing number of regular educators who are advocating for and devising methods to adopt instruction to meet the needs of diverse students (Fenstermacher & Goodlad, 1983; Wang & Walberg, 1983). (In Chapter 6, this volume, Margaret Wang describes the implementation of such methods.) There is a need for more representatives from both special and general education to join together in such efforts.

CONCLUSION

Three decades ago, racial integration in America was at the forefront of discussion and debate. In *Brown v. Board of Education,* Chief Justice Warren stated the position of the Supreme Court that separate education was not equal education. That landmark Supreme Court decision was an influential force in the passage of PL 94-142 (the Education for All Handicapped Children Act of 1975), affirming the right of all students to a free appropriate public education in the "least restricted environment."

In order to promote the placement of students into the least restrictive environment, the mainstreaming movement became popular. Mainstreaming basically involves the movement of students considered to be mildly handicapped into regular education for part or all of the school day.

Robert Bogdan (1983), a noted scholar in the study of policy issues in education, has recently completed a series of in-depth field studies of both successful and unsuccessful mainstreaming programs. Bogdan (1983) concluded:

> We have come to understand them [mainstreaming failures] not as indications that disabled children are inherently incapable of success in mainstream classrooms. Rather, these supposed failures of mainstreaming are problems of organizational arrangements, internecine politics, and a lack of will and skill of school personnel. (p. 428)

Unfortunately, unless adaptations occur in regular education, there is little likelihood that students being returned to the mainstream will be any more successful than they were before the advent of special classes. Special educators to date have not made concerted efforts to join regular educators in exploring ways of making instructional practices, evaluation procedures, and the underlying organizational structures of the schools more flexible and accommodating for all students.

Piecemeal and isolated efforts to help students and teachers function within the current system of regular education are not sufficient. The objectives inherent in the integration movement will never be fully realized until special and regular educators are willing to merge their expertise and resources to develop strong, flexible regular education structures that accommodate for individual differences. As Gilhool (1976) has noted, mainstreaming should not imply an integration of students defined as special into the mutual sameness of traditional regular education. Rather, the mainstream itself should be designed to appreciate differences, to celebrate differences, and to accommodate for differences.

Recently, the appropriateness of perpetuating the concept of the least restrictive environment for students considered disabled as a policy direction has been questioned (Taylor, 1988). As Taylor points out, while the least restrictive environment was forward-looking when it was conceived, it is now time to go further. Adherence to the concept of the least restrictive environment as a policy direction for the future appears neither warranted nor worthwhile for fostering the goals of achieving an integrated society. The reason is that the LRE assumes that segregated environments are appropriate in some circumstances.

There are a number of constraints that impede the achievement of an integrated system. The major constraint is attitudinal in nature. As noted by Lipsky and Gartner (1987): "the establishment of a separate system of education for the disabled is an outgrowth of attitudes toward disabled people" (p. 72). To continue making progress toward educating all students in the mainstream of regular education, the attitudes of educators, parents, and the general public will need to change. This will need to take place through education and daily contact with people labeled as handicapped or disabled.

The authors are optimistic. Historical trends indicate that increasing numbers of people (Stainback, Stainback, & Forest, in press) are adopting an attitude that people with disabilities should have the same rights as others, and should be accepted into the mainstream of school and community life. Similarly, people with disabilities are beginning to demand it (Gartner & Joe, 1987). As a result, we are beginning to "turn from the effort to perfect a separate special education system to the struggle of changing the educational system to make it both one and special for all students" (Lipsky & Gartner, 1987, p. 74).

REFERENCES

Biklen, D. (1985). *Achieving the Complete School*. New York: Columbia University Press.

Bogdan, R. (1983). Does mainstreaming work? is a silly question. *Phi Delta Kappan, 64*, 42–428.

Fenstermacher, G. (1983). Introduction. In G. Fenstermacher & J. Goodlad (Eds.), *Individual differences and the common curriculum* (pp. 1–8). Chicago: The University of Chicago Press.

Fenstermacher, G., & Goodlad, J. (Eds.) (1983). *Individual differences and the common curriculum*. Chicago: The University of Chicago Press.

Forest, M. (1986). Just one of the kids. *Entourage, 1*, 20–23.

Forest, M. (1987a). Keys to integration: Common sense ideas and hard work. *Entourage, 2*, 16–20.

Forest, M. (1987b). Start with the right attitude. *Entourage, 2*, 11–13.

Gartner, A., & Joe, T., (Eds.). (1987). *Images of the disabled, disabling images*. New York: Praeger.

Gartner, A., & Lipsky, D. (1987). Beyond special education. *Harvard Educational Review, 57*, 367–395.

Gilhool, T. (1976). Changing public policies: Roots and forces. In M. Reynolds (Ed.), *Mainstreaming: Origins and implications* (pp. 8–13). Reston, VA: The Council for Exceptional Children.

Goodlad, J. (1970). The nongraded school. *The National Elementary School Principal, 50*, 24–29.

Goodlad, J. (1984). *A place called school: Prospects for the future*. New York: McGraw-Hill.

Graden, J., Casey, A., & Bonstrom, O. (1985). Implementing a prereferral intervention system: Part II. The data. *Exceptional Children, 51*, 487–496.

Hayek, R. (1987). The teacher assistance team: A pre-referral support system. *Focus on Exceptional Children, 20*, 1–7.

Jacobs, J. (1986, November). *Educating students with severe handicaps in the regular education program, all day, everyday*. Paper presented at the 1986 annual conference of The Association for Persons with Severe Handicaps, San Francisco, CA.

Johnson, R., & Johnson, D. (1981). Building friendships between handicapped and nonhandicapped students: Effects of cooperative and individualistic instruction. *American Educational Research Journal, 18*, 415–424.

Lancioni, B. (1982). Normal children as tutors to teach social responses to withdrawn mentally retarded schoolmates: Training, maintenance, and generalization. *Journal of Applied Behavior Analysis, 15*, 17–40.

Lipsky, D., & Gartner, A. (1987). Capable of achievement and worthy of respect: Education of handicapped students as if they were full-fledged human beings. *Exceptional Children, 54*, 69–74.

Madden, N., & Slavin, R. (1983). Mainstreaming students with mild handicaps: Academic and social outcomes. *Review of Educational Research, 53*, 519–659.

McHale, S., Olley, J., Marcus, L., & Simeonsson, R. (1981). Nonhandicapped peers as tutors for autistic children. *Exceptional Children, 48,* 263–265.

Moran, M. (1983). Inventing a future for special education: A cautionary tale. *Journal for Special Educators, 19,* 28–36.

Nussel, E., Inglis, J., & Wiersme, W. (1976). *The teacher and individually guided education.* Reading, MA: Addison-Wesley.

PL 94-142, the Education for All Handicapped Children Act of 1975.

Reynolds, M., & Birch, J. (1982). *Teaching exceptional children in all America's schools* (2nd ed.). Reston, VA: The Council for Exceptional Children.

Ruttiman, A., & Forest, M. (1986). With a little help from my friends: The integration facilitator at work. *Entourage, 1,* 24–33.

Slavin, R. (1987). Grouping for instruction in the elementary school. *Educational Psychologist, 22,* 109–127.

Slavin, R., Madden, N., & Leavey, M. (1984). Effects of cooperative learning and individualized instruction on mainstreamed students. *Exceptional Children, 50,* 434–443.

Stainback, S., & Stainback, W. (Eds.) (1985a). *Integration of students with severe handicaps in regular schools.* Reston, VA: The Council for Exceptional Children.

Stainback, S., & Stainback, W. (1985b). The merger of special and regular education: Can it be done? *Exceptional Children, 51,* 517–521.

Stainback, S., & Stainback, W. (1988a). Classroom organization for diversity among students. In D. Biklen, D. Ferguson, & A. Ford (Eds.), *Disability and society.* Chicago: National Society for the Study of Education.

Stainback, S., & Stainback, W. (1988b). Needed changes in strengthening regular education. In J. Graden, J. Zins, & M. Curtis (Eds.), *Alternative educational delivery systems: Enhancing instructional options for all children* (pp. 17–34). Washington, DC: National Association for School Psychologists.

Stainback, S., Stainback, W., & Forest, M. (Eds.) (in press). *Educating all students in the mainstream of regular education.* Baltimore: Paul H. Brookes Publishing Co.

Stainback, W., & Stainback, S. (1984). A rationale for the merger of special and regular education. *Exceptional Children, 51,* 102–111.

Stainback, W., & Stainback, S. (1987). Educating all students in regular education. *TASH Newsletter, 13*(4), 1, 7.

Stainback, W., Stainback, S., Courtnage, L., & Jaben, T. (1985). Facilitating mainstreaming by modifying the mainstream. *Exceptional Children, 52,* 142–144.

Strully, J. (1986, November). *Our children and the regular education classroom: Or why settle for anything less than the best.* Paper presented at the 1986 annual conference of The Association for Persons with Severe Handicaps, San Francisco, CA.

Taylor, S. (1988). Caught in the continuum: A critical analysis of the principle of the least restrictive environment. *Journal of The Association for Persons with Severe Handicaps, 13,* 41–53.

Wang, M. (1980). Adaptive instruction: Building on diversity. *Theory into Practice, 19,* 122–127.

Wang, M. (1981). Mainstreaming exceptional children: Some instructional design considerations. *Elementary School Journal, 81,* 194–221.

Wang, M. (1982). *Effective mainstreaming is possible—provided that . . .* Pittsburgh: University of Pittsburgh, Learning Research and Developmental Center.

Wang, M. (1983). *Provision of adaptive instruction: Implementation and effects.* Pittsburgh: University of Pittsburgh, Learning Research and Development Center.

Wang, M., & Birch, J. (1984a). Comparison of a full-time mainstreaming program and a resource room approach. *Exceptional Children, 51,* 33–40.

Wang, M., & Birch, J. (1984b). Effective special education in regular classes. *Exceptional Children, 50,* 391–399.

Wang, M., & Walberg, H. (1983). Adaptive instruction and classroom time. *American Educational Research Journal, 20,* 601–626.

Will, M. (1986). *Educating students with learning problems—A shared responsibility: A report to the Secretary.* Washington, DC: U.S. Department of Education, Office of Special Education and Rehabilitative Services.

Ysseldyke, J., & Christenson, S. (1986). *The instructional environment scale.* Austin, Texas: PRO-ED.

chapter 4

The Educational, Social, and Vocational Integration of Students with the Most Severe Disabilities

Wayne Sailor

The unification of special and regular education is most definitely in the air. Whether the fragrance of this strange flower be sweet or acrid is very much in debate in the current literature. Whatever the judgment, it is certain that the seeds were sown in 1975 within the least restrictive environment (LRE) provisions of PL 94-142. Both the statute and its regulations are clear and consistent on the issue of where children with disabilities should receive their education. The environment that least restricts their involvement with their nondisabled peers is the most educationally desirable.

Years ago, the author participated in a series of workshops sponsored by the Midwest Regional Resource Center in Iowa. The workshops were conducted to assist local educational agency superintendents and special education directors from a number of midwestern states to begin to implement 94-142 in their respective regions. Not all of these directors were certain, by any stretch of the imagination, that this law and its extensive regulatory language was such a good idea. The LRE portion particularly rankled some participants. One vociferous administrator, in an oratorical denunciation of the process, shouted, "the logical extension of this LRE stuff is that we are going to be forced to put vegetables in the regular classroom!" The unfortunate culinary reference here was intended as an analogy rather than as a position statement on the nutritional needs of his district's students. Apart from his demeaning and pejorative language, was he prophesying? The argument advanced in this chapter is that he did indeed forecast correctly in essence, but only partially in form. For students with the most severe disabilities, more than 14 years after the beginning implementation of educational programs, the first glimmer of an educational design that truly em-

This manuscript was supported in part by the U.S. Department of Education Contract #300-82-0365 and Cooperative Agreement #G0087C3056. No official endorsement should be inferred.

bodies the LRE principle and its mandate (Gilhool & Stutman, 1978) is just beginning to take form, and yes, that form does include the regular classroom.

SEVERELY HANDICAPPED
PERSONS: POPULATION DEFINITION

Before examining the emerging form of this system in detail, some defining words are in order about the population under discussion. Brown and York (1974) have probably coined the most frequently cited definition of the phrase: "severely handicapped." They described the group as constituting the lowest 1% of the population on any measure of intellectual functioning. The problem with this definition is that many students labeled severely handicapped are un-testable, and thus unscorable, on any measure of intellectual functioning. This definitional issue was recently discussed in detail in a recent review of research literature pertaining to students with the most severe disabilities (Sailor, Gee, Goetz, & Graham, 1988).

For the purposes of this chapter, the term "zero rejection" is applicable. The emerging educational systems for students with the most severe disabilities are designed to serve all comers. *No* student is considered to be exempt from these systems. Exceptions to the zero rejection rule are so few (e.g., those for whom cumbersome life-support equipment or life-threatening behavior patterns preclude participation at the moment) as to be unworthy of serious concern as a legitimate separate system or subsystem of educational programmatic practice. Thus, these emerging designs, which are applicable to the unification of regular and special education, do not contain separate (or "segregated") special schools, either public or private. Nor do they include hospitals, institutions, or homebound instruction as options. These systems serve all eligible children in regular schools.

THE IMPORTANCE OF EDUCATIONAL ENVIRONMENTS

Do the above statements reflect a radical review of the situation? Perhaps, particularly to readers unfamiliar with the body of literature that has emerged in just the past few years dealing specifically with the issues of educational service delivery for students possessed of the most severe disabilities. Much of this literature has appeared in a series of books and in a journal associated with TASH, The Association for Persons with Severe Handicaps, and it may not be readily familiar to readers whose primary concern is occupied by other popula-tions of students in educational programs. For this reason, a brief review of some summary sources is presented here.

Historically, curriculum models for students with the most severe dis-abilities found their common origins in the works of Bereiter and Engelmann

(1966), who worked with preschool populations. Efforts to assess and determine the educational needs of such students were predicated on mental age/chronological age discrepancy models (Snell, 1987). The resulting curricula tended to cluster students in relatively homogeneous groups, by category of disability, in special schools. The students in these schools had little or no opportunity to interact with same-age, nondisabled peers (Sailor & Guess, 1983). The Bereiter and Engelmann system, which was strongly grounded in operant conditioning instructional tactics, led to rapid development and expansion. This was at least partly due to the often very dramatic early successes obtained with applied operant conditioning principles (cf. Gaylord-Ross & Holvoet, 1985; Snell, 1987). Development was also due to the data-based nature of these procedures in documenting changes referenced to specifiable goals and objectives (cf. Sailor & Guess, 1983). However, little attention was being paid to *where* students with severe disabilities were receiving their education during the early period of the populations' enfranchisement for educational programs (about 1974–1979). The honeymoon with operant instructional methodology in isolated settings was all the more enhanced during this period by the proliferation of volumes of studies documenting clear and rapid progress on a variety of skills with children who had been formerly written off by the medical establishment as ''untrainable'' (cf. Sontag, Smith, & Certo, 1977).

Then, in the early 1980s, what may be appropriately called the Lou Brown revolution got underway (cf. Madison Metropolitan School District, 1975–1988). Academics and practitioners across the country began to question the function and relevance of many of the skills that were being taught to severely disabled students within these strongly behavioral program practices. In their celebrated paper delineating the ''criterion of ultimate functioning,'' Brown, Nietupski, and Hamre-Nietupski (1977) managed to invalidate the antiquated, cognitive developmental curriculum model with its standard of mental age as the principal basis for deciding what to teach.

Two further conceptual developments during this period strengthened the growing importance of attending to the nature of educational environments with this population. The first was reflected in the emergence of a data-based literature documenting the relative importance in the child's social development of social and communicative interactions *among* children with and without disabilities. This was in contrast to the more characteristic pattern of disabled child/caregiving adult interactions (Bricker, 1978; Goetz, Schuler, & Sailor, 1979, 1981, 1983; Strain, 1983; Strain & Odom, 1986; Strain, Odom, & McConnell, 1984). The implications of this emerging literature increasingly suggested the need for opportunities for students with severe disabilities to interact with their nondisabled age mates. Goetz and Sailor (1988) have recently reviewed and summarized this literature.

The second development that challenged isolated, self-contained educational settings came in the form of a comprehensive analysis of the factors that produce generalized skill acquisition among students with severe disabilities.

What the bulk of this highly prolific research (recently summarized in Horner, McDonnell, & Bellamy [1986], and by Haring [in press]) clearly indicated was that for students with severe disabilities to generalize their skills to new situations where displays of the skills are called for and appropriate, the skills need to be taught in a variety of circumstances where each skill is utilized by a variety of personnel. Coupled with the admonition for the instruction of age-appropriate, functional skills (cf. Falvey, 1986; Sailor & Guess, 1983), there is clearly a need for community-based instruction and for a corresponding reduction of classroom instruction for students with severe disabilities. The resultant models of community-based instruction of this newer type have recently been reviewed and summarized by Sailor et al. (1986). In addition, Sailor, Goetz, Anderson, Hunt, and Gee (1988) have reviewed and summarized the research on both integration and community intensive instruction with the population of students with severe disabilities, including those with the most severe disabilities (see also Sailor, Gee, et al., 1988). At the leading edge of these instructional models (Meyer, Eichinger, & Park-Lee, 1987), the education of students with severe disabilities has shifted from a state of benevolent segregation and protectiveness to a state of social belonging and challenge in a mainstream social context.

What follows is an attempt to provide a concise summary of an educational model that embodies the long-range implications of these conceptual areas of research. This model (which is being published in detail with a supporting review of the literature in Sailor, Anderson, et al., 1989) represents a logical extension of the LRE mandate as it bears on the population of students with severe disabilities, the zero rejection population. The base of action for the model is, and must be, the regular public school. The broader implications for the unification of regular and special education have principally to do with the strategies and tactics employed at the regular school to facilitate interactions and involvement of students with severe disabilities with the general education population.

THE CONCEPT OF A COMPREHENSIVE LOCAL SCHOOL

It is argued here that, on the basis of a principle of zero rejection, the least restrictive, yet most appropriate, environment that the field of education has to offer students with severe disabilities is the comprehensive local school. If the local school is defined as the school the student would attend if he or she had no disabilities, then the comprehensive local school is that age-appropriate school nearest to the local school (if other than the local school) that meets the educational needs of all prospective students in the region. This would apply no matter how severely disabled the students are or what the nature of their disabilities are, and no matter how extensive or costly their special educational needs. The difference, then, between a local school placement and a comprehensive local school placement might come down to such transient and ultimately remediable problems as: 1) the lack of ramps or elevators at the local school, 2) problems of attitude with the local school administrators, 3) transportation problems, or 4) problems resulting from racial balance at the school. By this definition, the comprehensive local school is the same as the local school, or is a temporary substitute for the local school until such time as the local school can assume a policy of zero exclusion and, thus, become itself comprehensive.

The comprehensive local school has at least the following special characteristics:

1. It is age-appropriate for all of its students. If, for example, it is an elementary school, and there are no regular preschool children attending the school, location of a disabled preschool class at the school would be inappropriate.
2. Transportation to and from the school is accomplished in a reasonable time period, and is integrated to the maximum extent possible. That is, the students with disabilities are transported with nondisabled students, unless such transportation is justifiably impossible. In only the most rare instances should transportation from home to school exceed 45 minutes one way.
3. Where special classes are utilized at the school for the provision of educational programs to students with disabilities, those classes are located in the immediate proximity of regular classes serving nondisabled students in the same age group.
4. Procedures are carried out regularly to promote interactions between students with disabilities and nondisabled students throughout the school environment.
5. The school reflects, at all times, the natural proportion of students with disabilities in the school district at large. Thus, if a school serves a total of 500 students, and approximately 10% of the district's school population are in special education, then no more than about 50 students at the comprehensive local school would be expected to be special education students. About five of these students would be expected to have severe disabilities (10%).
6. The school program will at all times promote the inclusion of each disabled student in all school activities, including social, recreational, and administrative activities in which nondisabled students of comparable ages are included. Such activities would include, for example, aerobics classes, assemblies, field trips, graduation and other ceremonies, and dances.

These six factors constitute a working definition of integration for students with severe disabilities in regular schools. Obviously, there is more to the integration of students with disabilities on a zero exclusion basis than the location of such students on regular school campuses. It is, of course, possible to create conditions for severely disabled students at regular schools that are every bit as segregated and exclusionary as special school placements. This fact has now been recognized by a number of states. California, for example, has published state policy concerning placement in the least restrictive environment that contains language specific to some of the above six points.

Generalization and Social Interaction

The research literature that has appeared to date that examines student outcomes as a function of various instructional and curricular practices seems to suggest a particularly striking role for two of the above six points in facilitating student gains. These are the nature and frequency of interactions between students with severe disabilities and their nondisabled peers, and the range and number of environments in which instruction occurs (cf. Sailor, Goetz, et al., 1988 for a review of this literature). The data on multiple-site, multiple instructor teaching systems have grown largely out of the extensive literature on generalization of learning that has emerged in the past few years. Much of this research was recently summarized in Horner, Dunlap, and Koegel (1988).

MULTIENVIRONMENT INSTRUCTION

The author and his colleagues have used the terms "community intensive instruction" to describe the overall instructional design of a comprehensive local school program (Sailor, Anderson, et al., 1989; Sailor, Goetz, et al., 1988; Sailor et al., 1986). This design utilizes a multienvironmental assessment approach in which the natural characteristics (and demands) of a range of age-appropriate environments frequented by nondisabled peers are analyzed in relationship to the current skill levels of students with severe disabilities. A large component of this assessment process consists of parent and family input into the instructional plan for each student.

For the early childhood student, particularly one newly enfranchised for education through the recent passage of PL 99-457, the natural environment wherein the initial development of social skills takes place is in the regular public or private preschool program. The stress here is on *regular*. The present author suggests that segregating young children very early on the basis of disability by setting up, for example, special preschools, is to deprive those children of interactions with young nondisabled children. This would be taking place at an age when the resultant influence on subsequent social development, responsiveness, and attentiveness is very likely at a critical peak (Hanson & Hanline, 1989). The inclusion of young children with all ranges and types of disabilities in a maximum-contact situation with their nondisabled age-mates is quite likely to result in patterns of behavior characteristic of less severely disabled students later on (Sailor, Anderson, et al., 1989). Visitors to the integrated school programs of the San Francisco Unified School District, for example, are often struck by the relative absence of "medically fragile" students at the middle school and secondary age ranges. These students are not referred elsewhere, nor are they placed in segregated special programs within the District. The inescapable conclusion is that the full integration pattern of the District has now begun to result in the emergence of a less severely impaired group of students at later stages in their education. If this statement seems incredible, one has only to examine closely the content of the IEPs of the most severely disabled students who are still very young. For example, students who enter the District program with special medical apparatus, such as gastrostomy tubes to facilitate feeding, are targeted for oral soft food ingestion, and ultimately, tube independence. Students with poor muscle tone and abnormal positioning characteristics have specific goals established early for improved motor coordination, muscle tone, and head-body position. Mobility training is begun very early.

While full regular classroom placement of these students at very young ages is only now beginning to become a reality in the District, the long-term policy of placement of these young severely disabled students in regular, elementary school campuses, with extensive programmed interactions with nondisabled classmates, has proven to be a critical factor in the later success of integrated school placements. Other environments in which these young students receive instruction, often with assistance from regular education kids as "peer tutors" or "special friends," include playgrounds, cafeterias, bathrooms, hallways, libraries, and school offices. The principle of "general case instruction" (Horner et al., 1988) applied across these environments facilitates generalized skill acquisition and extension of newly learned performances to new environments where the display of these skills is appropriate.

As students advance in age through the educational system, fewer and fewer of their educational needs can be met in the context of a classroom, regular or special. Increasing amounts of time are required in natural community environments in order to facilitate generalized skill acquisition. The result of increased instructional time in natural community settings is progress in the acquisition of functional, useful, and age-appropriate skills that enhance the likelihood of an integrated postschool work and living situation in later years (Brown et al., 1987).

Integrated work and community living is, of course, the ultimate goal of a comprehensive local school educational model. It makes little sense to integrate and mainstream students with severe disabilities for the educational years, only to prepare them to enter a 20- or 30-bed residential institution where they will spend their days in a sheltered workshop or day treatment program. The Comprehensive Local School (CLS) model is thus closely linked to the concepts of transition and supported employment (Will, 1984, 1986, 1988). The social service system in the United States is at a stage wherein a sustained and intense effort is being made within and across states (and, for that matter, across countries) to coordinate planning for individuals with severe disabilities to move from school to integrated work and community living options.

To summarize briefly, the CLS model is predicated on data that support integrated, community intensive instructional programs for students with severe disabilities. The CLS model is the logical extension of the programmatic implications of LRE. The CLS model is also closely associated with the regular education initiative (Will, 1988) and with the unification of regular and special education programs.

Integration and Motivation

Keeping in mind the ultimate goal for the consumer of an integrated life-style with paid, meaningful work and a normalized living circumstance, the logic of CLS is as follows. Skill attainment, at any age, of a type that enhances progress toward normalized, independent living requires maximum motivation on the part of the student who has extensive special needs. What the student needs to learn is especially difficult relative to nondisabled peers. Research has demonstrated that motivation results from frequent and sustained interactions (cf. Anderson & Goetz, 1983); this motivation is at its highest levels in the earlier period (up to age 12) of social development (Sailor et al., 1986).

This motivation helps students succeed in the demanding circumstances encountered in regular community settings. Without this enhanced motivation, it is doubtful that young students with extensive and severe disabilities could master the demands of the postsecondary work and community life they encounter later on. It is axiomatic that people with severe disabilities have historically been sheltered, isolated, and protected through their life spans, so there is really no standard by which to evaluate progress in a more challenging set of circumstances. If the CLS model is grounded in correct assumptions and is successful in its outcome, a student with severe disabilities will be:

Immersed in a highly integrated social context early

Moved into the community for education in increasing increments as he or she advances in age

Prepared still later in real work settings for future job placement

Socialized in community settings to achieve a degree of independence and normal residential living in integrated circumstances, such as a cooperative shared apartment, an integrated group home, or in an integrated private setting with intensive attendant care

What remains is to describe the components of the CLS model. The model is futuristic to the extent that it does not exist in its entirety in any form or in any place at present. Many of the components are in place in the San Francisco Unified School District and in school districts in other parts of California. In Hawaii and Vermont, elements of a CLS model are in place; elements of the model are also present in Madison, Wisconsin; Syracuse, New York; parts of Oregon; and De Kalb County in Illinois. Such a model is presented here in its entirety, as a prediction of things to come. Combined with the progress described elsewhere in this book for other populations, it would seem to be a relatively safe and, most likely, a short-term prediction. The regular school is the place to be for all students, and the question for students with severe disabilities in the last decade of the twentieth century is not *whether*, but *how* to get there.

THE COMPREHENSIVE LOCAL SCHOOL MODEL (CLS)

The CLS model is multiphasic; that is, it manifests itself in sequential stages that correspond to age groupings with permeable boundaries. It is linear: it encompasses the life span of its students to the extent that they encounter public education programs. The model finds affinity with the writings of Nicholas Hobbs (1975), who argues that the answer does not lie in the development of more highly specialized technology fitted to the specialized needs of categorical groupings. Rather, the answer lies in improved perceptions. Children with disabilities will only come to full fruition as adult human beings when they are recognized as individuals who may be in need of special assistance, equipment, or modified environments as they grow. This approach contrasts with one in which children with disabilities are stereotyped as the retardates, the blind, the deaf, and so on.

For CLS to achieve its full potential, a certain amount of restructuring will be implicit. For example, the way teachers are trained and licensed for the provision of service to students with disabilities will need to change (see Chapter 8, this volume). These processes will necessarily have to become more generic and less specialized. As Hobbs has argued, we need teachers who know something of the special implications of blindness, not teachers of the blind. It is likely that schools will increasingly come to need teachers with specialized skills to assist as part of educational teams, rather than being classroom-based special education teachers. Specialized instructional teams will need to manage components of the educational process as delivered to heterogeneous groups of students with specialized educational needs. Such a model will likely supplant teachers of "deaf-blind" students or of "autistic" students who teach self-contained classes of their respective populations.

San Francisco Unified School District recently tackled one such component by hiring its first occupant of a new position called "transition specialist." Regardless of range, type, or extent of disability of the student, it is special education teacher Sara Murphy's job to team with other educational personnel in effecting the transition of students with disabilities in the District from school, job, and community living preparation efforts to the postschool world of integrated job placement and normalized community living. The District has plans to expand this highly successful concept to additional positions. A similar position has been developed by the Center for Advanced Study in Education at the Graduate Center of the City University of New York. The program will be implemented in the New York City public schools.

In addition to restructuring, full implementation of a CLS type model will involve the use of the community at large as the "classroom," particularly for students with severe disabilities. This has important social policy ramifications. From about fourth-grade equivalency on, instruction can occur in the student's home or in other homes or apartments dedicated to educational use. Instruction can also take place in restaurants, public pools, buses, streets, and at job training sites, as well as in all of the environments that constitute the school itself. Such a concept will affect school staffing and student grouping and transportation, as well as family, school, and community attitudes toward children with disabilities (see Sailor et al., 1989).

CLS consists of five distinct phases which correspond roughly to chronological age groupings. Two of the phases, I and V, overlap the responsibilities and functions of agencies other than schools, but they allow for the possibility of coordination, monitoring, and quality control of these transdisciplinary functions by the public education agency.

PHASE I: MAINSTREAMING

At this point, it may be useful to differentiate between two terms that are frequently used in discussions of the movement of students with severe disabilities to regular schools. The term "mainstreaming" is used here to mean the primary placement of a pupil in the regular classroom for educational purposes. The term "integration" is used here to mean the location of students with disabilities on regular school campuses (in accordance with the six characteristics delineated earlier in this chapter). "Partial mainstreaming" refers to placement of students with disabilities in the regular classrooms for a part of their instructional day, but not as the primary placement.

Phase I starts at the first point of contact with educational agencies. Under current legislation, this involves (in some states) children as young as newborns. More typically, such programs include children who are about 2–3 years of age. The term mainstreaming was selected for this phase in order to emphasize the primacy of placement in a regular educational context, that is, in the same physical unit (or class) that serves nondisabled children.

Groupings of nondisabled children before the age of public school placement typically take the form of day care at very young ages (0–3 years), and preschool at ages 4–5. In some areas, kindergarten begins at age 5, in others, at age 6. School districts in states that currently offer programs under PL 99-457 have, under current proposed regulations, a number of options for providing day care or preschool services. A district may, for example, choose to operate a special education day program—usually half-day, but sometimes full-day—on an isolated site or on a site with nondisabled children. It can group young children with disabilities into a Head Start program at a regular elementary school. It can also choose to contract with private preschool and day care providers for all or part of the educational program. The isolated, disability-only site is presently the least defensible, since the proposed regulations for PL 99-457 place a strong emphasis on service provision in the least restrictive environment.

The comprehensive local school model takes a clear position on this issue. School districts should contract for day care and preschool educational services with private providers who serve primarily nondisabled children. The reason for this preference is that the private provider is very likely to offer the only opportunity for full mainstreaming to occur with same-age children who are nondisabled. The elementary school has children who are too old for these toddlers to have a truly integrated experience. Amalgamations with other "problem" populations, such as the at-risk groups found in Head Start programs, do not constitute a true mainstream experience.

There are problems, however. As Filler, Baumgart, and Askvig (1989) point out, schools lack the resources to exert quality control over the selection of private day service providers. Some of these providers are quite substandard. The result is that an undue burden is placed on the parent of a disabled child to locate a suitable day care or preschool provider, and then to convince the district to fund the placement. Additionally, the child needs and is entitled to special services from the district under PL 99-457. In many cases, the district is unwilling to send specialized personnel, such as teachers and therapists, into a setting with which it is unfamiliar and over which it has no direct control.

In some cases, districts work out contractual agreements with private providers specifying IEPs at least yearly for each child funded under PL 99-457. The IEP then becomes the vehicle for deciding the conditions under which special personnel, equipment, and transportation are delivered through the private provider. In other cases, the district simply evaluates a total service plan from a private provider and then decides which portion, if not the whole plan, it will fund. In some cases, districts (such as the San Francisco Unified District, for example) provide combinations of services, with equipment and special personnel going out to mainstreamed day care and preschool programs for some days of the week, and with the child returning to a special class at an elementary school for other days.

The existing base of data from research on the early childhood population strongly supports a full mainstream model when child outcomes are the primary variables of interest (cf. Bagnato, Kontos, & Neisworth, 1987; Cooke, Ruskus, Apolloni, & Peck, 1981; Filler et al., 1989; Guralnick, 1981; Hanline, 1985; Hanson & Hanline, 1989). Only when administrative considerations and logistical barriers to mainstreaming become an issue does one find pressure to seek alternatives to a full mainstream model. No matter how severely or multiply disabled a child is, there is no aspect of his or her educational needs that cannot be met in a private day care or preschool context. The great advantage of such programs lies in the ready acceptance of nondisabled children to engage and interact with the special needs population of children. The single greatest educational need of early childhood is socialization, whether the child is disabled or not. The social behavior emerging at this age helps a child with disabilities cope with more complex demands of environments encountered later. There is strong evidence to suggest that interactions with nondisabled peers, particularly at the youngest ages, form the foundation upon which more complex skills are acquired (cf. Halvorsen, Doering, Farron-Davis, Usilton, & Sailor, 1989; Sailor, Anderson, et al., (1989).

The mainstreaming phase is thus preparatory for placement at the local school, rather than synonymous with it. Under the CLS model, the local school is responsible for meeting the educational needs of early childhood level students who will ultimately be eligible to go to that school later on. A partnership of the local school administration and the parent, by this model, can lead to joint selection and approval for placement of a child with disabilities into a regular day care or preschool setting, ideally, (but not necessarily) in the vicinity of the school. The preschool provider should accept children with disabilities into its regular program, but not in such large numbers as to deviate from the natural proportion of disability in the population at large. If a preschool serves 50 students, for example, no more than five or six should be students with disabilities, and of those, only one or two at most should be students with severe disabilities. The local school would have the responsibility to provide teaching consultation, equipment, therapists, training, and whatever else is required under the IEP process to administer the educational program. For a large day care or preschool provider, it might become feasible to fund one or more full-time, specialized staff members in order to at least partially meet the needs of the students with disabilities at such sites. But it would be important that these staff members team teach with all of the regular staff, in order to prevent situational isolation or segregation of the disabled children in the program.

What of the child of 5 or 6 years who is ready to enter kindergarten? Should this child, even if he or she is severely disabled, be separated from the normal peer group at this juncture? Not by the standards of the CLS model. The regular kindergarten classroom is the most appropriate (and least restrictive) environment for students with disabilities in that age range. Much, if not most, of the curriculum of the kindergarten is geared toward supervised, small-group activity that is important to the social development of disabled children. Again, specialized support services, including special education teaching staff, can be integrated into the regular kindergarten on at least a consultative or part-time basis.

Finally, there is a more subtle process that is set into motion by mainstream placement of infants, toddlers, and kindergartners. This process is recognizable to professionals and parents alike who experience these programs, but there is as yet little or no research about it. This process has to do with the effect on the family as a whole of not having their child kept apart from normal children as a consequence of disability. When their child is in a mainstream program, parents seem to see themselves as a part of general education and day care rather than as unique people faced with a lifetime of separate structures (Hanline & Halvorsen, 1988). The potential for greater acceptance, even within the family, of the disabled child, is obvious here (see Chapter 9, this volume). The developmental question for later ages becomes: "What is the difference between being a special child with unique needs versus being just another child who happens to have some special requirements to facilitate learning?'' The public ethos appears to be changing, and for good reason, from accentuating the specialness to accentuating inclusion.

PHASE II: INTEGRATION

At the age of first-grade equivalency, something different from the foregoing begins to occur. The regular education curriculum begins to become heavily academic. Less emphasis is placed on children's social development and play skills, and more on reading and mathematics. Most first-grade classes are physically oriented to a single point in the classroom to reflect the different pedagogy of this period. Less activity is occurring in this program that is programmatically appropriate for the severely disabled student. If this student were to retain a full-time placement in this classroom, he or she might begin to become increasingly isolated, as the intellectual requirements of the curriculum become less and less relevant. There is a point at which the advantages of social proximity to non-disabled peers are outweighed by the need for specialized skill instruction, particularly when the opportunities for direct social interaction with those peers diminishes by virtue of their attention being directed toward the class teacher.

The primary curricular needs of the age group of severely disabled students of first through about fourth-grade equivalency is for functional life skills (cf. Brown & York, 1974), not academic skills. The goal for students with severe disabilities is partial or total participation in all nonacademic activities that characterize their age group. The degree of exposure to academic skills, of course, varies with the level of severity of the intellectual disability of the student.

The term integration is thus used to describe the nature of the program from about first through fourth- or fifth-grade equivalency, that is, continuing contact with nondisabled peers, but without full-time, regular classroom placement. The integration phase of the CLS model calls for students with severe disabilities to be placed at the regular (comprehensive local or local) school, but with the possibility of some out-of-regular class time available in the program.

Under this model, the disabled student is assigned to a regular class. The regular first-grade teacher, for example, has primary responsibility for the student with severe disabilities. A desk (or other space) is reserved in the first-grade room for that student. When an activity is scheduled to take place in the regular class that meets an IEP objective, or that is generally appropriate for participation by the student with severe disabilities, he or she spends that time in the regular classroom. Assistance by specialized personnel may be called for. Thus, the child may be in a special class at the school for at least part of the school day.

The critical importance of ''horizontal interactions'' (Sailor, Goetz, et al., 1988), mentioned earlier in this chapter, determines much of the curricular effort in this phase of integration. Horizontal interactions are those that occur across children, particularly between students with severe disabilities and those with no disabilities. These interactions are qualitatively different from "vertical interactions," which are those that occur between children and adults, usually "top-down," that is, from the caregiving adult to the disabled child.

The research of Brinker (1985) and Brinker and Thorpe (1986), as well as Anderson and Goetz (1983), has shown that horizontal interactions play a major role in facilitating a range of positive outcomes (cf. Meyer et al., 1987) with students who have severe disabilities (cf. Sailor, Goetz, et al., 1988, for a review of these and related studies on the issue of social and communicative development). In short, the more frequent and diverse the social and communicative contacts between severely disabled and nondisabled students during Phases I and II, the greater will be the positive impact on a range of educational outcomes for severely disabled students.

Some methods that are frequently employed to increase these "horizontal" interactive contacts are practices called "peer tutorials" and "special friends" (cf. Voeltz, 1980, 1982; Sailor et al., 1986). Arrangements are made between special class teachers and regular teachers to allow volunteer regular class children to spend time in the special classroom. Those children who spontaneously show a nascent proclivity for teaching are provided those opportunities together with a little assistance on technique. Children who show no inclination toward tutoring, but who like to be with particular students who have severe disabilities, are encouraged to do so during these periods.

The phase of integration thus maximizes social contact with regular school children in two ways: by *in situ* regular class participation, both in and out of the regular classroom, and by participation of regular students in the special class situation through friendship and tutorial programs.

PHASE III: COMMUNITY INTENSIVE INSTRUCTION

This phase of the model, which roughly parallels fifth- through eighth-grade equivalency, marks a major shift in educational programming. The program shifts away from the concentrated development of social and communicative skills toward increased competence in functional community living skills. Research to date on community intensive instruction seems to suggest that for outcomes in Phase III to show dramatic gains, the social goals of the prior phases need to be realized. It is as if the motivation supplied by successful social development in the highly integrated context of Phases I and II fuels the student for the lonelier, more difficult tasks of community mobility. The evidence for this is anecdotal at present, but observations of severely disabled students who entered community intensive instruction at ages under 10 years from previous segregated (disabled only) schools, led to the observation that these students were (initially) less successful in comparison to those with equivalent levels and types of disability who had been formerly integrated into regular schools and classes (Sailor et al., 1989).

The main characteristic of the Phase III process is the rapidly increasing amount of time that students with severe disabilities spend away from school sites and in the community for their instruction.

As mentioned earlier, recent research on generalization, that is, the extension of skills taught in a purely instructional context to competent utilization in natural settings, indicates the importance of *in situ* instruction (cf. Haring, in press; Horner et al., 1986). In order for students with severe disabilities to extend competent performances of living and working skills into natural environments, they must be taught over time in a variety of those environments by several instructional staff members. The ultimate goal of all instruction with severely disabled students is to bring them to the point of maximum independence and self-sufficiency in normal integrated work and living environments. This is because those environments provide the highest quality of life opportunities by virtue of the extent of social integration and interdependence that is available (cf. Brown et al., 1987; Meyer et al., 1987).

When a student reaches age 12, during the middle school (or junior high school) period of Phase III, the first concentrated effort is begun to prepare the student for entry into the world of working life. The student at this time begins instruction in various jobs around the school to begin to develop various generic work skills. The first IEP that occurs following the student's 14th birthday is an occasion for the development of an individualized transition plan (ITP). At this time, in accordance with the CLS model, representatives of agencies that will ultimately be responsible for the student (or client) upon leaving the jurisdiction of the school system are invited to attend. Usually, this includes representatives of the Department of Vocational Rehabilitation and the Department of Developmental Disabilities (or their equivalents). These individuals will have the responsibility of tracking the student's progress through the remaining school years and preparing him or her for postschool living and working circumstances. It is the goal of the personnel working within the CLS model that no student should "graduate" from the school environment into segregated postschool living and day service circumstances. For such aspirations to be realizable, however, students must be worked with at a very early stage in their educational development to begin the attainment of such a level of relative self-sufficiency as to ensure integrated placements.

During Phase III, students will have job training experiences of a low level, beginning nature, often around the middle school environs. Conducting the internal school mail distribution route, for example, emptying trash, or washing tables and windows are typical vocational activities during the phase of community intensive instruction (cf. Sailor et al., 1986). Job training during this phase is only a small portion of the total IEP or ITP relative to the broader range of community living skills that are developed during this period, such as community mobility, recreation, and domestic living skills. Apartments, houses, and group homes are often utilized as training sites during this phase, to enhance generalized skill development.

PHASE IV: TRANSITION

The equivalent age of entry into high school marks the boundary for emergence into the phase of transition within the CLS model. Transition thus begins at about ninth-grade equivalency and lasts until graduation, or the point at which the student moves from the secondary educational program to the auspices of a postschool service provider agency. This process should be a smooth and coordinated one, with the least amount of disruption occurring in the lives of the family of the student with severe disabilities.

Programmatically, the phase of transition is characterized by a greatly intensified focus on vocational development. Since continued integrated living is the primary goal of CLS model education, work takes on an enormous significance because it constitutes, quite literally, the only integrated circumstance available after movement from public school programs. If a student cannot sustain integrated employment upon reaching age 18 or 22, or whatever age marks the passage from school, then the probability that such a student will encounter a segregated set of circumstances for permanent placement is very high (Brown et al., 1987). Brown and others have shown that even the most severely disabled clients can sustain integrated work with appropriate supports and adaptations (Sailor, Gee, et al., 1988). Thus, there is at present some validity for the CLS model's assertion that no student should have to graduate into sheltered or otherwise segregated circumstances.

During the phase of transition, students with severe disabilities use the local high school campus as a base. Those students in the upper ranges of the severe disability continuum may spend time in remedial programs such as math, reading, and computer instruction at the high school. At other times, such students will be in job training sites, possibly in conjunction with a vocational educational program (e.g., Gaylord-Ross, Siegel, Park, & Wilson, 1988).

The CLS model uses a vocational rotation job sampling strategy during this phase (e.g., Sailor et al., 1989). While in the high school program, each student experiences two or more community job training sites per year, where he or she will learn a job to a prespecified level of competence. Various job experiences (e.g., janitorial tasks, fast food tasks) are specified for each student depending upon the student's special needs for adaptive equipment, as well as preferences, or level of potential competence. As criterion is reached on any one job type, the student is moved (rotated) to another job site where a different type of job is learned to criterion. The intent of the rotation strategy is to provide experiences with a range of potential integrated job opportunities so that the prospect of matching each student's preferences and abilities with an appropriate vocational choice is ultimately realized.

The CLS model adheres strongly to the principle that students should receive educational experiences in age-appropriate environments. For this reason, every effort is made to complete the process of transition by age 18, which is the maximum age that involvement with a high school program is appropriate. In California, the maximum age for participation in educational programs under PL 94-142 funding is 22 years. For this reason, efforts are presently under way to develop community college sites as a vehicle for continuing education after 18 and until 22, if necessary. Students can, of course, affiliate with a community college placement after graduation from the secondary program, but this idea is not supported under the CLS model for the reason that a community college is not considered to be a suitable postschool provider agency. The college should be preparatory to integrated work and community living, rather than a terminal service provider in and of itself.

Another distinguishing characteristic of the transition phase is the recognition that it is not just the client who is in transition, but really the client's whole family. Parents of students with severe disabilities often have difficulty imagining a life for their child outside of the protection of the family home (cf. Halvorsen et al., 1989). Similarly, parents are often very concerned with the issue of who will provide for their disabled child after their death. The age of transition is the time when these factors are likely to surface in a significant way. Teaching staff as well as personnel at the postschool provider agency must work together during this period to assist the student and his or her parents in preparation for the moment of transition. (See Chapter 9, this volume, for details of such a partnership.)

Finally, it is the coordination and planning of services and their differential funding implications that is the hallmark of the phase of transition as well as its single biggest unresolved problem. The problem of coordinated service planning and funding for transition has recently been identified as world-wide in scope (Organization for Economic Co-operation and Development [OECD], 1987). The three primary agencies that are involved at this age are education, rehabilitation, and developmental disability agencies (or their equivalent state level departments). Each has regulations and sources of funding to carry out its specific mission on behalf of the client with severe disabilities, but none has the regulatory or statutory responsibility to carry out "bridge" functions, such as those that characterize transition programs.

Coordinated family information and counseling services, teaching and follow-up services, job site identification, and support services preparatory to placement—all are transitional functions that currently fall to educators. Unfortunately, educational facilities are not funded to carry out these functions, nor are educators particularly well-prepared or qualified to deliver these functions. What is needed is an identified transitional services provider at the state level for each state. A few states (such as Minnesota) have experimental systems to carry out these functions. Some countries, most notably Denmark (OECD Draft Report, 1987), have created fairly elaborate federal-level structures to handle the problem of multiagency coordination and cost-sharing to accomplish the transition of developmentally disabled persons. The problem at this writing, however, remains largely unsolved.

PHASE V: INTEGRATED WORK AND COMMUNITY LIVING

Phase V is really postschool, but it remains a part of the CLS model because it is the ultimate target of all of the efforts carried out in the first four phases. Ideally, this phase should begin at ages 17–18 and continue through adulthood, or as long as some form of agency support service is required. The primary role of the education agency in the Phase V program is to carry out follow-up and tracking of all the high school graduates with disabilities, in order to ensure that the transitional effort was and remains successful in meeting the clients' needs. Information from the tracking process should thus be used by the high school to revise and perfect its Phase IV program. Students with severe disabilities, for example, who fail to maintain an integrated work or living placement, might need follow-up efforts from high school personnel to reactivate the coordinated planning process. This would ensure that the program graduate is not placed in a segregated, sheltered environment.

Finally, the issue of integrated residential placement is undeveloped territory. Much emphasis has been put in recent years on group home development as an alternative to remaining in the family home (age-inappropriate after age 18–22 years), or being placed in some more restrictive environment, such as a facility for disabled people with more than six beds (i.e., institutional placement). Some models of foster home and cooperative apartment placement have been developing in the past few years (cf. Aneno, 1987; Haney, 1988; Shoultz, 1986; Walker & Salon, 1987), and many of these seem to be potential integrated alternatives to reliance on group homes. The problem with most group home models is that they perpetuate a system of separateness. The residents are usually disabled, and nondisabled people tend to be all paid staff. The cooperative apartment model, on the other hand, tends to create opportunities for shared living experiences between disabled and nondisabled people.

THE COMPREHENSIVE LOCAL SCHOOL MODEL: SUMMARY

Tom Bellamy, Director of the Office of Special Education Programs of the U.S. Department of Education, recently wrote that:

> Local schools should be for *everyone*. From the beginning, PL 94-142 established the presumption in favor of the regular education environment. The law stipulates

that we remove people from the regular education environment only when absolutely necessary, and only so far as absolutely necessary to meet individual educational needs. A personal paraphrase of the assumption or belief embedded in that provision is as follows: It is better for children; it is better for parents; it is better for communities; it is better for future employers; it is better for peers; and it is better for teachers when children with disabilities attend and are served well by the regular schools in their neighborhood.

In many ways, that is a simple extension of my first belief. If society is for everybody, then school logically should be for everyone as well. The potential of regular local schools to truly serve children with disabilities well, to meet individual educational needs, has expanded with each advance in knowledge during the decade since the passage of PL 94-142. Since then, advances in curricula, in peer support, in instructional procedures, in employment preparation and so forth, have gradually eliminated many of the justifications for removal of children and youth with disabilities from the regular classroom environment.

Today, the ability of a local school to serve most or all of these students with disabilities is closely related to the ability of that school to provide effective quality education for any student. To me, this value places special education exactly where it belongs: at the very center of the school reform movement. If we truly believe that schools are for everybody, then the first measure of an effective school should be the extent to which it can serve all of its students. (Irwin & Wilcox, 1987, p. 3)

The evidence to date supports Bellamy's assertion. What has been lacking is a coordinated local school delivery system with which to replace the segregated and parallel structure that has been built up over the past 2 decades or so, to meet the educational needs of students with severe disabilities.

A unification of regular and special education is called for, to reintegrate children into regular schools and classrooms and to ensure that children with severe intellectual disabilities are no longer secluded from mainstream life experiences during and after their school years.

REFERENCES

Anderson, J., & Goetz, L. (1983, November). *Opportunities for social interaction between severely disabled and nondisabled students in segregated and integrated educational settings.* Paper presented at the 10th Annual Conference of The Association for Persons with Severe Handicaps, San Francisco, CA.

Aneno, A. (1987). A survey of activities engaged in and skills most needed by adults in community residences. *Journal of The Association for Persons with Severe Handicaps, 12*(2), 125–130.

Bagnato, S.J., Kontos, S., & Neisworth, J.T. (1987). Integrated day care as special education: Profiles of programs and children. *Topics in Early Childhood Special Education, 7*(1), 28–47.

Bereiter, C., & Engelmann, S. (1966). *Teaching disadvantaged children in the preschool.* Englewood Cliffs, NJ: Prentice Hall.

Bricker, D. (1978). A rationale for the integration of handicapped and nonhandicapped preschool children. In M.J. Guralnick (Ed.), *Early intervention and the integration of handicapped and nonhandicapped children* (pp. 3–26). Baltimore: University Park Press.

Brinker, R.P. (1985). Interactions between severely mentally retarded students and other students in integrated and segregated public school settings. *American Journal of Mental Deficiency, 89*(6), 587–594.

Brinker, R.P., & Thorpe, M.E. (1986). Features of integrated educational ecologies that predict social behavior among severely mentally retarded and nonretarded students. *American Journal of Mental Deficiency, 91*(2), 150–159.

Brown, L., Nietupski, J., & Hamre-Nietupski, S. (1977). The criterion of ultimate functioning and public school services for severely handicapped students. In B. Wilcox, F. Kohl, & T. Vogelsberg (Eds.), *The severely and profoundly handicapped child. Proceedings from the 1977 statewide institute for educators of the severely profoundly handicapped.* Springfield, IL: State Board of Education, Illinois Office of Education.

Brown, L., Rogan, P., Shiraga, B., Zanella Albright, K., Kessler, K., Bryson, F., VanDeventer, P., & Loomis, R. (1987). A vocational follow-up evaluation of the 1984–1986 Madison Metropolitan School District graduates with severe intellectual disabilities. *Monograph of The Association for Persons with Severe Handicaps, 2*(2).

Brown, L., & York, R. (1974). Developing programs for severely handicapped students: Teacher training and classroom instruction. In L. Brown, W. Williams, & T. Crowder (Eds.), *A collection of papers and programs related to public school services for severely handicapped students* (pp. 1–18). Madison, WI: Madison Public Schools.

Cooke, T.P., Ruskus, J.A., Apolloni, T., & Peck, C.A. (1981). Handicapped preschool children in the mainstream: Background, outcomes, and clinical suggestions. *Topics in Early Childhood Special Education, 1*(1), 73–84.

Falvey, M.A. (1986). *Community-based curriculum: Instructional strategies for students with severe handicaps.* Baltimore: Paul H. Brookes Publishing Co.

Filler, J., Baumgart, D., & Askvig, B. (1989). Mainstreaming young children with disabilities. In W. Sailor, J. Anderson, K.F. Doering, J. Filler, L. Goetz, & A. Halvorsen. *The comprehensive local school: Regular education for all students with disabilities.* Baltimore: Paul H. Brookes Publishing Co.

Gaylord-Ross, R.J., & Holvoet, J.F. (1985). *Strategies for educating students with severe handicaps.* Boston: Little, Brown.

Gaylord-Ross, R.J., Siegel, S., Park, H.-S., & Wilson, W. (1988). Secondary vocational training. In R. Gaylord-Ross (Ed.), *Vocational education for persons with handicaps* (pp. 174–202). Mountain View, CA: Mayfield Publishing Co.

Gilhool, T.K., & Stutman, E.A. (1978). Integration of severely handicapped students: Toward criteria for implementing and enforcing the integration imperative of PL 94-142 and Section 504. In *Developing criteria for the evaluation of the least restrictive environment provision.* Washington, DC: State Program Studies Branch, Division of Innovation and Development, Bureau of Education for the Handicapped, U.S. Office of Education.

Goetz, L., & Sailor, W. (1988). New directions: Communication development in persons with severe disabilities. *Topics in Language Disorders, 8*(4), 41–54.

Goetz, L., Schuler, A., & Sailor, W. (1979). Teaching functional speech to the severely handicapped: Current issues. *Journal of Autism and Developmental Disabilities, 9,* 325–343.

Goetz, L., Schuler, A., & Sailor, W. (1981). Functional competence as a factor in communication instruction. *Exceptional Education Quarterly, 2,* 51–61.

Goetz, L., Schuler, A., & Sailor, W. (1983). Motivational considerations in teaching language to severely handicapped students. In M. Herson, V. VanHasselt, & J. Matson (Eds.), *Behavior therapy for the developmentally and physically disabled.* New York: Academic Press.

Guralnick, M.J. (1981). The efficacy of integrated handicapped children in early education settings: Research implications. *Topics in Early Childhood Special Education, 1* (1), 57–72.

Halvorsen, A., Doering, K., Farron-Davis, F., Usilton, R., & Sailor, W. (1989). The role of parents and family members in planning severely disabled students' transition from school. In G.H.S. Singer & L.K. Irvin (Eds.), *Support for caregiving families: Enabling positive adaptation to disability.* Baltimore: Paul H. Brookes Publishing Co.

Haney, J.I. (1988). Toward successful community residential placements for individuals with mental retardation. In L.W. Heal, J.I. Haney, & A.R. Novak Amado (Eds.), *Integration of developmentally disabled individuals into the community* (2nd ed., pp. 125–168). Baltimore: Paul H. Brookes Publishing Co.

Hanline, M.F. (1985). Integrating disabled children. *Young Children, 40,* 45–48.

Hanline, M.F., & Halvorsen, A. (1988). *Parent perceptions of the integration process.* Manuscript submitted for publication.

Hanson, M.J., & Hanline, M.F. (1989). Integration options for the very young child. In R. Gaylord-Ross (Ed.), *Integration strategies for persons with handicaps.* Baltimore: Paul H. Brookes Publishing Co.

Haring, N. (in press). *Generalization: Strategies and solutions for students with severe handicaps* (Final monograph). Seattle: University of Washington, College of Education.

Hobbs, N. (1975). *The futures of children.* San Francisco: Jossey-Bass.

Horner, R., Dunlap, G., & Koegel, R. (Eds.). (1988). *Generalization and maintenance: Life-style changes in applied settings.* Baltimore: Paul H. Brookes Publishing Co.

Horner, R., McDonnell, J., & Bellamy, G.T. (1986). Teaching generalized skills: General case instruction in simulation and community settings. In R. Horner, L. Meyer, & H.D. Fredericks (Eds.), *Education of learners with severe handicaps: Exemplary service strategies* (pp. 289–314). Baltimore: Paul H. Brookes Publishing Co.

Irwin, M., & Wilcox, B. (1987). *Proceedings of the National Leadership Conference. Least restrictive environment: Commitment to implementation.* Bloomington, IN: Indiana University, The Institute for the Study of Developmental Disabilities.

Madison Metropolitan School District (1975–1988). *Publications related to students with severe intellectual disabilities* (Vols. I–XVI). Madison, WI: Author and University of Wisconsin, Madison.

Meyer, L., Eichinger, J., & Park-Lee, S. (1987). A validation of program quality indicators in educational services for students with severe disabilities. *Journal of The Association for Persons with Severe Handicaps, 12*(4), 251–263.

Organization for Economic Co-operation and Development (OECD). (1987). *Handicap and adult status: Policy issues and practical dilemmas* (Draft report). Paris, France: OECD, Centre for Educational Research and Innovation.

PL 94-142, the Education for All Handicapped Children Act of 1975.

PL 99-457, the Education of the Handicapped Act Amendments of 1986.

Sailor, W., Anderson, J., Halvorsen, A., Doering, K.F., Filler, J., & Goetz, L. (1989). *The comprehensive local school: Regular education for all students with disabilities.* Baltimore: Paul H. Brookes Publishing Co.

Sailor, W., Gee, K., Goetz, L., & Graham, N. (1988). Progress in educating students with the most severe disabilities: Is there any? *Journal of The Association for Persons with Severe Handicaps, 13*(2), 87–99.

Sailor, W., Goetz, L., Anderson, J., Hunt, P., & Gee, K. (1988). Research on community intensive instruction as a model for building functional, generalized skills. In R. Horner, G. Dunlap, & R. Koegel (Eds.), *Generalization and maintenance: Life-style changes in applied settings* (pp. 67–98). Baltimore: Paul H. Brookes Publishing Co.

Sailor, W., & Guess, D. (1983). *Severely handicapped students: An instructional design.* Boston: Houghton Mifflin.

Sailor, W., Halvorsen, A., Anderson, J., Goetz, L., Gee, K., Doering, K., & Hunt, P. (1986). Community intensive instruction. In R. Horner, L. Meyer, & H.D. Bud Fredericks (Eds.), *Education of learners with severe handicaps: Exemplary service strategies* (pp. 251–288). Baltimore: Paul H. Brookes Publishing Co.

Shoultz, B. (1986, October). Wisconsin makes community integration a reality. *TASH Newsletter,* p. 11.

Snell, M.E. (Ed.). (1987). *Systematic instruction of persons with severe handicaps* (3rd ed.). Columbus, OH: Charles E. Merrill.

Sontag, E., Smith, J., & Certo, N. (1977). *Educational programming for the severely and profoundly handicapped.* Reston, VA: The Council for Exceptional Children, Division on Mental Retardation.

Strain, P.S. (1983). Generalization of autistic children's social behavior change: Effects of developmentally integrated and segregated settings. *Analysis and Intervention in Developmental Disabilities, 3,* 23–34.

Strain, P.S., & Odom, S.L. (1986). Peer social initiations: Effective intervention for social skills development of exceptional children. *Exceptional Children, 52*(6), 543–551.

Strain, P.S., Odom, S.L., & McConnell, S. (1984). Promoting social reciprocity of exceptional children: Identification, target behavior selection, and intervention. *Remedial and Special Education, 5*(1), 12–28.

Voeltz, L.M. (1980). Children's attitudes toward handicapped peers. *American Journal of Mental Deficiency, 84*(3), 455–464.

Voeltz, L.M. (1982). Effects of structured interactions with severely handicapped peers on children's attitudes. *American Journal of Mental Deficiency, 86*(4), 380–390.

Walker, P., & Salon, R. (1987, August). Creating residential supports: Centennial Development Services, Inc. A community-centered board serving Weld County, CO. *TASH Newsletter,* pp. 8–9.

Will, M. (1984). *OSERS program for the transition of youth with disabilities: Bridges from school to working life.* Washington, DC: Office of Special Education and Rehabilitative Services (OSERS), U.S. Department of Education.

Will, M. (1986). Educating children with learning problems: A shared responsibility. *Exceptional Children, 52*(5), 411–416.

Will, M. (1988). *Statement to Subcommittee on Select Education on the Rehabilitation Act of 1973* (March 16, 1988). Transmitted on *SpecialNet,* March 21, 1988; Message NGII-3426-3024.

chapter 5

Different Programs, Indifferent Instruction

Richard L. Allington and Anne McGill-Franzen

Remedial and special education programs have undergone substantial transformations in the past 25 years. Both categories of instructional support programs have expanded and evolved over this period as a result of various governmental and societal initiatives. As a result, virtually all American public schools now provide both remedial and special education services. In large part, these efforts derive from Chapter I of the Educational Consolidation and Improvement Act of 1980 (ECIA) and earlier related federal compensatory education enactments, and Public Law 94-142, the Education for All Handicapped Children Act of 1975 (EHA). These two federal initiatives (see footnote 1) provide substantial fiscal and legal incentives for school districts to offer extra instructional services for children who experience difficulties in regular education programs. While these two initiatives are "based on different assumptions about the etiology of the child's failure . . . and derive their legal and fiscal statuses from different judicial and legislative decisions . . ." (McGill-Franzen, 1987), they share the common feature of primarily serving children who have not been successful in regular classrooms through specialist teachers who remove children from the regular education classroom for some part of the school day.

Instructional efforts funded under the auspices of these programs are designed to resolve or alleviate the learning difficulties experienced by participat-

The research reported here was supported by funds from the Office of Special Education Programs, U.S. Department of Education (Grant #G008630480). The conclusions we report are our own.

[1]Chapter I of ECIA is a direct descendant of Title I of the Elementary and Secondary Education Act of 1965. Though the ECIA altered some provisions of the earlier act, in most respects Chapter I programs are similar to the earlier Title I programs. The special education programs for the mildly handicapped derive from PL 94-142, the Education for All Handicapped Children Act of 1975. Ysseldyke and Algozzine (1982) provide a fairly comprehensive analysis of the development of remedial and special education programs under these federal initiatives.

ing children. It seems clear that Chapter I programs are understood as efforts to remediate basic skill failure (e.g., reading, writing, and mathematics) through supplementary instructional efforts (Allington, 1986). It is less clear that special education programs, even for the mildly handicapped, are understood this way (Gartner & Lipsky, 1987). However, recent incentives to foster declassification activities suggest that some educators see resolving academic failure as an appropriate goal for special education programs. But, as Coles (1987) has suggested, others may understand the identification of students as handicapped to indicate the presence of a physiological deficit that is likely to impair learning capacity permanently. McGill-Franzen (1987) argues that our understanding of school failure, and reading failure in particular, has changed over time. She presents a variety of evidence illustrating a shift from "disadvantagement" to "disability" in explanations of reading failure. This shift can be seen in research, textbooks, and magazine articles, as well as in the enrollment patterns in various categorical programs. As our understanding has changed, so too has the nature of instructional support services and the characteristics of children served by each program.

Currently, most children identified as handicapped and entitled to special education services fall under the broad classification of mildly handicapped; children identified as learning disabled (LD) represent the largest category of participants. As McGill-Franzen (1987) has noted, this group of children is not only the largest but also the most rapidly expanding special education population. She notes that the increase in children identified as LD nearly matches the decline in Chapter I participants over the past decade. That is, the 1.5 million student decrease in Chapter I may be reflected in the 1.8 million student increase in LD identification. In any event, it is increasingly clear that remedial programs and special education programs for the mildly handicapped serve students who are similar in many ways, and strikingly similar in their academic diagnostic profiles (Algozzine & Ysseldyke, 1983; Bartoli & Botel, 1988; Bogdan, 1982; Jenkins, 1987; Mehan, 1984; Ysseldyke, Algozzine, Shinn, & McGue, 1982).

READING INSTRUCTION IN SPECIAL EDUCATION PROGRAMS

Most schools offer instruction support services for children through both Chapter I and special education, with little overlap in planning, personnel, or participating children. In the material that follows, the authors attempt to characterize how school districts respond to both federal initiatives. Basically, the opportunities for reading instruction available to students who were participants in these programs are described. Put another way, we have attempted to ascertain the extent to which participants in either program have access to larger amounts of higher quality reading instruction. In a quantitative analysis conducted earlier, we noted that Chapter I participants did, in fact, receive larger quantities of reading instruction than did mainstreamed mildly handicapped students (Allington & McGill-Franzen, in press). However, what remains to be more adequately addressed is the quality of instruction experienced and the potential sources for the differences that we found.

Our earlier findings were similar, in some respects, to those of Haynes and Jenkins (1986) and of Ysseldyke, Thurlow, Mecklenburg, and Graden (1984), who noted that mainstreamed mildly handicapped student participation in special education programs did not increase the quantity of reading instruction available to participants compared to the amount offered nonhandicapped children. Likewise, the enormous variability in quantity of reading instruction received by special education students was also reported by Haynes and Jenkins (1986), as well as Thurlow, Ysseldyke, Graden, and Algozzine (1984), Ysseldyke, et al. (1984), and Zigmond, Vallecorsa, and Leinhardt (1980). What seems clear, then, is that participation in special education programs, even when students are mainstreamed mildly handicapped learners, does not ensure access to larger amounts of reading instruction.

In the analyses that follow, two broad areas that influence the quality of instruction offered in schools were considered. First, aspects of district-level organizational policies were examined, since Dreeben and Barr (1983) have illustrated how administrative decisions about various resources (including instructional time allocation, curriculum/textbook selection, and grouping and placement decisions) constrain the actions of teachers in schools. Dreeben (1987) argues that learning deficits can "be attributed in part to the actions of district and school administrators before classroom instruction ever takes place" (p.32). By contrasting the instructional experiences of children in different districts with different district-level policies concerning Chapter I and special education for the mildly handicapped, the process by which such policies influence the opportunities for reading instruction is identified.

Second, the nature of the reading instruction that Chapter I and mainstreamed mildly handicapped students experience across the school day is examined. In this analysis, we have been particularly concerned with the issues of the quality of instruction experienced. The analyses were guided by the assumption that the quality of instruction is at least as critical as the quantity. That is, one could argue that even smaller amounts of higher quality instruction would serve the needs of children experiencing learning difficulties better than large amounts of ineffective instruction. In our analyses of instructional quality, we focused on several particular features of instruction that have been identified as characteristic of effective programs for the populations studied. We looked for evidence of coordination with regular education programs, and for curricular coordination in particular (Allington & Johnston, 1986; Griswold, Cotton, & Hansen, 1986; National RRC Panel on Indicators of Effectiveness in Special Education, 1986; Sarason, 1983). Since failure in the core curriculum was the primary determinant in identification of those who received services under either program, we examined the instructional experiences of the participants to determine the linkages between reading instruction in the instructional support programs and in the core curriculum of the regular education classroom. In addition, reading instruction was examined to determine the nature of the instructional activities that participants were assigned. We were particularly interested in the types of academic tasks that these students attempted. Thus, we noted task features such as the unit of text that was the focus of the instructional activity, the difficulty of the material, and the skill or topic that was being addressed. Our goal was to describe and explain the reading instruction that Chapter I students and mainstreamed mildly handicapped students experienced.

THE SCHOOLS AND THE STUDENTS

The school day experiences of 52 second and fourth grade children (26 at each grade level) from five school districts were analyzed. The school districts varied in size and community type, and included a rural, a suburban, and three small city school districts. These students were drawn from an array of regular education classrooms and were provided instructional support services by 22 different specialist teachers.

For our analyses we had several types of information available. In each district, interviews were conducted with district and school building administrators and with specialist and classroom teachers. Many of these interviews were available in a transcribed format; in other cases, an analytic summary and the original audiotape recording were available. The set of interviews was generally complete, although a few teachers did not consent to participate. We used the interview evidence to clarify district and school policies, as understood by the participating teachers and administrators, and to clarify the observed instructional experiences. The interviews also provided both a historical glimpse of the evolution of current policies and practices and personal comments about the issues in which we were most interested.

A single whole school day observational record for each participating student was obtained. This record was composed of several sorts of evidence. The primary data for analysis of student instructional experiences were drawn from the Student Observation Instrument (SOI). The SOI offered a combined system of structured coding categories with descriptive field notes which provided a chronological record of student experiences across the various instructional settings. (The Allington & McGill-Franzen [in press] report details an analysis of the quantitative data from the structured coding categories.) For the present analyses, the focused field notes were the primary source of data. These included a listing of the curricular materials in use and photocopies of these materials whenever possible.

Based upon the interview and observation records, a summary of each district's organization plan for the delivery of Chapter I and special education services was prepared. These summaries offered a framework for analyzing the "fit" of the services provided with organizational plans and a template for evaluating the influences of district and building plans on the participating childrens' instruction experiences.

The field notes available in the SOI were analyzed and each reading instructional activity was identified. We began our analyses by noting whether the observational record indicated engagement in the activity by the observed student. Those activities in which students were observed to be unengaged in the reading learning event were excluded, primarily because the evidence suggested that engagement in the instructional activity was central to enhanced achievement. That is, a scheduled opportunity for independent reading was one thing, but engagement in independent reading was another. We note this because the SOI system of structured coding categories included no differentiation in these instances; evidence of engagement, or the lack of it, was reported in the field notes only.

After the episodes of engaged reading, and after instructional activities had been identified and coded as to whether the activity occurred in the regular education or in the support instruction setting, each was analyzed further. We began by focusing on the academic work that children were engaged in, noting the size of the unit of text that was the focus of the response required by the task. We coded these as focused on word, sentence, or story levels based upon the unit of text presented the child. Then, we noted whether the evaluation of the response was centered on simple accuracy or on comprehension. On the one hand, words, sentences, or stories can be simply pronounced, or they can be read with little attention to the meaning of the text. On the other hand, one can focus on the meaning of text at each of these levels. Both the field notes and samples of the curricular materials were inspected to determine this focus. Next, we attempted to determine the difficulty of the task as represented by two indices: publisher's designation, and student error rate. Finally, the skill, strategy, and/or topic of the task were derived from the field notes and copies of the curriculum materials that were used.

These analyses, then, formed the basic data reduction process. Based on the results, the authors attempted to characterize the nature of the reading instruction that these children experienced across the school day. The analyses produced information that permitted a comparison of the reading instruction individuals received in various settings across the day and a comparison of the reading instruction in regular education classrooms, in Chapter I classrooms, and in special education resource rooms. From these comparisons, we drew our conclusions concerning the nature of reading instruction in various settings and the coordination of instruction across these settings.

By aggregating these data across school districts, it was possible to address patterns of response in the instruction offered children who participated in either Chapter 1 or in special education programs for the mildly handicapped. By examining the patterns of response to individuals against the backdrop of the district organization plan reported in the interviews, one may examine the effect of providing children with larger amounts of higher quality reading instruction.

In the sections that follow, a sketch of the organization patterns for remedial and special education services in the districts is provided; the patterns are drawn from our case studies of these districts. Following this is a discussion emphasizing the nature of the reading instruction provided to children served by the two categorical programs, and the influence of federal, state, and district level policies and plans on the design and delivery of these instructional interventions. The chapter concludes with a discussion of how we might consider reorganizing our efforts better to serve children who fail to learn to read on schedule.

ORGANIZATION PATTERNS

The study also examined descriptions by teachers and administrators. Specifically, the interest was in the ways that teachers and administrators described: 1) the purposes and organization of instructional services of the two support programs (Chapter I and special education resource room), 2) the instruction offered children who participated in either program, and 3) the similarities and dissimilarities of the children served and the services provided. Our interview data provided much information, but what we heard did not always match what we saw.

Common Features

The instructional support programs in these school districts shared some organizational features. First, it was more common for the two programs to be separated administratively, although in two districts a single district administrator was responsible for both. However, in four districts, the process of identification was separate from instructional planning, and classroom teachers had little opportunity to engage in the processes beyond initial referrals. Second, entry into Chapter 1 was generally determined by student performance on routinely administered group standardized achievement tests. In most cases, a cutoff score had been established and students whose scores fell below that point received services. Similarly, the structure of the identification process for special education varied little, conforming generally to the sequence mandated by PL 94-142. Third, few districts had an identified curriculum for the reading instruction provided in the support programs, though it was generally clear that little attention was paid to the reading curriculum of the regular education program. In most support programs the curriculum was created, or selected, by the specialist teacher. Finally, there was little overlap of participants in the two programs. That is, low-achievement children generally participated in either Chapter 1 or special education resource room programs, but only rarely did individuals participate in both. Thus, while many of the mainstreamed mildly handicapped students were eligible for remedial reading services under Chapter 1, most did not receive such services. This situation was similar to that reported by Birman (1981).

Unique Features

While similarities existed, these districts varied substantially in several organizational aspects. For instance, one district offered all remedial instruction through an in-class model in which the support teacher came into the regular education classroom to work with children. Another combined in-class and pull-out instruction, depending on the grade level and the teachers' preferences. Most used a pull-out model, but the size of the groups and the degree of heterogeneity of the participants varied. Additionally, the districts varied in the proportion of children served by the two programs. In one district, fewer than 5% of the students were identified as handicapped, while in another district, about 20% were so identified. Likewise, Chapter 1 eligibility varied from less than 10% to greater than 40%. These five school districts all offered instructional support funded through Chapter 1 and a state remediation program. All districts had special education programs for mildly handicapped children which involved substantial mainstreaming. Each district had created distinct administrative structures for these programs. By observing similarities and dissimilarities in the instructional intervention efforts across districts and between programs, we attempted to identify influences on the design and delivery of the instructional support offered to children who were failing to acquire reading skills on schedule.

THE NATURE OF THE READING INSTRUCTION OBSERVED

Although these instructional intervention programs differed in certain respects, important common characteristics of the reading instruction were observed. Because general descriptions almost always obscure unique cases, the following section portrays a few such cases while presenting what seem to be critical aspects of the instruction observed. In this characterization and analysis, we draw upon the available research describing the nature of instruction found to be effective in developing reading generally (e.g., Berliner, 1981; Good, 1983; Leinhardt, Zigmond, & Cooley, 1981). We also draw upon data focusing on the development of reading in low-achievement and mildly handicapped populations, such as those observed in this study (Allington, 1983; Crawford, Kimball, & Patrick, 1984; Greenwood et al., 1981; Haynes & Jenkins, 1986; Larrivee, 1985; Thurlow et al., 1984; Zigmond et al., 1980).

Quantity of Instruction

One difficulty in attempting to characterize the nature of reading instruction observed is that the diversity of instructional experiences was enormous. However, we would begin by noting that, generally, the instructional experiences we observed did not fulfill the expectation that remedial and mildly handicapped students would have access to larger amounts of significantly superior instruction. However, unlike Haynes and Jenkins (1986) and Ysseldyke et al. (1984), we had no direct observational data on regular education students; thus, we draw this conclusion from information that is less adequate than theirs. Nonetheless, the organizational plans that districts presented most often absented the observed children from all or part of the classroom reading instruction. In addition, for these remedial and special education students, the total time allocated for reading instruction (70–100 minutes per day) seemed comparable, in the best cases, to that reported in previous studies of regular education instruction (e.g., Berliner, 1981).

One striking feature of these observations was the enormous variability in reading instruction time experienced by the observed students, variability which seemed substantially larger than that found for regular education students. Some students received very little instruction, while others participated in reading instruction for fairly large segments of the school day. The reading instruction time data presented in Table 1 illustrate this variability. Students 6 and 41 obviously have an advantage over students 8 and 43, at least in terms of quantity of reading instruction. The instructional program that accounted for the allocated time also varied. Note that the student data provided in the table illustrate no consistent advantage for one program over the other in terms of quantity of reading instruction. (Across the whole sample, we did find an advantage for Chapter 1 participants, however.)

Differences in instructional time were also the result of differences in the quantity of reading instruction offered these students in the regular education program. Some students received most of their instruction in the regular classroom; others did not participate in classroom reading instruction. Some special education students had over an hour of reading instruction in the resource room, but just as many received no instruction during their resource room session. In

Table 1. Time allocated for reading instruction, examples of variability within schools

Student	School	Grade	Category	Minutes
6	2	4	SPED	123
43	2	4	CH 1	55
8	4	2	SPED	46
41	4	2	CH 1	132

SPED = special education students.
CH 1 = Chapter I students.

most cases, however, participation in instructional support programs did not seem to increase the quantity of reading instruction received compared to the amount that nonparticipating peers received.

We noted earlier, however, that simply increasing the quantity of instruction may not be an adequate response to reading failure, particularly if little attention is paid to instructional quality. While quantity of instruction is an important correlate of achievement, large amounts of instruction in materials that elicit high rates of error, on tasks with little relationship to reading development, or on fragmented and incoherent curricular tasks, are unlikely to enhance reading development. Thus, we examined the quality of the reading instruction from a task perspective in order to describe the instructional activities by noting features such as those mentioned above.

Quality of Instruction

Not all observed students served by either support program participated in classroom reading instructional groups. While only one Chapter 1 student did not participate in a classroom reading group, nearly one-third of the mainstreamed mildly handicapped students did not participate. Those students from either program who did participate in regular classroom reading, however, were typically grouped with other low achievers for basal reader instruction. These low achievement instructional groups frequently focused on oral reading accuracy and concentrated instruction at the word level. When larger units of text were the focus—stories, for instance—accuracy remained the critical feature of instruction, with oral reading tasks that evidenced little, if any, emphasis on comprehension, a frequent activity. Such activities and emphases are common features of instruction for low-achievement students in classrooms (Allington, 1983). The students also routinely participated in undifferentiated language arts activities in the classroom. They were assigned grade level spelling, transcribing, composing, and grammar tasks along with their normally achieving classmates. A few students were successful participants in both the classroom reading groups and language arts activities, but most were not. Success was more common in reading groups, but even that was far from universal. Finally, we observed little coherence in the various reading instruction activities that these students experienced in the regular classroom. Rarely, for instance, were decoding or vocabulary activities during reading instruction related to word structure or word meaning activities during spelling. Rarely were reading and composing tasks related on topic, genre, or text structures. Rarely were grammar or transcription tasks related to reading, writing, or composing activities, and rarely did we find sets of seatwork tasks that presented an extended focus on related topics or strategies. Instead, we observed an array of tasks, across the school day, that offered little evidence of coherence or attention to a unified curriculum plan.

Each of the observed students participated in reading instruction offered in an instructional support program; in most cases they left their regular classroom for this instruction. There were several distressing features of this instruction. First, we were surprised to find much of this instruction was also undifferentiated (McGill-Franzen, 1988). That is, students attending the instructional support programs simply participated in another instructional group, with common instructional activities, as a matter of course. Some students represented a better "fit" with the instructional focus of the group activity than others. In some cases, the instruction participants were more homogeneous, in terms of achievement levels, than in other cases. Rarely, however, in either remedial or resource room classes, did we observe instruction that seemed particularly tailored to the unique needs of individual students.

For instance, one fourth grade special education student accurately completed several activities in the resource room, including a worksheet. The worksheet required marking the letters that made the *at* sound in some three-letter words, identifying similar words to fit in a sentence deletion, and rapid reading of a short first grade paragraph with multiple-choice questions. We were not surprised since he had read aloud accurately from a grade level reader in his classroom reading group earlier that day and demonstrated good comprehension. However, the other special education student who also participated in these resource room activities was not particularly successful; the activities then seemed somewhat more appropriate for him. This pattern was frequently seen in support instruction classes (McGill-Franzen, 1988). What we commonly observed were children attempting to fit instructional material, or instructional routines, that were assigned all members of the group attending the support instruction at that time period.

We found similar materials, tasks, and instructional routines employed in both support programs, and we were unable to identify relevant features of the instructional sessions that would differentiate between the two support programs. These findings reflect a situation similar to that described by Allington, Stuetzel, Shake, and Lamarche (1986), Fraatz (1987), Haynes and Jenkins (1986), Morsink, Soar, Soar, and Thomas (1986), and Thurlow et al. (1984). In each of these studies, the authors report little evidence that instruction in resource rooms or remedial programs is differentiated by individual instructional needs. They also found little evidence that the reading instruction in the two settings was obviously differentiated by materials, tasks, or routines.

A second distressing aspect of the instruction in both support programs was the incredible fragmentation of curricular experiences. Not only did these students have to deal with unrelated reading activities in the classroom, but they were also assigned additional sets of unrelated activities and tasks in the support setting. Thus, the curricular fragmentation for these children occurred at several levels. First, they experienced the fragmentation in the classroom reading tasks. While attending support instruction, they were also assigned an incoherent array of unrelated tasks. Second, there was little coordination between the instruction offered in the two settings; students encountered different curricular materials developed from competing theories of reading development, varying levels of difficulty in curriculum materials, and differing task emphases. Similar findings have been noted by researchers studying resource or remedial instruction (Allington et al., 1986; Haynes & Jenkins, 1986; Holley, 1986; Johnston, Allington, & Afflerbach, 1985; Kimbrough & Hill, 1981; Rowan, Guthrie, Lee, & Guthrie, 1986). The extraordinary fragmentation of instruction experiences of these children simply undermined the good efforts we often saw—good efforts from both learners and teachers.

From the evidence available, we must conclude that the expectation that participation in remedial or special education will enhance access to larger amounts of higher quality instruction remains yet unfilled. While many good teachers attempted many good deeds, in the end, many of these students experienced instruction which appeared unlikely to resolve their reading failure.

INFLUENCES ON THE DESIGN
OF INSTRUCTIONAL SUPPORT PROGRAMS

In our analyses, we attempted to identify the factors influencing the instruction observed in the support programs. There exist several broad levels of influence, each having a potential role in shaping the nature of the instruction. The following is a discussion of how forces at each level constrained decisions made at other levels.

Federal Level

Chapter I and special education instructional support programs derive from federal initiatives. In both cases, program design is influenced by rules and regulations issued at the federal level. For instance, Chapter I has, by and large, precluded early intervention efforts with a focus on supporting programs enrolling students in grades 2–12. Thus, children are literally required to experience failure for at least a year before service can begin. In some cases, children who might have benefited from early remedial intervention were simply referred to special education programs, the only option for externally funded support instruction. The identification of clients is constrained by the practice of serving first those children "most in need," and by the inadequate funds available to serve all children who are eligible (Carter, 1984). Combined, these factors produced Chapter I programs that had varying entry criteria and differing standardized test score cutoffs in the four districts that relied on these measures for identification. In districts where the eligible Chapter I population was large, children had to obtain lower achievement test scores to qualify for services. In most districts, there were children who were having substantial difficulty in the classroom who were not served, usually because enrollments were restricted to those who had met the arbitrary standard.

Finally, the "supplement not supplant" provision of Chapter I influenced the instruction. There appeared to be two distinct effects. First, Chapter I children were more likely to participate in a regular classroom reading group than were the special education students. In some cases, the result was that children received larger amounts of reading instruction. Second, the lack of curricular consistency between classroom and Chapter I instruction also seemed to be derived from misunderstanding of this provision. In our interviews, we were told that Chapter I instruction had to be different by some informants. While this is not the case, it is a common misperception that has been noted for most of the 20-year history of the program (Allington, 1986).

Federal influences on special education were reflected in the composition of the Committee on Special Education (CSE), the group of professionals that evaluated referrals and recommended placement in one program option or the other. Regular educators, especially classroom teachers, were largely unrepresented on the CSE, since federal regulations did not require their membership. Thus, the mainstream classroom teacher typically had little voice in decisions about level of service, appropriate curriculum, or any of the other issues central to resolving academic failure. Often, this seemed to result in a lack of "ownership" of the problem or solution. The mandated individualized education program (IEP), with its reductionist emphasis on specific objectives for handicapped students, trivialized the learning process and produced a bias toward low level skills instruction as the emphasis of the intervention.

Perhaps the greatest influence at the federal level was the labeling, or categorical identification, of special students. In our interviews with teachers and administrators, we found a somewhat contradictory dual focus. On the one hand, educators often expressed skepticism about the reality of differences between students in various categories, with those closest to the children as the most skeptical. On the other hand, educators often alluded to the "special methods" that were necessary to teach these children, although what we observed most commonly were rather ordinary uses of common skill sheet tasks in both remedial and resource room instruction.

State Level

The majority of Chapter I participants received remedial reading instruction for 90–100 minutes per week, with no obvious differentiation by instructional need. Thus, whether the student was in grade two and reading at the first grade level, or in grade four reading at the first grade level, three 30-minute remedial group sessions were the standard for each student. We traced this standard to the New York State interpretation of the Chapter I "sufficient size, scope, and quality" provision. Since 90 minutes per week was the minimum service allowed, 90 minutes was what Chapter I participants received. If the state were to shift the minimum to 120 minutes, for instance, Chapter I students would undoubtedly receive that quantity of instruction. Similarly, state requirements for reimbursement for special education services established a participation minimum which was double that of Chapter I, and again, many participants received the minimum amount of instruction or only slightly more. These fiscal incentives led districts to design programs in particular ways (Gartner, 1986; McGill-Franzen, 1987; Singer & Butler, 1987). In our analysis, standards set for reimbursement (e.g., required minimum minutes of service, maximum group size, maximum number of students to be served), were more influential than were student instructional needs. In each district, there were children who needed more and better services than they were receiving. Typically, district personnel agreed that services were insufficient, but noted that the child was being provided what was required. In other words, it was rarely the case that a teacher or administrator argued that the services offered provided sufficient individualization or sufficient increases in learning opportunities. Rather, what was argued was that the services provided met the minimum established criteria, a criteria set for reimbursement approval.

Compared to special education regulations, state Chapter I guidelines suggested a substantially higher cap on the number of students a single specialist teacher should serve. Thus, Chapter I teachers often served two or three times as many pupils as special education teachers, and for shorter and less frequent periods. However, special education teachers seemed, more often, to find themselves instructing a more heterogeneous group of children. In most districts, it appeared that this occurred primarily as a result of the differing sizes of the participating populations. Frequently, the remedial class was drawn from a single grade level, and in some cases, from a single classroom. The special education teacher often drew her class from several grade levels and typically from multiple classrooms. Thus, the Chapter I groups tended to be more homogeneous, since both curriculum placement and age levels were similar, while the special education classes ranged more widely. The greater the heterogeneity of the participants scheduled for any period, the less likely that large amounts of high quality instruction were observed.

A final influence, we suspect, is a state policy that removes children identified as handicapped from the statewide achievement testing program. While the special education students can take part in the testing, there is no requirement that their scores be submitted to the state office. There exists no similar reporting exclusion for Chapter I participants. Thus, a second incentive to identify children as handicapped seems to operate, since by moving low-achievement children from compensatory to special education programs, their achievement scores are no longer reflected in the district's assessment profile. In the district with the highest achievement levels, fewer than 5% of the pupils were identified as handicapped, while in one of the lowest achievement districts, roughly 20% were identified as handicapped. In the first district, inclusion of the special education student scores on statewide assessments would have a minimal effect, although it would still depress average achievement levels. In the latter district, however, inclusion of those scores would have a potentially disastrous effect on the already depressed achievement levels, especially since state assessment profiles are released to the press with districts rank ordered on student achievement.

Gartner and Lipsky (1987) pointed out that New York state has organized fiscal incentives that encourage placing students in more restrictive educational environments, a set of policies at variance with the intent of PL 94-142. Similarly, in an era of concern about "overclassification" of students as handicapped, state policies offer several incentives for just that. Not only can larger amounts of reimbursement be attracted by shifting students from compensatory to special education, but also low-achievement students can be removed at the same time from the statewide assessment reports.

District Level

While two previous studies have described district level influences similar to this study, the authors arrived at different conclusions about the most appropriate strategies for resolution of the problem (Kimbrough & Hill, 1981; Moore, Hyde, Blair, & Weitzman, 1981). In both studies, the fragmented and often incoherent nature of the instructional support services were discussed. Both studies noted the lack of any district level plan to achieve coordination, and both argued that instructional support programs seemed to have little impact on modifying problems in the regular education program. Moore et al. (1981) suggest that most district administrators were ill-prepared for the task of developing coordinated approaches, since few had the necessary experiences or professional preparation needed to create curriculum plans or instructional interventions. They also attribute the lack of coordination to the fact that many of the district-level support program administrators did not consider their programs to be reading programs, even though reading failure was the common condition of students participating in virtually all such programs.

However, Kimbrough and Hill (1981) emphasize that "district officials have far greater resources for program coordination and integration than do principals and teachers" (p.42). Moore et al. (1981) suggest that leadership in coordination must come from principals. We observed three districts that had more detailed plans for instructional support services, and two that had rather meager plans. The effects of district plans on the operation of the various programs were quite evident in all districts. In the districts with more detailed plans, we observed more consistency within the support program instruction, though not necessarily between the support programs and the classroom. In districts without a defined program, we observed substantial variation in quantity and quality of instruction within the support programs.

Some aspects of the district plans seemed to have a greater effect on instruction than others. For instance, district decisions about curricular materials had an effect in one district, where special education students had a basal reader program different from that in the classroom. In this case, the basal reader dominated much of the resource room instruction; this often led to more story activities, more comprehension tasks, and greater consistency between tasks than was observed in districts where no curriculum plan existed for support instruction. At the same time, however, resource room teachers invariably offered less instruction than suggested in the manual, and often placed groups of students in a single basal level, whether or not it was the most appropriate level. In addition, these students typically did not participate in classroom reading groups. While this did reduce the curriculum fragmentation, it also failed to increase the quantity of reading instruction experienced. In a neighboring district, there was no mandated curriculum for either remedial or special education, and we observed little coherence within the support instruction tasks, few text reading activities, and little emphasis on comprehension tasks. The de facto curriculum here took the form of isolated skill sheets. We observed greater coherence of instruction in another district that had not purchased and mandated a commercial curriculum but that had invested in teacher training toward a particular philosophy of reading instruction. One district had separate plans for regular, remedial, and special education, and these plans did not mesh into a clear, unified plan. While individual program administrators devised plans, there was no encompassing district plan that could have guided these disparate elements into a coherent effort.

As recommended by Kimbrough and Hill (1981), our work points to the need for a well-defined district-level plan that would detail who should be collaborating with whom, on what, and why. We see the need for some district curriculum plan, though this obviously would not necessitate mandating particular material. In addition, such a plan should include basic issues, such as whether support instruction is to be supplementary and related to mastery of the classroom core curriculum, or whether this instruction is to supplant that in the regular education program. While we argue that district plans are necessary, we view the school principal as important in ensuring that the district plan is appropriately implemented and followed in the school.

In the main, however, we observed many aspects of district plans that seemed designed primarily to simplify the responsibilities of the district administrator. Arbitrary and fixed cutoff points on standardized achievement tests, inflexible schedules, and rigid and unsatisfactory assessment and evaluation procedures made it easy to "go by the book" and ignore the needs of individual children (see also Singer & Butler, 1987). Decisions to create maximum enrollments for the minimum amount of service necessary to obtain reimbursement resulted in situations that made it virtually impossible for specialist teachers to meet the original intent of the support instruction. Too often, children were simply scheduled for services that met the minimum mandated service levels, rather than for instructional interventions designed to meet their instructional needs. For instance, the quantity of instructional support in both programs typically reflected the minimum allowed by regulations. Children in third grade reading at the second grade level received the same amount of services, in the same size groups, as children in fifth grade reading at the same level. Scheduling, then, limited the ability of specialist teachers to offer instructional support that met individual needs. When districts develop poorly conceived organizational plans, and no true curriculum plan, then teachers and principals find their attempts to meet children's needs more difficult.

Each of the district-level decisions had an effect on the educators, both specialist and classroom teachers. Specialist teachers were often overwhelmed by the sheer diversity and numbers of students whose needs they were attempting to meet. Generally, children received what was available rather than what they needed (see Mehan, 1984). When districts had no clearly defined reading curriculum, classroom and support teachers invented their own. Some invented better curriculum plans than others, but whenever teachers had to invent curricula, fragmentation occurred. In the one district that had a reasonably detailed curriculum plan and a unified plan for reading instruction, we observed more coherence than elsewhere. Even here, however, district administrators elected not to monitor implementation of the plan, and instruction across settings often lacked the coordination desired.

Teacher

Of all the truisms associated with education, *the teacher makes the difference* is probably the most frequently cited. We concur with this observation, and thus we must attempt to describe the influence that the teacher exerts on the instructional experiences of children. It is easy to simply attribute most of what was observed, pleasant and unpleasant, to teacher influences. However, as outlined above, teachers are to some extent pawns in the influence game. Nonetheless, as Dreeben (1987) notes: "The decisions that district and school administrators make in selecting and distributing educational resources set limits on educational possibilities, but they do not directly determine how teachers organize and instruct their classes" (p.32). Although district decisions about enrollments, schedules, and curricula all restrict teacher decisions, there remain substantial arenas wherein teachers influence the instructional experiences of children.

Unfortunately, the instruction that was observed suggests that many classroom and specialist teachers simply lack the expertise necessary to deliver high quality reading instruction to low-achieving children. While substantial obstacles confronted teachers, it must concluded that many of the teachers were poorly trained or had training that was outdated. One can argue that school districts must share the burden of poorly trained teachers, along with the teacher training institutions and the teachers themselves.

Contrary to the concept of individualized instruction, McGill-Franzen (1988) argues that specialist teachers, as well as classroom teachers, develop instructional routines—routines employing known material and teaching activities—and simply present these routines repeatedly with group after group. Children must then conform to the routine if they are to be successful. Whether in the classroom or down the hall, children must fit the teacher's routine. The undifferentiated instruction we so often observed in both instructional settings suggests the appropriateness of that conceptualization. As noted in earlier studies (e.g., Allington et al., 1986), specialist teachers typically employed a limited set of teaching routines and, similarly, a limited set of curricular materials that virtually all students were presented. What we found most distressing was the lack of any clear and consistent superiority in the instruction offered by the specialist teachers as compared to the instruction available in the regular classroom. While groups were smaller and the teachers possessed more credentials, the specialist instruction did not routinely involve more direct instruction, more text reading activity, more higher-order tasks, or other features of high-quality instruction (Duffy et al., 1987). Individuals spent most of the time working alone, waiting, or in other nonacademic activities. When students were working alone or with the teacher or aide, the tasks rarely involved higher-order academic tasks.

WHERE DO WE GO FROM HERE?

This study was initiated for several reasons. First, the study sought to address directly the issue of how schools responded to children who were failing to learn to read on schedule. Because of dual backgrounds in remedial and special education, the authors were interested in the nature of the response, in terms of reading instruction particularly, to these two groups of students. This was of interest because, like so many other researchers (Bartoli & Botel, 1988; Birman, 1981; Gartner & Lipsky, 1987; Leinhardt, Bickel, & Pallay, 1982; Singer & Butler, 1987; Reschly, 1987; Reynolds, Wang, & Walberg, 1987; Ysseldyke & Algozzine, 1982), we have begun to doubt the validity of the distinctions that are used to differentiate low-achievement learners. What we attempted to describe were the instructional experiences of the two groups of students: students receiving services from two distinct federal initiatives. In the end, few differences worth attending to in the instructional experiences of the students were observed, and few differences were attributable primarily to the categorical program that they participated in.

Two Models for Change

The findings of this study of remedial and special education students' instructional experiences are remarkably consistent with those of earlier studies. None of the reports are heartening to those concerned with the educational futures of low-achievement children. There are, obviously, serious limitations in current conceptualizations about how best to deal with school failure. According to one researcher, the uniform standards for achievement and the uniform methods of instruction that exemplify schools create a group of students considered deviant

(Gelzheiser, 1987). The deviance is a result of learner differences and uniform expectations and may be exacerbated by instructional environments that give those most in need of high quality instruction, instruction that is qualitatively, and perhaps quantitatively, no better than that received by successful children.

In our view, current programs and policies must change if educational opportunities are to improve. We are quite unsure what type of change would best serve the interest of the low-achievement learners. We believe, as do Timar and Kirp (1987), that such changes cannot be coerced or legislated, but that providing access to larger amounts of substantially higher quality instruction for low-achievement children is a goal to which we should aspire. While providing such access has not been routinely achieved and will probably not come easily, we are quite sure that the knowledge about what kind of instructional opportunities low-achieving children need is generally available. We can implement that knowledge only after we alter current practice in substantial ways. It is in this spirit that we offer two suggestions for redesigning instructional support programs. Both, however, require shifts in current practices.

The Content Specialist Model

Our first suggestion would require the merger of all instructional efforts aimed at low-achievement children, regardless of current categorical label. Other researchers have proposed similar shifts (e.g., Gartner & Lipsky, 1987; Ginsburg & Turnbull, 1981; Jenkins, Pious, & Peterson, in press; Leinhardt et al., 1982; Moore et al., 1981; Reschly, 1987; Reynolds et al., 1987; Stainback & Stainback, 1984; Will, 1986), though the details of the various proposals differ. In our proposed unified effort, districts would create instructional intervention plans that focus on providing larger quantities of higher quality instruction to low-achievement students. Meeting the instructional needs of individuals is primarily a matter of providing some students with larger amounts of high quality instruction, and on focusing on differences in individual learning rates more than individual learning styles. In our unified plan, districts would select or create a reading curriculum, for instance, that all students would master. This curriculum plan would encompass all reading instruction efforts, at all levels.

Three recent papers (Allington & Johnston, in press; Idol, West, & Lloyd, 1988; Walmsley & Walp, in press) have discussed models for initiating such collaborative efforts. These papers suggest that to enhance the quantity and quality of instruction for low-achievement readers, attention must be directed to the core curriculum and instructional opportunities in the regular education program. Since failure in the core curriculum results in referrals to instructional support programs, effects must begin with strengthening instruction in regular education. Support instruction needs to focus on enhancing performance in the core curriculum; ideally, this would accelerate the mastery of core curricular goals, tasks, and activities. To do this, regular education and support teachers must work collaboratively on the design and delivery of instruction, ultimately developing the "shared knowledge" necessary to create coherent instructional opportunities across school settings (Allington & Broikou, 1988). In these models, regular and support teachers would hold "shared responsibility" for the instruction and achievement of low-achieving children. Most probably, the teachers would work as intact teams that address the instructional needs of a set of children. For instance, one support teacher might team with three or four classroom teachers and all would be jointly responsible for providing adequate quantities of instruction of sufficient quality to maintain normal progress through the core reading curriculum.

In our adaptation of these models, children who need larger amounts of instruction to attain mastery on schedule would receive just that—enhanced opportunities to learn. Such additional instruction would be provided by content specialists: specialist teachers who had much better training in the difficulties that students have in learning particular content. Rather than the current system of training by categorical classification, math, science, reading, and writing specialists would work with teachers and children. These content specialists would be trained to deal with all learners, and would focus on the particular difficulties that some learners have with specific school subjects. These specialists would conduct all of the assessment, focusing on identifying the particular difficulties the individual learners are having in completing the core curriculum tasks and activities. They would be far more knowledgeable about the core curriculum materials in use, about classroom instruction, and about the instruction histories of individual children than are the specialists who work in our schools today (Johnston et al., 1985). The instructional support offered would invariably be in addition to the instruction provided in the regular classroom, although improving upon the classroom instruction would be central to their role.

The Accountability Model

Our second proposal involves the elimination of all categorical programs as we now know them and, likewise, the elimination of specialist teachers. Actually, specialist teachers would still be in the schools, but they would become classroom teachers. In this accountability model, staff sizes would be reduced through the elimination of about half of the administrators and specialists that now, according to the U.S. Department of Education (1987), outnumber classroom teachers 2 : 1. While schools would still have the benefit of the expertise of specialist teachers, they would work as classroom teachers and would collaboratively assist other teachers in the preparation of lessons for learners with special instructional needs (Allington, in press).

In this design, each classroom teacher would be held accountable for the learning of all students, thus resolving the problem of "ownership." We would still have district plans, particularly coherent and complete curricula that teachers would develop and implement. With a class size of 12–15 students, teachers would be far better able to meet individual needs than in classrooms of 24–30 students. With no supplemental programs to send problem learners off to, class-room teachers would perhaps be more likely to seek out collaborative consulta-tion with other teachers with specialized training. Specialist teachers, school psychologists, special education, and Chapter 1 directors would now serve pri-marily as classroom teachers. Their expertise would then have to be refocused on meeting individual instruction needs in the practical world of classroom settings. In addition, the funding that now supports the various remedial, compensatory, and special education efforts would be redirected toward enhancing classroom instruction.

CONCLUSION

The central focus of both proposals is the assumption of responsibility by regular education programs for the academic achievement of low-achievement children. The current separation of remedial and special education from regular education has not only resulted in increased fragmentation in the learning experiences of participating children, it has resulted in diffused responsibility for the student's learning success or failure. Continued administrative, curricular, and instruc-tional separation of support programs from regular education, and the continued separation of different support programs designed to achieve similar goals with similar students, serve only to perpetuate unsatisfactory efforts to resolve the learning difficulties of off-schedule learners. Our proposals suggest a reorienta-tion of current programs so that resources are available to provide the instruc-tional support necessary to keep low-achievement children on schedule. The key goal is to dispel the seemingly pervasive belief that some children will neces-sarily attain low levels of achievement. Differential achievement is only neces-sary if instructional resources are allocated such that, at best, all children receive similar amounts of similar quality instruction. If, however, fewer of the critical instructional resources continue to be allocated to those students who need them the most, as is the current situation, the children cannot be blamed for their failure to achieve on levels comparable to their more advantaged peers.

The authors do not anticipate, however, that either of these proposals will be soon implemented. Unfortunately, it is likely that tradition, vested interests, and the lack of any powerful and organized constituency for the education of low-achievement children will impede anything but the most modest of changes in the current situation. Children come to school expecting to be successful; currently, some are and some are not. In neither case does the child hold the power to determine his or her fate; that power lies primarily with their educa-tional caregivers—teachers and administrators. Until instructional settings and programs are created that consistently provide low-achievement children with access to larger quantities of substantially enhanced instruction, we will fail our most important constituency: the children.

REFERENCES

Algozzine, B., & Ysseldyke, J. (1983). Learning disabilities as a subset of school failure: The over-sophistication of a concept. *Exceptional Children, 50,* 242–246.

Allington, R.L. (1983). The reading instruction provided readers of differing ability. *Elementary School Journal, 83,* 548–559.

Allington, R.L. (1986). Policy constraints and effective compensatory reading instruction: A review. In J. Hoffman (Ed.), *Effective teaching of reading: Research and Practice* (pp. 261–289). Newark, DE: International Reading Association.

Allington, R.L. (in press). What would you give up for 13 students? *Learning.*

Allington, R.L., & Broikou, K. (1988). The development of shared knowledge: New roles for classroom and specialist teachers. *Reading Teacher, 41,* 606–611.

Allington, R.L., & Johnston, P. (1986). The coordination among regular classroom reading programs and targeted support programs. In B.I. Williams, P.A. Richmond, & B.J. Mason (Eds.), *Designs for compensatory education: Conference proceedings and papers* (pp. 3–40). Washington, DC: Research and Evaluation Associates.

Allington, R.L., & Johnston, P. (In press). Coordination, collaboration, and consistency: The redesign of compensatory and special education interventions. In R. Slavin, N. Madden, & N. Karweit (Eds.), *Preventing school failure: Effective programs for students at-risk.*

Allington, R.L., & McGill-Franzen, A. (in press). School response to reading failure: Chapter I and special education. *Elementary School Journal,*

Allington, R.L., Stuetzel, H., Shake, M., & Lamarche, S. (1986). What is remedial reading? A descriptive study. *Reading Research and Instruction, 26,* 15–30.

Bartoli, J., & Botel, M. (1988). *Reading/Learning disability: An ecological approach.* New York: Teachers College.

Berliner, D. (1981). Academic learning time and reading achievement. In J. Guthrie (Ed.), *Comprehension and teaching: Research reviews.* Newark, DE: International Reading Association.

Birman, B.F. (1981). Problems of overlap between Title I and PL 94-142: Implications for the federal role in education. *Educational Evaluation and Policy Analysis, 3,* 5–19.

Bogdan, R. (1982). *Illiterate or learning disabled? A symbolic interactionist approach to the social dimensions of reading and writing.* Unpublished paper, Syracuse University School of Education.

Carter, L.F. (1984). The Sustaining Effects Study of compensatory and elementary education. *Educational Researcher, 12,* 4–13.

Coles, G. (1987). *The learning mystique: A critical look at learning disabilities.* New York: Pantheon.

Crawford, J., Kimball, G.H., & Patrick, A. (1984, April). *Differences and similarities in teaching effectiveness findings between regular classroom instruction and Chapter 1 compensatory instruction.* Paper presented at the AERA annual meeting, New Orleans.

Dreeben, R. (1987). Closing the divide: What teachers and administrators can do to help black students reach their reading potential. *American Educator, 11,* 28–35.

Dreeben, R., & Barr, R. (1983). Educational policy and the working of schools. In L.S. Shulman & G. Sykes (Eds.), *Handbook of teaching and policy* (pp. 81–96). New York: Longmans, Inc.

Duffy, G.G., Roehler, L., Sivan, E., Rackliffe, G., Book, C., Meloth, M., Vavrus, L., Wesselman, R., Putnam, J., & Bassiri, D. (1987). Effects of explaining the reasoning associated with using reading strategies. *Reading Research Quarterly, 22,* 347–377.

Educational Consolidation and Improvement Act of 1980.

Elementary and Secondary Education Act of 1965.

Fraatz, J.M.B. (1987). *The politics of reading: Power, opportunity, and the prospects for change in America's public schools.* New York: Teachers College.

Gartner, A. (1986). Disabling help: Special education at the crossroads. *Exceptional Children, 53,* 72–76.

Gartner, A., & Lipsky, D.K. (1987). Beyond special education: Towards a quality system for all students. *Harvard Educational Review, 57,* 367–395.

Gelzheiser, L.M. (1987). Reducing the number of students identified as learning disabled: A question of practice, philosophy, or policy? *Exceptional Children, 54,* 145–150.

Ginsburg, A.L., & Turnbull, B.J. (1981). Local program coordination: An alternative for federal aid to schools. *Educational Evaluation and Policy Analysis, 3,* 33–42.

Good, T. (1983). Research on classroom teaching. In L.S. Shulman & G. Sykes (Eds.), Handbook of teaching and policy (pp. 42–80). New York: Longmans.

Greenwood, C.R., Delquadri, J.C., Stanley, S., Sasso, G., Wharton, D., & Schulte, D. (1981). Locating opportunity to learn as a basis for academic remediation: A developing model for teaching. In R.B. Rutherford, Jr., A.G. Prieto, & J.E. McGlothlin (Eds.), *Severe behavior disorders of children and youth: Monograph in behavioral disorders.* Reston, VA: Council for Exceptional Children.

Griswold, P.A., Cotton, K., & Hansen, J. (1986). *Effective compensatory education sourcebook.* Washington, DC: U.S. Government Printing Office.

Haynes, M.C., & Jenkins, J.R. (1986). Reading instruction in special education resource rooms. *American Educational Research Journal, 23,* 161–190.

Holley, F.M. (1986). Program and staff structure: Reactions from a quarter century worker in compensatory education. In B.I. Williams, P.A. Richmond, & B.J. Mason (Eds.), *Designs for compensatory education: Conference proceedings and papers* (pp. 95–116). Washington, DC: Research and Evaluation Associates.

Idol, L., West, J.F., & Lloyd, S. (1988). Organizing and implementing specialized reading programs: A collaborative approach involving classroom, remedial, and special education teachers. *Remedial and Special Education, 9,* 54–61.

Jenkins, J.R. (1987). Similarities in the achievement levels of learning disabled and remedial students. *Counterpoint, 7,* 16.

Jenkins, J.R., Pious, C., & Peterson, D. (1988). Categorical programs for remedial and handicapped students: Issues of validity. *Exceptional Children, 55*(2), 147–158.

Johnston, P.H., Allington, R.L., & Afflerbach, P. (1985). The congruence of classroom and remedial instruction. *Elementary School Journal, 85,* 465–478.

Kimbrough, J., & Hill, P.T. (1981). *The aggregate effects of federal education programs.* Santa Monica, CA: Rand Corporation.

Larrivee, B. (1985). *Effective teaching for successful mainstreaming.* New York: Longmans.

Leinhardt, G., Bickel, W., & Pallay, A. (1982). Unlabeled but still entitled: Toward more effective remediation. *Teachers College Record, 84,* 391–422.

Leinhardt, G., Zigmond, N., & Cooley, W. (1981). Reading instruction and its effects. *American Educational Research Journal, 18,* 343–361.

McGill-Franzen, A. (1987). Failure to learn to read: Formulating a policy problem. *Reading Research Quarterly, 22,* 475–490.

McGill-Franzen, A. (1988). *Curriculum coherence: A qualitative dimension of at-risk second-graders experiences with reading instruction in special education, Chapter 1, and regular classrooms.* Manuscript submitted for publication.

Mehan, H. (1984). Institutional decision-making. In B. Rogoff & J. Lane (Eds.), *Everyday cognition: Its development in social context* (pp. 41–66). Cambridge, MA: Harvard University.

Moore, D.R., Hyde, A.A., Blair, K.A., & Weitzman, S.M. (1981). *Student Classification and the Right to Read*. Chicago: Designs for Change.

Morsink, C.V., Soar, R.S., Soar, R.M., & Thomas, R. (1986). Research on teaching: Opening the door to special education classrooms. *Exceptional Children, 53*, 32–40.

National RRC Panel on Indicators of Effectiveness in Special Education (1986). *Effectiveness indicators for special education: A reference tool*. Stillwater: Oklahoma State University, National Clearinghouse of Rehabilitation Training Material.

PL 94-142, the Education for All Handicapped Children Act of 1975.

Reschly, D.J. (1987). Learning characteristics of mildly handicapped students. In M.C. Wang, M.C. Reynolds, & H. Walberg (Eds.), *Handbook of special education: Research and practice* (Vol. 1, pp. 35–58). New York: Pergamon.

Reynolds, M.C., Wang, M.C., & Walberg, H.J. (1987). The necessary restructuring of special and regular education. *Exceptional Children, 53*, 391–398.

Rowan, B., Guthrie, L.F., Lee, G.V., & Guthrie, G.P. (1986). *The design and implementation of Chapter I instructional services: A study of 24 schools*. San Francisco: Far West Laboratory for Educational Research and Development.

Sarason, S.B. (1983). *Schooling in America: Scapegoat and salvation*. New York: The Free Press.

Singer, J.D., & Butler, J.A. (1987). The Education for All Handicapped Children Act: Schools as agents of social reform. *Harvard Educational Review, 57*, 125–152.

Stainback, W., & Stainback, S. (1984). A rationale for the merger of special and regular education. *Exceptional Children, 51*, 102–111.

Thurlow, M.L., Ysseldyke, J.E., Graden, J., & Algozzine, R. (1984). Opportunity to learn for LD students receiving different levels of special education services. *Learning Disability Quarterly, 7*, 55–67.

Timar, T.B., & Kirp, D.L. (1987). Educational reform and institutional competence. *Harvard Educational Review, 57*, 308–330.

Walmsley, S.A., & Walp, T. (in press). Toward an integrated language arts program: The North Warren project. *Elementary School Journal*.

Will, M. (1986). *Educating students with learning problems: A shared responsibility*. Washington, DC: Office of Special Education and Rehabilitative Services, U.S. Department of Education.

Ysseldyke, J., & Algozzine, B. (1982). *Critical issues in special and remedial education*. Boston: Houghton-Mifflin.

Ysseldyke, J.E., Algozzine, B., Shinn, M.R., & McGue, M. (1982). Similarities and differences between low achievers and students classified as learning disabled. *Journal of Special Education, 16*, 73–85.

Ysseldyke, J.E., Thurlow, M.L., Mecklenburg, C., & Graden, J. (1984). Opportunity to learn for regular and special education students during reading instruction. *Remedial and Special Education, 5*, 29–37.

Zigmond, N., Vallecorsa, A., & Leinhardt, G. (1980). Reading instruction for students with learning disabilities. *Topics in Language Disorders, 1*, 89–98.

chapter **6**

Adaptive Instruction
An Alternative for Accommodating Student Diversity through the Curriculum

Margaret C. Wang

General and special educators are being challenged to work together in the identification and implementation of effective alternatives for accommodating increasingly diverse student populations, including handicapped students and others with "special" learning needs (Wang, Reynolds, & Walberg, 1986, 1987; Will, 1986). This challenge is reflected in the growing movement toward improving and coordinating the educational services that traditionally have been provided by a multitude of separate programs in general, special, compensatory, and remedial education (e.g., Gartner & Lipsky, 1987; Wang, Reynolds, & Walberg, 1987).

Projected demographic trends indicate that the educational system will be expected to provide greater than usual education and related service support for an increasing number of children from poor families, for ethnically diverse groups of children, and for children with a variety of "special" learning needs. These trends include growing enrollments of minority students (U.S. Bureau of the Census, 1983), who typically are more likely than nonminority students to be identified as requiring special or compensatory education services (cf. Brantlinger & Guskin, 1987). Additionally, increases in the percentage of students under 18 who live in poverty and who have a strong chance of being singled out for remedial or other special services (Child Trends, 1985; U.S. Bureau of the Census, 1985) are also predicted. A third trend that has been projected is an epidemic rise in teenage pregnancies, which often produce low birth-weight babies who tend to develop lifelong health problems and learning difficulties (Hughes, Johnson, Rosenbaum, Simons, & Butler, 1987). Such student demographics are particularly prominent in large urban areas (Hodgkinson, 1985; Yancey, Goldstein, & Rigsby, 1986).

Because of these demographic trends and the growing number of students who will need greater than usual education and related service support, the problems inherent in current paths to educational excellence, whereby overall high standards are achieved by excluding segments of the population from schooling success, will intensify. Research and practical experience clearly suggest the inadequacy and legally questionable practice of maintaining a segregated, ineffective "second system" of programs and services for students with special needs (cf. Gartner & Lipsky, 1987; Wang, Reynolds, & Walberg, 1987–1988). (The term "second system" refers to special, compensatory, and remedial programs for students who might not prosper in the regular education system.) Schools are now being challenged to adjust to changes in the student population by providing coordinated, inclusive educational experiences that can overcome the effects of academic and social underdevelopment (Reynolds, Wang, & Walberg, 1987).

Reducing the separateness of second system programs requires careful attention to differences in the amount and types of education and related service support needed by individual students. It also requires the development of service delivery systems that are based in regular classroom settings (Wang, Reynolds, & Walberg, 1986, 1987). Adaptive instruction is rapidly gaining acceptance as one alternative educational approach for helping schools to accommodate a diversity of student learning needs in ways that are educationally effective, equitable, socially nonstigmatizing, and administratively efficient (e.g., Heller, Holtzman, & Messick, 1982; Reschly, 1987).

This chapter discusses two of the major tasks involved in the implementation of effective adaptive instruction programs. These tasks are: the identification of student learning characteristics that are relevant for instructional planning, and the adaptation of the curriculum to the unique characteristics of individual students. In the first section of the chapter, the adaptive instruction approach is briefly described, including its major design features and highlights from recent research on its effectiveness. The next two sections discuss the expanding research base on instructionally relevant learning characteristics and outline specific considerations in making appropriate curriculum adaptations. The concluding section of the chapter discusses the implications of adaptive instruction for integrating students and "special" education and related service supports in regular classrooms and schools.

RESPONDING TO THE CHALLENGE THROUGH ADAPTIVE INSTRUCTION

Adaptive instruction is an alternative educational approach designed to achieve the overall goal of enabling each student to experience schooling success through a systematic process of making instructional accommodations that meet the unique learning characteristics and needs of individual students. Improving instructional support to meet the individual needs of students is viewed as a twofold task. It involves, first, increasing the capabilities of schools to adapt the school learning environment to diverse student characteristics and needs. Second, it involves providing instructional interventions that enhance each student's ability to profit from the instructional accommodations and to experience schooling success.

Research and program development in adaptive instruction have incorporated a variety of instructional practices thought to be effective for individual students and various classroom settings. Among these are: mastery learning, cooperative teams, individual tutorials, large- and small-group instruction, and other practices shown by research to have positive effects on student learning (cf. Walberg, 1984b; Waxman, Wang, Anderson, & Walberg, 1985; Wang & Walberg, 1985). Thus, adaptive instruction programs are generally designed to use a variety of alternative instructional practices that have been shown to be effective. They also use a variety of instructional materials and technologies in ways that suit individual teachers, classes, and students. In his major review of research that links teacher behavior to student achievement, Brophy (1986) notes that the most effective way to accommodate students' learning needs is systematically to develop "comprehensive programs of curriculum and instruction that draw eclectically but planfully from the full range of available knowledge in devising effective methods of accomplishing specified goals" (p. IV–166). This view is also explicit in the design of adaptive instruction programs. In essence, the adaptive instruction approach calls for an evolving process that combines the best practices currently known to make systematic accommodations for meeting the learning needs of individual students.

Although adaptive instruction calls for individualized planning, it does not necessarily require that teachers work with individual students or that students work alone. Cooperative learning, small group instruction, one-to-one tutoring, and other instructional grouping patterns are all incorporated in the design of adaptive instructional programs. Their inclusion is generally based on the premise that the most efficient and effective structures for enhancing instructional effectiveness and for achieving intended learning outcomes (including basic skills acquisition, participation in group discussion, collaborative planning, development of social skills, and self-responsibility for learning) should be the basic criteria for designing school programs.

Thus, contrary to numerous portrayals in the literature on effective teaching, adaptive instruction programs are not the direct opposite of group-paced, teacher-directed instruction (e.g., Brophy, 1979; Rosenshine, 1979); nor are they strictly synonymous with open education or individualized instruction (e.g., Bangert, Kulik, & Kulik, 1983; Peterson, 1979). Instead, adaptive instruction is designed to meet the needs of each student through the purposeful use and combination of individualized instruction, small- and large-group instruction, and teacher-directed as well as student-initiated learning. Effective schooling through adaptive instruction is thus conceptualized to include a variety of teaching and learning strategies, instructional materials, and learning tasks (Wang, 1980; Wang & Walberg, 1985).

The following features have been identified as common to effective adaptive instruction programs (Wang & Lindvall, 1984):

1. Instruction is based on the assessed capabilities of each student. Teachers provide varying amounts of instruction and use a variety of approaches to work with students individually and in groups.
2. Materials and procedures permit each student to progress in the mastery of instructional content at a pace suited to his or her abilities and interests.
3. Periodic and systematic evaluations of student progress serve to inform individual students of their mastery of academic skills and content.
4. Each student undertakes, with teacher assistance and coaching, increasing responsibility for identifying his or her learning needs, as well as the resources required to perform tasks, plan learning activities, and evaluate his or her mastery.
5. Alternate activities and materials are available to aid students in the acquisition of essential academic skills and content.
6. Students have opportunities to make choices and decisions about their individual learning goals, their specific learning activities, and, consequently, their own learning outcomes.
7. Students assist each other in pursuing individual goals, and they cooperate in achieving group goals.

HIGHLIGHTS FROM THE RESEARCH BASE ON ADAPTIVE INSTRUCTION

During the past decade, the development and implementation of programs based on the adaptive instruction approach have been accompanied by stepped-up research on the impact of these programs on student learning (cf. Wang & Walberg, 1985). The results from two recent studies (Wang & Walberg, 1986; Waxman et al., 1985) are briefly described here.

A large-scale, observational study by Wang and Walberg (1986) was designed to characterize the features of instructional models aimed at providing for student diversity. Additionally, the study sought to increase understanding of how different combinations of features are integrated into working programs to produce the classroom processes and outcomes associated with effective instruction and learning as reported in the effective teaching literature. Findings from the Wang and Walberg study suggest that well-implemented programs that feature student choice, task flexibility, systematic teacher monitoring, peer tutoring, student-initiated requests for assistance from teachers, a wide variety of curriculum materials, and task-specific instruction are associated with high levels of self-management, more substantive than management-related interactions with teachers, and frequently include small group instructional activities.

The programs that utilized adaptive instruction practices and strategies also produced student achievement levels as great as, and often greater than, the achievement levels obtained under programs that are more characteristically teacher-directed and group paced. Moreover, several of the sample programs in the Wang and Walberg study had highly positive results for additional outcomes that are considered valuable by many educators, parents, and students. Among these outcomes were: 1) constructive student interactions with peers, 2) high levels of student self-responsibility, 3) ability to work independently, 4) close linking of diagnosis in the planning (prescription) and implementation of instructional accommodations, 5) student cooperation and helping each other with learning tasks, and 6) student self-responsibility and self-directed and peer-assisted exploration. Wang and Walberg also found that no single instructional practice or program feature seemed to distinguish effective programs from less effective programs. On the contrary, it was the combination and coordination of several features in carefully implemented programs that appeared to produce a wide range of positive student outcomes.

In their meta-analysis of findings from 38 studies, Waxman et al. (1985) made 309 comparisons between adaptive and nonadaptive (control) instruction programs. The studies that were included in the meta-analysis involved a variety of programs, social settings, grade levels, subject matter, and research methodologies. Waxman et al. synthesized the findings for three categories of student outcomes: cognitive (based mainly on performance on standardized achievement tests), affective, and behavioral (or process). They computed an effect size for each comparison as well as the overall weighted effect size for each study.

The findings from the Waxman et al. meta-analysis provide strong, consistent evidence for a positive relationship between adaptive instruction and desired student outcomes. The overall mean weighted effect size for the studies in the meta-analysis was .45, more than twice the average effect size of .20 standard deviations in classroom research of the past few decades. This effect size suggests that the average student in an adaptive instruction program scored at the 67th percentile of the distribution scores for the control group students (those in nonadaptive programs). The mean weighted effect sizes for cognitive, affective, and behavioral outcomes were .39, .60, and .69, respectively. These effect sizes did not vary significantly from one type of outcome to another. Nor did they vary significantly as a function of specific program characteristics, methodological rigor, social context of the study, subject-matter area, grade level, or student characteristics.

In contrast to the results from earlier reports of inconsistent and low or negative effects of adaptive instruction, the consistent outcomes reflected in the past decade's reports of research on the effects of adaptive instruction are particularly noteworthy. Tailoring instruction to respond to the learning characteristics and needs of individual students seems to be an educational alternative that can be effective in obtaining intended social and academic outcomes.

IDENTIFYING INSTRUCTIONALLY RELEVANT STUDENT CHARACTERISTICS

Efforts to improve the chances of schooling success for academically underserved students, including those who are categorized as requiring special and compensatory education, are often based on the assumption that instruction is the intentional manipulation of the learning environment to facilitate appropriate student responses. In such efforts, the teacher's primary task is to foster each student's competence so that his or her capability to profit from available learning alternatives is enhanced. The teacher must focus on identifying the unique, instructionally relevant characteristics of individual students and on finding ways to provide educational experiences that are responsive to the students' learning characteristics and needs.

While the deliberate attempt to link assessment to instruction in order to enhance student learning is an expressed goal of second system programs, in actual practice, special, compensatory, and remedial education tend to rely on traditional measures of learning ability, aptitude, and other social and personality attributes that are used primarily for normative and predictive purposes (cf. Glaser & Bond, 1981; Reschly, 1984, 1987). Typically, little attention has been given to the need to describe learner characteristics in terms of the cognitive-affective and social processes that are intrinsic to learning and performance.

The research base identifies a wide range of individual difference variables as correlates of learning (cf. Wang & Lindvall, 1984). Yet only a small number of these variables tend to be incorporated in actual instructional planning and delivery—either in general or in special education. Extant programs generally are concerned with individual differences in subject matter knowledge, or in school achievement as measured by standardized achievement tests and learning rates. Only a few programs consider process-related characteristics such as time on-task, cooperative learning, self-management, and self-instructive skills (e.g., Deshler, Schumaker, & Lenz, 1984; Slavin, 1983a; Wang, 1980).

Individual Differences in Learning

Although individual differences in learning have long been accepted as a given, fundamental conceptual changes have occurred over the last 2 decades in the type of information on individual differences that is examined and in the ways in which the information is used to provide instruction. Among the significant developments is an increased recognition that certain personal and learning characteristics are alterable (cf. Bloom, 1976). Some prime examples of variables that are no longer considered to be static are family characteristics, such as parent expectations and family involvement (e.g., Walberg, 1984a), cognition and processes of learning (cf. Chipman, Segal, & Glaser, 1985; Mussen, 1983; Segal, Chipman, & Glaser, 1985), and student's perceptions of self-competence (cf. Levine & Wang, 1983).

Perhaps the foremost change has been a major shift toward describing the unique processes of learning that are used by individuals to mediate their acquisition and retention of knowledge and skills. Instead of characterizing student learning solely by grossly defined outcome measures, learner differences are being examined in terms of the manner in which information is processed, the mental mechanics and rules that students bring to the instructional environment, the motivation and affective response tendencies involved in the acquisition and retention of knowledge, and the knowledge and competence of individual students (e.g., Glaser, 1976; Gordon, 1983; Messick, 1979; Mussen, 1983; Scandura, 1977; Segal et al., 1985; Snow & Farr, 1983; Wang & Lindvall, 1984). Recent developments also indicate a trend toward studying ways of altering the psychological processes and cognitive operations used by individual students (Bransford, Vye, Delclos, Burns, & Hasselbring, 1985; Brown, 1978; Dweck, 1975; Feuerstein, Jensen, Hoffman, & Rand, 1985; Palincsar & Brown, 1984). There is also a trend toward modifying learning environments and instructional strategies to accommodate learner differences beyond those that occur in the rate of basic skills acquisition (cf. Wang & Lindvall, 1984; Wang & Walberg, 1985).

Several student learning behaviors have been cited in the psychological and educational research literature as correlates of learning (cf. Wang & Lindvall, 1984; Wittrock, 1986). These student behaviors include, for example, task involvement (e.g., Grannis, 1978), energy deployment (e.g., Birch & Gussow, 1970; Thomas, Chess, & Birch, 1968), autonomy (e.g., Bandura, 1981; Thomas, 1980; Wang, 1983), time on-task (e.g., Carroll, 1963; Denham & Lieberman, 1980; Fisher & Berliner, 1985; Karweit, 1983; Underwood, 1949), and resource utilization and decision making (e.g., Bandura, 1977; Wang, 1983). Although this research base is still quite scanty in some cases, individual difference variables, beyond achievement in basic skills as measured by standardized tests, must be considered in instructional planning from both the theoretical and the pedagogical perspectives.

One of the salient implications of recent developments in the study of the learning process is that learning necessarily involves adaptation on the part of the learner (Wang & Peverly, 1987). School improvement efforts have focused on the need to develop students' abilities to function as active learners throughout their lives. In this context, successful learners are defined as active processors, interpreters, and synthesizers of information (Brown, 1978; Chipman, Segal, & Glaser, 1985; Flavell, 1979; Levine & Wang, 1983; Segal, Chipman, & Glaser, 1985; Zimmerman, 1986). Individual learners are expected not only to take greater responsibility for managing, monitoring, and evaluating their learning, but also to be instrumental in adapting the learning environment (e.g., identifying and obtaining learning resources to fit their needs and goals) and adjusting themselves to the demands of the learning process (e.g., Covington & Beery, 1976; Meichenbaum, 1985; Wang, 1983; Weiner, 1980). The concept of learning-as-adaptation is exemplified by student adaptation in the selection and use of resources in the learning environment and by student adaptation in the use of specific materials to enhance learning.

Synthesizing the Research Base and Practical Wisdom

Current systems for classifying and placing students with "special" learning needs in special, compensatory, and remedial education have repeatedly been shown to be ineffective for matching instruction to learner characteristics and needs. The differences in student characteristics, even within given categories of handicapping conditions (e.g., Keogh & Macmillan, 1983; Reschly, 1988; Wood & Lakin, 1982; Ysseldyke & Thurlow, 1983), and the wide variation in administrative arrangements for providing "special" services (e.g., Algozzine & Korinek, 1985; Comptroller General, 1981; Glass, 1983; U.S. Department of Education, 1985), have been cited as major reasons for the existing discrepancies between instruction and student needs.

A first critical step toward solving this problem is to develop a common language for delineating instructionally relevant characteristics, and then to develop and implement instructional practices that accommodate differences in those characteristics. A common language would facilitate communication among researchers and between researchers and practitioners. It is typical of special education research, for example, to describe subjects simply by citing the categorical labels used in the schools. However, the definitions and uses of such categorical labels have shown to be so variable and scientifically questionable as to make communication very difficult. As a result, it is not easy to replicate special education research or to synthesize findings across studies.

An attempt to address this concern was represented in a study by Wang that was designed to synthesize and communicate the extant research base on the wide range of variability in the cognitive and affective processes associated with students' learning (Wang, 1986). One of the major objectives of the study was to obtain consensus among researchers, leading practitioners, teacher educators, parents, and other advocates on specific marker and student outcome variables that have an important impact on student learning. To this end, a survey of identified "stakeholders" was designed that addressed the question: What is it about schools and instruction that causes students to learn?

Respondents to the survey were asked to rate the extent to which selected variables that have been frequently cited in the research literature, both in general and in special education, are related to student learning. The variables were selected based on: 1) the effective schools literature (e.g., Bennett, 1986; Brophy, 1986; Silverman & Taeuber, 1985; U.S. Department of Education, 1986a, 1986b; Walberg, 1984b; Wittrock, 1986); 2) relevant research in the field of special education (e.g., Kaufman, Agard, & Semmel, 1985; Mann, 1985-1986; Wang, Reynolds, & Walberg, 1987; Ysseldyke, 1987); and 3) other input from leading researchers and practitioners.

A preliminary analysis of results from the survey suggests findings that have particular relevance for the discussion in this chapter (Wang, 1988). In the category "student variables," the mean ratings of survey respondents indicated moderate to strong relationships between student learning and a variety of motivational, affective, social, behavioral, cognitive, and metacognitive variables. These variables included: positive, nondisruptive behavior; appropriate activity level; attitudes toward school and teachers; motivation for continual learning; attributions for success and failure; levels of general academic knowledge and knowledge in specific subject matter areas; self regulatory and self control strategies; comprehension monitoring; positive strategies for coping with failure; and positive strategies to facilitate the generalization of concepts.

In the category "implementation, classroom instruction, and climate," the highest ratings for relevance to student learning were given to variables that included the following:

Time on-task
Provision of frequent feedback to students about their performance
Setting and maintenance of clear expectations for content mastery
Appropriate challenging of students with tasks at appropriate levels of difficulty
Use of clear and organized direct instruction
Development of students' self-responsibility for independent study and planning
    of their own learning activities
Creation and maintenance of necessary instructional materials
Systematic sequencing of instructional events and activities
The use of assessment as a frequent, integral component of instruction

Finally, in the category "program design," the variables that received the highest mean ratings from survey respondents included the following:

Clearly presented academic, social, and attitudinal program goals/outcomes
Use of explicit goal/objective-setting for instruction of individual students
Use of mastery learning techniques, including instructional cues, engagement,
    and correction
Use of cooperative learning strategies
Use of prescriptive instruction combined with aspects of informal or open
    education
Degree to which the curriculum structure accommodates the needs of different
    learners
Availability of materials and activities for students with different abilities

ADAPTING THE CURRICULUM TO STUDENT DIFFERENCES

As discussed in preceding sections of this chapter, recent research in education, combined with results from reviews of the state of practice in schools, has contributed significantly to the current understanding of what makes learning productive. This information suggests alternative approaches to delivering instruction and related services that are substantially superior to widespread traditional practices (Brophy, 1986; Wang, Reynolds, & Walberg, 1986; Wittrock, 1986).

Figure 1 provides an overview of this extant knowledge base as derived from an integrative analysis of the recent research literature (Good, 1983; Walberg, 1984b; Wang, Reynolds, & Walberg, 1986; Wang & Walberg, in press). The first column of Figure 1 lists features of effective classroom learning environments. The corresponding expected outcomes are grouped into four categories: development of positive attitudes toward learning, acquisition of a variety of learning skills, mastery of subject-matter content, and development of positive self-perceptions. In many cases, the research findings summarized in Figure 1 corroborate the results from the survey on learning-related variables described in the preceding section.

It is interesting to note the documented student outcomes for two curriculum-related features that are widely associated with effective adaptive instruction. As shown in Figure 1, one of these features, "assessment and diagnosis that provide frequent and systematic assessment of progress and feedback," has been found to result in motivation for continuing learning, ability to study and learn independently, ability to plan and monitor learning activities, ability to obtain assistance from others, mastery of content and skills for effective functioning, mastery of content and skills for further learning, and confidence in one's ability as a learner. The curriculum-related feature "learning experiences in which alternative instructional strategies, student assignments, and activities are used" has been found to result in students' enjoyment in taking part in learning activities, in addition to the same outcomes listed above (except for "ability to obtain assistance from others").

Based on the findings indicated in Figure 1, as well as on practical experience in the implementation and development of demonstrably effective adaptive instruction programs (cf. Wang & Walberg, 1985), certain characteristics of an effective adaptive instruction curriculum can be delineated. When these characteristics operate as part of an overall adaptive instruction cycle in general education classrooms, a wide range of student diversity can be accommodated.

CHARACTERISTICS OF EFFECTIVE ADAPTIVE INSTRUCTION

The adaptive instructional approach is based on the premise that effective instructional interventions incorporate a variety of exemplary practices and delivery systems to meet the diverse needs of students. An adaptive instruction curriculum is distinguished by several characteristics. The curriculum objectives are clearly defined and are arranged in a pedagogically meaningful sequence to ensure student mastery of initial skills before more advanced skills are introduced (Gagne, 1968; Resnick, 1973; Wang, Resnick, & Boozer, 1971). Learning opportunities that include an assortment of materials and activities are incorporated to accommodate the diverse instructional support requirements of individual students. The implementation of adaptive instruction includes procedures for linking criterion-referenced diagnosis and assessment to the design and provision of instruction that enhances teacher effectiveness in improving students' chances for learning success.

During the 1960s and 1970s, several individualized curricula that were specifically designed for adaptive instruction programs were developed and field-tested (e.g., Individually Prescribed Instruction, Lindvall & Bolvin, 1967; Wang & Resnick, 1978). An essential characteristic of these programs is the linkage between assessment and systematically designed instruction, known as the criterion-referenced diagnosis and prescription process of designing and implementing instructional programs. This criterion-referenced concept of assessment and instruction had a profound effect on curriculum development in general. Most contemporary commercially published curricula include well-defined and hierarchically sequenced objectives, various text-embedded and adjunct practice activities, and procedures for assessing students' mastery of objectives. The incorporation of these curricula into an effective cycle of diagnosis, prescription, and teaching is one of the distinguishing characteristics of the adaptive instruction approach (Wang, 1987).

The Adaptive Instruction Cycle

Adaptive instruction may be viewed as a *cycle* of activities that accommodates the learning characteristics and needs of individual students. This adaptive instruction cycle is essentially a recurring sequence of diagnosis, prescription, teaching, and assessment. At each stage of the adaptive instruction cycle, the teacher utilizes a variety of curriculum resources.

Diagnosis Under adaptive instruction, diagnosis refers to the process of determining each student's level of functioning and learning needs with respect to particular curriculum objectives or units. Diagnosis may be based on the results from placement tests, diagnostic tests of students' specific learning competencies and difficulties, unit pretests, curriculum-embedded tests, or on informal means such as student work samples. Structured, systematic methods for recording students' progress through the curriculum on an ongoing basis are critical. Accurate, comprehensive, and up-to-date records are invaluable, not only helping teachers in management and instructional planning, but also serving as a reinforcement for students and as a data base for assessment of student learning.

Expected Student Outcomes	Development of positive attitudes toward learning			
	Enjoyment in taking part in learning activities	Viewing help-giving and help-receiving as positive experiences	Special interest in certain learning areas	Motivation for continuing to learn
Features of effective classroom learning environments				
Instructional content that is:				
Essential to further learning			X	
Useful for effective functioning in school and society			X	X
Clearly specified				
Organized to facilitate efficient learning				X
Assessment and diagnosis that:				
Provide appropriate placement in the curricula				X
Provide frequent and systematic evaluation of progress and feedback				X
Learning experiences in which:				
Ample time and instructional support are provided for each student to acquire essential content	X		X	X
Disruptiveness is minimized	X			X
Students use effective learning strategies/study skills				X
Each student is expected to succeed, and actually succeeds, in achieving mastery of curriculum content, and accomplishments are reinforced	X		X	X
Alternative instructional strategies, student assignments, and activities are used	X			X
Management of instruction that:				
Permits students to master many lessons through independent study				X
Permits students to plan their own learning activities	X			X
Provides for students' self-monitoring of their progress with most lessons	X		X	X
Permits students to play a part in selecting some learning goals and activities	X		X	X
Collaboration among students that:				
Enables students to obtain necessary help from peers	X	X		
Encourages students to provide help	X	X	X	
Provides for collaboration in group activities	X	X	X	

Figure 1. Examples of features of classroom learning environments and expected student outcomes.

Acquisition of a variety of learning skills			Mastery of subject matter content		Development of positive self-perceptions			
Ability to study and learn independently	Ability to plan and monitor learning activities	Ability to obtain assistance from others	Mastery of content and skills for effective functioning	Mastery of content and skills for further learning	Confidence in one's ability as a learner	Confidence in oneself as a contributing member of the school/community	Confidence in one's ability to take self-responsibility for learning and behavior	Perceptions of internal locus of control
			X	X	X			
			X	X				
X	X		X	X	X		X	
X	Y		X	X	X		X	
X			X	X	X			
X	X	X	X	X	X			
			X	X	X			X
X	X		X	X	X		X	
X	X	X	X	X	X		X	
			X	X	X	X	X	
X	X		X	X	X			
X	X		X	X	X			X
x	X		X	X	X			X
X	X		X	X	X		X	X
X	X		X	X	X		X	X
	X	X	X	X	X		X	X
		X	X	X		X		X
	X	X	X	X	X	X	X	X

The [X] indicates that extant findings from studies on effective teaching and learning suggest relationships between the implementation of specific features and the achievement of particular student outcomes. (Source Wang, M. C., Reynolds, M. C., & Walberg, H. J. [1986]. Rethinking Special Education. *Educational Leadership, 44*, 28–29; reprinted with permission of the Association for Supervision and Curriculum Development. Copyright [1986] by ASCD. All rights reserved.)

Prescription After a student's current level of functioning is assessed and his or her specific learning needs are diagnosed, the teacher uses this information to prescribe appropriate learning activities, including group and individual instruction and independent assignments.

Teaching The next stage in the adaptive instruction cycle is teaching students to acquire the knowledge and skills required to complete their learning tasks. Instruction may be directed toward the introduction of new content or the reinforcement/extension of old content, depending on students' needs and prescriptions. Although instructional planning in accordance with systematically derived student prescriptions is an important aspect of the adaptive instruction cycle, the accommodation of student diversity also incorporates on-the-spot decision making by teachers (Joyce, 1978–1979; Peterson & Clark, 1978; Shavelson & Stern, 1981; Smith & Sendelbach, 1979; Zahorik, 1970). If adaptive instruction is to operate at the optimum level, consideration must be given to in-class strategies, or interactive instructional decisions, that are aimed at immediately clarifying students' misconceptions. Such strategies must also foster adequate learning progress, and must consider preplanned curricula and lessons formulated outside the classroom.

Assessment Both formal (unit or lesson posttests, level tests, teacher-constructed tests) and informal (work samples) means can be used to determine whether and to what degree each student has achieved mastery of curriculum objectives. Performance on curriculum-based tests yields valuable information about the objectives mastered by each student over given periods of time as he or she progresses through the curriculum.

Research and development have pointed to the need for assessment procedures that produce holistic profiles of learning, instruction, and curriculum for individual students. This approach, which is sometimes referred to as assessment-in-context (Messick, 1984, 1987; Tyler, 1967), is aimed at providing a broad perspective of student learning performance and, consequently, linking appropriate instruction to the findings from student assessments. Such multifaceted assessments would take into account a range of variables, including:

Subject-matter competence

Learning processes and cognitive strategies applied as students acquire and use their knowledge and skills

Structure and objectives of the curriculum

Opportunities students may or may not have had to learn the assessed knowledge and skills and to use this information in the monitoring of their own learning

Contextual characteristics such as features of classroom instruction, teacher effectiveness, and functional requirements or operating systems of the classroom and of each student's home

The general sociocultural environment of the community

Assessments-in-context have particular implications for improving the current classification system of certifying and entitling students for special and compensatory services. Using this approach, the focus could be shifted from labeling students according to predefined categories to identifying specific steps for improving the quality of instruction for students with special needs.

In the adaptive instruction cycle, both teachers and students are held accountable for student progress through the curriculum. Teachers are responsible for diagnosing individual student needs correctly, making appropriate assignments, providing needed instruction, monitoring student work, adjusting assignments as necessary, and assessing student mastery of objectives. Students are responsible for completing assigned tasks in a timely manner, having them checked, and ultimately, mastering the objectives. Thus, even in light of the diversity of student abilities, interests, and ways of functioning in most classrooms, all students, including those who require greater than usual instructional support, can have access to a variety of learning options under adaptive instruction.

CONCLUDING REMARKS

Extant programs designed systematically to link classroom instruction with the research findings on instructionally relevant learner characteristics and demonstrably effective instructional practices include: the Adaptive Learning Environments Model (Wang, 1980; Wang, Gennari, & Waxman, 1985), Mastery Learning (Anderson, 1985; Bloom, 1968), and Team-Assisted Individualization (Slavin, 1983b). (For a more detailed description of such programs, see Brophy, 1986; Cantalician Foundation, Inc., 1983; Dawson, 1987; Epps & Tindal, 1987; Heller et al., 1982; Mayor's Commission on Special Education, 1985; Nevin & Thousand, 1987.) Although they differ in design and specific instructional strategies, all of these programs, when well-implemented in school settings, have been shown to be effective for their use of the adaptive instruction approach to serve diverse student populations. Such populations include special education students and other academically underserved students in general education settings. Thus, they may be viewed as intact models for further experimentation and collaboration aimed at providing learning experiences based on a broad continuum of academic and social goals that accommodate a wide range of individual learning characteristics and needs.

Research and field experience have shown that the integration of students from the second system programs and of their required services in regular classroom settings is both feasible and instructionally effective (e.g., Gartner & Lipsky, 1987; Madden & Slavin, 1982; Morsink, Thomas, & Smith-Davis, 1987; Wang, Peverly, & Catalano, 1987). Curriculum adaptations based on individual learning characteristics and needs are key factors in successful educational integration. By replacing fragmented systems of classification, placement, and instruction with effective core curricula that incorporate the best practices of special and general education, improved learning can be expected for all students (e.g., Allington, 1987; Brophy, 1986; Wang, Reynolds, & Walberg, 1986). Likewise, the need for special classes, remedial services, and resource rooms is likely to be reduced for many, if not most, students.

REFERENCES

Algozzine, B., & Korinek, L. (1985). Where is special education for students with high prevalence handicaps going? *Exceptional Children, 51*(5), 388–394.

Allington, R.L. (1987). Shattered Hopes. *Learning 87,* (July/August), 60–66.

Anderson, L.W. (1985). Opportunity to learn. In T. Husen & T. Postlethwaite (Eds.), *The International Encyclopedia of Education.* Oxford: Pergamon Press.

Bandura, A. (1977). *Social learning theory.* Englewood Cliffs, NJ: Prentice-Hall.

Bandura, A. (1981). Self-referent thought: A developmental analysis of self-efficacy. In J.H. Flavell & L.R. Ross (Eds.), *Social cognitive development: Frontiers and possible futures* (pp. 200–239). New York: Cambridge University Press.

Bangert, R.L., Kulik, J.A., & Kulik, C.C. (1983). Individualized systems of instruction in secondary schools. *Review of Educational Research, 59,* 149–158.

Bennett, W.J. (1986). *First lessons: A report on elementary education in America.* Washington, DC: U.S. Department of Education.

Birch, H.G., & Gussow, J.D. (1970). *Disadvantaged children: Health, nutrition, and school failure.* New York: Harcourt, Brace & World.

Bloom, B.S. (1968). Learning for mastery. *Evaluation Comment, 1*(2), 74–86.

Bloom, B.S. (1976). *Human characteristics and school learning.* New York: McGraw-Hill.

Bransford, J.D., Vye, N.J., Delclos, V.R., Burns, M.S., & Hasselbring, T.S. (1985). *Improving the quality of assessment and instruction: Roles for dynamic assessment* (Learning Technology Center Technical Report Series). Nashville, TN: George Peabody College of Vanderbilt University.

Brantlinger, E.A., & Guskin, S.L. (1987). Ethnocultural and social psychological effects on learning characteristics of handicapped children. In M.C. Wang, M.C. Reynolds, & H.J. Walberg (Eds.), *Handbook of special education: Research and practice: Vol. 1: Learner characteristics and adaptive education* (pp. 7–34). Oxford, England: Pergamon Press.

Brophy, J.B. (1979). Teacher behavior and its effects. *Journal of Educational Psychology, 71*(6), 733–750.

Brophy, J.B. (1986). Research linking teacher behavior to student achievement: Potential implications for instruction of Chapter 1 students. In B.I. Williams, P.A. Richmond, & B.J. Mason (Eds.), *Designs for compensatory education: Conference proceedings and papers* (IV, pp. 121–179). Washington, DC: Research and Evaluation Associates.

Brown, A.L. (1978). Knowing when, where and how to remember. In R. Glaser (Ed.), *Advances in instructional psychology* (Vol. 1). Hillsdale, NJ: Lawrence Erlbaum Associates.

Cantalician Foundation, Inc. (1983). *Technical assistance and alternative practices related to the problem of the overrepresentation of Black and other minority students in classes for the educable mentally retarded.* Buffalo, NY: Author.

Carroll, J.B. (1963). A model for school learning. *Teachers College Record, 63,* 722–732.

Child Trends, Inc. (1985). *The school-age handicapped* (NCES 85-400). Washington, DC: U.S. Government Printing Office.

Chipman, S.G., Segal, J.W., & Glaser, R. (Eds.). (1985). *Thinking and learning skills: Vol. 2. Research and open questions.* Hillsdale, NJ: Lawrence Erlbaum Associates.

Comptroller General. (1981). *Disparities still exist in who gets special education.* Washington, DC: General Accounting Office.

Covington, M.L., & Beery, R. (1976). *Self-worth and school learning.* New York: Holt, Rinehart & Winston.

Dawson, P. (1987). Preface. In A. Canter, P. Dawson, J. Silverstein, L. Hale, & J. Zins (Eds.), *NASP directory of alternative service delivery models.* Washington, DC: National Association of School Psychologists.

Denham, C., & Lieberman, A. (Eds.). (1980). *Time to learn.* Washington, DC: National Institute of Education.

Deshler, D.D., Schumaker, J.B., & Lenz, B.K. (1984). Academic and cognitive interventions for LD adolescents: Part 1. *Journal of Learning Disabilities, 17*(2), 108–117.

Dweck, C.S. (1975). The role of expectations and attributions in the alleviation of learned helplessness. *Journal of Personality and Social Psychology, 31,* 674–685.

Epps, S., & Tindal, G. (1987). The effectiveness of differential programming in serving mildly handicapped students: Placement options and instructional programming. In M.C. Wang, M.C. Reynolds, & H.J. Walberg (Eds.), *Handbook of special education: Research and practice: Vol. 1: Learner characteristics and adaptive education* (pp. 213–248). Oxford, England: Pergamon Press.

Feuerstein, R., Jensen, M., Hoffman, M.B., & Rand, Y. (1985). Instrumental enrichment, an intervention program for structural cognitive modifiability: Theory and practice. In J.W. Segal, S.F. Chipman, & R. Glaser (Eds.), *Thinking and learning skills: Vol. 1: Relating instruction to research* (pp. 43–82). Hillsdale, NJ: Lawrence Erlbaum Associates.

Fisher, C., & Berliner, D. (Eds.), (1985). *Perspectives on instructional time.* New York: Longman, Inc.

Flavell, J.H. (1979). Metacognitive and cognitive monitoring: A new idea of cognitive development inquiry. *American Psychologist, 34*(10), 906–911.

Gagne, R.M. (1968). Learning hierarchies. *Educational Psychologist, 6,* 1–9.

Gartner, A., & Lipsky, D.K. (1987). Beyond special education: Toward a quality system for all students. *Harvard Educational Review, 57*(4), 367–395.

Glaser, R. (1976). Components of a psychology of instruction: Toward a science of design. *Review of Educational Research, 46,* 1–24.

Glaser, R., & Bond, L. (1981). Testing: Concepts, policy, practice, and research. *American Psychologist, 36*(10), 997–1000.

Glass, G.V. (1983). Effectiveness of special education. *Policy Studies Review, 2*(1), 65–78.

Good, T.L. (1983, April). *Classroom research: A decade of progress.* Paper presented at the annual meeting of the American Educational Research Association, Montreal.

Gordon, E.W. (Ed.). (1983). *Human diversity and pedagogy.* Westport, CT: Mediax.

Grannis, J.C. (1978). Task engagement and the consistency of pedagogical controls: An ecological study of differently structured classroom settings. *Curriculum Inquiry, 8*(1), 3–36.

Heller, K., Holtzman, W., & Messick, S. (Eds.). (1982). *Placing children in special education: A strategy for equity.* Washington, DC: National Academy of Sciences Press.

Hodgkinson, H.L. (1985). *All one system: Demographics of education—Kindergarten through graduate school.* Washington, DC: Institute for Educational Leadership, Inc.

Hughes, D., Johnson, K., Rosenbaum, S., Simons, J., & Butler, E. (1987). *The health of America's children: Maternal and child health data book.* Washington, DC: Children's Defense Fund.

Joyce, B. (1978–1979). Toward a theory of information processing in teaching. *Educational Research Quarterly, 3,* 66–67.

Karweit, N. (1983). *Time on task: A research review* (Research Report No. 322). Baltimore: Johns Hopkins University, Center for the Social Organization of Schools.

Kaufman, M., Agard, J.A., & Semmel, M.I. (Eds.). (1985). *Mainstreaming: Learners and their environments.* Cambridge, MA: Brookline Books.

Keogh, B.K., & Macmillan, D.L. (1983). The logic of sample selection: Who represents what? *Exceptional Education Quarterly, 4*(3), 84–96.

Levine, J.M., & Wang, M.C. (Eds.). (1983). *Teacher and student perceptions: Implications for learning.* Hillsdale, NJ: Lawrence Erlbaum Associates.

Lindvall, C.M., & Bolvin, J.O. (1967). Programmed instruction in the schools: An application of programming principles in individually prescribed instruction. *Sixty-sixth yearbook of the National Society for the Study of Education, Part VII.* Chicago: University of Chicago Press.

Madden, N.A., & Slavin, R.E. (1982). *Count me in: Academic achievement and social outcomes of mainstreaming students with mild academic handicaps* (Report No. 329). Baltimore: The Johns Hopkins University, Center for the Social Organization of Schools.

Mann, L. (Ed.). (1985–1986). Research synthesis in special education [Special Issue]. *The Journal of Special Education, 19*(4), 381–526.

Mayor's Commission on Special Education. (1985). *Special education: A call for quality.* New York: Author.

Meichenbaum, D. (1985). Teaching thinking: A cognitive-behavioral perspective. In S.F. Chipman, J.W. Segal, & R. Glaser (Eds.), *Thinking and learning skills: Vol. 2: Research and open questions* (pp. 407–426). Hillsdale, NJ: Lawrence Erlbaum Associates.

Messick, S. (1979). Potential uses of noncognitive measurement in education. *Journal of Educational Psychology, 71,* 281–292.

Messick, S. (1984). The psychology of education measurement. *Journal of Education Measurement, 21,* 215–237.

Messick, S. (1987, May). *Assessment in the schools: Purposes and consequences.* Paper presented at the Inaugural Conference on the Benton Center for Curriculum and Instruction, University of Chicago.

Morsink, C.V., Thomas, C.C., & Smith-Davis, J. (1987). Noncategorical special education programs: Process and outcomes. In M.C. Wang, M.C. Reynolds, & H.J. Walberg (Eds.), *Handbook of special education: Research and practice: Vol. 1: Learner characteristics and adaptive education* (pp. 287–311). Oxford, England: Pergamon Press.

Mussen, P. (Ed.). (1983). *Handbook of child psychology* (4th ed.). NY: John Wiley & Sons.

Nevin, A., & Thousand, J. (1987). Avoiding/limiting special education referrals: Changes and challenges. In M.C. Wang, M.C. Reynolds, & H.J. Walberg (Eds.), *Handbook of special education: Research and practice: Vol. 1: Learner characteristics and adaptive education* (pp. 273–286). Oxford, England: Pergamon Press.

Palincsar, A.S., & Brown, A.L. (1984). Reciprocal teaching of comprehension-fostering and comprehension-monitoring activities. *Cognition and Instruction, 1,* 117–125.

Peterson, P.L. (1979). Direct instruction reconsidered. In P.L. Peterson & H.J. Walberg (Eds.), *Research on teaching: Concepts, findings, and implications* (pp. 57–69). Berkeley, CA: McCutchan.

Peterson, P.L., & Clark, C.M. (1978). Teachers' reports of their cognitive processes during teaching. *American Educational Research Journal, 15*(4), 555–565.

Reschly, D.J. (1984). Beyond IQ test bias: The National Academy panel's analysis of minority EMR overrepresentation. *Educational Researcher, 13*(3), 15–19.

Reschly, D.J. (1987). Learning characteristics of mildly handicapped students: Implications for classification, placement, and programming. In M.C. Wang, M.C. Reynolds, & H.J. Walberg (Eds.), *Handbook of special education: Research and practice: Vol. 1: Learner characteristics and adaptive education* (pp. 35–58). Oxford, England: Pergamon Press.

Reschly, D.J. (1988). Introduction. In M.C. Wang, M.C. Reynolds, & H.J. Walberg (Eds.), *Handbook of special education: Research and practice: Vol. 2: Mildly handicapped conditions.* (pp. 3–5). Oxford, England: Pergamon Press.

Resnick, L.B. (Ed.). (1973). Hierarchies in children's learning. *Instructional Science, 2,* 311–362.

Reynolds, M.C., Wang, M.C., & Walberg, H.J. (1987). The necessary restructuring of special and regular education. *Exceptional Children, 53*(5), 391–398.

Rosenshine, B.V. (1979). Content, time, and direct instruction. In P.L. Peterson & H.J. Walberg (Eds.), *Research on teaching: Concepts, findings, and implications* (pp. 28–56). Berkeley, CA: McCutchan.

Scandura, A. (1977). *Social learning theory.* Englewood Cliffs, NJ: Prentice-Hall.

Segal, J.W., Chipman, S.G., & Glaser, R. (Eds.). (1985). *Thinking and learning skills: Vol. 1: Relating instruction to research.* Hillsdale, NJ: Lawrence Erlbaum Associates.

Shavelson, R.J., & Stern, P. (1981). Research on teachers' pedagogical thoughts, judgments, decisions, and behavior. *Review of Educational Research, 51*(4), 455–498.

Silverman, L.J., & Taeuber, R.C. (Eds.). (1985). *Synthesis of invited papers: Elementary-Secondary education data redesign project* (NCES 85-114). Washington, DC: National Center for Education Statistics, Office of Educational Research and Improvement, U.S. Department of Education.

Slavin, R.E. (1983a). *Cooperative learning.* New York: Longman, Inc.

Slavin, R.E. (1983b). *Team-assisted individualization: A cooperative learning solution for adaptive instruction in mathematics.* Baltimore: The Johns Hopkins University, Center for the Social Organization of Schools.

Smith, E.L., & Sendelbach, N.B. (1979, April). *Teacher intentions for science instruction and their antecedents in program materials.* Paper presented at the annual meeting of the American Educational Research Association, San Francisco.

Snow, R.E., & Farr, M.J. (Eds.). (1983). *Aptitude, learning, and instruction: Cognitive and affective process analysis.* Stanford, CA: Office of Naval Research.

Thomas, A., Chess, S., & Birch, H.G. (1968). *Temperament and behavior disorders in children.* New York: New York University Press.

Thomas, J. (1980). Agency and achievement: Self-management and self-regard. *Review of Educational Research, 50*(2), 213–240.

Tyler, R.W. (1967). Changing concepts of educational evaluation. In R.W. Tyler, R.M. Gagne, & M. Scriven (Eds.), *Perspective of curriculum evaluation.* Chicago: Rand McNally.

Underwood, B.J. (1949). *Experimental psychology: An introduction.* New York: Appleton-Century-Crofts.

U.S. Bureau of the Census. (1983). Projections of the population of the United States:

1982 to 2050. *Current Population Reports* (Series P25 No. 922). Washington, DC: Author.

U.S. Bureau of the Census. (1985). *Statistical abstract of the United States, 1986* (106th ed.). Washington, DC: U.S. Government Printing Office.

U.S. Department of Education. (1985a). *Indicators of educational status and change.* Washington, DC: Author.

U.S. Department of Education. (1985b). Seventh annual report to Congress on implementation of Public Law 94-142: The Education for All Handicapped Children Act. Washington, DC: Author.

U.S. Department of Education. (1986a). *Effective compensatory education sourcebook: Vol. 1: A review of effective educational practices.* Washington, DC: Author.

U.S. Department of Education. (1986b). *What works: Research about teaching and learning.* Washington, DC: Author.

Walberg, H.J. (1984a). Families as partners in educational productivity. *Phi Delta Kappan, 65*(6), 397–400.

Walberg, H.J. (1984b). Improving the productivity of America's schools. *Educational Leadership, 41*(8), 19–30.

Wang, M.C. (1980). Adaptive instruction: Building on diversity. *Theory into Practice, 19*(2), 122–127.

Wang, M.C. (1983). Development and consequences of students' sense of personal control. In J. Levine & M.C. Wang (Eds.), *Teacher and student perceptions: Implications for learning.* (pp. 213–247). Hillsdale, NJ: Lawrence Erlbaum Associates.

Wang, M.C. (1986). *Designing and evaluating school learning environments for effective mainstreaming of special education students: Synthesis, validation, and dissemination of research methods.* [Technical Proposal]. Philadelphia: Temple University Center for Research in Human Development and Education.

Wang, M.C. (1987, October). *The wedding of instruction and assessment in the classroom.* Paper presented at the Invitational Conference of the Educational Testing Service, New York.

Wang, M.C. (1988, April). Findings on the expert opinions and outcome variables of programs designed to integrate students with special learning needs into regular educational settings. In H.J. Walberg (Chair), *Synthesis of research findings and consensus of expert opinions on relevant variables of improvements in instruction and learning.* Symposium conducted at the annual meeting of the American Educational Research Association, New Orleans.

Wang, M.C., Gennari, P., & Waxman, H.C. (1985). The Adaptive Learning Environments Model: Design, implementation, and effects. In M.C. Wang & H.J. Walberg (Eds.), *Adapting instruction to individual differences* (pp. 191–235). Berkeley, CA: McCutchan.

Wang, M.C., & Lindvall, C.M. (1984). Individual differences and school learning environments. In E. W. Gordon (Ed.), *Review of research in education* (pp. 161–225). Washington, DC: American Educational Research Association.

Wang, M.C., & Peverly, S.T. (1987). The role of the learner: An individual difference variable in school learning and functioning. In M.C. Wang, M.C. Reynolds, & H.J. Walberg (Eds.), *Handbook of special education: Research and practice: Vol. 1: Learner characteristics and adaptive education* (pp. 59–92). Oxford, England, Pergamon Press.

Wang, M.C., Peverly, S.T., & Catalano, R. (1987). Integrating special needs students in regular classes: Programming, implementation, and policy issues. In J. Gottlieb (Ed.), *Advances in special education* (Vol. 6, pp. 119–149). Greenwich, CT: JAI Press.

Wang, M.C., & Resnick, L.B. (1978). *The Primary Education Program (PEP).* Johnstown, PA: Mafex.

Wang, M.C., Resnick, L.B., & Boozer, R. (1971). The sequence of development of some early mathematics behavior. *Child Development, 41*(6), 1767–1778.

Wang, M.C., Reynolds, M.C., & Walberg, H.J. (1986). Rethinking special education. *Educational Leadership, 44*(1), 26–31.

Wang, M.C., Reynolds, M.C., & Walberg, H.J. (1987, October). *Repairing the second system for students with special needs.* Paper presented at the Wingspread Conference, Racine, WI.

Wang, M.C., Reynolds, M.C., & Walberg, H.J. (1987–1988). *Handbook of special education: Research and practice* (Vols. 1–3). Oxford, England: Pergamon Press.

Wang, M.C., & Walberg, H.J. (1985). *Adapting instruction to individual differences.* Berkeley, CA: McCutchan.

Wang, M.C., & Walberg, H.J. (1986). Classroom climate as mediator of educational inputs and outputs. In B. J. Fraser (Ed.), *The study of learning environments 1985* (pp. 47–58). Salem, OR: Assessment Research.

Wang, M.C., & Walberg, H.J. (in press). Exemplary implementation of eight innovative instructional models. *International Journal of Educational Research.*

Waxman, H.C., Wang, M.C., Anderson, K.A., & Walberg, H.J. (1985). *Adaptive education and student outcomes: A quantitative synthesis.* Pittsburgh: University of Pittsburgh, Learning Research and Development Center.

Weiner, B.A. (1980) May I borrow your class notes? An attributional analysis of help giving in an achievement-related context. *Journal of Educational Psychology, 72,* 676–681.

Will, M.C. (1986). Educating children with learning problems: A shared responsibility. *Exceptional Children, 52*(5), 411–416.

Wittrock, M.C. (1986). *Handbook of research on teaching* (3rd ed.). A Project of the American Educational Research Association. New York: Macmillan.

Wood, F.H., & Lakin, K.C. (1982). Defining emotionally disturbed/behaviorally disordered populations for research purposes. In F.H. Wood & K.C. Lakin (Eds.), *Disturbing, disordered or disturbed? Perspectives on the definition of problem behavior in educational settings.* Reston, VA: Council for Exceptional Children.

Yancey, W., Goldstein, I., & Rigsby, L. (1986). *The ecology of educational outcomes: A preliminary report.* [Research on Philadelphia and the Greater Delaware Valley Region]. Philadelphia: Temple University, Institute for Public Policy Studies.

Ysseldyke, J.E. (1987). Classification of handicapped students. In M.C. Wang, M.C. Reynolds, & H.J. Walberg (Eds.), *Handbook of special education: Research and practice: Vol. 1: Learner characteristics and adaptive education* (pp. 253–271). Oxford, England: Pergamon Press.

Ysseldyke, J.E., & Thurlow, M.L. (1983). *Identification/classification research: An integrative summary of findings* (Research Report No. 142). Minneapolis, MN: University of Minnesota, Department of Educational Psychology.

Zahorik, J.A. (1970). The effect of planning on teaching. *Elementary School Journal, 71* (3), 143–151.

Zimmerman, B.J. (Ed.). (1986). *Contemporary Educational Psychology, 11*(4).

chapter 7

Multiple Paths
to Educational Effectiveness

Jenifer Goldman and Howard Gardner

Jamie, a shy but cheerful child, is playing alone in the reading corner of his kindergarten classroom, where he is engrossed in one of his many favorite books. As he leafs through its pages, Jamie softly chants songs in which he invents elaborate stories of his own about the different pictures he encounters in the book. The rich language that Jamie spontaneously produces to himself and to others during free play in the classroom is not to be found at storytelling time, however; instead, he quietly watches as other children offer their ideas. And, later, during the structured reading and writing time consisting of repetition drills and letter copying, the child who earlier in the day was so intently examining a book is easily distracted and becomes quickly frustrated.

As the year progresses, Jamie's reading and speech appear to his teacher to lag increasingly behind the other children in his class. Consequently, she decides to refer Jamie to the school psychologist for psychoeducational assessment. He is given the Wechsler Intelligence Scale for Children-Revised (WISC-R), a standardized test typically used by school personnel for the identification and placement of children with learning problems. The examiner is a stranger to Jamie, the testing takes place in a room in which Jamie has never been before, and it focuses primarily on his verbal and logical skills. During the 1–2 hour test, Jamie is asked such questions as: "Why do we wear shoes?" and: "In what way are a pencil and crayon alike?". He is asked to define words like "ball," "summer," and "book." Additionally, he is asked to complete a series of mazes, to solve arithmetic problems, and to copy different geometric and block designs.

Afterward, the examiner analyzes Jamie's answers and determines a

The work described in this chapter was funded by generous grants from the W.T. Grant Foundation, the James S. McDonnell Foundation, Spencer Foundation, The Rockefeller Foundation, and The Bernard Van Leer Foundation. We thank the editors for their comments on an earlier draft.

number that quantifies his "intelligence." It is safe to say that this resulting intelligence quotient, based on verbal and logical skills, does not adequately represent Jamie's full range of abilities. The rich vocabulary and complexity of sentence structure that Jamie demonstrates through his chosen form of expression, singing, seldom surface during the more formal activities in the familiar classroom. It is not surprising, then, that Jamie's performance on this standardized test, administered by a stranger and without any reference to music or musical ability, is far below the norm.

In the ensuing conference, the examiner explains to Jamie's parents that their son produced a subnormal score on the test, and that it would be wise to conduct further tests to determine his eligibility for special education services. Several standardized tests later, it is concluded that Jamie is "learning disabled." A course of education is prescribed for the child who is now classified as "mildly handicapped"; Jamie will go to special and separate rooms to learn with other "special needs children." Tragically, the only thing special about the education Jamie will probably receive is that it will revolve around especially small expectations that perpetuate minimal academic achievement (Granger & Granger, 1986). If Jamie is lucky, he will pass through the educational system with moderate success. But if Jamie is like many of the 4.37 million children enrolled in special education classes in the United States, he may find himself locked into a cycle of learning failure that will affect the course of his educational career, his resulting self-concept, and ultimately, his future as a productive member of society (Armstrong, 1987; Coles, 1988; Gartner & Lipsky, 1987).

THE INADEQUACY OF CURRENT CLASSIFICATION SYSTEMS

The circumstances that lead children like Jamie to be classified as "learning disabled" are not readily justified. Rather than accurately describing his profile of skills and deficits, they may well reflect serious conceptual and practical problems with the current system of classifying children. The problems begin with the classification "learning disabled," an ill-defined and poorly conceptualized term that is used to characterize a vast number of children who are unsuccessful in school. One interpretation of "learning disabled" is that children's learning difficulties find their source somewhere as yet undetermined in the brain. The term also connotes psychological or social causes, such as emotional disturbance or ill-treatment at home, that might explain why a child is experiencing academic problems. Although there do exist children with neurological problems, as well as children who experience learning difficulties for psychological reasons, the fact that *millions* of school children are classified as having "minimal neurological dysfunction" calls the classification into question (Armstrong, 1987; Coles, 1988; Ysseldyke & Algozzine, 1983; Ysseldyke, Algozzine, Richey, & Graden, 1982; Ysseldyke, Thurlow, et al., 1983).

The inadequacies of current classification practices, however, go beyond the conceptual problem of defining "learning disabled." Experts indicate that the instruments used to classify children are often inappropriate and, even worse, are of questionable reliability and validity (Salvia & Ysseldyke, 1987; Sattler, 1988; Ysseldyke, Algozzine, Regan, & Potter, 1980). Moreover, studies have shown that those who administer the tests and make placement decisions are often not knowledgeable enough to interpret the results appropriately (Davis & Shepard, 1983; Gartner & Lipsky, 1987; Ysseldyke & Algozzine, 1983; Ysseldyke, Algozzine, & Epps, 1983; Ysseldyke, Thurlow, et al., 1983).

In the present authors' view, the inadequacy and misapplication of assessment may reflect another order of difficulty as well. We question the theoretical basis on which the learning disabled literature and its classification system are founded. All too often the assumption is made that there is a certain form of ability, or intelligence, on which all children can be readily compared, and that children can be reliably rank ordered in terms of intellectual power. In the following pages we explore an alternative view of intelligence and assessment, one that challenges the idea that a child's intellectual capacities can be captured in a single intelligence quotient, and one that seeks to view productively the difference in children's abilities and proclivities.

THE THEORY OF MULTIPLE INTELLIGENCES

Traditionally, intelligence has been conceptualized as a single overall construct that encompasses all cognitive processes of significance, one that changes very little with age and experience, and that can be adequately summarized as a single metric unit. The notion of the mind as a quantifiable faculty has spawned the vast collection of intelligence tests and short-answer instruments that are designed to be administered and scored within a brief time. These instruments yield cognitive behavioral profiles; however, the information they elicit is largely dependent on the restrictions of the particular tests. For example, standardized tests typically involve responding to rapid-fire questioning asked in a setting remote from familiar and comfortable surroundings. Such testing conditions tend to highlight areas of weakness rather than locate areas of strength.

Perhaps most strikingly, intelligence tests also primarily highlight only two kinds of tasks: those requiring linguistic skill and those requiring skill in logical problem solving. An individual who has relatively developed linguistic and logical capacities should succeed on these tasks; an individual with significant limitations in one or both of these areas will perform poorly. This emphasis on logical and verbal abilities has traditionally characterized the Western view of cognition and intelligence, and is a bias commonly associated with both psychological and educational settings.

Many educators and scientists, along with much of the lay public, still subscribe to this view of intelligence. Even so, the articles of faith upon which it was founded have undergone searching critiques in recent years. Part of the critique has simply involved a recognition that particular mental processes, like learning and memory, are far more complicated and multifaceted than had generally been held. Another critique has proposed that the mind is itself composed of different modules or "intelligences," each of which operates according to its own principles. As a frequent corollary, it is held that power in one intellectual domain holds little if any predictive value for power in other intellectual domains—thus the notion of a unidimensional intelligence makes dubious scientific sense. Continuing in this vein, Howard Gardner, the second author of this chapter, has presented a theory of multiple intelligences known as MI-theory (1983) that contests the existence of a single intelligence or of general intellectual operations. Instead of accepting the notion of intelligence as a single entity, no matter how simple or complicated, Gardner posits the existence of several separate families of abilities. According to the theory, intelligence is not adequately captured by the ability to answer items on standardized tests. Instead, the scientific investigation and the educational evaluation must move beyond the stereotypical pupil abilities that happen to be valued in the West to encompass a broader range of abilities.

A NEW DEFINITION OF INTELLIGENCE

Gardner redefines intelligence as the ability to solve a problem or to fashion a product in a way that is considered useful in one or more cultural settings. Armed with this definition, Gardner sets up a number of criteria for what counts as a human intelligence. The evidence on which he draws comes from numerous disparate sources: knowledge about the breakdown of cognitive capacities under different forms of brain damage, for example, and the existence of isolated capacities in "special" populations, such as prodigies, idiot-savants, and autistic children. He also draws on the scattered evidence obtained from studies of cognition in different cultures, of cognition in diverse species, from psychometric correlations, and from studies of training and generalization of skills (Gardner, 1987d).

Weaving together these many lines of evidence, Gardner arrived at seven candidate intelligences: linguistic, musical, logical-mathematical, spatial, bodily-kinesthetic, interpersonal, and intrapersonal. It is important to stress that these seven intelligences should not be interpreted as the only acceptable candidates. Most, if not all, of the intelligences harbor several separate skills, and careful analysis can be readily conducted in order to identify a yet richer spectrum of intellectual facilities. The nomination of these seven different intelligences is most crucially intended to support the notion of a plurality of intelligence, rather than to insist on the absolute priority of the particular intelligences cited thus far (Gardner, 1987b).

Let us briefly summarize each of the seven intelligences. The first entry, linguistic intelligence, is a mainstay of traditional psychological analyses. The linguistic intelligence is exemplified, for example, in the poet, orator, or lawyer. One of the most heavily studied intelligences, the linguistic faculty can be broken into subcomponents, including syntactic, semantic, or pragmatic aspects, and certain kinds of more specific skills, such as written expression, oral expression, and verbal memory.

A second intelligence, logical-mathematical, is the intelligence which Jean Piaget probed in great detail (Piaget, 1983). As with language, an inventory of subskills can be delineated for logical-mathematical intelligence. The archetype of the problem-solving faculty, this intelligence is exemplified, for example, in the scientist or mathematician.

These two companion intelligences, language and logical-mathematical reasoning, are awarded the highest value in the school and form the basis for standardized assessment. Hence, it is predominantly lack of skill in one of these intelligences that contributes to a child's difficulties in school and increases the probability that the child will be classified as "learning disabled." The utility of these intelligences outside of school, however, is much less certain.

The next entry, spatial intelligence, entails the capacity to represent and manipulate spatial configurations. Spatial problem solving is required, for example, in navigation. Other kinds of spatial problem solving are brought to bear in playing chess, or in visualizing an object seen from a different angle. Visual artists also employ this intelligence in the use of space. Thus, a wide range of vocational and avocational roles, including geographers, surveyors, architects, sculptors, painters, and engineers all possess considerable spatial intelligence. Though little valued in the current educational system, spatial intelligence can be an important constituent of success in many cultural pursuits.

Fourth on the list is musical intelligence, which involves the ability to think in musical terms, to be able to hear themes, to understand how they are transformed, to be able to follow those themes in the course of a musical work and, in the best cases, to be able to produce music. Musical intelligence is exemplified by the composer, performer, or other individual with a keen musical ear and music analytic abilities. A fifth intelligence, termed bodily-kinesthetic, refers to the ability to use all or part of one's body to perform tasks, fashion products, or solve problems. Actors, mimes, dancers, athletes, surgeons, and mechanics are distinguished by considerable bodily-kinesthetic intelligence. Except in certain special situations, the musical and bodily-kinesthetic intelligences are not valued educationally. Subsequently, many children who are musically or bodily inclined are more likely to experience learning problems because they are not exposed to the kinds of knowledge which they are fully capable of learning.

Finally, we speak of two other intelligences. Interpersonal intelligence involves the ability to understand other individuals, to develop viable models of how they function and how they are motivated, and to act productively on the basis of that knowledge. In more developed forms, this intelligence permits a skilled adult to read the intentions and desires of others, even when these have been hidden. This skill appears in a highly sophisticated form in religious or political leaders, teachers, therapists, and parents. Most of us experience inter-personal intelligence as a tacit knowledge that carries us successfully through life and its social interactions. For those children who are not skilled in this intel-ligence and who have difficulty engaging in successful peer relationships, school may be an unhappy burden which their schoolwork might reflect (Gardner, 1987c).

The companion social intelligence, intrapersonal, involves knowledge of the internal aspects of a person: access to one's own range of emotions, the capacity to effect discriminations among these emotions and eventually to label them, and the ability to draw upon them as a means of understanding and guiding one's own behavior. It is difficult to pinpoint an individual or a vocational role that exemplifies this form of intelligence, but it may be useful to think of a psychologically-oriented novelist, or an individual whose degree of self-insight has been notably enhanced by psychotherapy. The autistic child is the pro-totypical example of an individual with impaired intrapersonal intelligence; in-deed, the child may not even be able to refer to him- or herself. At the same time, such children often exhibit remarkable abilities in the musical, computational, and/or spatial realms.

All normal members of our species have the potential to develop each of these intelligences to some degree. Theoretically, it is possible that an individual could excel in all intelligences or could perform at the same level in all intel-ligences; however, such outcomes are empirically rare. In most cases, indi-viduals exhibit a fairly jagged profile of intelligences, revealing relative strengths in some areas and comparative weakness in others. The differences in individual levels of achievement hinge upon the notion that each intelligence proceeds along its own developmental trajectory; hence, the intelligences are manifested in different ways at different developmental levels. Each of the multiple parts of the mind, then, is organized in terms of its individual content rather than reflect-ing across-the-board laws of development.

Operating within the separate developmental trajectories of each intel-ligence are one or more "core" operations that are relatively autonomous from the "core" operations in other intelligences. Syntactic and phonological analy-ses are core operations in the linguistic sphere. Similarly, sensitivity to numbers and causality are "core operations" in the logical-mathematical sphere, and appreciation of pitch and rhythm occupy "core roles" in music. Given the independence of core operations, strength in a particular intelligence does not necessarily predict strength or weakness in another intelligence. By the same token, it is difficult to strengthen a given intelligence by exploiting the core operations of another intelligence.

Thus, individuals differ in the extent to which they are "at risk" or "at promise" in each intelligence. Given an equal number of exposures to a material or exercise, children who advance very rapidly through a set of developmental milestones are considered "at promise," while those who remain at or near the novice status are considered "at risk". In the absence of special aids, those "at risk" in an intelligence will be most likely to fail tasks involving that intelligence. Conversely, those "at promise" will be most likely to succeed. Intensive intervention at an early age may bring a larger number of children to an "at promise" level in an intelligence in which they may initially appear "at risk" (Walters & Gardner, 1985).

MI-BASED ASSESSMENT

Our perspective of multiple intelligences, while viewed initially as a contribution to psychological theory, has come increasingly to be considered with reference to educational formats. In particular, we have focused on ways in which to assess the range of intelligences in school children, and particularly among children on the threshold of formal school. Following is a description of the authors' general philosophy of assessment. This is followed by a detailed description of a particular program, Project Spectrum, on which we have been working for a number of years. Abandoning the IQ test, with its nearly exclusive emphasis on linguistic and logical-mathematical skills, we have moved to implement assessment that captures the expanse of human potential in all intelligences and that identifies each child's unique intellectual propensities. Rejecting the stylized circumstances that surround most standardized measures, the authors utilized a more naturalistic and unobtrusive means of assessment which takes place *within* the classroom. Rather than reducing a child's cognitive capacities to a number, or a set of reading or math indices, we hold that the most valuable depiction of a child's intelligences is conveyed in the rich format of a narrative profile (Malkus, Feldman, & Gardner, 1987).

We envision such a profile as a portrait of distinctive intellectual patterns that focuses on areas of strength and delineates areas where a child is less proficient. Instead of simply "photographing" a child at the moment of testing, our portrait strives to present a holistic and more balanced view, which covers the gamut of each child's intellectual potential. In addition, the profile serves as a guide to the kinds of activities that serve to nurture and support each child's particular abilities. Thus, instead of simply serving to rank and pigeonhole students, this type of assessment could help determine an optimal educational regime.

An important characteristic of this approach is that it does not look at all abilities through the window of logic or language. Rather, it assesses a capacity directly, in terms of its own constituent skills. Thus musical abilities are assessed by having children sing or play tone bells; social abilities are assessed by observing the particular social skills of children during situations that arise naturally in the class. In other words, the assessing of intelligences must include the individual's ability to solve problems or create products using the materials that typify the intellectual realm in question.

An equally important dimension of this assessment approach is the determination of which intelligence is favored when an individual has a choice. One technique for pinpointing this activity is to expose the individual to a sufficiently complex situation that can stimulate several intelligences. Alternatively, one may provide a set of materials drawn from different intelligences and determine toward which one an individual gravitates and how deeply he or she explores it.

As an example, consider what happens when a child sees a complex film in which several intelligences figure prominently: music, people interacting, a maze to be solved, or a particular bodily skill that is exhibited. Subsequent debriefing with the child should reveal the features to which the child paid attention; these should be related to the profile of intelligences in that child. Or, consider a situation in which children are presented with several different kinds of equipment and games. Simple measures of the regions in which children spend time, and the kinds of activities they engage in, should yield insights into the individual child's profile of intelligence.

Another essential criterion of our assessment is that the process of evaluation should be integrally linked to ongoing classroom activities, as children demonstrate their strengths and weaknesses over the course of every school day. We believe that furnishing the classroom with engaging materials and activities that span the many realms of intelligence will maximize the chance of eliciting children's abilities. The materials should be open-ended in design so that children have the opportunity to express themselves in their preferred form of expression. Moreover, the activities and materials should possess challenges that are meaningful for the child and to which the child will wish to return again and again. In other words, we seek to make assessment as enjoyable for the child as it is informative for the adult.

It should be clear, at this point, that the assessment we support is as much a part of curriculum as a self-standing means of evaluation. By linking assessment closely to the regular events of the school year, it may be possible to dissolve the traditionally observed boundary between learning and assessment. Children can be offered games and exercises that expand their horizons, hold their interest, and provide instruction over the course of time. With occasional scaffolding on the part of the teacher, the children may learn from these activities in expected as well as unanticipated ways. And while the child is learning, we (as researchers, evaluators, and teachers) are given an opportunity to look, in an unobtrusive way, at the ways in which the child approaches his or her work and, in the process, assess his or her potential. This integration of assessment into the curriculum serves both to expand and individualize the curriculum, thereby creating an environment that welcomes children who may have special needs.

PROJECT SPECTRUM: APPLICATIONS OF THE THEORY

With both eyes fixed on the above criteria, the authors have developed an assessment technique for use in a preschool environment. Project Spectrum, a joint research project at Harvard and Tufts Universities, features a number of ecologically valid monitoring procedures; these procedures allow us to identify young children's preferences for, and competence in, activities in the several cognitive domains delineated by MI-theory. To date, Project Spectrum has developed 15 specifically targeted exercises that provide rough measures of skill levels in approximately 2 dozen intellectual realms, ranging from music and narrative to social-analytic skills.

Every child in the class is given the opportunity to engage in all the Spectrum activities but is not forced to participate if he or she is reluctant or uncomfortable. In the Spectrum program, the participation of as many children as possible is encouraged by offering the activities within the context of the classroom and having them administered by a familiar adult. Each child's performance on the structured activities and interaction with our materials is recorded in detail during or immediately after the activity, using observation and score sheets that describe the skills involved in negotiating the tasks. In addition, incidental information about each child's activities in the daily classroom is regularly recorded throughout the school year. This assessment procedure secures a considerable amount of information on the intellectual propensities and styles of each child enrolled in a "Spectrum Classroom."

At the end of the school year, all recorded information is culled into a Spectrum Report, an essay of two or three pages that serves as a portrait of the child's distinctive intellectual patterns. The report focuses on areas of strength but also indicates areas where the child could benefit from extra support. A crucial part of the Spectrum Report is a list of suggested activities that can be carried out by the child at home, in school, or elsewhere in the community. The report, then, serves not only as a descriptive form of assessment, but also as a guide to the kinds of activities in which a child with this "spectrum of abilities" might profitably be engaged.

In order to indicate how the Spectrum program's assessment techniques differ from traditional standardized tests, it is helpful to describe one of the activities in some detail. In the area of language skills, Spectrum offers the children the opportunity to create a story of their own with the aid of a "storyboard"; the board is replete with interesting and ambiguous figures and props. The cast of characters includes such *personae* as a king, a queen, a turtle, and a dragon; the props range from a treasure box filled with colorful "jewels" to caves, arches, and other transformable abodes with which the children can arrange their own scenery.

These materials may inspire children to deliver cohesive narratives and can afford the teacher a detailed view of the kinds of linguistic skills on which children rely when asked to invent a story. For research purposes, each child's story is tape-recorded and then analyzed on dimensions such as thematic coherence, inclusion of temporal connectives, use of dialogue and narrative voices, sentence structure, and level of vocabulary. At the end of the year, the child's performance on this linguistic measure, on other related Spectrum activities, and on any incidental observations, are qualitatively discussed in the Spectrum Report. For those children who create a distinctive story, a segment from their story is included in the report. In our experience, parents and teachers appreciated and were sometimes surprised by the length and scope of their children's stories. Parents of a child with a linguistic flair also appreciated particular suggestions about games, activities, and community resources which might prove of special interest to their child.

For all activities, assessment takes place chiefly within the classroom, with the teacher observing and noting particular levels of skill which the children demonstrate on the different tasks. The assessments inform the teacher about children's particular skills in the multiple domains of knowledge; in addition, they may reveal children's interests in materials that they may not have been exposed to otherwise. For example, another Spectrum activity involves the disassembly and reassembly of a simple but real tool: a food grinder. This task elicits skills not readily tapped in the typical preschool classroom: fine motor control, analysis of the detailed structure of an object, and capacity to plan a lengthy sequence of activities in order to reach a novel goal. In addition, it affords the opportunity for children to reveal their mechanical skills. While some children are easily frustrated by the task, or do not become engaged at all in the activity, others demonstrate keen interest and/or skill in the dismantling and reassembly of this real-world object.

At best, the Spectrum assessment technique plays an integral part in the classroom, serving as both a measurement instrument and a source of learning and enjoyment for the children. Spectrum's philosophy is one of dynamic interaction between assessment and learning, with emphasis both on learning about children and on helping to teach them on the basis of that knowledge. We would like to think that it differs from the typical standardized forms of assessment, which are designed specifically not to teach and are often distinctly unenjoyable. The results, at least so far, have been promising. It is in part on the basis of our experience with Project Spectrum, and in reaction to the present tendency to classify inordinate numbers of children as "learning disabled," that we are motivated to speculate on the impact that MI-based assessment could make on special education.

IMPLICATIONS OF MI-BASED
ASSESSMENT FOR SPECIAL EDUCATION

The theory of multiple intelligences and its conceptualization of assessment has a number of significant implications for special education and its current classification system. First, MI-theory challenges the current definition of "learning disabled" as one based on impairment etiology in combination with the concept of a unitary intelligence. To talk about a child as "learning disabled" assumes there are problems across-the-board and ignores a child's potential skill in intelligences other than language and logic. In contrast, multiple intelligence theory questions whether strengths or weaknesses can be seen as occurring across-the-board.

In addition, the theory reduces the impact of mild to severe neurological dysfunction on a child's educational regimen by focusing on those areas where the child *is* functioning. Further, it suggests that strength in one area can sometimes compensate for or even be used to teach effectively in an area of apparent weakness. Thus, a child with difficulties in logical-mathematical reasoning may be able to master certain mathematical concepts and problems by exploiting his or her spatial or linguistic skills. Indeed, intelligences can be used either as the content of an instruction (one teaches the area of language) or as a means of communicating content (one uses language to teach mathematics). As an illustration of the way in which the intelligences can be mobilized, let us return to the case of Jamie described at the beginning of the chapter.

Had Jamie been evaluated using the kind of assessment which we propound, his prognosis may well have been different. An example of this may be seen in his natural proclivity for singing, which he demonstrates repeatedly during free play, but seldom in the presence of a group. This incidental information was overlooked by his teacher and disregarded by the tests that deemed Jamie "learning disabled." A more naturalistic and curriculum-oriented assessment that works within the context of the classroom would, for example, take into account the length of time Jamie remained engrossed in the book that particular day and the way he focused on its story through song. Regular observations would record areas in which he spent the most time and indicated the most interest, and would also include remarks on differences in his approach to the various activities in the classroom. A more structured assessment could be conducted to determine the scope of Jamie's musical ability, perhaps by having him play with tone bells or learn musically complex songs.

With this kind of information, Jamie's musical intelligence would not be overlooked. On the contrary, Jamie would be identified as possibly having musical potential; his teacher could provide him with materials and activities to nurture his musical ability and could perhaps suggest to his parents that he take music lessons. To put it directly: seen through the lens of impairment etiology, Jamie was a child intellectually "at risk"; viewed through the prism of multiple intelligences theory, Jamie is now "at promise" in one of the "spectrum" of intelligences.

From the kind of information amassed through naturalistic, MI-based assessment, a different picture of Jamie can emerge—one that portrays a serious and intent child, who is able to focus for lengths of time on things that he finds interesting, and who is especially oriented to singing. His intense interest in looking at the book would indicate that Jamie may be longing to read, but for some reason is unable to do so. With an understanding that this child is potentially interested in learning how to read, has the capacity to focus and become engaged in a task, and is perhaps skilled in a domain of intelligence other than verbal ability, some rays of hope emerge. This is probably not a child who is "learning disabled." Instead, this is perhaps a child who, like many others, has abilities and propensities that are neither elicited nor nurtured by standard curricula and tests.

Based on Jamie's musical orientation, an alternative route could be devised to meet educational goals and serve as a remedy for difficulties. By focusing on Jamie's exploration of vocabulary and language skills through singing, it may be possible to engage enough of his interest and utilize his naturally occurring talent to foster the development of reading skills. For example, Jamie's musical ability might be used to smooth the way into reading, perhaps by learning to read lyrics and stories to songs. Or his musical ability could be used in the service of mathematical learning, by building lessons around rhythmic or metrical analyses or intuitions.

Clearly, the traditional and typically exclusive focus on linguistic and logical skills by formal schooling and assessment seriously shortchanges those children, like Jamie, whose skills lie primarily in other intelligences. Assessment emphasis needs to be spread across the many domains of knowledge so that children are no longer evaluated strictly on the basis of standards that are culturally biased and reflect a narrow view of schooling.

Accommodating modes of instruction to the specific intelligences, however, is not in itself enough. Teachers need to be sensitive to the manner in which each individual intelligence develops and to the kinds of interventions that are likely to be productive in light of that particular development. In other words, the role of instruction must relate to changes across the development of the intelligences. Thus, a knowledge of the normal developmental trajectory of language is extremely important: this knowledge will suggest when it is appropriate (or inappropriate) to begin formal instruction in reading, writing, public speaking, or foreign languages. The typical curriculum in formal schooling, which approaches intelligence as a unitary entity with a universal developmental pattern, shortchanges the education of the intelligences developing within their uniquely prescribed trajectories.

A SPECIAL EDUCATION FOR ALL

Multiple intelligences theory, with its focus on the development and nurturing of each individual's different proclivities, dictates the need for a more diverse and individual-centered curriculum. From the earliest years, students should have available to them the means to explore and be identified as skilled in areas other than those traditionally located in the pedagogical canon. While there would still be some subjects studied by all youngsters, subject matter and teaching approaches would be keyed to the inclinations of particular students. To be sure, students ought to take some core subjects, even as they ought to be offered electives. But whether the emphasis falls on a common curriculum, or on specialized options, there is every reason to tailor the mode of instruction as much as possible to the inclinations, working styles, and profiles of intelligence of each individual student.

The need to identify individual abilities as fully as possible, early in a child's academic career, calls for a new system of assessment and evaluation. In lieu of standardized tests, the type of innovative assessment developed by Project Spectrum would be used to tap the capabilities of younger children. For older youngsters, assessment and evaluation would involve student, teacher, and "outside expert" review of projects and other activities in which students had been involved for sustained periods of time. Desirable school outcomes would be expanded to encompass a range of vocational and avocational roles, with achievement in standard academic areas as one of a number of goals. The school should be a place where students can follow their own intellectual interests, while mastering the materials that will enable them to become productive members of society (Gardner, 1987a).

Providing students with a wider range of materials with which to work and explore their individual skills does not, however, necessitate the development of ability in *every one* of those areas. Quite to the contrary, it has become increasingly clear that individuals cannot hope to be expert in all areas of human knowledge. Even within specific disciplines, such as physics, economics, or the law, no single person can hope to master all the subspecialties of the field.

Just as we have come to acknowledge the impossibility of a universal education, we are now becoming familiar with the notion that individuals do not necessarily master subject matter in the same way. It is not only the individuals with frank learning impairments, such as mild or severe neurological dysfunction, who require special forms of instruction and individually designed strategies; each of us has idiosyncratic learning styles and strengths and can benefit from instructional approaches that speak to our particular configuration of intellectual skills and interests.

The imperative for some form of specialized education for *all* children, not just those with evident learning difficulties, and the desirability of teaching that takes into account an individual's cognitive profile, calls for a radically different approach to education. It no longer makes sense for everyone to learn the same materials in the same way; it is this outmoded approach that explains why so many children were once termed "ineducable" and are now labeled the essentially equivalent "learning *dis*-abled."

It is important to help teachers and those children with manifest special needs, as well as those children whose particular needs are less discernible, to discover the particular curricula and the particular educational approaches that are best suited to each individual. It is equally imperative that individual skills be nurtured outside the school—at home and in the community—as well as within the school program. To help carry out the mission of servicing students' intelligences both in school and extracurricularly, we call for the creation of two new roles: the *student-curriculum broker* and the *school community-broker*.

While not necessarily an expert in particular curricula, the student-curriculum broker would be familiar with the range of curricula appropriate at a particular age and with the ensemble of teaching approaches that might prove effective for a given curricula with selected children. Aided by technological resources, ranging from computerized files of activities to instructional programs especially crafted for certain kinds of learners, the broker attempts to devise a curriculum (or, more precisely, a set of curricula options) that can be considered by the child, his parents, and/or his teachers. The broker would work together with teachers and with an assessment specialist to ascertain whether the plans that have been devised are effective and, if not, would consult on the optimal means for refashioning the plan.

Although the student-curriculum broker would be needed most upon the commencement of formal schooling, the role can be briefly illustrated in terms of the framework that we are using with younger children in Project Spectrum. The broker begins with knowledge of an individual child's intellectual proclivities and styles, as measured by the techniques utilized in Project Spectrum. The broker next considers the range of knowledge areas or domains that are suitable for students of this particular age. The broker would take into account areas previously studied by the child, his or her own preferences, and the expertise of teachers and others in the community. Having collated all of this information, the broker then lays out several suggested lines of study and activities, and reviews them with all of the interested parties designated above.

It should be stressed that the student-curriculum broker's role extends well beyond the recommendation of particular courses or programs. Even when students are taking exactly the same courses as their peers, there is no need for these courses to be presented in the same way. Individual children, and especially those with special problems or unusual abilities, often are particularly able to tackle a subject matter in one way (say, through language), while exhibiting marked difficulties when the curriculum is presented in another way (say, through logical or spatial meanings). The broker should recommend teachers, curricula guides, and ancillary hardware and software materials that would facilitate the student's mastery of a "uniform" curriculum.

The school-community broker carries out an analogous set of matching operations, but does so within the wider community. Whereas the student-curriculum broker works chiefly within the confines of the school, the school-community broker is concerned with those opportunities that are unavailable in the school, but that may be found at home or in the wider community. The school-community broker has available considerable information about mentorships, apprenticeships, organizations, clubs, and other institutions that can provide opportunities for students who exhibit particular cognitive interests, strengths, and styles. It is the broker's job to help students make the appropriate connections with such institutions and to make sure that the connections are in fact working effectively. While the broker owes allegiance to all students in the school, his or her chief services would be provided to those students who exhibit unusual cognitive profiles, or who indicate special needs and/or special skills which the school could not readily handle.

The success of the specialists and brokers would depend in part upon the extent to which their roles can be systematized and rationalized. If every student turns out to be utterly different from the other, the brokers' tasks would be overwhelming. It is therefore important to ascertain whether there may be families of suggestions or coordinated lines of growth that are applicable to groups of individuals within a community. By encouraging the intelligences within the school environment *and* in the extracurricular community, the wide range of different needs presented by any student population would be better addressed.

THE ROLE OF THE TEACHER IN AN INDIVIDUALIZED SCHOOL

The teacher's primary role has been to introduce students to the intellectual domains that are valued by society: basic skills such as reading and writing in the elementary grades, traditional subject matters like history and biology at the secondary level, and academic subspecialties at the college level. In our view, some of the newly defined educational functions would be taken over by other kinds of specialists, such as the assessors of intelligences and the curriculum and community-brokers introduced above. This division of labor would free the teacher to do what he or she ought to be doing: presenting the accumulated knowledge and skills of the past in appropriate ways to students so that they are given the best possible opportunities for learning (Gardner, 1987a).

Should our general approach to schooling be adopted, we anticipate the following kinds of changes in the teacher role. First of all, demonstrated expertise in the domain would become the primary criterion for entrance and advancement in the field of teaching (Shulman, 1986). Second, teachers would develop expertise in various approaches to the subject matter. Either they would specialize in an approach deemed appropriate to certain kinds of students, such as students with special needs (e.g., dyslexic or dyscalculic children), or they would develop an arsenal of techniques, which could then be deployed appropriately for students who exhibit distinctive strengths and weaknesses. Thus, knowledge of "pedagogical styles" would be wedded to expertise in "domain knowledge."

Our vision also includes a new form of "master teacher" who would work regularly with the other kinds of specialists. The master teacher would have five major assignments:

1. To serve as a role model for new teachers, exhibiting at least some of the alternative ways in which subject matters can be presented to students with different "intelligence" profiles
2. To monitor novice teachers with particular attention to their approaches to subject matter and their teaching techniques
3. To keep abreast of new findings in the area of teaching and to disseminate them to other members of the school community, ranging from principals to apprentices
4. To collaborate with the curriculum, community, and assessment specialists in designing programs of study for individual students and in making sure that the appropriate teachers and sites are available for each student
5. To intervene when the program is not successful and to suggest alternative regimens for the student

Clearly, the roles of teacher and master teacher would be extremely important in this new scheme. Teachers would have the primary responsibility for disseminating knowledge and would be judged by their effectiveness in this central task. Master teachers would be the school generalists, having as their assignment the orchestration of the activities of curricular, community, assessment, and domain specialists, and ensuring that the methods being used are current and effective. Anyone capable of carrying out these functions would have to be a highly trained and skilled professional.

If a school along these lines is to be effective, it is important that all members of the teaching staff, as well as the various specialized brokers, have the mechanisms whereby they can communicate on a regular basis and can register their opinions and impressions, both with each other and with master teachers. This means that periods for conversation and reflection must be built into the regular school schedule; it also indicates the need for efficient communication mechanisms, such as computer networks, whereby teachers can readily share their findings and impressions with their colleagues. Optimally, such opportunities for exchange would lead teachers to develop common ways to think about learning problems and produce suggestions for how best to tap the skills of those children who are not academically successful. Over time, teachers would internalize the ways in which their colleagues think about students and be able to anticipate the kinds of steps their colleagues are likely to take when confronted with particular challenges or opportunities. The time and energy required for such exchange, as well as a convenient means for preserving and accessing the information accumulated through such discourse, are essential.

If teachers are to be trained to review students' options using evaluative information from assessment in context, schools that operate on such a system need to be established and monitored carefully to make sure that they are fulfilling their tasks. They should then be made available as sites for those who wish to implement a similar approach. On an apprenticeship basis, teachers could enter the school to observe and participate. We are currently involved in one such pioneering effort, a "Key School" in Indianapolis, where a serious attempt is being made to nourish all of the intelligences and to coordinate the diverse forms of information being gathered about all the students (Olson, 1988).

If widely adopted, such an approach to teaching would radically change the appearance of special education programs. Rather than special education connoting the need for an intervention to help a victim, it would instead be embraced in a positive sense. Indeed, fashioning the curriculum so that it is centered on each individual student, and altering current teacher-training standards so that individual gifts and styles are featured, would make special education the norm rather than the exception. According to such a curriculum, it would be *expected* that "special" services would be needed for every child. Indeed, every child has his or her own particular style of learning. Such individuality is too often overlooked and can suffer under the burden of a uniform curriculum. It is our philosophy that every child is entitled to and can benefit from a more personalized form of schooling.

The benefits gained by children currently depicted as having "special needs" are manifold. No longer would they need to be classified as very different from their peers and segregated into separate classes, for everyone in the school would be accommodated by the curriculum. The vicious circle of labeling, and fulfillment of that label, could perhaps be broken; there might no longer be a need for classifications such as "learning disabled." Rather than being separated from their peers, children could flourish in a community of special education. Further, children with special needs would be exposed to the kind of curriculum which they are largely being denied under the current special education system, and to a richer and more stimulating curriculum that encompasses multiple areas of knowledge.

CONCLUDING NOTE

A narrow view of intelligence has cast a long shadow over schools during the past century. As long as it was assumed that individuals could be arrayed in terms of a single intellectual metric, it followed that the majority of students would consider themselves to be of modest intellectual endowment, and that those with the poorest performance on "approved measures" would be stigmatized.

Building upon recent work in cognitive, developmental, and neuro–sciences, we have put forth a view of the mind as a far more capacious instrument, exhibiting a number of relatively distinct talents. In this view, most children are intelligent in at least some respects, and nearly all can develop a set of potentials that will be socially useful and personally satisfying. Applied to an educational setting, this perspective proves to be an optimistic one: it should be possible to devise methods that reveal intellectual strengths at an early age as well as techniques that can exploit those strengths in the service of wider and deeper learning.

We have no illusions that it will be easy to set up schools that are built around the idea of individual strengths, curricula, and growth patterns. Schools forged in this image should be possible, however. The failure of our society thus far to guide schools in this direction reflects less a lack of resources than a failure of will. Still, unless we are willing to push for educational programs that are committed to developing each individual potential to the fullest extent, we are designed to have a society in which many problems will lie unsolved, and many lives will be incompletely realized.

REFERENCES

Armstrong, T. (1987). *In their own way*. Los Angeles: Jeremy P. Tarcher, Inc.

Coles, G. (1988). *The learning mystique*. New York: Pantheon Books.

Davis, W.A., & Shepard, L.A. (1983). Specialists' use of test and clinical judgment in the diagnosis of learning disabilities. *Learning Disabled Quarterly, 19,* 128–138.

Gardner, H. (1983). *Frames of mind: The theory of multiple intelligences*. New York: Basic Books.

Gardner, H. (1987a). *Balancing specialized and comprehensive knowledge: The growing educational challenge*. Paper presented at the Breckenridge Forum, San Antonio, Texas.

Gardner, H. (1987b). The assessment of intelligences: A neuropsychological perspective. In M. Meier, A. Benton, & L. Diller (Eds.), *Neuropsychological rehabilitation* (pp. 59–70). London: Churchill Publishers.

Gardner, H. (1987c). The theory of multiple intelligences: Educational implications. In *Language and the world of work in the 21st century*. Boston, MA: Bureau of Transitional Bilingual Education.

Gartner, A., & Lipsky, D.K. (1987). Beyond special education: Toward a quality system for all students. *Harvard Educational Review, 57*(4), 367–395.

Granger, B., & Granger, L. (1986). *The magic feather: The truth about special education*. New York: E.P. Dutton.

Malkus, U., Feldman, D., & Gardner, H. (1987). Dimensions of mind in early childhood. In A.D. Pellegrini (Ed.), *The psychological bases of early education* (pp. 23–38). Chichester, England: Wiley.

Olson, L. (1988). Children flourish here: Eight teachers and a theory changed a school world. *Education Week, 7*(1), 18–19.

Piaget, J. (1983). Piaget's theory. In P. Mussen (Ed.), *Handbook of child psychology.* New York: John Wiley & Sons.

Salvia, J., & Ysseldyke, J.E. (1987). *Assessment in special and remedial education.* Boston: Houghton Mifflin.

Sattler, J. (1988). *Assessment of children's intelligence and special abilities.* San Diego, CA: Author.

Shulman, L. (1986). Those who understand: Knowledge growth in teaching. Presidential Address at 1985 Annual Meeting of the American Educational Research Association. *Educational Researcher, 15*(3), 4–14.

Walters, J., & Gardner, H. (1985). The development and education of intelligences. In F. Link (Ed.), *Essays on the intellect* (pp. 1–21). Washington, DC: Curriculum Development Associates.

Ysseldyke, J., & Algozzine, B. (1983). LD or not LD: That's not the question! *Journal of Learning Disabilities, 16,* 29–31.

Ysseldyke, J., Algozzine, D., & Epps, S. (1983). A logical and empirical analysis of current practice in classifying students as handicapped. *Exceptional Children, 50,* 160–166.

Ysseldyke, J., Algozzine, B., Regan, R., & Potter, M. (1980). Technical adequacy of tests used by professionals in simulated decision-making. *Psychology in the Schools, 17,* 202–209.

Ysseldyke, J., Algozzine, B., Richey, L., & Graden, J. (1982). Declaring students eligible for LD services: Why bother with the data? *Learning Disabilities Quarterly, 5,* 37–44.

Ysseldyke, J., Thurlow, M., Graden, J., Wesson, C., Algozzine, B., & Deno, S. (1983). Generalizations from five years of research on assessment and decision-making. *Exceptional Education Quarterly, 4,* 75–93.

part III

Teachers, Parents, and Students

chapter 8

Teacher Preparation

M. Stephen Lilly

Unification of education[1] and special education is no longer an abstract possibility to be discussed in theoretical terms on the pages of professional journals. Nor is it merely the dream of a few special educators who question the efficacy of standard practice in their own field of endeavor. The movement in education toward deregulation and empowerment of teachers and principals at the building level is having a substantial effect. Increasingly, the logic and practicality of special education programs that remove students from the classroom for services that often are only tangentially related to classroom instruction is being questioned (Lilly, in press). Change is coming, and the purpose of this chapter is to assess the potential impact of this change on teacher education programs throughout the field of education, and particularly in special education.

THE TRADITIONAL NATURE OF SPECIAL
EDUCATION TEACHER PREPARATION PROGRAMS

Pugach and Lilly (1984) have pointed out that "teacher education programs tend to follow rather than lead the field of practice" (p. 48). This is somewhat understandable for two reasons:

---

[1]In special education circles, distinction is commonly made between "special education" students and professionals and "general education" students and professionals. In this author's experience, the use of the term "general education" or "regular education" is usually restricted to special educators. Classroom teachers and building/district administrators consider themselves educators, not "general" or "regular" educators. Further, they consider their work with children to be education, not "general" education, and they often resent the inference that educational programs of incredible variety are characterized by a single term with decidedly neutral or even negative connotations. Would any of us be thrilled to have our job termed "general" or "regular," especially if other colleagues were labeling their own work as "special"? Thus, in this chapter, the terms "general education" and "regular education" will be replaced by the term "education." "Education" will be used to denote the educational experience that most students receive, and which we want all students to have, in a given school or school district.

1. Universities prepare students to compete for real jobs in real schools and must therefore be sensitive to professional conditions, as well as hiring practices and criteria, in K–12 schools.
2. Universities offer teacher education programs through a maze of state regulations for program approval and teacher certification that are nearly always reflective of current and past practice in education, not future trends or directions.

Thus, it is not surprising that special education teacher preparation programs in the United States have been and continue to be largely categorical in nature and based on assumptions of student deficit rather than notions of teacher efficacy. Also, it is understandable that there has been considerable psychological (and often physical) space between special education faculty and education faculty in our colleges and universities.

Pugach (1988) argues that the traditional nature of special education programs has acted as a restraint not only on the nature of special education programs in the K–12 schools and the relationships between educators and special educators in the schools, but also on the nature of *all* teacher education programs in the university. The latter effect is described as follows:

> The relationship between the general and special preparation of teachers, then, can be thought of as an implicit agreement that goes something like this: Teacher educators in special education will prepare graduates to accept the role of working with students who do not readily fit classroom teachers' conceptions of whom they are prepared to teach, while general teacher educators will agree to ensure that their graduates are prepared from the outset to seek out and expect the services special education provides. As a result, three fundamental and natural functions of classroom teaching have, by tacit agreement, been parcelled out in part or in full to special education: the pedagogical function, the metacognitive function, and the universal learning function. Each affects the potential for reform [of teacher education] in a particular way. (Pugach, 1988, p. 54)

Thus, much as the nature of special education programs in the schools has a direct effect on teachers' perceptions of children as learners and of their own roles as teachers, separate, segregated special education teacher preparation programs in universities encourage a maladaptive view of students and teachers *throughout* the teacher education enterprise.

The purpose of these introductory comments is twofold: to provide a brief perspective on the nature of the issues to be dealt with in the chapter, and to introduce a contextual framework for analysis of the issues. The following points are posited:

1. Special education is undergoing fundamental change in its definition and its relationship to education in our schools.
2. These changes will have a direct effect on teacher training programs of all types. In particular, special education teacher preparation programs should be prepared to make major changes in focus, underlying assumptions, locus in the college and university, and philosophical underpinnings.

3. Such basic reanalysis will not be easy. In most cases, it will be undertaken only after it is absolutely clear that modifications are necessary to be in tune with changes occurring in the K–12 schools.
4. Existence of traditional programs of special education teacher preparation serves as a deterrent both to preparing all teachers to teach heterogeneous classes of students and to instill a strong sense of self-efficacy in all new teachers.
5. Even though restructuring of teacher education will be difficult and challenging for all concerned, it *will* occur when colleges and universities determine it is necessary in order for graduates to compete successfully for teaching positions and to meet the expectations associated with teaching in the common schools.

The remainder of this chapter provides a discussion of the contextual factors that can be expected to affect teacher preparation (particularly in special education) in the next decade. This will include an analysis of trends in special education definition and service delivery in the K–12 schools, and a discussion of the significant new directions in teacher education, both in special education and in elementary/secondary education. In addition, a description of salient characteristics of a unitary system of teacher education ("beyond special education"), and a description of extant or anticipated barriers to change is provided. We will begin, however, at the end. The next section describes teacher education programs of the future, particularly in relation to the characteristics of programs that are affected by the traditional bifurcation of special education and education. Thus, the chapter starts with describing the "conclusion" of the chapter, then proceeds to present information supporting that conclusion.

CONCLUSION: WHAT SHOULD TEACHER EDUCATION LOOK LIKE?

What should be the role of special education in teacher preparation in the future? Should there be departments of special education within colleges of education, or should the personnel and functions be folded into departments of curriculum and instruction, or elementary/secondary education? Should "school specialists" be prepared? If so, should this be done through special education? How will teacher education models reflect emerging conceptions of teachers' roles in the schools? These questions and others must be answered in order to gain a reasonable perspective on the nature of teacher education in the future. This section describes one vision for the future that is based on analysis of current major reform efforts in teacher education, special education, and professionalization of teaching. It is a "walk in the future," as defined by this author, with additional background information to be presented in subsequent sections.

Present evidence of directions and processes of educational change lead to the conclusion that separate systems of teacher preparation in special education will go the way of separate systems of education for children. That is, special education-based teacher preparation systems will fade into obscurity as educators increasingly recognize their limitations and liabilities (Hagerty & Abramson, 1987; Pugach & Lilly, 1984; Stainback & Stainback, 1987). Specifically, in relation to programs for preparing the teachers of students labeled "mildly handicapped" (or "learning disabled," "behaviorally disordered," or "educable or mildly mentally retarded"), special education as a separate entity in teacher education will disappear. A new focus will emerge on differentiation of specialty area expertise for teachers.

The new system of teacher preparation will be built on a basis of initial preparation of teachers for early education, elementary education, and secondary education. Beginning teachers will, according to the state or institution in which they study, be prepared at either the undergraduate or graduate level. This program will include a strong general education, expanded subject area preparation, professional education (including historical, philosophical, social, and psychological foundations and both general and subject-specific pedagogy), and substantial clinical experience, including a supervised internship in the schools at least one semester in duration. Beginning teachers will be provided induction experiences and supervision by mentor teachers who will help them bridge the gap between their preparation experiences and their assumption of full teaching duties.

Included in this scenario is a system of national teacher certification, including a basic and advanced national teaching certificate (Carnegie Forum, 1986), and state and district incentives for continuing education and attainment of advanced degrees by teachers. Thus, in their advanced preparation phase, teachers will have opportunities to specialize in a variety of subjects and to assist colleagues in those areas. For example, some teachers will pursue advanced work in specific subject areas such as mathematics, sciences, reading, writing, social studies, or physical education. Others might concentrate their advanced studies on important topics such as student assessment, critical thinking and problem solving, cooperative learning, outcome-based education, classroom management, multicultural education, or international education. Still other teachers might concentrate on the educational needs of students with vision impairments, hearing impairments, or severe multiple disabilities. Undoubtedly, many educators would elect to concentrate their advanced studies on the challenges and opportunities of meeting the educational needs of students who are in nearly all ways similar to other students in the school, but who have particular difficulty in learning the curriculum as quickly or easily as most students. (These specialists will focus on adaptation of instructional programs rather than isolation, overprotection, and denial of standard curriculum opportunities to students.)

The teacher education system just described is based largely on concepts embedded in the "second wave of educational reform," which focuses on teacher empowerment, professionalization of teaching, and deregulation of education accompanied by increased decision-making and accountability at the school and classroom level (Carnegie Forum, 1986). It assumes that given the authority to design school programs based on meeting the needs of students, many teachers and administrators would make different decisions than are often required by the current maze of laws and regulations that are designed to produce quality education, but are destined instead to "make a camel out of a horse." The proposed teacher education model assumes a system in which teachers have the time and opportunity to plan together to establish school-based excellence and to meet the needs of all students who come to school. The model assumes that decisions about children focus on *how* to help them learn all the school strives to teach them, rather than *whether* to offer them a total, challenging school program. Tucker and Mandel (1986) describe such a school as follows:

> Groups of teachers would gather periodically to determine how best to cluster and distribute among the staff those students for whom they were responsible. Class times and sizes might be varied across the school day, and teachers might not be confined to a single classroom. Students as well as teachers might be encouraged to move about—the former to master an assigned lesson or to search for an engaging learning experience, the latter to consult with a colleague or to monitor a particular group of students in need of periodic oversight. (p. 26)

Obviously, state licensing patterns would be different in the teacher education system just described. (State licensing is distinguished from national certification in that a state license is required to ensure that *minimum* standards of preparation are met. National certification is awarded for meeting predetermined standards of excellence. Education currently confuses the notions of licensure and certification, which are more clear in other professions.) *Levels* of licensing would be distinguished, with relatively common expectations for teachers (differentiated by age level of students to be taught) for initial licensure, and encouragement of diverse programs of study in varying specialty areas for advanced licensure of experienced teachers. Separate licenses for special educators would be unnecessary in this system, and specialization in traditional special education areas would be at the advanced level of study and would *always* build upon basic teacher preparation. Studies in areas traditionally associated with presumed "mild handicapping conditions" would not be identified with special education at all, and there would be no distinction between "special educators," remedial teachers, or subject area specialists in terms of preparation, licensure, or deployment in the schools. Essentially, schools would be expected to ensure that an appropriate array of qualified personnel were employed to provide effective instruction for the variety of students in the school, and *all teachers would be expected to teach children and to assist each other in meeting individual students' needs.* The outcome of such a system is a community of teachers in a school who act as creative problem solvers, defining instructional problems and solving them collaboratively (Bickel & Bickel, 1986).

A teacher education system for preparing classroom teachers at the initial level and experienced teachers with advanced preparation and varying specializations would lead to different organizational structures not only in K–12 schools, but in colleges and universities as well. Departments of special education would cease to exist, and special education faculty would be expected to define their expertise in functional terms meaningful to school practitioners (such as classroom management or cooperative learning), rather than categorical (or noncategorical, but equally debilitating) descriptions of children. Disciplinary boundaries between teacher educators and "special education" teacher educators would break down as faculty discover, by working together, that they are dealing with similar functional problems among school children and teachers in training. Research by former special education faculty would focus more on school context and student learning variables, and less on student descriptors and placement issues. Fewer arguments would occur in the professional literature about discrepancies between the knowledge base in special education and the knowledge base in education (arguments based largely on inappropriate assumptions regarding student characteristics). In addition, there would be less finger pointing by individuals convinced that "general educators" care less for the educational welfare of all children than "special educators." There would be little patience for esoteric arguments among special educators about such issues as the "real" definition of learning disabilities or the true incidence of behavior disorders. The clear and primary focus of teacher education would be the preparation of all teachers for commitment to universal student learning, the encouragement of a sense of self-efficacy in helping all students to learn, and the establishment of collegial approaches to problem solving in schools.

EDUCATIONAL REFORM: THE IDEAL

By now, many readers are undoubtedly questioning the reality base of the author, asking where such teacher preparation programs, professional commitments, and conditions for teaching and schooling exist. Indeed, what has been presented is an ideal vision present in selected schools and universities that contrasts with the isolation, overspecialization, and compartmentalization of many schools and universities today. The ideal, however, is within reach in the next 10 years if we capitalize on the impetus for educational reform based on teacher empowerment and school-based decision making. If the ideal is desirable, we must work to make it reality, and we must refrain from implementing, supporting, or continuing educational programs that impede such educational improvement.

Special education in the K–12 schools, and teacher preparation in special education, are both impediments to reaching (or approaching) the educational conditions described above. The vision as described requires a basic reconceptualization of special education as we know it, a restructuring described and advocated by Gartner and Lipsky (1987), Lilly (in press), Stainback and Stainback (1984), and many other authors in the professional literature. It also requires dramatic changes in traditional special education teacher preparation.

Such changes are advocated by Hagerty and Abramson (1987), Pugach (1987, 1988), Pugach and Lilly (1984), and Stainback and Stainback (1987). We must see special education, both in service delivery and in teacher education, as an inhibitor to basic educational reform in order to escape our inaccurate and maladaptive tendency to see it as a "savior" for children and disgruntled professional educators.

Are the "conclusions" presented in this section reasonable and justifiable? What contextual factors would lead to such conclusions? Subsequent sections of the chapter will discuss special education in the K–12 schools, teacher education, and special education teacher preparation, citing the factors in each system that make these conclusions viable and realistic. Finally, the chapter concludes with an analysis of barriers to change and steps to success in creating ideal systems of student and teacher education.

ISSUES IN SPECIAL EDUCATION

An obvious, explicit assumption in the foregoing discussion is that separate, heavily regulated systems of special education are dysfunctional; they must be dismantled and replaced with coordinated systems of support for students and teachers based in education, not in special education. This topic is the subject of many other chapters of this book, and will not be covered fully here. It is useful, however, to review the basic arguments supporting such a conclusion.

Lilly (1986) identified the following basic problems and shortcomings in the current special education system. Specifically, he addresses service provision to students with "mild learning and behavior problems":

1. The "referral to placement" process is complex, costly, and of questionable validity.
2. Special education pull-out services are disruptive to classroom routines and of questionable utility in helping students meet the expectations of classroom teachers.
3. Special education pull-out programs exist in schools alongside other pull-out services, but they are seldom coordinated with such programs. Examples of such services include: remedial education, Chapter I programs, bilingual programs, and special subject instruction. The result is fragmentation of services and needless bureaucracy as a consequence of attempting to achieve "nonoverlap" of services to students.
4. Special education diagnostic and placement procedures are time consuming and prevent timely attention to instruction problems in the classroom.
5. Rules governing delivery of special education services often discourage direct help to classroom teachers or prevent the delivery of help to students within the classrooms in which the original instructional problems were identified.

6. Rules typically prevent "special education" teachers from working with groups of students experiencing common classroom learning problems unless all such students are identified as "handicapped." Such roles also inhibit the use of other academic specialists to teach identified special education students. (Such functional approaches to teaching assignments typically threaten ongoing program funding.)
7. Special education labels are often inaccurate and invite overgeneralization and inappropriate reductions in expectations for identified students.
8. The philosophical tenets underlying special education encourage teachers to see themselves as incapable of teaching certain students, and to assume that identified students are incapable of succeeding in learning the standard curriculum.

These and other criticisms of existing special education assumptions and practices have been chronicled by numerous researchers (e.g., Carlberg & Kavale, 1980; Gartner & Lipsky, 1987; Hagerty & Abramson, 1987; Reynolds, Wang, & Walberg, 1987; Stainback & Stainback, 1984; Will, 1986; Ysseldyke, Algozzine, & Epps, 1983). This criticism has led to increasing calls for "merger" of education and special education (Stainback & Stainback, 1984), development of a unitary system of education for all students (Gartner & Lipsky, 1987), and elimination of traditional forms of special education for students labeled "mildly handicapped" (Lilly, in press). These analyses, and the current interest in schools and school districts across the country in implementing new support programs for students and teachers, form the basis for the new system of teacher preparation described in this chapter.

ISSUES IN TEACHER PREPARATION

The new system of teacher education presented in this chapter is supported not only by an analysis of problems and trends in special education service delivery, but also by observations of current trends in teacher education. Clearly, teacher education is a focus of the "second wave" of educational reform cited earlier. The first wave of educational reform, characterized best by the 1983 report of the National Commission on Excellence in Education, *A Nation at Risk: The Imperative of Educational Reform,* was characterized by a regulatory approach to improvement of education (Romanish, 1987). The dominant theme was that students needed to be forced to learn more through increased graduation requirements, frequent testing, and increased school assignments. The report also stated that teachers needed to be forced to perform better through increased accountability and testing. The results of this first wave of reform are best seen in the legislation adopted in many states, particularly in the southeastern states. This new legislation concerns minimum competency testing, increased graduation requirements, and new testing requirements for initial and continuing teacher certification.

These early education reform reports, which called for the general public to "get tough" with educators and students, have given way over the past few years to a new and more promising focus on creating conditions that empower and encourage teachers to provide the best possible education for students. This second wave of reform is best characterized by the 1986 report of the Task Force on Teaching as a Profession of the Carnegie Forum on Education and the Economy, entitled *A Nation Prepared: Teachers for the 21st Century*. This report calls for a fundamental redesign of public education, recognizing that teachers are the *sine qua non* of educational excellence and that true reform can occur only *because of*, and never *in spite of*, the nation's teachers. The report states:

> Properly staffed schools can only succeed if they operate on the assumption that the essential resource is already inside the school: determined, intelligent and capable teachers. Such schools will be characterized by autonomy for the school as a whole and collegial relationships among its faculty . . . Professional autonomy is the first requirement . . . Within the context of a limited set of clear goals for students set by state and local policymakers, teachers, working together, must be free to exercise their professional judgment as to the best way to achieve these goals . . . This autonomy will work only if the school staff work collaboratively, taking collective responsibility for student progress. (p. 58)

Obviously, this approach to educational reform places a premium on excellence in teacher education, and the last few years have seen a spate of reports calling for improvements in teacher education programs. Such reports have been issued by various organizations, including:

American Association of Colleges for Teacher Education (1985)
Association of Teacher Educators (1986)
California Commission on the Teaching Profession (1985)
Carnegie Forum on Education and the Economy (1986)
Holmes Group (1986)
National Governors' Association (1986)
Southern Regional Education Board (1985)
Western Interstate Commission for Higher Education (1985)

The Carnegie Forum

Without question, the most influential of these reports has been that of the Carnegie Forum (1986), which contains the following major recommendations regarding improvement of teaching conditions and teacher education:

1. Create a National Board for Professional Teaching Standards, organized with a regional and state membership structure, to establish high standards for what teachers need to know and be able to do, and to certify teachers who meet that standard;
2. Restructure schools to provide a professional environment for teachers, freeing them to decide how best to meet state and local goals for children while holding them accountable for student progress;
3. Restructure the teaching force, and introduce a new category of Lead Teachers with the proven ability to provide active leadership in the redesign of the

schools and in helping their colleagues to uphold high standards of learning and teaching;

4. Require a bachelor's degree in the arts and sciences as a prerequisite for the professional study of teaching;
5. Develop a new professional curriculum in graduate schools of education leading to a Master in Teaching degree, based on systematic knowledge of teaching and including internships and residencies in the schools;
6. Mobilize the nation's resources to prepare minority youngsters for teaching careers;
7. Relate incentives for teachers to school-wide student performance, and provide schools with the technology, services and staff essential to teacher productivity; and
8. Make teachers' salaries and career opportunities competitive with those in other professions. (p. 55)

While not all of the recommendations of the Carnegie Forum will become reality in the near future, the report has had a major impact on teacher education already. Space limitations preclude a complete review of trends in teacher education in this chapter. However, it is sufficient to assert that substantial changes have already taken place in teacher education nationally over the last several years, and that more changes will occur in the near future. Specifically:

1. Admission standards have been raised in the majority of teacher education programs in the country, resulting in an overall increase in the qualifications of students entering teacher education.
2. Many institutions of higher education are recognizing the need for extended programs of teacher education; 5-year programs are gradually becoming the norm rather than the exception. (In institutions that have not formally adopted an extended program format, the reality is that all or most students take closer to 5 years than 4 years to complete the program.)
3. There is considerable debate on the question of graduate versus undergraduate preparation of teachers (see Howey & Zimpher, 1986). The concept of requiring graduate preparation for either initial or continuing teacher licensure is growing in popularity.
4. Institutions and states are increasingly requiring new teachers to have undergraduate degrees or majors in the arts, humanities, or sciences. (This has traditionally been a requirement in most institutions for students seeking secondary licensure, and it is being considered as a requirement for aspiring elementary teachers as well.)
5. Many institutions of higher education and various state governments are increasing the requirements for general education and subject area preparation for teachers at all levels.
6. Efforts are being made to develop a "knowledge base" for teacher education, particularly as it relates to more effective integration of disciplinary content and pedagogy.
7. Increased clinical experience is being required in many state standards and university programs. Also, identification of clinical experience sites is

more selective, and observation and evaluation of students in clinical teaching settings is more systematic.

8. National teacher certification is gaining in popularity and prestige, and is being perceived as a viable method of recognizing excellent teachers. It is also being regarded as a means of increasing the stature of the teaching profession (see Kowalski, 1988).

9. Teacher assessment continues to be a popular topic among those calling for teacher education reform. The development of assessment devices for use by the National Board for Professional Teaching Standards encourages widespread availability and use of appropriate teacher assessment systems.

10. Programs are being developed and implemented to promote midcareer entry into the teaching profession for individuals who have degrees in the arts, humanities, or sciences and who decide to enter teaching after completing their undergraduate work. (Some states have implemented "alternative" routes to teacher licensure that require little or no formal teacher education. In contrast, some states offer complete teacher education programs to serve these individuals.)

Thus, there are many exciting and progressive developments in teacher education. Such developments make it likely that teacher preparation programs will be able to prepare the type of teachers called for in the Carnegie Forum report and in the "conclusion" section of this chapter. The extent to which current special education teacher preparation can and should be a part of this effort is discussed in the next section.

ISSUES IN SPECIAL EDUCATION TEACHER PREPARATION

Many of the relevant issues of special education teacher preparation have already been covered in earlier sections of the chapter. It has been pointed out that traditional special education teacher education acts as an impediment to preparation of teachers for the roles described earlier (Pugach, 1988). This is due largely to the categorical nature of the majority of special education preparation programs (Chapey, Pyszkowski, & Trimarco, 1985), despite evidence of the lack of efficacy of categorical training (e.g., Marston, 1987), and the underlying assumptions of student deficit and teacher incompetence that tend to be taught to students preparing to teach.

In addition, there is increasing evidence that the knowledge base for teacher education is largely the same as the knowledge base for special education teacher preparation. Bickel and Bickel (1986) reviewed the literature on characteristics of effective schools, classrooms, and instructional processes and concluded:

> that there is a growing knowledge base about how to organize schools and instruction that is relevant to both special and regular educators and that there is a growing rationale for special and regular educational programming to become more integrated at the school level . . . . Special and regular educators have much to learn from each other. (p. 497)

Likewise, Larrivee (1986) concluded from a study of teaching practices associated with desirable outcomes for "mildly handicapped students in regular classroom settings" (p. 173) that "the descriptive profile that emerges for teachers effective with mainstreamed students is remarkably similar to that of the effective overall teacher" (p. 176). Larrivee concludes that "instructional strategies that meet the needs of mainstreamed students are also likely to be effective practices for the majority of students" (p. 177).

In other words, there are no compelling reasons to maintain separate systems of teacher preparation for classroom teachers and teachers for students labeled mildly handicapped. We have available to us both the knowledge base and the incentives to implement the "ideal" teacher preparation system described earlier. In the opinion of this author, we have more goals and interests in common among faculty members in teacher education and special education than we realize, because the current separate systems often prevent direct communication. Teacher preparation is, then, directly analogous to K–12 school programs, in that a merger of education and special education programs is in the best interest of students and professional educators alike, and creation of a unitary system of teacher education would serve important social and professional goals. Why, then, do we not proceed? The final section of this chapter will present some barriers to change, and suggest ways to start the ball rolling.

BARRIERS TO CHANGE AND STEPS TO SUCCESS

If logic were the primary determinant of educational change, the current K–12 and higher education systems would look very different. In fact, change is difficult, painful, and slow in an institution as conservative as education. Barriers to the merger of teacher education systems include:

1. Professional identities as reflected in organizational affiliations, collegial groupings, and administrative structures
2. Professional inertia, as represented in the common cliches that "we've always done it this way," and "we must be careful not to throw out the baby with the bathwater"
3. Deeply held beliefs on the part of many special educators that there really are fundamental differences among children that are reflected well in the current categorical system and that must be honored for the sake of children
4. Professional isolation that has resulted in lack of knowledge and understanding between educators and special educators (see, e.g., Spodek, 1982)
5. The ease associated with operating in one's comfort zone, and fear of breaking the barriers of that zone (e.g., the hesitancy that a university faculty member might have in forsaking the standard journals that are well known to the person and seeking new publication outlets for professional writings).

Obviously, some of these barriers are easier to break than others. Many, in fact, can be addressed by arranging for increased communication and problem solving among teacher educators. Perhaps the best way to set the occasion for increased communication is to create an organizational structure in which such communication is necessary in order for all the various parties to have their needs met.

This line of reasoning supports the elimination of departments of special education and the incorporation of those faculty into departments of curriculum and instruction, teacher education, or elementary/secondary education. In doing so, it is not necessary to predetermine the exact nature of new programs to be developed. Rather, it should be assumed that faculty who are working together under new environmental conditions will be able to produce positive reforms in teacher education. While specifics should not be predetermined, certain values must guide discussions. It should be recalled that the Carnegie Forum report called for greater autonomy for teachers, within a larger structure and framework in which expectations for students are set. Likewise, merger of teacher education faculties is not likely to succeed unless it is accompanied by a clear statement of expectations regarding the goal of developing a single, unified system of teacher education. Given this expectation, and the time and opportunity for increased communication, there is reason to believe that significant change could occur.

THE REAL CONCLUSION

Change is difficult, but inevitable. It is guided first by vision, then by planning, then by action. No matter how much we want to hurry, change is methodical and slower than we might wish. But it does occur. Ideas that were considered heretical in special education 20 years ago—such as consultation and collaboration with classroom teachers—are established concepts (if not practice) in the field today. Likewise, many of the merger notions that form the basis of this book could not be discussed in friendly terms only a few years ago. Current open discussions of the shortcomings of traditional special education service delivery and teacher preparation, along with increased emphasis on deregulation of teaching and teacher empowerment, will produce the changes called for in this book. The vision is being developed, the planning is occurring, and the action is beginning. Education in 2009 will not resemble education in 1989, and the changes will be more dramatic than any which have occurred in the past century.

The shape of the future is unknown, but one may speculate about what it will not be. One need only look around to see systems and practices that will not stand the test of time. One must see the changes to come as evolutionary, based on what we have learned from our experimentation with different ways of viewing children, professionals, and the educational process. Special education is not "evil" or "mischievous," it is merely unsuited for education in the 21st century, when the majority of students will have "special needs" by today's standards, and when all students must be taught to be problem solvers and consumers of increasingly complex information.

This chapter focuses on preparation of teachers for the 21st century, and on concepts that must guide us in development of quality teacher education programs for the future. These programs will be much more integrated than current teacher education programs, and will make use of a variety of professional teacher educators working together to create optimum conditions for teacher education. The present authors have not dealt with administrator preparation; it is simply not possible to do so within the confines of the chapter. However, many of the principles enumerated here apply equally to administration preparation programs.

In the title of an article reporting on a survey of teacher educators in California, Marks (1987) asked: "Can teacher education shape its own destiny?" Teacher educators in special education might well ask the same question. The answer presented in this chapter is "Yes," but it can only be done by becoming a part of the community of teacher educators, by accepting the challenge of broadening our vision and committing ourselves to collaboration with peers in teacher education to develop excellent programs for the preparation of all teachers. If special educators continue to insist on separate, deficit-based approaches to education of children and teachers, they will have little or no influence on the reform of education for the next century. Special educators stand to gain influence and new knowledge by giving away turf, and the need for movement is most evident in the area of teacher education.

REFERENCES

ATE Blue Ribbon Task Force. (1986). *Visions of reform: Implications for the education profession.* Reston, VA: Association of Teacher Educators.

Bickel, W.E., & Bickel, D.D. (1986). Effective schools, classrooms, and instruction: Implications for special education. *Exceptional Children, 52,* 489–500.

California Commission on the Teaching Profession (1985). *Who will teach our children? A strategy for improving California's schools.* Sacramento: California Commission on the Teaching Profession.

Carlberg, C., & Kavale, K. (1980). The efficacy of special versus regular class placement for exceptional children: A meta analysis. *Journal of Special Education, 14,* 295–309.

Carnegie Forum on Education and the Economy. (1986). *A nation prepared: Teachers for the 21st century.* New York: Carnegie Corporation.

Chapey, G.D., Pyszkowski, I.S., & Trimarco, T.A. (1985). National trends for certification and training of special education teachers. *Teacher Education and Special Education, 8,* 203–208.

Gartner, A., & Lipsky, D.K. (1987). Beyond special education: Toward a quality system for all students. *Harvard Educational Review, 57,* 367–395.

Hagerty, G.J., & Abramson, M. (1987). Impediments to implementing national policy change for mildly handicapped students. *Exceptional Children, 53,* 315–323.

Holmes Group. (1986). *Tomorrow's teachers: A report to the Holmes Group*. East Lansing, MI: Author.

Howey, K.R., & Zimpher, N.L. (1986). The current debate on teacher preparation. *Journal of Teacher Education, 37*(5), 41–49.

Kowalski, T.J. (1988). One case for national certification of teachers. *The Teacher Educator, 23*(4), 2–9.

Larrivee, B. (1986). Effective teaching for mainstreamed students is effective teaching for all students. *Teacher Education and Special Education, 9*, 173–179.

Lilly, M.S. (1986). The relationship between general and special education: A new face on an old issue. *Counterpoint, 6*(1), 10.

Lilly, M.S. (in press). The regular education initiative: A force for change in general and special education. *Education and Training of the Mentally Retarded*.

Marks, M.B. (1987). Can teacher education shape its own destiny? *Teacher Education Quarterly, 14*(1), 67–77.

Marston, D. (1987). Does categorical teacher certification benefit the mildly handicapped child? *Exceptional Children, 53*, 423–431.

National Commission for Excellence in Teacher Education. (1985). *A call for change in teacher education*. Washington, DC: American Association of Colleges for Teacher Education.

National Commission on Excellence in Education. (1983). *A nation at risk: The imperative for educational reform*. Washington, DC: U.S. Government Printing Office.

National Governors' Association (1986). *Time for results: The Governors' 1991 report on education* Washington, DC: National Governors' Association.

Pugach, M. (1987). The national education reports and special education: Implications for teacher preparation. *Exceptional Children, 53*, 308–314.

Pugach, M. (1988). Special education as a constraint on teacher education reform. *Journal of Teacher Education, 39*(3), 52–59.

Pugach, M., & Lilly, M.S. (1984). Reconceptualizing support services for classroom teachers: Implications for teacher education. *Journal of Teacher Education, 35*(5), 48–55.

Reynolds, M.C., Wang, M.C., and Walberg, H.J. (1987). The necessary restructuring of special and regular education. *Exceptional Children, 53*, 391–398.

Romanish, B. (1987). A skeptical view of educational reform. *Journal of Teacher Education, 38*(3), 9–12.

Southern Regional Education Board. (1985). *Improving teacher education: An agenda for higher education*. Atlanta: Southern Regional Education Board.

Spodek, B. (1982). What special educators need to know about regular classrooms. *The Educational Forum, 46*, 295–307.

Stainback, S., & Stainback, W. (1984). A rationale for the merger of special and regular education. *Exceptional Children, 51*, 102–111.

Stainback, S., & Stainback, W. (1987). Facilitating merger through personnel preparation. *Teacher Education and Special Education, 10*, 185–190.

Tucker, M., & Mandel, D. (1986). The Carnegie report: A call for redesigning the schools. *Phi Delta Kappan, 68*(1), 24–27.

Western Interstate Commission for Higher Education. (1985). *Quality in teacher education: A crisis revisited*. Boulder, CO: Western Interstate Commission for Higher Education.

Will, M.C. (1986). Educating children with learning problems: A shared responsibility. *Exceptional Children, 52*, 411–415.

Ysseldyke, J.E., Algozzine, B., & Epps, S. (1983). A logical and empirical analysis of current practice in classifying students as handicapped. *Exceptional Children, 50*, 160–166.

chapter 9

The Roles of Parents

Dorothy Kerzner Lipsky

Parent involvement in the education of students is essential, especially for students with disabilities. For example, parents were the major force in the passage of PL 94-142 and in protecting the law from the early efforts of the Reagan Administration to ravage it. While sometimes viewed by professionals in negative ways, parents have been increasingly recognized as playing a substantial role in the effective education of children, in both general and special education (Lipsky, 1985). Their roles have been conceptualized as being that of decision makers, advocates and protectors, and teachers (Turnbull & Turnbull, 1982).

Despite their importance, validated research studies of parental involvement in special education have been few and limited. Most studies focus on a particular activity, such as participation in the individualized education program (IEP) conference, or the number of contacts between parent and teacher. In practice, there is little professional recognition of: 1) the nature of parental involvement and how it changes over the course of the child's life, 2) the differing cultural understandings of disability and their meaning for the nature of parental involvement, and 3) the potential range of parental roles that depend upon parents' conditions, interests, and desires.

LABELING PARENTS

> The most important thing that happens when a child is born with disabilities is that a child is born. The most important thing that happens when a couple becomes parents of a child with disabilities is that a couple becomes parents. (Ferguson & Asch, in press, p. 1.)

The authors of this quotation suggest such a statement is obvious. Yet, as they point out, far too often parents become a curious trait associated with the disability. Just as the patient with a disease of the liver becomes, in the flip phrase of the hospital personnel: "the liver," the parents of a child with spina bifida become "the spina bifida parents." The damaging consequences of labeling for the child are extended to the parents as well (Ferguson & Ferguson, 1987; Sarason & Doris, 1979). They become disabled parents.

The problem is not only that parents are labeled; the same model of pathology that is used in describing the child with a disability is applied to the parents as well. Just as the handicaps that the child faces are ascribed solely to the impairment, not to the societal response, the parents' reactions are also seen in an intrapsychic mode, a melange of shock, sorrow, denial, and rejection. The parents' reactions are never viewed as rational responses to the burdens imposed by inadequate services, the insults of professional ignorance, or the lack of social and economic supports (Lipsky, 1985b). Indeed, it is rare to find reports in the professional literature of parents' positive adaptive responses.

Lusthaus (n.d.) has cataloged the professional literature's ascription of parental responses and offered interesting alternative explanations. To the shock that is often described, she counterposes Farber's (1960) point that: "In refusing to consider disappointment and tragedy as normal modes of existence . . . we magnify frustration and suffering for families with a disabled child" (p. 36). Accepting this does not require a disregard of reality. As a parent (Pieper, n.d.) writes:

> Jeff is neither my burden nor my chastisement, although his care requires more than I want to give at times. He is not an angel sent for my personal growth or my future glory; he is not a punishment for my past sins. He is a son. (p. 88)

Most parents of children with disabilities have acknowledged feeling sorrow at varying degrees at various times. While there is little research to substantiate their feelings of happiness, many parents express a mixture of joy as well as sorrow. And at particular developmental benchmarks or transition points, there may be a heightened sense of one or the other emotion. When parents do not express sorrow, or express too much joy, however, they are often considered as using denial.

Denial is a complex phenomenon that ranges from denying the existence of the handicap altogether to minimizing its severity. Of course, as Lusthaus (n.d.) points out; "parents can be mistakenly accused of denial when they have a legitimate difference with professional opinion" (p. 9). And the often criticized "shopping around" behavior may in other contexts be seen as an appropriate form of seeking a second (or third) opinion.

Another aspect of "denial" is expressed by Rousso (1984) in her description of her mother's response to the way she walked.

> She made numerous attempts over the years of my childhood to have me go for physical therapy and to practice walking more normally at home. I vehemently refused all her efforts. She could not understand why I would not walk straight. Now, I realize why. My disability, with my different walk and talk and my involuntary movements, having been with me all of my life, was part of me, part of my identity. With these disability features, I felt complete and whole. My mother's

attempt to change my walk, strange as it may seem, felt like an assault on myself, an incomplete acceptance of all of me, an attempt to make me over. (p. 9)

The other side of denial is over-involvement or inappropriate involvement. The child, or his or her disability, becomes a "project." As Asch (Ferguson & Asch, in press) points out; "making the child's disabilities and differences into a project [loses] sight of the rest of the child . . . " (pp. 20). Speaking about herself and her parents, she says, "[Disability] was something that had to be thought about and contended with; sometimes it got them and me into humorous situations, and at other times it provoked struggle, but it never was what our relationship was about" (p. 20).

As Gallagher (1956) indicates, parents are put in an untenable position when discussing rejection. If they express the honest feelings of not liking their child—as if only parents of children with a disability ever have such feelings—they are condemned for rejecting their child. If they say they like and love their child, they are being unrealistic. The constant analyzing of parental behavior by professionals often produces parental anger. And then, this too is analyzed.

> The belief that parents displace their anger onto the professional is a kind of "Catch-22." That is, whenever the parent disagrees with or confronts the professional, that behavior can be dismissed as an expression of inadequate adjustment, frustration, displaced anger, or a host of psychological problems. Any interpretation is possible other than the parent may be correct! (Lipsky, 1985b, p. 616)

Indeed, much of professional-parent relationships are power struggles, "around that most valuable cultural commodity of knowledge. . . . [T]he worth of knowledge parents have about their own children is devalued. Concerns are dismissed. Requests are patronized. Reports of home behavior are distrusted" (Ferguson & Asch, in press, p. 25). The extreme of this was described by parents of a young boy who did not read at school. Refusing to believe the parents' report that the child read at home, the school diagnosticians subjected him to batteries of tests to explain why he did not read. And, of course, they found explanations, although the boy did read (Granger & Granger, 1986).

It is not that the child with a disability has no differences; it is a matter of the appropriateness of the response to them. Describing her experiences in an integrated classroom before the implementation of PL 94-142, Asch (Ferguson & Asch, in press) writes:

> Some classroom teachers emphasized my differentness—overpraising me for ordinary things, not disciplining me when I deserved it, or vainly protecting me from problems with my peers. Others scolded me for knitting in class or for not turning in a homework assignment on time. From my standpoint such disciplining gave the message to me and my classmates that the teachers thought I was subject to the same treatment as everyone else. Some teachers too readily intervened when I was teased, whereas others recognized I would have to fight the battle of acceptance myself and would not get too far if authorities scolded my tormentors. (p. 29)

Her last point rings close to home. A young boy in a wheelchair came home from school disheveled and happy. He had been "punched out" by another boy, and had thereby been recognized as a peer.

Summarizing the attitudes special and general educators have about families of children with handicapping conditions, Nevin and Thousand (1987) list the following beliefs:

> (a) parents are not willing or able to work with their handicapped children; (b) parents have unrealistic expectations for their handicapped children; (c) parents do not know how to teach their handicapped children; (d) parents need professionals to help them; and (e) parents contribute to the problems of their handicapped children. (p. 280)

Their assertion that these views are more of the past than current may be too optimistic. For example, in a recent survey of special education professionals by Donnellan and Mirenda (1984), 78 percent believed parents were not competent to choose appropriate goals for the children's education, 40 percent thought parents uncooperative, and 38 percent thought them unrealistic (Educators, 1987, p. 3). However, the authors correctly pointed out that not only were these views erroneous, but they tended to foster an adversarial relationship between parents and professionals, in which the parties perceive their efforts as being at cross-purposes (Donnallan & Mirenda, 1984). Such feelings, of course, make it difficult for parents to play the roles set out for them in PL 94-142. Similarly, the view fails to recognize the range of characteristics, circumstances, and conditions of parents.

A recent poll on special education conducted by Louis Harris and Associates provides a more positive, although still mixed, picture. The majority of parents of children with handicaps (77 percent) report that they are "very" or "somewhat satisfied" with the special education system. However, when asked specifically about various services and programs, the proportion of satisfaction drops, particularly among parents whose children have been labeled as emotionally disturbed, visually handicapped, or learning disabled. This is also true among parents whose children have been categorized as having "moderate" or "somewhat severe" levels of disability, or who are served in separate classrooms in regular schools (*ICD Survey III*, 1989, Tables 4-1-A, 4-1-C).

CHANGING FAMILY LIFE PATTERNS

The changing reality of American family life, while often noted, is not often addressed in practice within human services agencies or schools. The standards, content, and service delivery arrangements continue to operate as if the old picture of the "normal" family continues. Until recently, the so-called "normal" family was characterized as being white and middle-class, and possessing 2.3 children, with a working father and a mother who stayed home. Additionally, all family members were assumed to be able-bodied and healthy. Of course, while never entirely correct, recent research has clearly established that the old definition is inaccurate.

A recent report of the House of Representatives Select Committee on Children, Youth, and Families gives ample evidence of these changes for the population at large (*U.S. Children,* 1987):

Of the 63 million children 0 to 17 years of age in 1985, 19 percent were nonwhite and 10 percent of Spanish-origin. By the year 2000, these percentages are estimated to be 21 percent and 13 percent, respectively.

In 1970, 45 percent of households had one or more children 0 to 17 years of age, by 1986 the figure dropped to 36 percent. And in those same years, the percentage of single parent households grew from 5 percent of family households to 8 percent, with an increasing proportion of them male-headed.

The percentage of families with children that are female-headed grew from 7 to 19 percent between 1960 and 1986. Among blacks, the growth was from 21 to 48 percent.

The percentage of children under 18 living with two parents dropped from 84 percent in 1970 to 73 percent in 1986. Among blacks, the figures for the two years were 58 and 40 percent, respectively.

The number of children per family has dropped. Between 1960 and 1986, families with no children grew from 43 to 50 percent, those with three children dropped from 11 to 7 percent, while those with four or more children dropped from 10 to 3 percent.

The participation of mothers in the labor force has increased substantially. For all children under 18 years of age, it grew from 39 percent in 1970 to 58 percent in 1986; from 29 to 50 percent for children 0 to 5 years of age, and from 43 to 62 percent for those 6 to 17 years of age.

The median income of families with children dropped (in constant dollars) between 1975 and 1985 for all types of families and especially for mother-only families.

The percentage of children under 18 years of age living in poverty grew between 1970 and 1985, from 14 to 20 percent; this growth was true for all racial and ethnic groups.

There are no comprehensive data on families with disabled children. The data reported by the Select Committee give breakdowns by race, sex, age, and income, but do not distinguish families with a child with a disability. Furthermore, one of the few studies examining characteristics of families with disabled children that specifically sought to identify single parent families, reported they were "unable to locate any systematic national or statewide data indicating the number or percentage of families of handicapped children headed by single parents" (Bristol, Reiche, & Thomas, 1987, p. 57). They note a number of individual studies that report prevalence of separation and divorce ranging from the same rate as that of the general population to three times the national average. In assessing the validity of these studies, they note methodological problems such as anecdotal accounts cited as evidence for prevalence rates, lack of clarity as to evidence used, sweeping conclusions from small and sometimes biased samples, effects of factors such as race or class ignored, and the lack of adequate comparative data (pp. 57). While subject to some of these limitations, Vadasy (1986) offers a useful survey of the experience and needs of single mothers.

While the Bristol et al. (1987) study concludes that the necessary data are not available to determine the prevalence of single-parent families with a handicapped child, they do offer a valuable set of dicta as to the basis for serving families:

(1) Father involvement is a continuum, not a dichotomy, in both single-parent and two-parent families of handicapped children; (2) Persons other than parents contribute significantly to child rearing in these families; (3) Socioeconomic differences between two-parent and single-parent families of handicapped children are important in interpreting research results and family assessments for intervention; (4) Single-parent families of handicapped children do not constitute a homogeneous group; (5) Coping with single parenting of a handicapped child is a process that changes over time; and (6) The deficit model of "broken homes" is not useful or constructive in advancing our knowledge or in providing improved services for families of handicapped children. (p. 63)

The presence and involvement of fathers is infrequently acknowledged in the literature. While it is true that child care responsibilities (for all children) fall disproportionately upon mothers, the roles of fathers can be expanded. Meyer (1986) examines these roles over the course of the child's life cycle. One of the few programs to have operated long enough to have collected follow-up data is located at the University of Washington (Vadasy, Fewell, Greenberg, Dermond, & Meyer, 1986).

While limited by its data base of five cities, The Collaborative Study of Children with Special Needs offers a great deal of information (Singer & Butler, 1987). The authors report that students receiving special education services differed from the districts' student population as a whole in that they were more likely to be members of a single-parent family. Such families generally had: 1) incomes below 150% of the poverty line, 2) incomes below $15,000 a year, 3) a mother who did not graduate from high school, and 4) the head of household did not hold a full-time job.

DIFFERING RESPONSES

Not only are there variations of class, size, race, composition, and education among families with disabled children (as is the case among all families), there is among these families differences in cultural response to disability. Distinguishing the factors that determine responses to children with disabilities among Asian-American, Black-American, and Mexican-American families, Florian (1987) identifies differences in family structure and composition, experience with service systems, and cultural values. For example, he notes the prevalence of the extended family in the black community; extended families tend to assume (or at least share) the responsibility for child rearing. Florian suggests that this may account for the finding that black mothers had more positive attitudes toward having a retarded child at home than did white mothers.

Florian's research on culture and disability distinguishes between "shame" and "guilt" as the basis of family response:

> Shame and guilt differ from other effects in that they may be understood through their direct references to internalized social norms: the disruption or violation of these social norms may lead to 'shame'—a response to role transgression or 'guilt'—a response to moral transgression (Piers & Singer, 1953). . . . [I]n a 'shame oriented' society most individuals' reactions to a stigmatizing condition, such as a physical disability, may involve attempts to hide the condition from the immediate surrounds, while in a 'guilt-oriented' society individuals' reactions to such a condition may involve ongoing self-blame and a strong sense of personal responsibility for the condition. Shame interrupts, exposes and disrupts a unitary sense of an individual and his/her family, while guilt evaluates, judges and condemns the individual and his/her family. (p. 41)

Another dimension of parental response concerns the differing needs of the family depending upon the age of the child. There is considerable evidence in the professional literature that the following events are considered to be particularly stressful for families: initial diagnosis, enrollment in school, age of puberty, and transition to adulthood (Bray, Coleman, & Bracken, 1981; Fewell & Vadasy, 1986; Hanline, 1988; Marion, 1981). This concept, combined with a broad understanding of family composition and dynamics, is the basis for the family systems approach (Turnbull, Brotherson, & Summers, 1985). A virtue of this approach is seeing the "essential similarity in many respects between families of disabled children and families of non-disabled children. . . . In general, families meet the day to day problems created by the child's disability in ways that are fairly typical of the behaviour of any other family" (Mittler, Mittler, & McConachie, 1987, p. 18).

A topic requiring far more inquiry concerns the family conditions present when one or both parents are themselves disabled. Too often, the same assumptions regarding incapacity that afflict persons with disabilities in other areas of life also apply to their role as parents (Browne, Connors, & Stern, 1985; Kirshenbaum, 1985; Tiffany Callo, 1988). One program, Through the Looking Glass, provides services in Berkeley, California, to such parents. A unique feature of the program is the involvement of the parents with nondisabled parents of a child with a disability. This allows the nondisabled parents to see in the disabled parents the future of their own children. Also, the program appropriately presents people with disabilities as experts.

THE ROLE OF THE PARENT IN THE EDUCATIONAL PROCESS

Building on earlier federal mandates, PL 94-142 provides an extensive set of guarantees for parents concerning their child's education. Among these are: 1) due process rights, 2) rights of notification and consent, 3) access to records, and 4) participation in the development of the child's IEP. While not entirely achieved, by and large the procedural rights, items 1–3 above, have been assured. However, the Louis Harris survey report that 61 percent of the parents said they knew little or nothing about either PL 94-142 or Section 504 of the Rehabilitation Act is striking. Perhaps this accounts for the finding that 46 percent of the parents felt they needed an individual independent of the school system to act as an advocate for their children's rights in school (*ICD Survey III,* 1989, Tables 2-1-A, 9-2). More complex, and less well achieved, is parental involvement in the IEP. This is reviewed in the following section for school age and transitional students; the involvement of parents with preschool children, as mandated by PL 99-457, is then addressed.

Parents and the IEP Process

Although parental involvement in the IEP is a legal requirement of PL 94-142, the benefits expected from that involvement are nebulous. There are few hard data to answer the question: "what types of parent involvement with what types of children under what types of conditions with what types of support produce what types of effects?" (Dunst & Snyder, 1986, p. 275). At a basic level, the provisions of PL 94-142 expressed an apparent belief by Congress that school personnel had not adequately served children with handicaps, nor could they be entrusted alone to do so in the future. Parents were seen as protectors of and advocates for their child(ren)'s interests: both in terms of procedural fairness and, as necessary, ensuring appropriateness and adequacy of services. Other roles for parents, such as providers of information, reinforcers of school activities, direct providers of educational or therapeutic services, and involvement in general aspects of school life, were left vague and have been little examined, except in early childhood programs (Castro & Lewis, 1984; Castro & Mastropieri, 1986; Hocutt & Wiegerink, 1983; Strain & Smith, 1986). A contribution to determining the effectiveness of parent participation is the recent development of a standardized instrument to measure their participation (Cone, DeLawyer, & Wolfe, 1985).

There has not been a comprehensive study of parent involvement in the United States such as the one carried out by Rogers in Great Britain (1986). The studies that have been conducted reveal results that vary over time and location and from one impairment type to another. While there appears to have been short-term increases in parent involvement, overall parent involvement in the IEP process is limited, both in the extent to which parents are involved and in the nature of that participation.

Summarizing a number of studies, one review states that these "reports suggest that up to half of the parents fail to participate . . ." (Meyers & Blacher, 1987). One study reported that in 70 percent of the cases, parents provided no input to IEP development (*A National Survey,* 1980). A more recent study reports that only half of the parents attended IEP meetings (Scanlon, Arick, & Phelps, 1981), and that when they did, professionals believed that they contributed little (Goldstein, Strickland, Turnbull, & Carry, 1980; Lynch & Stein, 1982).

In contrast, the Louis Harris study reports that 79 percent of the parents said they attended their child's most recent IEP conference, while 9 percent reported that either they were not informed of the meeting or the school did not offer such meetings. Among those parents who participated in the IEP conference, 73 percent felt they contributed to the development of objectives for their child's IEP, 64 percent felt that the IEP goals "very much" reflected their child's needs, and 20 percent felt that the goals of their child's IEP were not being properly carried out (*ICD Survey III,* 1989, Tables 7-1-A, 7-1-B, 7-3-A, 7-3-B, and 7-4). There are some data to suggest that parents of more severely impaired children participate more in the IEP process (Meyers & Blacher, 1987; Morgan, 1980), while those with less severely impaired children are less involved in the process (McKinney & Hocutt, 1982). Another set of factors affecting the extent of parental involvement concerns race, class, and education. "[A] white, married mother who graduated from high school was 5.4 times more likely than a non-white, single mother who had not graduated from high school, to have attended the most recent IEP conference held for her child" (Singer & Butler, 1987, p. 146).

Several studies indicate that parents "feel intimidated or are provided only limited opportunity" to become involved (Meyers & Blacher, 1987). This is true even when the parents are themselves professionals (Turnbull & Turnbull, 1978). And this point is emphasized in a Department of Education report to Congress which notes: "several studies have reported that in the majority of IEP conferences, the IEP was completely prepared prior to the meeting. . . ." The report concludes: "presenting parents with what may appear to be decisions the school has already reached rather than recommendations, and the failure to directly communicate and provide appropriate opportunities for involvement, can obviously limit parent participation in the IEP decision making process" (*Ninth Annual Report,* 1987, p. 71).

Several factors appear to account for this limited involvement of parents in the IEP process. They include such factors as: 1) parents' desire not to participate, 2) parents' inability to participate, or 3) parents' belief that the school does not welcome them. These factors are as true for parents of children without disabilities as for those with them. For example, a recent national study reports from one-fifth to one-third of all parents either never or only once a year participate in any activity involving their child's school (*Strengthening Links,* 1987).

Professional factors may be a reason why parents do not feel welcomed in school settings. One example of this would be school personnel who have not been trained to work directly with parents, that is, with other adults, who have adult knowledge and emotions. Another inhibiting factor would be the difficulty that arises when parents are regarded as threats because they hold differing values or because they may challenge the professionals' expertise.

Parents and the Transition Process

Transition is the term now used to describe the process by which students move from secondary education to postsecondary education or employment. In general, as students become older, parental involvement in their school activities lessens. While over three-quarters of elementary school parents have a "high" or "medium" degree of involvement with their child's school, this drops to barely two-fifths among parents of high school students (*Strengthening Links,* 1987). The drop in involvement reflects the increased maturity of the child, as well as a greater percentage of mothers in the labor force. For example, in 1984, 39% of mothers with children 0–5 years old were not in the labor force, while among those with a child 12–17 years old, the figure dropped to 28% (*U.S. Children,* 1987).

While these factors are also true for parents of teenage children with disabilities (Lynch & Stein, 1982; Morgan, 1980), for these parents there is a counter set of factors. They see their children "aging out" of the PL 94-142 entitlement, and are increasingly concerned that successful adult opportunities will not be available to their children. Such pressures are made all the greater when the previous years of schooling have not provided a sure enough base (Gartner & Lipsky, 1987).

There have been a few surveys of parent views and expectations for their children. Such studies were recently conducted in Oregon (Benz & Halpern, 1987; Brodsky, 1983; McDonnell, Wilcox, Boles, & Bellamy, 1985), Virginia (Hill, Wehman, Kregel, Banks, & Metzler, 1987) and in Colorado (Mithaug, Horiuchi, & McNulty, 1987). In Washington a follow-up study (Schill, Mc-Carten, & Meyer 1985) investigated students' employment status and family structure. Similarly, Liebert, Lipsky, and Horowitz (1987) surveyed parental needs for information and compared those with professional perceptions.

Considerable discussion concerning the necessity for parental involvement in transition planning appears in the literature (Everson, Barcus, Moon, & Marton, 1987; Kelker & Hagen, 1985; McDonnell, Sheehan, & Wilcox, 1981; McKinney & West, 1985; McNair & Rusch, 1987; Mendelsohn & Mendelsohn, 1986). The need for parental involvement was further expanded upon in two extensive studies that identified the major significance of family and friend networks in successful job finding for students with disabilities (Hasazi, Gordon, & Roe, 1985; Hill et al., 1987).

The reality of parental participation, however, is "not particularly encouraging'' (Halpern, 1985, p. 484). In large part this reflects the factors previously discussed; overall low level of parental involvement in IEP development and in educational activities. Specifically concerning transition, more than two-thirds of special education teachers in an extensive Oregon study were "dissatisfied" or "very dissatisfied" with the support and involvement of parents of teenage students. This is not surprising, given that over half of the parents reported one or fewer meetings per term with teachers (Benz & Halpern, 1987, p. 509). This lack of involvement is reflected, according to the study's authors, in the high percentage of parents who reported that they did not know what their high school–age child would be doing occupationally 1 or 10 years in the future, 36 percent and 35 percent, respectively. There were similar high "Don't know" responses to a question about the child's future residence arrangements (Benz & Halpern, 1987, Table 3).

The Louis Harris survey reports the highest level of parental dissatisfaction concerns the transition from school to work; only 44 percent of the parents said it was "effective." This judgment is not surprising given the report of parents of children 17 years of age or older that a transition plan was a part of the IEP in only 38 percent of the cases, that job counseling and placement occurred in only 40 percent of the cases, and contact with a vocational rehabilitation agency occurred in only 43 percent of the cases (*ICD Survey III*, 1989, Tables 8-2, 8-4-A, and 8-6).

While the Benz and Halpern (1987) study avoids explicitly blaming the parents for noninvolvement, other studies either place blame on the parents or imply it. Indeed, in calling for "parent education," the implication is that the cause of the absence of appropriate parental involvement is parental ignorance. Again, alternative explanations are available, including the nature of professional response to parents (Gartner, 1988; Lipsky, 1985), the inappropriateness of the service arrangements, and the lack of support for families (Lipsky, 1985). For example, only 6 percent of the Oregon districts had formal written agreements with other agencies to coordinate transition services, and 15 percent of the districts had no coordination mechanisms. These findings are not surprising given the report that one-third of the special education administrators do not regard such coordination as important (Benz & Halpern, 1987, p. 509). Equally rare are efforts to see parents as possessors of valuable knowledge about both their child's employment potential or of parents' as potential "trainers" of the professionals (Gartner, 1988) or to ascertain from parents what information they need to be effective participants in the transition process (Liebert et al., 1987).

Parents and Early Childhood Programs

Parent involvement in programs serving very young children with handicaps is becoming an increasingly central issue with the implementation of PL 99-457, which gives support to states to provide early intervention programs to all handicapped preschool children, from birth through 5 years of age. The requirements of PL 99-457 replace the PL 94-142 IEP for children from birth to 3 years of age with an IFSP (Individualized Family Service Plan). As the name indicates, it is the needs of the family, both as a unit and for each member, that the Plan must address. This shift raises a great many issues, including:

1. The balance to be struck between the needs of the child with a disability, other family members, and the family as a unit
2. Given the likelihood that the service providers will be nondisabled, the extent to which this will affect the way this balance is struck between the needs of the disabled child and the nondisabled family members   (A pertinent set of issues is raised, for example, when considering respite services and the extent to which in their design they give focus primarily to the family's needs or to the needs of the child. Both are important. For a discussion of a similar issue, attendant care for adults with disabilities, see Litvak, Zukas, and Heumann, 1987.)
3. The willingness of service system providers, including health and welfare departments, not-for-profit organizations, and school systems, to play the role of implementers of parent decisions
4. The ability and willingness of parents to play the goal setter role
5. The capacity of "parent education programs" to prepare parents for such roles, especially in light of the rapid changes in the life prospects of currently very young handicapped children
6. The willingness and ability of service systems to meet the wider needs of families, including housing, nutrition, health care, employment, and education of family members

Indeed, the provisions of PL 99-457 force a broadening of attention from the topic of parental involvement to that of support for families with a disabled child.

The largest body of information about parent involvement in programs for young children with handicaps draws upon the experience of the federally funded Handicapped Children's Early Education Projects. While parent involvement varied in nature and extent across the projects, one study of projects in their 3rd year found that those projects operated by public schools had lower levels of parent involvement than ones conducted by private nonprofit organizations. Additionally, there was a high correlation in all programs between the extent of parent involvement and their overall satisfaction with programs (Hocutt & Wiegerink, 1983). More recently, there are reports in the literature concerning programs involving parents of children making the transition from preschool to public school (Bailey et al., 1988; Hains, Fowler, & Chandler, 1988; Hanline, 1988; Hanline & Knowlton, 1988). These and other programs are exploring and developing new models of parent involvement.

FAMILY SUPPORT SYSTEMS

Family support services are increasingly being utilized to serve persons with disabilities. Such programs develop when individuals recognize that the consequences of disability affect both the individual with disabilities and others in the family. The issue then becomes the nature of that support; this will be affected by the characteristics of the family and its dynamics and the individual who is disabled and his/her characteristics.

The definition of "family support" varies widely around the United States and in other countries. However, the rationale behind the development of family support systems is similar; it stems from the belief that "An intact family offers stability, consistency, and close relationships which cannot be duplicated. . . . Like other people, the quality of life for developmentally disabled people is at its best when they can live in their home" (*Family Support*, 1986, p. 1). Recognition that governments may have endorsed family support services in order to cut costs does not gainsay the potential benefits for the individuals involved, nor deny their need. We must be careful, however, to avoid the exclusionary consequence of terms such as "intact family," especially given the previously noted increasing number of single-parent families.

The range of family support services may be categorized in the following 10 broad groupings.

Outreach, including information and referral, prevention and public information;
Family member/care giver training, including training of primary family care givers, specialized behavioral services, sibling services;
Counseling, including genetic counseling, personal adjustment to a disabling condition, and counseling dealing with the dynamics of family relationships;
Respite, including day or overnight respite, homemaker service, family care, community residencies, volunteer respite, drop-in centers, sitter companions, host families, guest homes, and parent exchange networks;
Transportation;
Special assistance services, including home habilitation, home care, and nutritional services;
Financial assistance;
Housing assistance services, including adaptive equipment and home modification;
Recreation; and
Crisis intervention services (Lipsky, 1987, pp. 5,f).

No state in the United States provides all or even most of these services (Agosta & Bradley, 1985). While not exhaustive of all components of a comprehensive family support system, this list suggests the range of issues that need to be considered. In doing so, there are at least five sets of factors to consider in shaping family support systems:

1. The dangers in most professional formulations of the consequences of disability for a family, which emphasize pathology and ascribe deviancy, necessitating professional treatment to any family response
2. The potential that in understanding the family consequences (i.e., the impact upon the nondisabled members), the special and unique needs of the individual with the disability will be downplayed if not ignored
3. The need to recognize that families differ, in composition, needs, cultural heritage, and life stage, each of which affect their understanding of and reaction to disability

4. The need to address a set of gender issues—both the special issues involved
   for women with disabilities (Fine & Asch, 1988) and the special caregiver
   responsibilities that many cultures assign to women
5. The unique feature that unlike traditional minority families seeking to buffer
   and protect each other from the hostility of the larger society, the child with
   a disability is (most often) a member of a family which does not share in the
   experience (or culture) of disability. Thus, in addition to the strengthening
   that comes from a strong system of family supports, children with disabilities need opportunities to be with and learn from other persons with
   disabilities

With ongoing research and project implementation, various designs of family support systems continued to emerge. These include: thirty projects funded by
units of the Department of Health and Human Services (*Family Caregiving
Project, 1987*), several projects being conducted by the Community Services
Society in New York City (McKaig, 1986), a new family project funded by the
National Institute on Disability and Rehabilitation Research being conducted by
the Human Services Research Institute, and from projects conducted in other
countries (Lipsky, 1987) and a 1988 international conference on family support
systems at the Wingspread Conference Center (Gartner, Lipsky, & Turnbull,
1988). Among the characteristics of an effective family support system would
be:

Early initiation, that is, the system reaches out to the family at the beginning of the
    family's involvement
Integrated services, while families will begin with one or another need, most often there
    will be a variety of needs, that can be met by differing agencies. Whatever the
    institutional reasons for this, from the family's perspective, receipt of the array of
    needed services should not be a function of agency territorial lines or eligibility
    criteria or service plans or professional prerogatives
A concomitant of this is *universal access,* that is, wherever a family enters the system, all
    parts should be available to them
While the totality of services may run a wide range, for any individual family it is its
    unique set of needs that must be addressed—in effect selection from a cafeteria of
    services
While we have talked of a family's needs, in fact the members of the family have unique
    needs, both the disabled person and the other individual members, so that services
    must be *individualized*
While supports are designed to respond to needs, they should be designed to *build on and
    bolster strengths* and not focus on deficits
The shared experiences of families with a disabled member offer the basis for *mutual
    support* among such families
Paramount recognition needs to be given to the family's capacity, including the ability to
    determine their own needs. Thus, in the determination of needs and the ways to meet
    them, the *wishes of the family* and of its members should be given priority. (Lipsky,
    1987, pp. 10–11)

The potential for the development of such systems is enhanced by the model
of efforts in Great Britain's Family Fund, as well as the increasing attention in

the United States to family policy (Edelman, 1988; Kagan, Powell, Weissbrod, & Zigler, 1987; Moroney, 1986; Zigler, Kagan, & Kleigman, 1983). In hailing this development, a *New York Times* editorial emphasized the need to strengthen families. The editorial noted that among the characteristics of successful pilot programs were: building on the family's strengths, treating parents as partners, providing comprehensive services, and integrating family and community ("Family Values and Good Intentions," 1988). More particularly, there is the beginning in several states of trust fund arrangements for ongoing support (Teltsch, 1988).

PARTNERSHIPS OF PEERS

While the family support system concept provides an essential broader frame, this closing section focuses on the issue of parent-professional relationships in the education of students labeled as handicapped.

> Parent-professional relationships have become a concern largely because of parents who have broken the quiet saint stereotype to articulate their need for services, and their desire not to be disenfranchised recipients of these services. (Healy, Keesee, & Smith, 1989, p. 43)

Drawing from the broad consumer advocacy efforts of the 1960s, and from a growing understanding of the value of parental involvement in their child's development, both parents and professionals talk increasingly of "partnership." What needs to be worked through is the meaning, shape, and terms of the partnership. Among the elements of such a partnership, Mittler and colleagues (1987) cite the following factors:

1. Growth and learning in children can only be understood in relation to the various environments in which the child is living.
2. Parents and professionals concerned with the development of children with disabilities share a number of basic goals.
3. Parents and the extended family are the adults who are normally most accessible to the child.
4. Parents and professionals each have essential information which needs to be shared among all who are concerned with the child's development. (p. 5)

In characterizing what they mean by partnership, Mittler et al. (1987) emphasize that real collaboration rests on the basic recognition that both sides have areas of knowledge and skill that can contribute to the joint task of improved programs and services for the benefit of the child. In doing so, roles are complementary rather than separate and distinct. The partnership concept is built on professional accountability to parents. It includes mutual respect, sharing in a common purpose, joint decision-making, sharing feelings, and flexibility in dealing with each other.

While discussing the transactions between professionals and parents of young children with handicaps, Healy, Keesee, and Smith (1989) offer guidance appropriate to the development of partnerships at all levels:

1. While parents with at-risk and disabled children may at times be parents in crisis, they are not disabled parents. They have capacities for creative problem solving and coping that professionals need to respect, promote, and encourage.

2. Parents and involved professionals may have widely differing perspectives, experiences, and goals for a particular at-risk or disabled child. The difficult process of sharing and learning to understand these differing perspectives is an important part of care for the child.

3. To foster independence and competence in families, and to make the most effective use of services, it is critical for both parents and professionals to distinguish between times when professional participation is important for good decisions, and times when the parent is singularly competent to make decisions in the child's and family's best interest. Inappropriate dependence is encouraged when professionals make decisions that should be made by parents.

4. Finding the professional balance between promoting competence and independence in families, on the one hand, and providing needed expertise and emotional support on the other, is part of a developmental process. A particular kind of support at one time may, at a later time, promote inappropriate dependence.

5. The goals of a partnership and teamwork between parents and professionals are difficult ones. The easiest pattern is for the professional to adopt the traditional role of knowledgeable decision maker and the parents to adopt that of passive recipients. Changing these roles takes commitment by both parties.

6. Lack of time and discontinuity of personnel are important and very real barriers to effective parent-professional collaboration.

7. The professional needs to share large amounts of information, often of a technical nature, with the parents of special needs children. This process can be aided by appropriate translation of technical language, the provision of relevant written materials, open acknowledgment of unknowns, and direction to other service resources.

8. Professional collaboration with families who have very young special needs children has a strong interpersonal component. Case management should allow professionals who develop a rapport with a particular family to take more responsibility for working with that family, and should also ensure that every family has an advocate.

9. Parents and professionals need to be drawn into a problem-solving diagnostic process that leads to answers for questions such as "What should be done?" and "What should it be called?"

10. Articulate, active parents have brought the issues of parent decision making into the spotlight, but not many start their careers as "special needs" parents with the skills to make it happen. It is part of the professionals' job to help parents identify goals and develop resources within themselves and within the service community to achieve them. (pp. 63–64)

CONCLUSION

Parent involvement since the passage of PL 94-142 has paved new ground and opened new areas for further development. Just as new meaning has been given to parent and community involvement in general education, there is need for increased parental participation in the education of students labeled as handicapped. This involves an understanding of the range of families and their characteristics, and of children and their needs. It involves a reconceptualization of professional and parent relationships, and of societal and family relationships. In the latter case, it involves transcending the dispute concerning which responsibilities are those of the family and which are those of the government, focusing more on ways government and society at large can support the family in all of its roles. Professional and parent relationships will need to be redefined. Neither parents nor professionals will be subordinate to the other, nor will one group assume the role of the other. Instead, they will be equal partners with differing strengths in addressing a shared task, that is, the education and growth of children.

REFERENCES

A National Survey of Individualized Education Programs (IEPs) for Handicapped Children. (1980). Triangle Park, NC: Research Triangle Institute.

Agosta, J.J., & Bradley, V.J. (Eds.). (1985). *Family care for persons with developmental disabilities: A growing commitment.* Boston, MA: Human Services Research Institute.

Bailey, D.B., Jr., Simiarcsson, R.J., Isbell, P., Huntington, G.S., Winton, P.J., Comfort, M., & Helm, J. (1988). Inservice training in family assessment and goal-setting for early interventionists: Outcomes and issues. *Journal of the Division for Early Childhood, 12*(2), 126–136.

Benz, M.R., & Halpern, A.S. (1987). Transition services for secondary students with mild disabilities: A statewide perspective. *Exceptional Children 53*(6), 507–514.

Bray, N., Coleman, J., & Bracken, M. (1981). Critical events in parenting handicapped children. *Journal of the Division for Early Childhood, 3,* 26–33.

Bristol, M.M., Reiche, N.C., & Thomas, D.D. (1987). Changing demographics of the American family: Implications for single-parent families of young handicapped children. *Journal of the Division for Early Childhood, 12*(1), 56–69.

Brodsky, M.J. (1983) *A five year follow-up of the graduates of school programs for trainable mentally retarded students in Oregon.* Unpublished doctoral dissertation, University of Oregon.

Browne, S., Connors, D., & Stern, N. (Eds.). (1985). *With the power of each breath.* Pittsburgh: Cleis Press.

Castro, G., & Lewis, A.C. (1984). Parent involvement in infant and preschool programs. *Journal of the Division for Early Childhood, 9,* 49–56.

Castro, G., & Mastropieri, M.A. (1986). The efficacy of early intervention programs: A meta-analysis. *Exceptional Children, 52*(5), 417–424.

Cone, J.D., DeLawyer, D.D., & Wolfe, V.V. (1985). Assessing parent participation: The Parent/Family involvement index. *Exceptional Children, 51*(5), 417–424.

Donnallan, A.M., & Mirenda, P.M. (1984). Issues related to professional involvement with families with individuals with autism and other severe handicaps. *The Journal of The Association for Persons with Severe Handicaps, 9*(2), 16–22.

Dugan, M.J., & Brooks, N. (Eds.). (1985). *Women and disability: The double handicap.* New Brunswick, NJ: Transaction.

Dunst, C.J., & Snyder, S.W. (1986). A critique of the Utah university early intervention meta-analysis research. *Exceptional Children, 53*(4), 269–276.

Edelman, M.W. (1988). *Families in peril: An agenda for social change.* Cambridge, MA: Harvard University Press.

Everson, J., Barcus, M., Moon, S., & Marton, M. (Eds.) (1987). *Achieving outcomes: A guide to interagency training in transition and supported employment.* Richmond, VA: Rehabilitation Research and Training Center, Virginia Commonwealth University.

Family caregiving project. (1987). Washington, DC: U.S. Department of Health and Human Services.

Family support services: Expanding alternatives for families with developmentally disabled individuals. (1985). Albany, NY: Office of the Mental Rehabilitation and Developmental Disabilities.

Family values and good intentions. (1988, March 19). *New York Times,* p. 26.

Farber, B. (1960). Perception of crisis and related variables and the impact of the retarded child on the mother. *Journal of Health and Human Behavior, 1,* 108–118.

Ferguson, P.M., & Asch, A. (in press). Lessons from Life: Personal and parental perspectives on schooling, childhood, and disabilities. In D. Biklen, D.F. Ferguson, & A. Ford (Eds.), *Schooling and disability.* Chicago: National Society for Study of Education.

Ferguson, P.M., & Ferguson, D. (1987). Parents and professionals. In P. Knoblock (Ed.), *Introduction to Special Education* (pp. 181–203). Boston: Little, Brown.

Fewell, R.R. (1986). A handicapped child in the family. In R.R. Fewell & P.F. Vadasy (Eds.), *Families of handicapped children: Needs and supports across the life span* (pp. 3–34). Austin, TX: PRO-ED.

Fewell, R.R., & Vadasy, P.F. (Eds.) (1986). *Families of handicapped children: Needs and supports across the life span.* Austin, TX: PRO-ED.

Fine, M., & Asch, A. (Eds.) (1988). *Women with disabilities.* Philadelphia, PA: Temple University Press.

Florian, V. (1987). Family supports in Israel. In D.K. Lipsky (Ed.), *Family supports for families with a disabled member* (pp. 37–56). New York: World Rehabilitation Fund.

Gallagher, J.J. (1956). Rejecting parents? *Exceptional Children, 22,* 273–276.

Gartner, A. (1988). Parents, no longer excluded, just ignored: Some ways to do it nicely. *Exceptional Parent, 18*(1), 41–42.

Gartner, A., & Lipsky, D.K. (1987). Beyond special education: Toward a quality system for all students. *Harvard Educational Review, 57*(4), 367–395.

Gartner, A., Lipsky, D.K., & Turnbull, A. (Eds.). (1988). *A cross-cultural conference on supports for families with a child with a disability.* New York: The Graduate School and University Center, The City University of New York.

Goldstein, S. Strickland, B., Turnbull, A.P., & Carry, L. (1980). An observational analysis of the IEP conference. *Exceptional Children, 46,* 278–286.

Granger, L., & Granger, B. (1986). *The Magic Feather.* New York: E.P. Dutton.

Hains, A.H., Fowler, S.A., & Chandler, L.K. (1988). Planning school transitions: Family and professional collaboration. *Journal of The Division for Early Childhood, 12*(2), 108–115.

Halpern, A.S. (1985). Transition: A look at the foundations. *Exceptional Children, 51*(6), 479–486.

Hanline, M.F. (1988). Making the transition to preschool: Identification of parent needs. *Journal of the Division for Early Childhood, 12*(2), 98–107.

Hanline, M.F. & Knowlton, A. (1988). A collaborative model for providing support to parents during their child's transition from infant intervention to preschool special education public school programs. *Journal of the Division for Early Childhood, 12*(2), 116–125.

Harris, A., & Wideman, D. (1988). In M. Fine & A. Asch (Eds.), *Women with Disabilities.* Philadelphia, PA: Temple University Press.

Hasazi, S.B., Gordon, L.R., & Roe, C.A. (1985). Factors associated with the employment of handicapped youth exiting high school from 1979 to 1983. *Exceptional Children, 51*(6), 455–469.

Healy, A., Keesee, P.D., & Smith, B.S. (1989). *Early services for children with special needs: Transactions for family support* (2nd ed.). Baltimore: Paul H. Brookes Publishing Co.

Hill, M.L., Wehman, P.H., Kregel, J., Banks, P.D., & Metzler, H.M.D. (1987). Employment outcomes for people with moderate and severe disabilities: An eight-year longitudinal analysis of supported competitive employment. *Journal of the Association for Persons with Severe Handicaps, 12*(3), 182–189.

Hocutt, A., & Wiegerink, R. (1983). Perspectives on parent involvement in preschool programs for handicapped children. In R. Haskins & D. Adams (Eds.), *Parent Education and Public Policy.* Norwood, NJ: Ablex.

ICD Survey III: A report card on special education. (1989). New York: Louis Harris and Associates.

Kagan, S.L., Powell, D.R., Weissbrod, B., & Zigler, E.F. (Eds.). (1987). *America's family support programs: Perspectives and prospects.* New Haven: Yale University Press.

Kelker, K., & Hagen, M. (1985). Overview: Transition issues and directions for individuals who are mentally retarded. In R.N. Ianacone & R.A. Stodden (Eds.), *Transition issues and directions* (pp. 99–122). Reston, VA: The Council for Exceptional Children.

Kirshenbaum, M. (1985). The disabled parent. In L. Aurenshine & H. Fenriquiez (Ed.), *Maternity nursing: Dimensions of change.* Belmont, CA: Wadsworth Press.

Liebert, D., Lipsky, D.K., & Horowitz, M. (1987). *Identification of parent needs for transition planning.* Unpublished manuscript.

Lipsky, D.K. (1985a). *Family supports in rehabilitation in Israel.* New York: World Rehabilitation Fund.

Lipsky, D.K. (1985b). A parental perspective on stress and coping. *American Journal of Orthopsychiatry, 55*(4), 614–617.

Lipsky, D.K. (Ed.). (1987). *Family supports for families with a disabled member.* New York: World Rehabilitation Fund.

Litvak, S., Zukas, H., & Heumann, J.E. (1987). *Attending to America: Personal assistance for independent living. A survey of attendant care programs in the United States for people of all ages with disabilities.* Berkley, CA: World Institute on Disability.

Lusthaus, E. (n.d.) *Parental response to their children with mental disabilities: Reinterpreting the negative assumptions.* Unpublished manuscript.

Lynch, E., & Stein, R. (1982). Perspectives on parent participation in special education. *Exceptional Educational Quarterly, 3,* 56–63.

Marion, R. *Educators, parents, and exceptional children.* (1981). Rockville, MD: Aspen Publishers.

McDonnell, J., Sheehan, M., & Wilcox, B. (1981). *Effective transition from school to work and adult services: A procedural handbook for parents and teachers.* Eugene, OR: University of Oregon.

McDonnell, J., Wilcox, B., Boles, S.M., & Bellamy, G.T. (1985). Transition issues facing youth with severe disabilities: Parents' perspectives. *Journal of The Association for Persons with Severe Handicaps, 11*(4), 53–60.

McKaig, K. (1986). *Beyond the threshold: Families caring for their children who have significant developmental disabilities.* New York: Community Service Society.

McKinney, J.D., & Hocutt, A. (1982). Public school involvement of parents of learning-disabled and average achievers. *Exceptional Education Quarterly, 3,* 64–73.

McKinney, L., & West, C. (1985). Family and friends. In L. McKinney (Ed.), *Extending horizons: A resource for assisting handicapped youth in their transition from vocational education to employment* (pp. 71–85). Columbus, OH: National Center for Research in Vocational Education.

McNair, J., & Rusch, F.R. (1987). Parent survey: Identification and validation of transition issues. *Interchange, 7*(4), 1–2.

Mendelsohn, B.L., & Mendelsohn, J.Z. (1986). Families in the transition process: Important partners. In L.G. Perlman & G.F. Austin (Eds.), *The transition to work and independence for youth with disabilities* (pp. 42–56). Alexandria, VA: National Rehabilitation Association.

Meyer, D.J. (1986). Fathers of handicapped children. In R.R. Fewell & P.F. Vadassy (Eds.), *Families of handicapped children: Needs and supports across the life span* (pp. 35–74). Austin, TX: PRO-ED.

Meyers, C.E., & Blacher, J. (1987). Parents' perceptions of schooling for severely handicapped children: Home and family variables. *Exceptional Children, 53*(5), 441–449.

Mithaug, D.E., Horiuchi, C.H., & McNulty, B.Z. (1987). *Parent reports on the transition of students from Colorado special education programs in 1978 and 1979.* Denver: State Education Department.

Mittler, P., Mittler, H., & McConachie, H. (1987). Family supports in England. In D.K. Lipsky (Ed.), *Family supports for families with a disabled member* (pp. 15–36). New York: World Rehabilitation Fund.

Morgan, D. (1980). Parent participation in the IEP process: Does it enhance appropriate education? *Exceptional Children, 46,* 446–454.

Moroney, R.M. (1986). *Shared responsibility: Families and social policy.* New York: Aldine.

Nevin, A., & Thousand, J. (1987). Avoiding or limiting special education referrals: Changes and challenges. In M.C. Wang, M.C. Reynolds, & H.J. Walberg (Eds.), *Handbook of special education research and practice* (Vol. 1: Learner Characteristics and Adaptive Education) (pp. 273–286). New York: Pergamon Press.

Ninth annual report to the Congress on the implementation of the Education of the Handicapped Act. (1987). Washington, DC: U.S. Department of Education.

Pieper, E. (n.d.) *Sticks and stones: The story of loving a child.* Syracuse: Human Policy Press.

Piers, G., & Singer, M. (1983). *Shame and guilt: A psychoanalytic and a cultural study.* Springfield, IL: Charles C Thomas.

PL 94-142. The Education for All Handicapped Children Act of 1975.

Rogers, R. (1986). *Caught in the act; What LEAs tell parents under the 1981 education act.* London: Centre for Studies on Integration in Education.

Rousso, H. (1984). Fostering healthy self-esteem. *Exceptional Parent, 9,* 9–11.

Rousso, H. (1988). Daughters with disabilities: Defective women or minority women? In

M. Fine & A. Asch (Eds.), *Women with disabilities*. Philadelphia, PA: Temple University Press.

Sarason, S., & Doris, J. (1979). *Educational handicap, public policy, and social history*. New York: Free Press.

Scanlon, C.A., Arick, J., & Phelps, N. (1981). Participation in the development of the IEP: Parents perspective. *Exceptional Children, 47,* 370–375.

Schill, W.J., McCarten, R.M., & Meyer, K. (1985). Youth employment: Its relationship to academic and family variables. *Journal of Vocational Behavior, 26,* 155–163.

Singer, J.D., & Butler, J.A. (1987). The Education for All Handicapped Children Act: Schools as agents of social reform. *Harvard Educational Review, 57*(2), 125–152.

Strain, P.S., & Smith, B.J. (1986). A counter-interpretation of early intervention effects: A response to Castro and Mastropieri. *Exceptional Children, 53*(3), 260–265.

Strengthening links between home and school. (1987). The Metropolitan Life Survey of the American Teacher, 1987. New York: Louis Harris and Associates, Inc.

Teltsch, K. (1988, April 4). Illinois project gives families a new way to aid disabled kin. *New York Times,* pp. A1–A10.

Tiffany Callo and the disability movement. (1988). *Disability Rag, 9*(2), 20–22.

Turnbull, A.P., Brotherson, M.J., & Summers, A.J. (1985). The impact of deinstitutionalization on families: A family systems approach. In R.H. Bruininks & K.C. Lakin (Eds.), *Living and learning in the least restrictive environment* (pp. 115–140). Baltimore: Paul H. Brookes Publishing Co.

Turnbull, A.P., & Turnbull, H.R. (1978). *Parents speak out: Views from the other side of the mirror.* Columbus, OH: Charles E. Merrill.

Turnbull, A.P., & Turnbull, III, H.R., (1982). Parental involvement in the education of handicapped children: A critique. *Mental Retardation, 20*(3), 115–122.

U.S. children and their families: Current conditions and recent trends. (1987). Washington, DC: Select Committee on Children, Youth, and Families, U.S. House of Representatives.

Vadasy, P.F. (1986). Single mothers: A social phenomenon and population in need. In R.R. Fewell & P.F. Vadasy (Eds.), *Families of handicapped children: Needs and supports across the life span* (pp. 221–249). Austin, TX: PRO-ED.

Vadasy, P.F., Fewell, R.R., Greenberg, M.T., Dermond, N.L., & Meyer, D.J. (1986). Follow-up evaluation of the effects of involvement in the fathers program. *Topics in Early Childhood Special Education, 6*(2), 16—31.

Vincent, L.J., Laten, S., Salisbury, C., Brown, P., & Baumgart, D. (1981). Family involvement in the education process of severely handicapped students: State of the art and direction for the future. In B. Wilcox & B. York (Eds.), *Quality education services for the severely handicapped: The federal investment.* Washington, DC: U.S. Department of Education.

Zigler, E., Kagan, S., & Kleigman, E. (Eds.). (1983). *Children, families and government: Perspectives on American social policy.* Cambridge: Harvard University Press.

chapter 10

Has the Law Made a Difference?
What Some Disabled Students Have to Say

Adrienne Asch

When The Rehabilitation Act of 1973 and the Education for All Handicapped Children Act of 1975 were passed, I believed wonderful things would happen for people with disabilities. I pictured disabled children finally going to school with nondisabled students of their age and grade. I pictured disabled and nondisabled children taking the same classes, reading the same books, and taking the same tests. I pictured them participating in the same clubs, sometimes becoming friends and other times not, getting into the same scrapes, and learning how to solve the same problems. I believed that the integrated education that had been atypical for me and other blind students of New Jersey in the 1950s and 1960s would be standard and unremarkable for this generation of disabled students. I assumed that today's high school graduates and college students would have experiences comparable to or better than my own of many years ago. Elsewhere I have described some of the trials and triumphs of my own experience as a blind child in a public school with sighted children (Ferguson & Asch, in press), and I assumed that what my parents and I had had to fight for would now be the right of all disabled youth.

In the 1980s, I find that my expectations are only sometimes met. By and large, disabled students still face physical separation, or even if they are physically integrated, many still face social isolation from the nondisabled school population. Furthermore, we know woefully little about how disabled people of yesterday or today feel about their school experiences. In these pages, I reflect on what I and other disabled people who supported the legislation had wanted it to achieve and present what some articulate disabled students have to say about how their experience compares with the promise.

At the outset, I should make clear that these reflections and the supporting data are drawn neither from the survey findings of a national sample of disabled elementary and secondary school students from Louis Harris and Associates (ICD survey III, 1989), nor from a selected sample of college-bound students surveyed by the Educational Testing Service (ETS). They are acquired through 20 years of reading and writing, and through participating and observing in the field of disability issues. Thus, I have had the opportunity to learn from disabled young people and adults during formal conference presentations, informal meetings, in-depth interviews, group discussions, brief conversations, and scattered writings. These thoughts also result from discussions with parents of today's disabled students, as well as with professionals in elementary, secondary, and postsecondary education who have worked with nondisabled and disabled students.

For two reasons, I focus on those people whose primary disabling condition is physical or sensory. First, I have had greater personal, professional, and political experience with that portion of the disabled population. My second reason for this focus is that I am concerned that in the necessary and appropriate current attention to educating and integrating people whose disabling conditions affect intellectual capacity, the learning process, or emotional well-being and behavior, professionals may conclude that all is well for that smaller group of youngsters whose "only" problems are in seeing, hearing, managing objects, or walking. All is not well, and although for some it is definitely better than what disabled people of yesterday faced, for others, it is either the replica of what people hated or something different but also negative.

My yardstick is part common sense and part professional expertise. School is the place where young people discover themselves through the development of skills and personal relationships. We hope that students will have the chance to learn not merely subject matter but also the necessary skills to acquire more information on their own, or in Eriksonian terms, a sense of mastery and of industry. In school, young people learn how to deal with others their own age and with adults other than their parents. They also learn how to develop friendships, and learn who they are and what values they hold. This knowledge is acquired partly by exposure to many people with a range of interests and values. My yardstick for judging whether today's disabled students are getting what they should out of school is one that concentrates on mastery of skills and knowledge for functioning in the world, on social life and relationships, and on a sense of personal identity. My question is not: Is mainstreaming working? PL 94-142 is not a law solely about mainstreaming. My question is: Do disabled people, their parents, educators, and disabled adults feel that the law, with its range of options, affords disabled students an educational experience comparable to that of their nondisabled counterparts? A corollary question is this: Should I and others who have advocated maximal integration rethink our position in light of what we are learning, or are the problems ones of implementation or practice and not of basic philosophy? If the goal of maximal integration is to be pursued, does the entire educational system for all students—disabled and nondisabled—need to be revamped, or can disabled youngsters flourish in the existing system with all its flaws?

A PRELIMINARY REPORT CARD

Academic Life: Separate But Not Equal

Recent professional and popular literature has decried the academic achievements of the nation's typical student in general education and has not even commented on the performance of the student body certified as receiving special education. Authorities have blamed the students' generally poor performance on school curricula, the lack of parental commitment, the low pay and low prestige of the teaching profession, its tendency to attract ill-prepared and unimaginative people to the job, and more. Schools may be falling down on the job for the nondisabled student, but is the disabled student getting at least as much as his or her nondisabled counterpart? Does the academic experience vary with the type of disability or educational placement? Is the disabled student of today getting more than a student with a similar disability educated before PL 94-142?

With very rare exceptions, today's adults with disabilities who recall segregated facilities, separate classes, or home instruction cannot say enough about how inadequate was their academic training. They compare their education with that of siblings or neighbors who were not disabled and speak only of the gaps. For example, they mention subjects, such as science, that they never studied, maps they never saw, field trips they never took, books that were never available, assignments that were often too easy, expectations of their capacity (by nearly all teachers) that were too low. Given the dismal descriptions of the previous era, one would expect that disabled students who received most of their elementary and secondary school education in the 1980s must be getting better opportunities. For those disabled people who have spent these years placed in separate schools or separate classes, many of the complaints are the same. Those in "regular" classes believe themselves better off than segregated disabled students, but they frequently feel disadvantaged compared to their nondisabled classmates.

Separate But Not Equal Running throughout my conversations with disabled students, parents, or professionals is the message that today's education is still largely separate and rarely equal. Separate means not only the segregated school or class but the *separate standards* used to measure the opportunities provided, or the progress made, by the student with a disability who is physically integrated. Whether speaking of such "basics" as reading, writing, mathematics, science labs, organizing ideas and organizing time, or such "frills" as physical education, field trips, computer literacy, art, music, home economics, industrial arts, driver education, or enrichment programs, the nation's disabled students are deprived. In many instances, standards of attendance, discipline, participation, and performance are different and lower for disabled students than for nondisabled members of the same class, grade level, school district, or state.

Adapting without Patronizing Unanimously, disabled students and parents of students in every educational setting complain that adapting or accommodating to disability all too often results in lowered expectations and patronization. Instead, they contend that disability sometimes requires modification and adaptation but never patronization. Accommodating without patronizing requires students, their parents, fellow classmates, and professionals to adopt a standard of inclusion in activities and of expectations of meeting norms of performance set for the activity. Variations from inclusion and performance norms should be the exception, not the rule, and should be accepted only after all involved have assessed the environment and activity carefully to determine how and under what circumstances and with what consequences should disability be considered relevant. For the disabled child and his or her parent, such evaluations begin long before school in deciding how and with whom the child will play. They last into all adult life in such areas as employment, friendship, family life, and community involvement. Some decisions are relatively straightforward; others are difficult, subtle, and vary with the same individual over time and between individuals with the same type and level of impairment.

Students and parents have a wealth of illustrations of appropriate, and more often inappropriate, accommodation to disability. Pat, Michelle, and Wendy, who attend different New York City high schools and who have mobility impairments from spina bifida, congenital limb deficiency, and cerebral palsy, respectively, all told of being penalized for school absences or class lateness because of elevator or schoolbus problems. Pat and Wendy received low grades when they were late for classes because elevators packed with teachers and nondisabled students failed to stop for them. Michelle failed to get credit for a semester of school because the special education bus was irregular in picking her up, and she was frequently absent. In these instances, the students were penalized when neither their motivation nor their disabilities, but the unaccommodating environment, was to blame.

Wendy provided another example of inappropriate handling of her disability. "When I took one of my first mainstream courses in ninth grade, I was absent because of bladder infections and missed a lot of book reports. I was not marked down when other students would have failed. I spoke with the teacher and said that I didn't need extra help, that I wanted to earn my grade. Then she treated me the same." Although a more sensible solution would have been to give Wendy, as any other student who missed work because of illness, the opportunity to complete the work, Wendy's protest demonstrates what today's disabled students still face in integrated as well as segregated settings. Teachers' lowered expectations and grading policies that over-reward disabled students lead to distorted views for the student her- or himself. Cynthia said: "You begin to question yourself. Are you smart, or are they making exceptions? It confuses you."

Zach, a legally blind college student from a Philadelphia suburb, said that he was often excused from requirements in physics and other classes because his teachers didn't want to take the time to explain lab work, material on the blackboard, or other things to him that he could not see. "Looking back on it now, I think my teachers couldn't do enough to let me out of things. I didn't care enough to challenge them." In Zach's case, fearful or resentful teachers may have believed that giving a student with a disability help after class was not as much a part of ordinary teaching responsibility as providing similar help to a nondisabled student. Had his teachers believed in his right to the same opportunities for learning as his classmates, they could not have neglected their educational obligations to him by the convenient method of exempting him from course requirements.

Lowered expectations are at least as common for professionals in special education as for the public school teacher meeting his or her first deaf, blind, or mobility-disabled student in the typical school program. Special educators tell Chicago public school teachers that blind students should be expected to complete only half as many math problems as their sighted classmates. In comparing separate schools to integrated programs, students interviewed by Marjorie Ragosta of the Educational Testing Service had various comments. As one student observed: "I think the teachers in my school (a residential school for the blind) were too easy and didn't give enough academic classes to prepare those of us who decided to go to college." "A special environment makes it all the more difficult to adjust to college or work. I think blind students would be better prepared in a public school." A student who is deaf said: "My advice to hearing impaired students is to go to regular public schools. Teach others to adapt to you."

Fortunately, some students receive quality education in public school programs that are characterized by perceptive, creative adaptation and a minimum of patronization. Annee, a senior from a small rural district in Washington State, was proud of the opportunities she had received. Her blindness did not stop her from conducting lab work in chemistry or from being selected to participate in a 2-month exchange student program in Latin America through the American Field Service. April, a high school senior from a city in South Carolina, who is blind, participated in much of her school's physical education program. Her itinerant teacher demonstrated the physical skills she needed in order to participate in activities, and her classmates took over from there by guiding her when she ran and by warning her of balls she couldn't see during volleyball games.

A mother persuaded the school to furnish her 7-year-old daughter who was blind with gymnastics, a physical education activity available to sighted students. The youngster gained not only skill and exercise but also the admiration of her classmates. "Now they see that she can *do* things and not just sit around."

Genuine commitment to including the student with a disability in the life of the class requires using teaching techniques that do not impose avoidable hardship on such a student. Many people complain of how teachers do not face the class during lectures but move around the room, often out of the line of vision of the student who must lip-read. Or, teachers fail to speak what is being written on blackboards so that the blind or partially sighted student can keep abreast of what is happening. A commitment to inclusion is a commitment to minimizing or eliminating such practices. During the period of many years that may be required for teachers to retrain themselves out of long established patterns, class members must be encouraged to realize that providing their classmates with disabilities with missing information is a legitimate, not burdensome, part of class activity.

Other apparently harmless accommodations can deprive students of achieving their full potential. If taking notes and participating during classroom lectures and discussions are essential for the nondisabled student, they are equally important for the one with a disability. The Supreme Court erred when it decided in the case of Amy Rowley that amplification and tutoring were as adequate as a full-time interpreter. It is common for fellow students to act as note takers for students with hearing, visual, and motor disabilities. Students who are deaf may be provided with note takers or tutors; providing interpreters might make it possible to dispense with both. If students are to develop the ability to sift out the essential from the illustrative in a lecture, they must themselves have the full text of that lecture communicated to them. If they are to join in class discussions, they must know what other students have said. For the student who must get information from lip-reading or sign, the only efficient and equivalent substitute for hearing is the interpreted class lecture and discussion. By giving the student who is deaf all that is spoken in the classroom, whether by teacher or fellow students, the interpreter provides the student information comparable to that provided the hearing students, and the student learning through lip-reading or sign is placed on a par with the rest of the group for knowing all that is going on in the room. Interpreters give deaf students an equal chance at classroom life. Note takers and tutors may be less expensive for the school but more costly for the student.

Note taking is itself a critical skill, and disabled students should be given the means to take their own notes rather than being forced to rely on others' judgments of what is important. Equip students whose manual, hearing, or visual disabilities preclude note taking in print or braille with silent lap top computers and teach them to touch-type. If manual disability precludes using a computer, resort to tape recorders with steno masks so that students can speak their notes into a tape recorder without being heard by those around them. Purporting to solve the note-taking problem by letting students tape lectures for study at home is efficient only for the school and not for the student. Students should have the equipment they need to do work in class during the class period itself.

Testing standards for disabled students also present problems of accommodation that can become patronizing and can actually harm the student in future life and work. Many teachers conclude that the blind student or the student with manual disabilities cannot write adequately and should take oral exams. If the purpose of a test is to determine whether the student can express ideas in clear, organized, uninterrupted discourse, an oral exam does not demonstrate the same abilities as those measured in the written tests taken by the others in a class. If the school intends to teach students how to write, it must give that same training to the disabled members of the class. Typing, dictating to others, tape recording a prepared answer, or taking additional time to write or type slowly would all give the student the chance to demonstrate the skill purportedly being measured by the test.

A more vexing question about testing is the matter of how much, if any, additional time should be allowed for the student whose motor or visual disability appears to cause the student to work more slowly than the rest of the class. Before deciding the question of granting additional time, teachers should first determine whether better equipment and techniques would put the disabled student on a footing that would be equal to the nondisabled. If so, provide appropriate equipment, test media, and testing conditions and do not modify time. If the student with a disability simply cannot accomplish as much classwork in the time allotted the rest of the class, decide whether time matters for anything more than the convenience of class schedules of teachers and students. If it is really more important to see what a student can communicate, regardless of how long it takes, modify time. If, for some reason, time matters to the test's purpose, then insist that disabled students be measured within the equivalent time parameters.

Sometimes schools think they are appropriately adapting to and meeting the needs of a student with a disability by providing him or her with one-to-one aides during the school day. A student who is deaf may very well need an interpreter throughout the day, and one who has spina bifida may need someone's assistance in catheterization. Students who cannot manipulate books, paper, or art materials, or who cannot feed themselves, will need assistance at mealtimes or at other parts of the class day. Aides should accompany the student only during activities in which individual assistance is essential, and should never mediate between the disabled student and his or her teacher and classmates. Many schools inappropriately provide the mobility-disabled or visually-disabled student an adult to act as wheelchair pusher, guide, or amanuensis rather than equipping the student with an electric wheelchair, a typewriter, and the skill of touch-typing, or instruction in cane travel. The student with a disability deserves to master skills for as much independence as possible, and providing aides or even assigning students as guides, wheelchair pushers, and writers of assignments may needlessly thwart development of self-sufficiency or discourage typical interactions with classmates and adults.

Choosing the Educational Setting The preceding discussion about appropriate accommodation presumes that the student who needs to learn lip reading, sign language, braille, or cane travel does so. Although I have met no students or parents who favor increased segregated schooling, students, their parents, and concerned adults with disabilities voice many reservations about whether any educational setting provides the basic skills for learning and living. Some members of leading disability rights organizations noted for advocacy of civil rights and equal opportunity, believe that current integrated programs give disabled youth neither the skills nor the attitudes about disability to permit adequate functioning. They wonder whether some system of group teaching of skills and attitudes for parts of the day, or for months, or years, is needed to prepare disabled youth for life in the mainstream.

Reports from students and their parents in New York and other urban districts that currently concentrate disabled students in particular classes and schools for some or all of their education do not suggest that such plans are successfully teaching either skills or positive attitudes. In New York, students with physical, visual, or hearing disabilities typically are not placed in classes with nondisabled students of their age and grade. Rather, they start out in special education classes that often persist in whole or in part through high school. As of 1988, not all New York City schools are architecturally accessible, thus limiting some people's options to those schools with elevators. Selected schools thus become the site for large groups of students with physical disabilities, who often are grouped together in special education classes. For the administrative convenience of the Board of Education and not as a consequence of environmental barriers or educational logic, blind and partially sighted students from throughout a borough are bussed to a few schools and grouped in a "braille room," even if they attend some or all of their classes with nondisabled students.

Some New York students and parents have succeeded in winning their battles for total integration, but they are the exception and not the rule. Students must prove themselves worthy of integration both by protesting their placements and by achieving superior academic records in the classes for disabled youth. Pat, who emigrated to this country from South America at age 9, said that most of her elementary and junior high school years were spent in special education courses that were far too easy. Comparing special education with mainstream classes, she said: "In ninth grade I had four special education classes. They were very, very easy. I told my mother I wanted out. Now that I'm in all mainstreamed classes, even homeroom, I don't think I'm favored because I'm disabled. I have to work for my grades. Some other disabled kids are passed along."

Currently high school juniors, Dorris and Wendy still spend a portion of their time in special education classes such as mathematics, English, acting, physical education, and homeroom. When asked to evaluate how disabled students fare in the New York schools, Wendy said, "Most kids are below average and pass with exceptionally high marks because they're disabled. Special education doesn't do any good. It passes you anyway with simple work." Dorris had never tried to take acting classes with nondisabled students, although she liked her adapted acting class and would have enjoyed the chance to participate with more of her schoolmates. Creating adapted classes makes it harder for people to imagine themselves entering the mainstream setting.

Annee, who was totally integrated into her public school, favorably contrasted her opportunities with those available at her state's school for the blind. Roy, a recent graduate of a school for the blind in the Midwest, said: "I would go home and see friends at home and find out what they were doing that I had never done. I had no chance to take calculus or chemistry in high school." During spirited discussion at the 1988 National Federation of the Blind Convention on the problems in educating blind students, one woman remarked to me: "I'm the mother of three children with RP [retinitis pigmentosa]. I'm not completely happy with what they are getting in the public schools, but I don't want them away in a residential school and to be a weekend mom. I'd rather fight to get what they need where they are."

Marjorie Ragosta of the Educational Testing Service, who interviewed several students who were deaf or who had significant hearing impairments, reported that most preferred the struggle to keep up with academic work in public school with hearing students to the alternative of special schools or classes for deaf students (M. Ragosta, personal communication, June 16, 1988). "You learn more with hearing kids when you are mainstreamed, and you get the background for college." A California student who is deaf told her that he chose the mainstream program because he thought it would be a better program. He could keep up because he had an interpreter with him at all times. "The education was good. Not belonging was bad. I socialized with deaf friends after school."

Although many of those in special classes saw no reason why they were there, they participated rarely, if at all, in the IEP (individualized education program) meetings that might have affected their placements. Similarly, many of the parents did not participate. Most students, whether satisfied or dissatisfied with their education, had failed to make use of the IEP process, or if they had been involved with it, had considered it a waste of time. Despite indications of motivation, intelligence, and interest in their schooling, they seemed never to have been informed that the IEP process represented an available and important vehicle for influencing their own education. If IEPs are to be retained, educators should work to ensure that students and parents realize the values of the IEP process and thus attend and participate actively in designing the program.

IEPs or PEAs (Programs for Educational Accessibility) Students with motor, visual, or hearing impairments logically should require little or no special programming in order to be successfully functioning members of the first, fifth, or twelfth grade. Such a statement takes the following features for granted, features that frequently are missing from the school situation:

A barrier-free school with classrooms and classroom furniture and equipment
Cafeteria, auditorium, library, schoolyard, and physical education facilities accessible to and usable by people with disabilities
Reading and writing instruction and materials in media other than standard print
Oral communication made understandable to people with hearing impairments

If schools met these criteria, it could be contended that for no child would the free appropriate public education in the least restrictive environment mean segregated day or residential programming or more than minimal time spent in separate classes with only disabled students. It could also be argued that no child with a motor disability would ever require an individualized educational program, and that programs for those with sensory impairments would be necessary only to ensure that they acquired the basic skills needed for independent functioning within the class and school. Such skills include: 1) fluency in comprehending and expressing themselves either orally or in sign, 2) fluency in reading and writing for people who are deaf or who have hearing impairments, and 3) proficiency in reading, writing, and traveling around the school for people who are blind or who have visual disabilities. After all, as Alan Gartner succinctly puts it: "There is no spina bifida spelling" (A. Gartner, personal communication, November 8, 1984). There is also no algebra or spelling for the deaf or blind.

In thinking about today's education for disabled students, I have argued that either every child (disabled or not) needs an IEP, or that no one does. If the spirit of Section 504 animated the educational system, professionals would develop plans not for individual disabled children but for bringing schooling environments into conformance. It is not so much that the child needs individualized evaluations and goals with which to measure progress, but that the school environment needs evaluations and goals with which to measure its ability to serve all its students, including those with disabilities. I would therefore urge educators to construct what I am coining Programs for Educational Accessibility (PEAs) and to locate the problem where it belongs: in program accessibility and in the attitudinal barriers of teachers, and not in the disabilities and deficits of students.

Life Beyond the Classroom

Socially: we were isolated. Symbolically, and appropriate to the prevailing attitudes, the handicapped and retarded classrooms were tucked away in a corner of the school basement. Our only activity with other children was the weekly school assembly. We never participated in any school program. We watched. Although the school lunchroom was also in the basement, we ate lunch in our classrooms. . . . Summing it up, the only contact we had with the normal children was visual. On these occasions I can report my own feelings: envy. Given the loud, clear message that was daily being delivered to them, I feel quite confident that I can also report their feelings: yuch"! (B. Davidson, personal communication, October 29, 1987).

This poignant statement captures the social life of many who were educated in special classes in public schools or in partly integrated, partly segregated public school programs of 40, 30, or 20 years ago. Reflecting on the lives of many disabled people in their late twenties and thirties who today seek assistance with independent living, Julie Shaw Cole (1988) vividly describes what many such students failed to get from their school days:

. . . those basic skills when you beat up a pal on the playground, choose up sides for sandlot ball, when you sit around a daycamp snickering over dirty stories you just barely understand; when you wrestle after a birthday party waiting for your mom. . . . the Halloween raids, sleep-overs, cliques in high school. . . . Even the smallest occasions for honing those kinds of social skills are often missing from the lives of many people who are today seeking independent living. (p. 15)

By contrast to the social isolation, loneliness, and ever-present sense of rejection faced by disabled adults in special classes in public schools, some aspects of residential or special school life in programs for blind, deaf, or physically disabled students were more tolerable. The range of activities may not have compared favorably with those offered the typical public school student, and the enforced segregation often engendered feelings of inferiority, fear of the "normal," and apprehension about the world beyond school. Nonetheless, some of the segregated schools for disabled students provided opportunities to participate in athletics, art and music programs, student government, the newspaper, clubs, and dances resembling those of public schools. In addition, the segregated disabled students of necessity created their own cliques and teams, had some friendships, and learned how to compete with or confide in one another.

Many of those who have become involved in extracurricular activities believe that exploring their interests and making friends have been invaluable activities that were at least as crucial to them as any academic accomplishments. For me, and for other disabled people who grew up in the 1950s and 1960s, joining in school chorus, student government, debating, sports, youth groups, or scouting profoundly influenced our lives. Unfortunately, even many of those who were academically successful in the mainstream of 20 and 30 years ago recall the lack of opportunity for clubs, sports, and friends. As I have heard about the lives of today's disabled youth, I again appreciate my relatively enjoyable and active after-school life and ask what conditions favor some people's participation and thwart that of others.

After-School Activities Those disabled students who are the most pleased with their school experiences generally participated in after-school activities alongside disabled or nondisabled peers and formed at least some friendships. The students whose teachers and schools expected the most from them academically were often, although not always, the happiest about their social lives. Schools that expect disabled students to participate and perform on a par with nondisabled students communicate an important message that facilitates social integration: that regardless of physical characteristics and disabilities, students are more similar than different.

April, a bubbly graduate of a South Carolina city high school who is blind, put it this way:

If a teacher treats me normally, that helps a lot of students. They realize this is just a normal person. We don't have to be especially nice to this person like they're going to get offended or to act as if this person's going to break. Clubs helped a lot. Being outside of the classroom itself and in extracurricular activities is good. You get to do a lot of things, to talk about a lot of things besides what you're doing in class that day.

Of course, many students with or without disabilities may prefer to do other things with their free time than to join in structured activities. However, participating in some organized group activities may be one of the best ways for people with disabilities to break down the barriers of fear and awkwardness that may exist between themselves and nondisabled classmates. Mere classroom participation, no matter how full and exemplary, may not be enough. Participation in the interest group, or after-school project, as well as attendance at plays, sporting events, or dances, can be ready-made vehicles for letting people know that a disabled student is interested in the world, in others, in fun and good times, and in making friends.

School budgets and overworked faculty and administrators often have failed to take into consideration that access to an integrated and appropriate education for disabled students includes access to the school's nonacademic life. Lack of interpreters for after-school activities and rigid schoolbus schedules have prevented many people who are deaf or who must take special transportation from joining clubs or attending school events. Many people who are deaf have spoken of great isolation in the public school, because they are prevented from participating in groups by the unavailability of interpreters for anything beyond classroom work. The writings of Nancy Becker (1984) and Frank Bowe (1987) attest to the loneliness some people who are deaf have experienced during mainstream public school life, and Marjorie Ragosta's interviews with recent high school graduates bear out the fact that PL 94-142 as implemented has not aided those deaf students who wish to join the give-and-take of nonacademic life. "You don't get a chance to socialize with other people," is Ragosta's summary of her interviews with deaf and hearing-impaired students from around the country.

Dorris, a junior in a New York City public school who uses a wheelchair and is required to ride the special education bus, was unable to join her school Spanish club even though it is her favorite subject. "It meets after school, and I would like to stay, but I would have no transportation. I take the schoolbus, and it leaves right after school gets out." Wendy, also mobility-impaired, talked of missing plays, sporting events, programs about college, and her yearbook picture because of the schoolbus schedule. Virtually all disabled students in New York are required to use the special education buses, all of which pick them up immediately after school, leaving them no way to join in the after-school life of their classmates. Because many students who are blind do not receive training in independent mobility until very late in high school, they too, are rendered captives of the special education system of transportation.

Remembering my own enthusiastic participation in debating, drama club, and high school music groups, I was shocked and appalled to discover how many people were prevented from enjoying similar activities by the transportation restrictions. I then remembered my own simple solution of negotiating with the cab driver hired by the school to merely pick me up 2 hours later two afternoons a week. On days when this was impossible, I paid for a cab myself, or, after some friends learned to drive, got rides from them. Such simple solutions were born of a middle-class family and a small town, where accommodation meant a few telephone calls, and not a 10-page policy in quadruplicate moving through innumerable layers of bureaucracy and requiring a major policy and budgetary decision.

Today, students from middle-class backgrounds and smaller communities are similarly advantaged. They too, are more likely to find ways to arrange simple accommodations for themselves that permit greater participation. Annee, for example, said that her community was not particularly welcoming to new people, but that her family had been there for years and was well-known, and consequently, people were generally willing to include her in everything going on in the school. Leslie, an eighth grader with vision and hearing disabilities who attends a private school in a New York suburb, has joined service clubs at her school and has signed up for weekend playwriting courses.

The yearning for an ordinary social and recreational life by many excluded students is obvious not only from their comments during discussions but also from their enthusiastic participation in any program that provides transportation or communication for them. Generally, this has meant programs serving exclusively people with disabilities, forcing them into segregated recreation. Those who are deaf, even if fully involved in classes with nondisabled students, join with others who are deaf after school because there is no problem communicating. For many disabled youth throughout the nation, the only form of recreation is the segregated scout troop, sporting event, or other program or summer camp of a philanthropic agency serving only the disabled. A notable New York exception that should inspire other communities and school systems is that of The Door, a city multi-service center for youth that has set out to ensure the participation of those with disabilities in all its programs. By publicizing its availability to adolescents and young adults with disabilities, and by providing such services as transportation to and from programs, The Door has become an important resource for developing the interests and the social lives of disabled youth. To the extent that schools expect to do such things for their nondisabled students, they fail in their responsibilities by not working to bring their disabled students into organized activities.

Forming Friendships Parents and professionals automatically assume that typical children need friendships. Being liked and having playmates and confidantes preoccupies most children for some or all of the time when they are growing up. Such matters concern most parents as well, as I witnessed recently when a friend told me that she would soon have to go back into therapy for herself if she could not stop worrying about how many play dates and party invitations her 4-year-old son received. "I'm always asking him," she said. "He's much better about it and says, 'Ma, why are you asking me all these silly questions?'"

The same concerns preoccupy disabled youth, as reflected in their conversations and in the autobiographies of scores of adults (Asch & Sacks, 1983; Brightman, 1984; Hahn, 1983; Heinrich & Kriegel, 1960). Yet, some parents, and many professionals, may feel that whether disabled youth make friends warrants less of their attention than whether a nondisabled child does so. Parental and professional attitudes on this matter could stem from many sources. They may believe friendships are less important to disabled youth than to others. They may feel that academic work, medical care, and the demands of physical or speech therapy are more important than friendships. Similarly, they may feel learning sign and lip reading, cane travel, or Braille are higher priorities for the student—and, thus, their time with the student—than having a social life. They may feel it inappropriate for adults to concern themselves with a problem that young people themselves must resolve. Or they may, without realizing it, assume that genuine intimacy and friendship between disabled and nondisabled people or between disabled people is beyond the reach of persons with disabilities. Further, they may feel that loneliness is simply something that goes with disability and something disabled people must "accept" about their situation.

Researchers who have studied children's friendships and young people's sexuality have almost never concerned themselves with the friendships or dating behavior of disabled youth, and students of disability have given scant attention to the arenas of friendship and romantic love in the lives of disabled youth or adults. (See Browne, Connors, & Stern, 1985; Fisher & Galler, 1988; Mest, 1988; Pogrebin, 1987; Rousso, 1988; and Schneider, 1988 for a discussion of these topics.) Sociologist Constantina Safilios-Rothschild (1970, 1982) maintains that disabled people will be more successful at integrating themselves into school, work, or community life than at finding true friendship or love, especially if they seek such relationships with nondisabled people.

Rationales for ending racial and sex discrimination have included increasing the opportunities for achievement of oppressed groups and ameliorating the psychological consequences of second-class treatment. Some researchers also hoped that ongoing positive contact between blacks and whites and females and males would promote better personal relationships between members of these groups. Blacks did not emphasize any aspirations for friendships with whites and did everything they could to make clear that ending school or housing segregation was not beginning wholesale intermarriage. Similarly, advocates of coed Little League teams were not advocates for neutering male-female relationships. It is necessary to understand the expectation and the experience of disabled youth resulting from PL 94-142 when it comes to relationships with people who have and do not have disabilities.

Disabled children generally grow up in families with nondisabled parents and siblings. They live in neighborhoods with nondisabled people. Most of their parents' friends do not have disabilities. Historically, people with disabilities have wanted friendships with nondisabled people whether or not they had friends with disabilities. Sometimes they have spurned others with disabilities because they were taught to devalue their own disability and consequently to devalue others with this ugly or shameful characteristic.

My own experience shapes my reflections on what I have heard about the social lives of disabled young people today. I feel very fortunate to have grown up knowing and becoming friends with children who were disabled and children who were not. Because my family valued having friends and a social life, they took seriously my interests in having a social life, and worked with me and with the school to encourage them. Parent narratives and autobiographies of disabled people all attest to the fact that building friendships can be especially difficult for the disabled person, but that active effort by parents, school personnel, and disabled children can make it happen (Ferguson & Asch, in press; Killilea, 1952, 1963; Massie & Massie, 1984; Zimmerman, 1984). Without active efforts, it is unlikely that simple proximity in class or clubs will be enough to turn acquaintances into friends.

Friendships with Nondisabled Classmates It would be gratifying to provide data and policy recommendations in this section regarding all of the factors that influence the ability of the disabled student to form what he or she considers satisfying friendships with nondisabled counterparts. It would be gratifying to report solid conclusions about the influence of such factors as age, type of disability, gender, participation in activities, assertiveness on the part of the student or the parent, the student's attitude about disability, the student's skills in functioning within the limits disability imposes, the size of the school, the teachers' attitudes toward disabled students, the amount of class time spent in group projects, teacher sensitivity to group dynamics, and school concern with intergroup relations. It would also be gratifying to know whether the disabled student's perception of his or her own experience would be confirmed by nondisabled people in their own class or school. Would whatever disabled people as a group say about their own experiences differ from what a group of nondisabled students would say about their own experiences? (When disabled teenagers say they weren't in the "in crowd," for example, how different is that from what virtually all nondisabled teenagers would say about their own experiences? Does the "in crowd" know it is the "in crowd"?)

I cannot provide these answers, but I can give some impressions and can say that the variables I have listed probably are among the ones that matter. If disabled youth report that they do not have friends and do not feel they fit in, they and everyone else they know can easily attribute their situations to the disability itself rather than to their own attitudes, the school environment, their own skills, or the like. A blind man in his early thirties, educated in a New Jersey public school nearly identical in student composition and size to mine of 10 years earlier, attributed his sense of isolation to his blindness until he returned from a week-long meeting of blind people. Conversations with them made him realize that many people were far more comfortable with people than he, that he had difficulty socializing with blind people as well as with sighted people, and that other blind people's experiences in school differed from his. "When you're blind, it's easy to blame things on blindness. Probably lots of other people don't feel they fit in, but they don't have such a convenient thing to hang it on. I have to realize that there are other things going on with me than just blindness alone."

I can safely say the following: many, perhaps most, people with disabilities feel some frustration and disappointment with their place in the social world of the mainstream school, but many of these same people do make friends. Some people with disabilities have made and continue to make friends with whom they are happy among their nondisabled classmates. They see those friends both in school and out, they participate in a range of activities, and they feel valued by those friends. Some of those friendships survive many years after people leave school, and after they go on to college or work, and through marriage, divorce, children, and new lives. Two months ago, Dana, a day-care center director from New England, spent a weekend in the big city with her lifelong best friend, Jean, a blind woman who works with senior citizens. Their friendship goes back to grade school, when they were playing pranks on their parents, skipping school, and getting into drugs in high school, and they have stayed friends through 20 years of being in separate places.

That some people with disabilities make friends underscores that more can. It is as important to learn about the ones who do as those who don't to see what lessons can be imparted to students, faculty, and parents about making things easier for the disabled children of the future. Marjorie Ragosta reports a nearly universal sense of isolation among deaf students in school with hearing students. "It's very lonesome," she says of their experience. She spoke with students fluent in English, fluent in sign, and fluent in both, and with those who were prelingually and postlingually deaf. In general, the mode of communication and the age of onset of the deafness did not differentiate those who felt isolated from those who did not. Yet one or two of the deaf students reported their friendships with their classmates as the most satisfying part of their school experiences. One deaf student who was fluent in English described his school experiences like this: "I felt good about being needed by my peers, being trusted and looked up to as a friend. I was not in a clique, but I got along with everyone. I think my personality was rounded out to make up for my academic weaknesses."

If we care about promoting friendships between disabled and nondisabled students, the following appear crucial:

The amount of integration

The expectation that the disabled student meet class norms of participation, behavior, and cooperation

Creation of situations where the disabled student must interact in projects with nondisabled classmates and can make a positive contribution

Assertiveness on the part of parents when children are young to create opportunities for children to play with others outside of school

Similar assertiveness by the disabled student to create opportunities if others do not initiate them

Equipping disabled students with skills to function as independently as possible in the widest possible range of activities

An accessible environment for communication, mobility, and transportation

Being a member of the second, fifth, or twelfth grade, and not a part-timer in a science class nor a member of the "braille room," or the "health class," is far better for the disabled student and his or her nondisabled schoolmates. If the disabled student is viewed and views himself as a member of that class, the stigma of disability is not compounded by that of the "special ed" label. Clustering groups of disabled students in a school class is a disaster for true acceptance by the nondisabled students, not much different today than the "yuch" of 40 years ago which Betty Davidson described. Pat, who went through high school mainstreamed in New York City, unlike most of the disabled people she knows, says about her relationships with her nondisabled classmates: "They accept me when they see that I can do the work. They are surprised that I'm not in the special ed. classes, but when they see I can do the work, it's okay." Wendy, whose mobility disability is not readily apparent but whose membership in special education is known to her classmates, says that she makes friends more easily if she first gets to know them in the halls. "My classmates know I'm in special ed, and they treat me as if I'm different." Dorris, who as a junior has spent almost all her time in segregated classes, says: "I had to make the first move in the mainstreaming, and I didn't know how to interact. I introduce myself and sit next to a friendly person."

The class itself can provide opportunities for getting to know other students if teachers create group projects and assist each student in finding tasks they can perform as well as tasks on which they need help from others. A seventh grade teacher turned my school life around by focusing our class social studies year on a project on Washington, DC. Working together on reports on history of the city, building models of its structures, and planning a 2-day field trip did wonders for all of us as a class, and for me as a member of it. A deaf student interviewed by Marjorie Ragosta spoke of how she got to know others because students sought her out on projects where communication was important. She had developed her own language skills sufficiently to help hearing people in some of their work. The mothers of 7-year-old Jo and 8-year-old Sherri, who are blind, each expressed pleasure in their daughters' friendships with their classmates. They talked about how their daughters, one from Maine and one from Michigan, integrated into classes from first grade, had learned to play with other students, tried to keep up in outdoor games, and were invited to other children's houses for parties and sleep-overs.

Integration is not enough. This is evident from the comments of the man who is blind whom I described earlier. It is also evident from the comments of

Leslie, who, in eighth grade, feels that she has no real friends with whom to do things outside of school. Pat and Wendy also feel that the friendships they have made in school have not carried over into socializing much beyond school activities. Pat says, "I don't see them outside schools, but I'd like to. I'd like to be invited to go out, but they don't ask. I say I'd like to go, but they don't ask." Wendy believes they don't ask because, "They think you'll fall." Wendy says that her school friends forget that she has to walk more slowly than they, and that she has trouble with curbs. They get impatient and make her feel that it's too much trouble to have her with them.

At least three crucial factors are amenable to action by parents, the disabled person, school personnel, and the larger society: 1) an environment that does not itself put barriers in the way, 2) the optimal skills for functioning within the limits of disability, and 3) assertiveness on the part of parents and the disabled person. No matter how many friends Dorris, Wendy, and Pat make in school, they must contend with inaccessible streets and transportation. Even if their schoolmates wanted to invite them to a movie, theaters are inaccessible. Similarly, public buses and subways have not been designed for someone using crutches or a wheelchair, or for someone who cannot walk stairs. Leslie, whose disabilities of sight and hearing do not preclude her from following conversation or participating in classroom life, does not have the same environmental restraints but appears constrained, as are the others, from taking initiative. Of those disabled students who have formed friendships with schoolmates that included doing things outside of school, all of them (or their parents) took the initiative to get things started. When they were young, their parents invited neighborhood children into their yards and invited people to their houses. As students get older, they take over the initiating role.

Ability to take initiative depends on the matter of skills and clarity about the place of disability in one's life. People who hide their disabilities or try to "pass" often have more trouble than those with what are considered more severe disabling conditions. John hides his epilepsy from his classmates, although he knows that he might have a seizure that would reveal it to all the world. Trying to cover it up prevents him from suggesting outings to people he might otherwise get to know. Helping him and his friends deal with difference is an appropriate task for classroom teachers, as well as parents and special education professionals.

Sam, a legally blind college sophomore from a Boston suburb, said that he had several good friends since fifth grade that he still knows now they are all in college. He also said that he had always felt as though he was pretending to be something he wasn't: sighted. "I never carried a cane; I didn't know braille; I held books up to my nose and tried to read." During college, he decided to learn cane travel and braille. His sight has not changed, but his attitudes have. I asked whether his friends had changed in their attitudes toward him: "Yeah, they like me better now that I'm more confident about myself."

April, with less sight but more clarity and self-confidence, said this about making friends:

> I was frank with my friends about being blind. I was friends with someone for about 3 months without his ever asking questions. I finally asked him whether there was something he wanted to know and said that he shouldn't be afraid to ask questions about my blindness. Show a good sense of humor. Crack a couple of blind jokes. It puts people at ease about asking you questions. It keeps people from being so amazed. If you make a mistake and make a joke about it, it makes you feel better and it makes the other people involved feel better.

Some disabled students feel that trying to pass is not worth it. Some say that forcing themselves to use crutches to walk when they could move more quickly in a wheelchair is ultimately more restricting than the wheelchair would be. Pat, who uses both, is not sure, and points out the difference that being on crutches makes with her friends: "When I'm sitting down, they treat me like I'm stupid. I'm more confident when I'm on crutches. I'm at their level. When they see me on crutches, they treat me different and better."

Professionals who prevent people from learning all the skills they can— Braille and cane travel, for example, as well as print, sign, and lip reading, or using crutches or a wheelchair—harm their disabled students and make them less comfortable, less functional, less confident than they could be. The process of learning skills matters in making friends as well as in competing in the classroom. Good skills and confidence may not solve all problems, but managing with poor skills leads to low confidence that creates far more problems.

Although people may make some friends during school, virtually all express some sense that they do not "fit in" as much as they would like. Vicky, who has dyslexia and is blind and was one of the top students in her class of over 600, joined in rock-climbing groups and made friends with whom she went ice skating and to movies. "We did all kinds of stuff. But I was never invited to parties. I just was viewed as not the partying type. I didn't date in high school and haven't dated in college, either. I don't feel comfortable at parties. I can't mingle. I don't always know who I am talking to." Annee said she was liked by everyone but was not in a clique. Zach, who had girlfriends as well as a close group of male friends, said he never went to parties or football games. Wendy said, "When my friends get to know me, they don't mind that I'm disabled, but they say I am not like the rest of the disabled kids. That hurts me and makes me feel weird, because they are going by stupid stereotypes about disability."

Today's young disabled people are having more chances than many who went before them. They are not totally excluded, and they are breaking in. But breaking in is hard, uncertain, and unpredictable. At any moment they may feel there is a party to which others they knew were invited and they were not. An individual with disabilities may feel that he or she has been accepted, but may also know of others who have disabilities who are looked down upon. This individual may then question how genuine is their inclusion and may wonder when he or she will not be looked down upon.

Unfortunately, this remains the reality for people with disabilities in our society. Figuring out how to survive being teased at age 6, and left out at age 15, and how to appreciate the friends one has are necessary for life after high school. The mainstream youth of today are not having a blissful time (not that non-disabled youth do either), and they are having harder times than the nondisabled people they know. But the ones who are integrated and are finding ways to communicate and participate are not always, or as often, experiencing the "yuch" of Betty Davidson's childhood. They are getting closer to learning those social skills Cole (1988) describes.

Friendships with Disabled People The growth of the disability rights movement, the greater visibility of disabled people in the world, and the opportunities for mainstreaming all have, I believe, had the remarkable side-effect of making it easier for people with disabilities to recognize their need for and value of others with disabilities. For the deaf students Ragosta interviewed, such feelings may be especially great because they are failing to communicate well with hearing classmates, and they long for others with whom to have unfettered conversations. In addition to these deaf students, other physically disabled people are also seeking out the company of others who can "understand." They want people with whom to compare notes. Annee and April, in many ways very happy with their schooling and friends, loved the chance to meet other people who were their age and who were also blind. Leslie joined a group where she could meet young disabled women. They were older than she, had different disabilities, and came from more economically deprived backgrounds than hers, but she wanted to get to know them. I asked her if she would like to have others with disabilities in her school. "It might be easier. Sometimes I feel very alone, as though there is no one to talk with. I bottle a lot up. I'd like someone to let off steam with."

Hearing her, I have mixed feelings. I remember how much I appreciated a summer camp with other blind children, where I made friends and compared notes with others about how we were surviving with overprotective parents, teachers who embarrassed us by not letting us do things, and trying to get to know the kids in our classes. But I also remember the pleasure and relief of sharing my fifth-grade difficulties in being teased with a fellow fifth grader, who wasn't disabled but was my friend. It was important at 10 and is important now to feel that "you don't have to be disabled to understand or to be friends." As a camp counselor at a camp for blind children, I noticed that many teenagers were talking to me about problems connected with growing up, they weren't seeking out potentially perceptive and helpful counselors with sight. Having a disability alone is no reason to be a friend or become a role model.

I applaud those disabled youth who recognize the value of knowing others with disabilities. I applaud Pat's friendship with Hope, whom she considers her best friend, and with whom she plans to share an apartment. She is not embarrassed or ashamed to have a best friend who is disabled, as many people were 20 years ago. Zach is right when he says that knowing other blind people earlier would have helped him realize he could do more than he was doing in his school. Because Chuck and his parents know others who are blind and like them, he doesn't wince when, at the age of 6, he is teased and called "blind" with derision on the playground. He can say, "Yeah, but so what"!

Those disability rights leaders who fear that mainstreaming may be depriving the movement of future leaders and fighters are, I think, not hearing what I have heard from disabled youth about how glad they are to know others with disabilities. A man with cerebral palsy, who met disabled people during college, said, "I was glad not to be the only one. I saw other disabled people doing what I was doing, and it reaffirmed my faith in myself. Disabled people aren't my only friends, but I'm glad to know other disabled people and to have them as my friends." A partially sighted woman said she learned an enormous amount about how to deal with her own disability from getting to know someone who had a spinal cord injury and had quadriplegia. "She was clear, assertive, not embarrassed, outgoing. She knew when to ask for help and when not to. I learned a lot by seeing her in action."

I would conclude that integrating disabled people, no matter how partial it is at the moment, and the awareness of laws and of a disability rights movement, all are building solidarity for people with disabilities. Schools can foster such solidarity by linking up disabled youth with disability rights groups, not by re-segregating them. Schools can also direct students with disabilities to independent living centers, and to the growing number of recreation programs that teach disabled youth outdoor sports such as skiing, canoeing, and camping. They can then set up programs for disabled and nondisabled young people to do things together. If I am right, and I admit that I am extrapolating from limited data, perhaps one of the best results of PL 94-142 is not its integration of the disabled with the nondisabled community, but rather, its fostering of appreciation of disabled people for one another. Backed up by a disability rights movement, and told by the law that they are not *required* to be segregated and not *required* to be second-class, they are able to come together by choice, when they want to, not because they must.

RECOMMENDATIONS AND CONCLUSIONS

Many, too many, disabled youth of average or above intelligence are going to school in segregated classes, looking out at the nondisabled students, being taught easier subjects than others, earning high grades for little work, and having no chance to socialize with anyone outside of school because they are taken away the minute the class day ends. These youth are passive and frightened around disabled or nondisabled people; they have no preferences they will express, exhibit no interests, no dislikes, no goals. By any measure, they lag behind nondisabled people of their chronological age and stated grade in school. They are not challenged academically and have no social life with disabled or nondisabled peers. About to graduate, they are not ready for life beyond their sheltered special education settings and their family homes.

Fortunately, some people's experiences demonstrate that education for disabled youth is and can be far better than that. Some people are getting many of the benefits the law was designed to achieve: challenge comparable to their classmates, activities to explore, a chance at friendship. Others are getting some, but not all of these. What the law is doing best today is giving parents, advocates, and disabled students something against which to measure what they have. Before there was nothing. Betty Davidson and millions like her had no way to imagine a future. No law entitled them to be in school, and in law and practice, they were there on others' sufferance. They got crumbs and were never given any reason to think they should have more.

Too many disabled children are still getting crumbs—or if not crumbs, far less than students without disabilities, and far less than the law's drafters and supporters dreamed. But the law itself helps Pat know that she should fight to get the school to fix the broken elevator, and she does. The law helped April convince skeptics to let her play volleyball and could have given Zach a chance at physics labs instead of excuses from them. Properly implemented, it might have helped Roy to leave a school for the blind and attend his local sixth grade when he first expressed an interest 7 years ago. Today it is helping Dan and his parents compel his neighborhood school to accept him, to teach him braille, and to let him play games in physical education. It has not been interpreted by courts or school districts as requiring interpreters for deaf students or arguing for the teaching of sign to hearing students. It should be. Just as it should be understood to require equal access to all of the school's life for all the students who are in it.

I conclude with 10 recommendations that embody the major concerns in this discussion. Implementing these recommendations constitutes no basic attack on the current educational system, or upon PL 94-142, but would go far toward meeting goals of providing to disabled students the academic, nonacademic, social, and identity-building experiences expected of education for all students.

1. Equip students with disabilities to function with the autonomy and self-direction of their nondisabled peers in self-care, communication, mobility, and classroom life. Create a barrier-free environment in the school and teach whatever will permit the disabled student to read, write, communicate, and navigate in school at the level expected of others of the same grade. Braille, lip reading, sign language, and independent mobility should be taught in kindergarten and first grade in the same way that children are taught to read and write, to speak in class, and to travel around part of the school.

2. End the clustering of disabled student in separate classes for any part of the school day as soon as basic skills of cane travel, touch-typing, Braille, sign, and lip reading are taught. Whenever possible, arrange individual teaching before or after school to minimize removal from class.

3. Before modifying expectations of, or requirements for, the disabled student, analyze the educational purpose of such requirements and expectations for all students. If practices, requirements, and expectations turn out to be arbitrary conventions rather than representing valid goals for all students, change them for everyone. Before adapting or accommodating, decide whether the accommodation fosters the inclusion of the disabled student and the learning of a skill, or exempts the student from meeting a norm expected of others. If it is impossible to adapt a task to meet the needs of a disabled student in learning a particular skill (e.g., music appreciation or singing for deaf students, or art appreciation and drawing for blind students), provide tasks that teach equivalent or comparable skills (e.g., dance or sculpture). Make only adaptations that foster learning rather than ones that excuse someone from learning a skill.

4. Make adaptations that promote inclusion of the disabled student in an activity, as long as inclusion does not defeat the purpose of the activity for others. For example, minimize blackboard writing by using handouts for everyone, thus avoiding the need for students to get notes from others or to ask others what has been written. In the same spirit, modify physical education team activities to include the disabled student by using a ball with a bell in it for the person who is blind or by permitting someone with a mobility impairment to use a wheelchair on a volleyball or basketball court. This need not be carried over to interschool sports, but there is no reason to exclude a disabled student in a regular physical education program. Other students who would not make a varsity team are expected to take their time to learn skills.

5. Abolish IEPs for students with disabilities until all students receive them. Instead, substitute PEAs.

6. Until IEPs are abolished, arrange for parents and students to have far greater involvement in their creation and approval than they now do. Arguably, no IEP should be concluded without the participation of the student from age 12 or 13 on.

7. Make sure that all school events are open and accessible to students with disabilities.

8. Create opportunities for disabled students to contribute to class projects and use the class as a vehicle for breaking down social barriers between the disabled and the nondisabled students.

9. Communicate with students and parents about the value of their own assertiveness in getting the law to work for them in the education process. Similarly, explain the need for equal assertiveness in reaching out to nondisabled students as potential friends.

10. Reach out to disability rights groups and independent living centers as resources for school staff and for disabled students and their parents. Promote linking disabled students with one another through such groups. Professionals and parents should look to disability rights groups for aid in improving the education of their children, and the disabled community should make education a high priority item on its agenda. Kenneth Jernigan of the National Federation of the Blind is right when he says that: ''Morally and ethically (even if not biologically) these are our children, and we must not fail them'' (Jernigan, 1988, p. 237).

I posed the question at the outset of whether the law was working, whether its supporters should rethink its goals in light of the decade of experience, and whether integration would only work if education for all were revamped.

The law provides the right guidelines when thoughtfully applied. Although it works far too little of the time, it does work sometime, and it can work far better. It is clear that some disabled youth are flourishing in the existing system with sensible accommodation. More can. Providing top quality education to disabled youth can be done in the same systems that provide education to the nondisabled. If the educational system of the nation should be revamped, it is not because disabled people cannot manage in the one that exists if given the chance. It is that they are not yet given the chance. If we want to revamp the educational system for everyone because it is failing millions of poor people, minority youth, youth for whom English is not a first language, and disabled people, by all means do it. But do not claim that disabled people cannot manage in the system as it is. They can and do manage to the extent that the system lets them in and equips them with the tools and the environment to survive.

REFERENCES

Asch, A., & Sacks, L. (1983). Lives without, lives within: The autobiographies of blind women and men. *Journal of Visual Impairment and Blindness, 77*(6), 242–247.

Becker, N.V. (1984). Being deaf and surprised. In A.J. Brightman, (Ed.), *Ordinary moments: The disabled experience* (pp. 51–67). Baltimore: University Park Press.

Bowe, F. (1986). *Changing the rules.* Silver Spring, MD: J & J.

Brightman, A.J. (Ed.). (1984). *Ordinary moments: The disabled experience.* Baltimore: University Park Press.

Browne, S., Connors, D., & Stern, N. (Eds.). (1985). *With the power of each breath.* Pittsburgh: Cleis Press.

Cole, J.S. (1988, May). Getting out. *Disability Rag,* pp. 15–17.

Ferguson, P., & Asch, A. (in press). Lessons from life: Personal and parental perspectives on schooling, childhood, and disability. In D. Biklen, Ferguson, D., & A. Ford, (Eds.), *Schooling and Disability.* Chicago: National Society for Studies in Education.

Fisher, B., & Galler, R. (1988). Friendship and fairness: How disability affects friendship between women. In M. Fine & A. Asch (Eds.), *Women with disabilities: Essays in psychology, culture, and politics* (pp. 172–194). Philadelphia: Temple University Press.

Hahn, H. (1983). "The good parts": Interpersonal relations in the autobiographies of physically disabled persons. *Wenner-Gren Foundation Working Papers in Anthropology,* 1–38.

Heinrich, E., & Kriegel, L. (1960). *Experiments in survival.* New York: Association for the Aid of Crippled Children.

ICD survey III: A report on special education. (1989). New York: Louis Harris and Associates.

Jernigan, K. (1988, May-June). Focus on the education of blind children. *Braille Monitor,* 232–237.

Killilea, M. (1952). *Karen.* Englewood Cliffs, NJ: Prentice-Hall.

Killilea, M. (1963). *With love from Karen.* Englewood Cliffs, NJ: Prentice-Hall.

Massie, R., & Massie, S. (1984). *Journey.* New York: Knopf.

Mest, G. (1988). With a little help from their friends: Use of social support systems by persons with retardation. *Journal of Social Issues, 44*(1), 117–125.

Pogrebin, L.C. (1987). *Among friends: Who we like, why we like them, and what we do with them.* New York: McGraw-Hill.

Rousso, H. (1988). Daughters with disabilities. Defective women or minority women. In M. Fine & A. Asch (Eds.), *Women with disabilities: Essays in psychology, culture, and politics* (pp. 139–171). Philadelphia: Temple University Press.

Safilios Rothschild, C. (1970). *The sociology and social psychology of disability and rehabilitation.* New York: Random House.

Safilios-Rothschild, C. (1982). The social and psychological parameters of friendship and intimacy for disabled people. In M. Eisenberg, C. Griggins, & R. Duvall (Eds.), *Disabled people as second-class citizens* (pp. 40–51). New York: Springer.

Schneider, J. (1988). Disability as moral experience: Epilepsy and self in routine relationships. *Journal of Social Issues, 44*(1), 63–78.

Zimmerman, D. (1984). The way I see myself. In A.J. Brightman (Ed.), *Ordinary moments: The disabled experience* (pp. 33–51). Baltimore: University Park Press.

chapter 11

Beyond Obligation
Students' Relations With Each Other in Integrated Classes

Douglas Biklen, Cathleen Corrigan, and Deborah Quick

Ruell, a boy in a fourth grade classroom, was asked what it would be like if his friend Eric were not permitted in the class with him. Eric uses a wheelchair and an electronic communication board and has cerebral palsy. At first, when asked this question, Ruell had difficulty making sense of it. Perhaps the question reflected a set of professionals' or adults' assumptions about schooling and organization of students that simply did not fit Ruell's experience. It was as if he could not figure out why someone would suggest that Eric should not be in the class.

According to Ruell, it would be bad: "I wouldn't feel too good because he should be able to see the world just as well as anybody else. That's how I feel. Other people may feel different but that's just the way I feel."

For Ruell, it was a matter of justice, something he felt personally. Eric, his classmate, was a friend, someone he respected. While he saw Eric as "special," Ruell's meaning of "special" differs from how special educators and most of the public generally interpret it. According to Ruell, "Eric, he's special just like everyone else thinks they are. Everyone is special in some ways. Cripple, any kind of way, handicap, anything, they're still special."

For Ruell, everyone has special and unique qualities. They cannot be taken away simply because you have another quality, such as a disability. In Ruell's

Preparation of this chapter was partially supported by the U.S. Department of Education, Office of Special Education and Rehabilitative Services, National Institute on Disability and Rehabilitation Research (NIDRR), under Cooperative Agreement No. G0085C03503 awarded to the Center on Human Policy, Division of Special Education and Rehabilitation, Syracuse University, Syracuse, N.Y. The opinions expressed herein are solely those of the authors and no official endorsement of the U.S. Department of Education should be inferred.
Authors' note: All names of individuals appearing in this chapter are pseudonyms.

definition, disability is not something that makes you special, but rather something that might keep you from being seen as special.

Ruell felt that if Eric were kept out, he would not have the teachers who knew him and who worked so well with him. In a special class, Ruell felt that Eric might be shy and not have people around him that he could talk to, and Eric would not have regular students to learn with. In addition, Eric would not have anybody with whom to share his sense of humor, and Ruell would not be able to do "special things" with Eric, such as going to a swimming pool or performing together in a school musical. Ruell sees the regular class as the place where Eric can find the kinds of instruction he needs.

Did Ruell imagine himself in Eric's place? When asked how the class would be different without Eric, Ruell explained that the class would probably run the same way, but that he'd miss Eric and "maybe his desk might not be there." Clearly, Ruell has strong, well thought-out feelings about what it means to go to school with a friend. The fact that his friend had a disability was not central to how he thought about him. We can infer this from the fact that when he entertained the idea of what it would be like for his friend to be forced out, he thought about his friend's sense of humor, his shyness, his friendships with students in the class, and his relationships with the teachers: all of the kinds of things that might be raised with a student who is not disabled.

At the same time, Ruell had thought about what it means to have a disability. He saw himself as an ally in helping Eric get around. He thought of negative labels or name-calling as reflecting badly on the labeler: "I'm not gonna call anybody dumb or anything like that, 'cause that's just a figure of speech. That's just making yourself look dumb."

And he did not interpret having a disability as being a reason to deny someone's individual worth. In effect, his thoughts about disability did not mimic cultural stereotypes.

STUDY FORMAT AND PURPOSE

We have observed many children and heard such original thoughts in classrooms where labeled and unlabeled children go to school together. In this chapter we describe other similar accounts from several students, and include observations of how students interpret and interact with each other. Also, some of the classroom conditions or strategies that facilitate such feelings and expressions are discussed. The chapter is based on accounts from children who were interviewed for the documentary videotape *Regular Lives* (1987). The chapter is also based on comments from students in other classrooms in the same school where the documentary was made, and on observations by two of the authors who are also teachers in two of the classrooms in the school.[1]

---

[1]The transcripts of narrative from *Regular Lives* are from interviews conducted by Gerardine Wurzburg, State of the Art, Inc.

Other authors have discussed the rationale and importance of relationships between students labeled disabled and their nondisabled peers (Strully & Strully, 1985). Also, researchers have explored the attitudinal effects of educating students together in the same schools. This research reveals increased acceptance as a result of mere physical proximity of students (Towfighy-Hooshyar & Zingle, 1984), increased interaction of students when the curriculum is structured to foster interaction (Voeltz, 1982), improved attitudes correlated with length of time integrated (i.e., number of years) (Voeltz, 1982), and evidence that students with severe disabilities are able to have interactions and relationships with students who are not disabled (Biklen, 1985; Knoblock, 1982). The research for this chapter focuses on a slightly different question.

Our purpose is to explore what it means for students with and without disabilities to be educated together. Specifically, we examine their relationships with each other, and how they act when they are encouraged to spend time together, learn together, and appreciate each other. At the same time, we identify and discuss strategies that teachers employ to foster positive interactions between students. Also, we note some lessons that the students and student relationships convey to their teachers, parents, and each other.

A WORD ABOUT THE SETTING

All of the examples for this chapter are drawn from experiences in one school: Edward Smith Elementary School in Syracuse, New York. The school has 810 students, 40 teachers, 38 assistants, and 26 other specialists. Up until 1973, students with severe or even moderate disabilities had not been allowed in the school. That year, a parent filed a class action lawsuit on behalf of his daughter and two dozen other children who had been kept out of the public schools. Some had been judged too disabled. Others were deemed "dangerous to self and others." And for all of them, the school district had declared that it did not have sufficient teaching staff and space. Within a few weeks after the legal papers were filed, the school district relented and created self-contained, special classes, two of them at the Ed Smith School. The students in these classrooms participated in many aspects of school life with their nondisabled peers—for example, mealtimes, school performances, recess, and field trips—but they were not integrated for instruction. Still, today, some of these students are not integrated for instruction. In the late 1970s, however, the school began to experiment with "integrated classes," bringing together students with severe disabilities and nondisabled students in a common class that would be taught by a special and "regular" educator. In the 1980s, that model has expanded and been modified, so that while there are still some students with moderate disabilities who attend self-contained classes, students with severe disabilities, including students with autism, currently attend integrated classes.

Since the early, contentious years, Ed Smith has come to pride itself on its innovations in "integrated schooling." Visitors arrive at least every month, and often daily, from other school districts, from other parts of the country, and even from such distant places as Australia, New Zealand, Canada, Austria, Japan, and England. Books have detailed some of the methods and approaches of the school for educating students with severe disabilities in the same classrooms with non-disabled students (e.g., Berres & Knoblock, 1987; Biklen, 1985; Knoblock, 1982). Much of the videotape *Regular Lives* was filmed at Ed Smith. Teachers and the principal have given presentations about the program at professional conferences.

One of the early models still being used for integration in the school teamed a special and regular educator together, and provided them with the space of two classrooms. The educators were provided with teaching assistants who would typically have worked in a self-contained classroom for students with severe disabilities, and with classes containing the same number of students who would have populated the two classrooms if they had not been combined. Within this model, 25–31 so-called typical students would be grouped in a class with 5 or 6 students who have severe disabilities. Over time, the teachers and administrators came to regard this approach as unwieldy. Two teachers were kept together, but in a number of instances, the class size was reduced to 20 and 4, or 24 and 6. Then, after several years, as the teachers and the school had come to have more experience with integration, the fourth grade of the school decided to abandon the combined classes model ("integrated class"). Instead, the teachers agreed to disperse the fourth-grade age students with severe disabilities throughout the fourth grade classes. In effect, most of the classes at that grade level became integrated classes.

In one of the classes where we did our observations for this chapter, there were 23 students (the average class size in the entire school is now 24). One of the students had a learning disability. Another student was labeled autistic. Eight of the students in the class were classified as gifted. In the other class, there were 21 students. One student had multiple handicaps (Eric), one was classified as autistic, two students received remedial help, and two were classified as gifted. In both classes, the majority of students ranged in age from 9–11. One of the children with a disability was 12 years old.

One of the teachers had training in elementary and special education, with a master's degree in special education, with an emphasis on working with children with autism. She trained at the Jowonio school, an innovative preschool program that integrates students with severe disabilities and students with no disabilities. The other teacher did not have a special education background, but she had experience in working with students with a wide range of abilities. She had taught previously in private middle-class schools, in an urban school that served students from very poor families, and in a school for students age 5–13 who had failed in public schools. She credited these experiences as well as her interactions with other teachers at the Ed Smith School with preparing her for teaching a class that included students with severe disabilities and students who had no disabilities.

BEHAVIOR IS NOT WHAT YOU ARE, IT IS SOMETHING YOU HAVE

Several years ago, in one of the integrated classes, it was recognized that only three of the nondisabled students had ever been in an integrated classroom before. Most of the nondisabled students did not have any experience with students with severe disabilities. Two strategies in particular proved helpful to the process of enabling students to think through some of the events that took place in an integrated class. Our notes record the following teacher comments:

> I felt I was having to do a lot of talking in front of the students, explaining what I was doing and why. Also, I had a question and answer box in the room. Students could put in questions, anonymously, and then we talked about them in class. Sometimes I would "plant" notes that would ask: "Why does Sheila always bite herself and other people?" or other things, as if they came from the kids. I did this because I knew they were thinking things like these. It gave me a way to talk about them.

Teachers felt as if they were searching for natural ways to present issues and interpret experiences or events that the students had not seen before. They felt also that students learned to interpret each other positively and not just to place blame. For example, one of the students with severe disabilities, Andy, had been having tantrums, and throwing things. His difficulties, we believed, stemmed either from the fact that one of the teaching assistants had been out of school because of the flu or that the student himself had a cold. According to the notes:

> We had one of the other students in the class meet his bus and go to breakfast with him. Later, he did act up in reading. He took the stapler off my desk and started running around the room. He threw the stapler. Then he went over to where the science projects are and, luckily the math, reading, and homework papers went down first. We talked about what had happened. I spoke with Andy and then with the class, out loud. I explained that Andy has a cold and doesn't feel well, and that Mr. Adams is out. These are confusing to Andy and therefore he is going to test anybody. The kids helped to pick up the papers and parts of one science project. Nothing was broken. One of the kids noted, "Andy hasn't acted like that in a long time." Another student said, "He hasn't been spinning the globe in a long time either." Early in the year, Andy had a habit of spinning the globe, to the point where we thought we might have to put it away. But we got him to stop spinning it by first requiring that he do his work before going over to the globe and then by looking at the globe with him, pointing out the colors, and so on.

Since students do not throw heavy objects in the classroom, after Andy threw the stapler, the students were encouraged to talk about it, to think about why it might have happened, and how it might be stopped. They talked also about how the behavior was an event and not a defining statement about the person who did it.

The students were encouraged to see that their classmate was responsible for what he did, but that there might have been a reason for the action. The teacher mentioned to her class that "If you were upset about something, imagine how frustrating it must be to not know how you can get them to understand, to know something that you know." Also, the teacher explained to the students, "Andy is going through some behaviors now that he hasn't exhibited before, because he is upset about something." By talking about Andy's acts as "going through some behaviors," it was possible for his classmates to think of Andy not just in terms of the negative action.

Students began to look for reasons for each others' behaviors rather than just blaming the behavior as "bad" or the person who was doing it as "bad." A student in another class, for example, was heard explaining to her teacher that "Marissa is really upset because she can't find her snack," or, "She's upset because somebody is in the bathroom and she can't get in." The teachers found that the classmates become each others' allies, often keeping the teacher informed or asking the teacher to recognize what their peers with disabilities needed or wanted. For example, a student informed her teacher, "Eric really wants to do that too," or "Eric needs to be moved. He's been in that position for a long time, and he's uncomfortable." Similarly, students often advocated for their classmate's right to have some of the same opportunities they had. In one instance, for example, several students told their teacher that Eric should get to go down the same two-story high slide that they were, using the teacher's assistance. They were speaking for his right to take risks, knowing that he would derive the same kind of enjoyment they had from the slide.

Learning to think about behavior as something that is related to circumstance, and not just to the person, is a valuable lesson. The lesson appears to survive the test even when Andy bit his classmates. As the teacher records indicate:

> There was a substitute teacher assistant on the playground today. By the time that I got out there, several of the kids had been bitten by Andy. They went to the school nurse. She deemed them all right, though they did have some marks on them. But the kids were all sticking up for Andy. They told me that he just felt caged in and frustrated when he found himself in a tight group of them.

Instead of blaming, students began to look for explanations for each others' behavior. The explanations they selected, as in the case of Andy being "caged in," also gave them a role to play in helping their fellow student to behave differently. In this case, by not crowding Andy, they believed he would not feel trapped and would, therefore, probably not bite a fellow student. In this way, the students came to see what was expected of them. The teachers modeled an interpretive process for them and they learned to do it themselves.

Students began to use this interpretive process with all of their peers. In one of the two classrooms, for example, a nonlabeled student had tantrums. He had gotten upset, spoken loudly, and accused other students of pulling his hair or taking his pencil when in fact they had not. The other students in the class, because of their recognition that behavior is not the person, began to look for reasons for their classmate's taunting and argumentativeness. They were also able to ignore his behavior, much as they had learned to ignore some of the behavior of students labeled severely disabled.

MAKING CONNECTIONS TO YOUR OWN LIFE

Educating nondisabled students together with students who have severe disabilities would appear to be a new and unique experience for most students. In practice, however, the experience is not an entirely new one, for many students see parallels between their interactions together and other relationships and events in their lives. The experiences of an integrated education program are interwoven with the feelings, skills, and relationships that the nondisabled students have at other times and places.

This interconnectedness between disability issues and other aspects of the students' lives becomes apparent in a number of different contexts. For example, one afternoon, we gathered a group of 8-year-old students to look at a video news story from CBC in Canada, entitled *Becky's Story*. The documentary recounts the experience of a child their age who had spent years in a nursing home, who had been crowded into a single room with 18 other children to live, who had been dangerously malnourished because the institution had failed properly to diagnose an esophageal hernia, and who had effectively been cut off from all of the typical experiences of childhood. The students who watched the video were shocked. Can you imagine, they asked, how awful it must be not to go outside and feel the wind and touch the leaves? How could she have been put in such a place? Isn't it wrong, they asked, that Becky didn't have her own home, a family to grow up in, friends to be with? "Everyone needs a family," one child told us. "Wasn't it wrong that the nursing home director didn't try to get her throat fixed?" another queried. The students talked about their own families, and how they would feel if their parents didn't keep them at home. One student spoke about her brother who had a disability and how he was a part of her family and how nice it was that Becky had come out of the nursing home and now had her own family too. Other children talked about how good it was that Becky could now go to Girl Scouts, play the family piano, be a part of things, and be loved. The children saw Becky as someone with whom they had some things in common: a need to be loved, family life, and protection against being mistreated.

We found students often making such connections between their experiences and feelings in the integrated school program and other aspects of their lives. A boy who had developed a close friendship with a classmate who had a disability talks about how he came to have such a friendship: "Before we got in this class together, we didn't know each other very well. But when the kids used to tease the kids who have a little bit of a problem, I'd just stick up for them."

He was queried as to why he defended another student that others might have made fun of:

> I don't know. There's a little boy that lives next door to me, and he has a little bit of a learning disability too. It didn't make me feel right making fun of him, so I don't make fun of him anymore. Me and him are friends.

In this case, the boy's experience in class was being interpreted through the lens of his prior experience in his neighborhood.

Another student discussed what she saw happening in class in relation to her feelings about her baby brother. According to her, she saw her classmate, Max, playing with his friend Daniel, and she observed that he could do various jobs in school. She knew, also, that he could do household chores, the types of things that she and other children do, like taking out the garbage, pulling down the blinds, and running errands. This gave her positive feelings about her brother's future. According to her:

> My baby brother, he's only one years old and does a lot of hard things. He's walking, he's talking, he's standing up in his bed. He's doing a lot of things (so) that my mother and granny (are) impressed with my baby brother. So if Max can do a lot of little things, I think my brother could grow out of his 47 chromosomes.

When a group of students began to talk about how they related to each other, particularly about teasing, the students again connected their experiences in class with experiences outside of class. In one instance, for example, a student said to another student: "Toby, that [example of teasing that the teacher had mentioned] is like you were telling me one of the kids where you live did to your sister [who has a disability]." Another student, speaking about how sometimes students make fun of another student for being a friend to a student with a disability, said:

> Well there is a kid, not in this class, but in the fourth grade, and we're best friends. She lives in my neighborhood and kids started teasing me because she is my best friend. I can't help it. She is my best friend. I can't help it that she's a girl!

The students then had an opportunity to talk about why other students made fun of each other. In this situation, they had a chance to discuss their good and bad feelings about themselves, as well as qualities they admired in others, making choices, and other lessons for daily living.

In still another instance, a student talked with classmates and his teacher about how different family members related to his brother who had autism, and about his brother's likes and dislikes. Due to being a part of a family with a disabled member, he recognized more readily than others that some students were "really good at getting Andy" to say words or to become involved in a game.

SEEING EACH OTHER'S WORTH

When students are together for extended periods of time, they come to know each other. They can see change in each other, feel comfortable with each other, notice who has a particular type of humor, who is shy, who talks too much and so forth. Such insights suggest acceptance of individual differences. A student goes home and tells her mother, for example, that "Sharell is doing much better. She's not refusing to do stuff." In another instance, a student is seen "fooling around" with another student. The teacher's notes record the incident:

I asked Terry if she wanted to move. She sits next to Andy. I asked her this because I thought maybe sometimes this (sitting next to Andy) is distracting her. But, no, she doesn't want to move. Today I caught her at snack time poking him like you would tease a typical kid. She was just poking him and what not and he was reacting to it every time. So I said to myself, she enjoys being next to Andy. Then, yesterday, Terry's mom said, "I understand Andy is trying to speak." Apparently, Terry went home and described how we in the class are working hard to try and understand Andy's sounds. It's kind of exciting.

In another case, a student mentioned to her father the situation of a classmate:

Sarah was coming to school looking really rough. She had on the same clothes every day and she was dirty and her hair wasn't combed. Then she didn't come to school for about two weeks. But now she's back and she looks a lot better. She's clean. And she's smiling again. She had her home changed. She was moved to a new family.

The student was reporting on the experience of a child who had apparently been neglected and had to have her foster placement changed. The student's report of her classmate's situation made no mention of the fact that Sarah is blind.

In our notes of daily interactions in the classroom, we see expressions of the belief in individual value:

It comes out even in little ways. Even today, Andy circled the room at snack time and grabbed Janet Copeland's plastic bag of Ritz crackers and they spilled on the floor. Of course Andy was going to eat them. Shannon McCarthy [another student in the class] was wonderful. She went right over and told Andy to pick up the crackers and said, "Andy put them in the bag and throw them away. They're dirty. You can't eat them after they've been on the floor." And she helped him throw them away, all the time getting it across to him that "No, you can't eat them. You shouldn't take somebody else's snack. You shouldn't throw food on the floor. You can't eat them now that they're dirty." She wouldn't let him eat one of them. She wasn't belittling him. She was just saying: Its not right for you to do that. And there are consequences now that you have done it.

As the example of Shannon and Andy suggests, there is a fine line between being a supportive friend and being too much the teacher, caregiver, or master. Teachers can help students work out the difference in their minds. As we discovered, however, students sometimes appear to be grappling with the proper role themselves. One student wrote in her journal about her efforts to decide how much help was appropriate. She wrote:

> Emily, Deena, and Stewie were bothering me about how much I help Eric, like pushing him to Art and things like that. And some people say I'm the boss of Marissa. This morning, I didn't shut the locker with Eric and so Melissa shut the lockers. Is it wrong that I shut the lockers with Eric? Or can he do that?

Their teacher believed that other students may have been jealous of the time she spent with Eric and Marissa, and of the success she had in getting Marissa to respond to her. But whatever the cause of the criticism, the prospect of students pondering the balance between a supportive friendship and control suggested that students were learning about each others' and their own feelings.

Not all of the interactions between students involve negative "incidents." For example, in the same class where Shannon set limits for her fellow student Andy, another student asked the teacher if he could vote for Andy in a school election. In a different class, one student talked about his friend who had severe cerebral palsy and what he especially liked about him:

> When he goes like this [stretching his arms and legs straight out] you think he's hitting you, and he starts moving his hands all over. He's really strong, too. Then he starts moving around like he's driving a car and stuff. The thing is that he's nice and everything. He acts casual. Sometimes he can act funny. He makes us laugh a lot. That's the *real* thing about him.

FRIENDSHIPS AND RELATIONSHIPS

Students can make friendships, talk to each other, and otherwise interact without being formally asked, required, or coaxed to do so. Most students can make their own way socially, without much in the way of external support. Nevertheless, the context of a class or other setting can either facilitate or hinder social relations. For example, teachers can group students so that they feel comfortable or supported. One teacher notes:

> I consciously grouped her with the kinds of girls who like to play hand games. Monica would really watch them. They automatically assumed that she would be part of that and learn how to do it. At the time she was basically nonverbal. But that didn't really matter to them. She was still part of their group. She has one very close friend in the group. Monica will do anything when Mary is there. She has a really hard time when Mary is out.

Teachers can use a whole range of strategies to promote the interactions of all students and their sense of belonging. They include:

1. Selection of curricula that allow students of very different skill levels to participate in different ways, often partially (e.g., a student with severe cerebral palsy has the task of throwing the switch in a class lesson about electric circuits)

2. Parallel curricula (e.g., if most of the students are working on alphabetizing words, some of the words used could be those that are being taught to one of the students as sight words)
3. Choice time when students select games or other group activities to play
4. Circle time for talking about feelings
5. Pairing students for jobs so that if a student needs assistance, another student is automatically available
6. Finding a role for all students in class events, irrespective of disability (e.g., one student's disability prevents him from participating in timed math quizzes, but he serves as the timekeeper; one student stands next to and supports another student in the class chorus)
7. Cooperative goal structuring/cooperative learning
8. Individualized instruction or projects that allow the entire class to participate (e.g., science projects)
9. Normalized routines and procedures so as to minimize the special or different status of a student with a disability (e.g., making sure that when some students have homework, report cards, class presentations, or awards, all have the same opportunities)

The most important learning strategy, however, does not deal with time and activities of students, but rather involves how teachers communicate their feelings about persons with disabilities through their interactions and behaviors.

TEACHERS AS MODELS

Teachers are important role models. A teacher explained how she used her own behavior consciously:

> We talk about "positives" and the kids pick up on that. They start to notice Andy's clothing and comment on his new red shirt, for example. Now, they always notice how he has his hair brushed or if he has a haircut. They focus on the pleasant things about him. That's part of them really making him a regular kid in their minds. Adult attitudes and actions are so important. We had a substitute who came in last week. She came in and immediately said, "Oh, he's drooling" and got a towel. Well nobody in here [in the class] *ever* focuses on something like that. We just don't do it. If you focus on those kinds of things, he is not going to be thought well of in society.

For the same reason, it would be inappropriate and would teach the wrong lesson if a teacher or other adult in the class spoke to a student who has a disability in a patronizing tone of voice or with a patronizing message. For example, "Oh, isn't he [a 10-year-old] cute," or, "Oh, don't you feel sorry for him," or: "Isn't that amazing that she can do that?" And, given just cause, it is not only appropriate but may even be obligatory for a teacher to reprimand a student with a disability in much the same manner, same tone of voice, and same affect as for a student who has no disability.

At the same time, teachers must recognize and respond to the uniqueness of each child. Our notes of a classroom scene provide us with an example of such a situation:

> One afternoon when the kids were doing something at their desks, I stood up at the board with Tommy [a boy who has autism] and started writing math multiplication problems on the board. I was writing them and he was writing the answers almost as fast as I could finish writing the problems. All of a sudden, the other kids were just looking at us. They were very impressed with Tommy's math skills. I had deliberately done this because I wanted to make sure they saw Tommy's ability. I purposely try to point out those kinds of strengths, find some way to make it come up. It's especially important to do that right in the beginning of the year, to present kids in a real positive light.

Another teacher modeled communication skills with a student who was nonverbal. She often spoke out loud, describing what she was doing with the student so that the other students in the class would informally pick up the skills that she used. The teacher described how her students learned from her example:

> I was really impressed this year that the kids picked up on how to communicate with Eric. It was only the second day of school and they were asking him questions, looking for his yes/no responses. They learned how to form questions in a way that he could respond.

While modeling behavior may be stressful for teachers, the educative power of such actions is clear. The same teacher who focused on teaching communication skills and helping a student to demonstrate his excellent math skills, discussed the handling of a crisis:

> Fighting, scratching, kicking! I really feel strongly about not removing kids from the classroom when that is happening, for a variety of reasons. One of them is that the kid may be trying to get out of the class. Another is that it is important for the other students to see how you process through with it, when the child is upset. In such a situation, it is important to express aloud the feelings that the student may be experiencing, so that the other students can see how you, the teacher, are interpreting the episode.

While a teacher may want to remove the child who is acting out from the classroom so that he or she will not be "on stage," such events are an opportunity to model problem solving and conflict resolution behavior.

The tension for teachers and for anyone concerned with the hidden messages of behavior is to identify what to model and the appropriate time to do so. Obviously, no one can be conscious all of the time about the messages given off by certain behavior. Perhaps it is enough that teachers and students discuss modeling as an important aspect of the learning process. For example, a teacher may wish to point out to a student those instances where he or she "took over" for another student, and did a task that the student could do for him- or herself. Similarly, students are often good critics of teachers' not recognizing a student's abilities to accomplish a task independently or without the teacher's intervention. A teacher wrote:

The kids are often more in touch with "special" kids even than we are. That was really apparent to me for example at last year's awards ceremony. We had the whole fourth grade sitting in the cafetorium. The vice principal had been calling kids names out and each student had gone up to the stage, gotten his or her award, and so on. So when they called Marissa's name, I wasn't really sure if she was aware enough of what was going on to know to go up to the stage. I leaned over to Jane, because Marissa was next to her, and said she should show Marissa how to get through the row and up to the stage. Then I started to get up myself and one of the kids turned around and said, "Mrs. Quick, sit down. She knows what she is doing." I sort of was set aback, in a good way. I felt good about that. Sure enough, Marissa did get through and up to the stage. I felt as if Katie [the student who had told her to sit down] had more of an idea about Marissa than I did. The kids really do get in touch with each other.

CONCLUSION

Our observations, interviews, and discussions with students, and parents' comments (which are not included here), all confirm that students of widely varying abilities can come to accept, appreciate, and interact with each other. Further, we learned that the nature of the school setting and, particularly, teachers' strategies, can foster the effective interaction of all students. The situations and examples described in this chapter suggest four principles for facilitating students' interactions.

First, *teachers can help students present themselves in the best possible light.* The following examples highlight this principle. When a 10-year-old student wet his pants while on his way in from the playground, the teacher helped him get changed and back into the routine of the class without drawing attention to the event, indeed, while keeping the other students from learning about it. A teacher continued her reading lesson and allowed the teacher aide to assist a student who was throwing a tantrum on the floor. Then, after the lesson and after the tantrum, the teacher discussed with the students what had happened. When several students asked the teacher why she did not assist the teacher aide, she explained, "How would you feel if you had everybody focusing on you when you were upset?" Such strategies are designed to ensure students' dignity.

Second, *teachers can use structured activities or events to help process students' experiences with their classmates and their understanding of issues related to disabilities.* In one instance, for example, a teacher and teacher aide role-played a scene in which one student coaxed another student (one with a disability) into saying words that made her look silly. The teacher who tried this strategy reported: "One of the students said, 'That looks like Marissa.' Then, nobody ever again mentioned that it concerned Marissa."

Third, *special adaptations in the curriculum or activities can be implemented in an unobtrusive fashion.* A student who needed support in getting undressed and dressed for gym received help from a fellow student. A relationship resulted that extended beyond this one type of assistance. The teacher reported, "He's terribly appropriate with him. I mean he can get him to do anything, throw a ball, pick up the jump ropes, things that he likes." Similarly, students are encouraged in one class to assist each other with their science projects. The effect of such a policy ensured that when a student with a disability received help from classmates, such assistance was normative. In another instance, one student's communication lesson occurred at the same time as a parallel subject for other students, for example, reading. Other normalizing adaptations included: report cards for all students, cooperative learning groups, and awards for students of every ability level.

Finally, *group planning can help increase teachers' creativity with the task of integration.* In the programs we have observed, the teachers, specialists (e.g., speech/language consultant, psychologist), and assistants met at least weekly for lesson planning, goal setting, problem solving, and idea sharing. In one such meeting, for example, the staff talked about how they could help Eric, a student without verbal language, to initiate conversations with his classmates. A conversation could involve fellow students asking him yes/no questions, giving him options from which to choose, or using the communication board to communicate. The staff discussed when such a conversation could most successfully be initiated, when it would be least successfully initiated, and how Eric could elicit a classmate's attention. In another case, the teachers planned to gather data on a student's disruptive behavior so that they could see when it occurred, under what circumstances, and how it might be altered. Planning meetings were also a time for sharing anecdotes, including accounts of successes. The effects of such meetings, the teachers told us, were that the teachers and other staff generated ideas and became advocates within their group of particular students.

The results of these approaches, principles, and strategies are encouraging. Students developed relationships with each other that were personal rather than stereotyped, interactive rather than one-sided, and caring rather than obligatory. And, students learned to interpret each others' intentions or frustrations.

For some students, interaction turned into friendship. As Ruell described his friendship with Eric:

> Yeah, I've learned how to use his light talker and his computer. I've been to his house a lot of times. We play and watch his fish. He has millions of stuffed animals on his bed, and its fun to play with Eric. They have a dog and cat.

Ruell has learned how to help Eric get around the school, how to interpret Eric when his body physically tenses up, and how to have fun with him. What was impressive about such accounts was not merely that students appreciated each other or saw each others' personal qualities, but that in their eyes and in their experiences, disability was not an all-defining characteristic.

REFERENCES

Berres, M., & Knoblock, P. (1987) *Program models of mainstreaming: Integrating students with moderate to severe disabilities.* Rockville, MD: Aspen Publishers.

Biklen, D. (1985). *Achieving the complete school: Effective strategies for mainstreaming.* New York: Teachers College Press.

Knoblock, P. (1982) *Teaching and mainstreaming autistic children.* Denver: Love Publishing.

Strully, J., & Strully, C. (1985). Friendship and our children. *The Journal of The Association for Persons with Severe Handicaps, 10*(4), 224–227.

Towfighy-Hooshyar, N., & Zingle, H. (1984). Regular-class students' attitudes toward integrated multiply handicapped peers. *American Journal of Mental Deficiency, 88,* 630–637.

Voeltz, L. (1982). Effects of structured interactions with severely handicapped peers on children's attitudes. *American Journal of Mental Deficiency, 86,* 180–190.

part **IV**

Next Steps

chapter **12**

The Politics of Special Education

Harlan Hahn

Although relatively little attention has been devoted to the controversy in the special education literature, the study of disability is currently experiencing a massive conflict between opposing paradigms that may have a critical impact on the fate of this discipline and related areas. The conventional approach to research on this subject has been shaped by a "functional limitations" model, which assumes that the principal difficulties of people with disabilities reside within these individuals, and that solutions can be found by surmounting or transcending such deficits to the maximum extent possible (Hahn, 1985a). Inspired in part by the growing disability rights movement, however, this orientation has been challenged by a "minority group" paradigm, which posits that the primary problems facing disabled[1] citizens are external rather than internal, and that remedies can be achieved through efforts to alter the environment in which they live, instead of their personal characteristics (Hahn, 1985b). While the field of special education traditionally has been dominated by the former model, which stresses the development of effective methods of instruction compatible with the restrictions imposed on students with various types of disabilities, the latter construct implies a comprehensive new agenda that promises to introduce significant changes in the content as well as in the techniques of elementary, secondary, and higher education. Since the minority group perspective identifies different problems and solutions as crucial issues in the lives of children or adults

---

[1]The nomenclature of this presentation differs slightly from the terms employed by other studies in that "disabled" is sometimes used here as an adjective to describe the person. This usage implies the expectation that disability can someday be redefined as a trait that conveys pride and dignity instead of stigma and shame. Thus, it also suggests the hope that disability can be transformed into a positive source of personal and political identity rather than simply an attribute that is incidental to an individual's other interests or capabilities. However, an effort is made to avoid the use of words such as "disabled" as nouns, which seems to infer that this characteristic is the sole defining feature of all individuals included in this category. Language is obviously a crucial component of political change; while agreement has not yet been reached on some of the nuances of these terms, it is important to specify their intended meaning as clearly as possible.

with disabilities, educators need to become increasingly familiar with the major tenets of this theoretical framework and with the distinctions between these two viewpoints.

THE DEFINITIONS AND POSTULATES OF CONTRASTING MODELS IN THE STUDY OF DISABILITY

The contrasts between the functional limitations and the minority group models are based in large measure on divergent definitions of disability. Whereas the functional limitations orientation has been supported by medical and economic concepts that concentrate almost exclusively on the physical or vocational needs of disabled individuals, the minority group approach is founded on a new sociopolitical concept that reflects a broader range of interests and objectives (Hahn, 1982). Each of these definitions has been incorporated into research and is evident in government policy concerning disability. But different phrases in this formulation are stressed by the medical, economic, and sociopolitical definitions, respectively. These variations in emphasis have important implications for the future of special education.

The Medical Definition

Undoubtedly, the most popular understanding of disability is represented by medical concepts that stress physical inabilities or limitations. This orientation reflects the clinical focus of medicine and psychology on efforts to strengthen the anatomically or psychically internal resources of the individual as the principal vehicle of rehabilitation (Stubbins, 1982). Yet, in many respects, the relatively permanent nature of disabilities or chronic conditions seems inconsistent with Parson's (1951) characterization of the "sick role," identified by Siegler and Osmond (1974) as a major component of the medical model. The medical model exempts individuals from ordinary social obligations in exchange for their promise to submit to professional authority and to devote all of their energies to the ultimate goal of complete recovery. Perhaps even more importantly, the emphasis in medicine on etiology, or the study of the causes of health problems, has spawned a vast range of diagnostic categories that not only disclose an implicit striving for prevention and eradication as eventual solutions to the problem of disability, but that may also bear little, if any, relationship to the functional or other skills of the persons labeled by these diagnoses. This system of categories has probably impeded the development of testing procedures that would permit forming valid extrapolations about the capabilities of individuals with various types of disabilities. As a result, there is a heavy reliance on medical classifications, which are concerned with the causes rather than the consequences of impairments. Such reliance raises serious questions regarding the validity of any measurement of the association between disabilities and physical, intellectual, or emotional capacities.

The Economic Definition

By contrast, the definition of disability most widely endorsed by public policy signifies an economic focus on the performance of expected roles and tasks. Since work probably constitutes the principal role expected of most individuals in an industrialized nation, disability has been defined in government surveys and in research by economists as a "health-related" inability or limitation on the "amount or kind of work" that a person can perform (Berkowitz, Johnson, & Murphy, 1976). Perhaps in part because of the strong influence of vocational training on rehabilitation programs during the period surrounding World War I, educational activities became closely linked with an economic understanding of disability that concentrated on preparing disabled individuals for entry-level jobs offering few opportunities for advancement. This association was strengthened by policies that defined disability as an inability to engage in "substantial gainful activity" (Berkowitz, 1987). Examples include worker's compensation indemnification policies for lost wages and the eventual adoption of income maintenance plans such as Supplemental Security Income and Social Security Disability Insurance. Hence, the primary goals of educators as well as rehabilitation personnel have been to improve the occupational skills of specific disabled individuals rather than to ameliorate the social and economic conditions that have produced endemic poverty and unemployment among this segment of the population (Howards, Brehm, & Nagi, 1980). At an individual level, this orientation has resulted in criticism of school programs. One such criticism was expressed by a young man with cerebral palsy who complained that he spent so much time learning how to tie his shoes (a task he subsequently delegated to his attendant) that he was never given an opportunity to pursue an appreciation of art, literature, or music, which later became important to his enjoyment of life. The tendency to use disability as a criterion for excluding persons from the labor force (except during World War II, when the waiver of these restrictions permitted disabled adults, women, and other minorities to demonstrate their productivity) supports the charge that workers with disabilities have been educationally and economically relegated to the "industrial reserve army." Such a practice reduces pressure that would otherwise be engendered by the intrinsic failings of a capitalist economic system (Hahn, 1987b).

The Sociopolitical Definition

The third major definition of disability directs attention to the sociopolitical significance of the interaction between persons and the environments that surround them. From this perspective, the basic problems encountered by citizens with disabilities can be traced to the external configurations of a disabling environment rather than to the internal traits of so-called personal defects or deficiencies. The sociopolitical approach also suggests that the most effective solutions to the difficulties confronting disabled people can be attained by efforts to improve the status of this group as a whole rather than by actions focusing on distinct individuals. As a result, this definition is the primary foundation of the minority group model of disability, whereas the essentially clinical orientation of the medical and economic viewpoints constitutes the primary support of the functional limitations paradigm. The most significant expressions of the sociopolitical understanding in public policy can be found in legislation such as Section 504 of the Rehabilitation Act of 1973, which explicitly identifies disability as a source of discrimination and which seeks to outlaw this kind of prejudice (Scotch, 1984). Hence, measures prohibiting discrimination, and programs designed to alleviate physical or occupational disadvantages, are based on two fundamentally distinct analyses of the origins of the problem of disability that cannot be readily be treated as reconcilable or complementary.

In addition, the sociopolitical definition of disability seems to encompass a radically new assessment of expectations concerning the behavior of children and adults. In the past, the ability to achieve mastery of the existing environment was usually considered a necessary prerequisite to the exercise of the rights of citizenship. Such rights include the freedom to vote or to participate in political deliberations, as well as the opportunity to receive an education and to pursue a livelihood. Consequently, judges have been reluctant to redress the grievances of persons using wheelchairs whose access to polling booths, juries, and legislative or judicial chambers is barred by steps or other architectural barriers. Similarly, many early court cases have upheld the decisions of school boards and administrators to exclude students who could not gain entrance to their classes for comparable reasons (Burgdorf, 1980). And yet, there has been an increasing tendency for many localities to adopt regulations requiring, at least in new construction of schools and other public buildings, that facilities be made accessible to people who use wheelchairs. This transition has reflected a growing realization that mastery of the human-made environment is not an appropriate criterion for participation in the life of the community.

Contrasting Models

This change has vast implications for the development of educational practices. In fact, the origins of special education probably can be traced to the parochial constraints of conventional pedagogical techniques that have penalized students with hearing or vision impairments. Such programs relied exclusively upon verbal communication in the classroom and upon written communication in the dissemination of instructional materials. From a sociopolitical perspective, a clear solution to easing the difficulties of persons with disabilities can be achieved through the use of multiple modes of communication, just as universal accessibility represents a crucial step toward fulfilling the needs of persons who use wheelchairs. These principles might also be fruitfully applied to the mental and physical skills ordinarily required of children and adults as part of the so-called "activities of daily living." Obviously, the creation of an environment adapted to the needs of everyone is a distant vision. But the attainment of this goal may ultimately be determined both by technology and by the limits of the human imagination. In many respects, this environmental objective might be a more appropriate standard for evaluating the capabilities of people with disabilities than are assessments of their functional capacities that fail to recognize the constraints imposed by their surroundings.

The logical implications of the functional limitations and the minority group paradigms, therefore, appear to indicate alternative educational strategies. From the former perspective, which locates the principal problem within disabled individuals, a primary task is the remediation of their functional deficits to the maximum extent possible. Hence, attempts are made to provide disabled young people with the skills that they must acquire in order to be productive in an environment that is usually not adapted to their interests or needs. The success of these efforts is measured by the comparability of proficiency displayed by such students and by their nondisabled peers. However, the characterization of disabled individuals by functional deficiencies has meant that remedies that focus solely on this dimension of their problems can never be fully successful. By contrast, the minority group model ascribes the source of the basic problem of disability to external instead of internal phenomena, and strives to adapt the environment to the aspirations of disabled people rather than to adapt the individual to the demands of the environment. In addition, since a disabling environment is regarded as inherently discriminatory, this approach views efforts to instill a positive sense of identity among persons with disabilities as a crucial component of educational objectives. Instead of concentrating on the task of remedying alleged functional defects, educational policies based on the minority group concept encourage disabled youth to extend their academic strivings both to improve their own lives and to enhance the status of the group of which they are members. As a result, these programs seek to avoid the imposition of restrictive limits on the potential of disabled students by building upon their distinctive experiences and capabilities.

The competing models in research on disability are also based on different postulates. Whereas the functional limitations orientation asserts that the primary difficulties of disabled individuals stem from their physical deficits, the minority group approach assigns primacy to the environment, and specifically to public attitudes, which reveal extensive evidence of aversion toward people with disabilities (Jones, 1984). In many respects, the appearance of traits signifying disability represents an almost Rorschach-like stimulus that usually evokes a powerful visceral or even irrational impulse to draw away from others who are perceived as alien or strange. No matter how much energy is expended to smother these emotions with sympathy or benign support, the propensity to avoid people with disabilities usually is stronger than the instinct to offer acceptance. This fact underscores the need to integrate disabled students in school classrooms. As a result, efforts to attack the origins of the problems of children and adults with disabilities from a minority group perspective concentrate on attempts to change pervasive attitudes rather than on efforts to alter the disabled individual.

The second major proposition of the minority group concept also emphasizes external circumstances by pointing out that all aspects of the environment are fundamentally molded by public policy. The configurations of the social and other human-made structures that shape human behavior are not the products of immutable natural laws; they are basically determined by the fact that governmental decisions either permitted or required them to be designed and constructed in that manner. Hence, legislation can be effectively utilized to create an increasingly favorable educational, social, economic, and even physical climate for persons with disabilities. On the other hand, the functional limitations approach treats the environment almost as a given, and focuses instead on the benevolent assistance provided by professional training and expertise. Consequently, this orientation has been closely allied with dominant models of education based on the conviction that learning is most likely to occur under the tutelage of a professional educator.

The final principle of the functional limitations paradigm, therefore, is founded on the alleged efficacy of professional intervention. Even though the functional deficiencies of disabled students may be ultimately incurable, this approach assumes that professional help offers the best promise for them at least to approximate equivalency with their nondisabled counterparts. By contrast, the third postulate of the minority group perspective joins the two prior statements by concluding that public policies are a reflection of prevalent attitudes and values. Hence, facets of the environment that tend to separate or segregate disabled and nondisabled citizens might not be accidental or coincidental (Hahn, 1986). The pervasive nature of social institutions that impede interactions between disabled and nondisabled persons in the classroom or elsewhere have produced a milieu in which the former group has been denied the equal treatment to which they are legally entitled in the United States. While the functional limitations model views disability primarily as a personal misfortune, the minority group perspective considers it a source of collective discrimination. Similarly, whereas the functional limitations orientation tends to prescribe compensatory adaptations as a principal remedy for their difficulties, the minority group approach contends that solutions to the major problems of disabled Americans can be found through the strict enforcement of legal guarantees of freedom and equality. Perhaps even more significantly, the three major principles of the minority group concept support a strong case that disabled citizens should be considered from a legal point of view as a "suspect class." This calls for rigorous judicial scrutiny to determine whether or not distinctions made on the basis of disability reflect discriminatory practices, within the meaning of the "equal protection" clause of the Fourteenth Amendment to the U.S. Constitution (Hahn, 1987b).

CHARACTERISTICS OF THE DISABLED MINORITY

The description of disabled children and adults as a minority group is also supported by the major characteristics of this segment of the population. Disabled Americans have one of the highest rates of unemployment, poverty, and welfare dependency in the country (Bowe, 1978, 1980). Although each of these statistics may be attributed to functional incapacities as well as to attitudinal discrimination, the prejudicial origins of these patterns is underscored by the prevalence of segregation between disabled and nondisabled persons in education, transportation, housing, and public accommodations (Hahn, 1983). In fact, citizens with disabilities have been subjected to more rigid and pervasive segregation practices than those imposed under apartheid.

Discriminatory practices have had an indelible imprint on the lives of disabled women and men. According to a Louis Harris survey, a plurality of disabled Americans feel that they "are a minority group in the same sense as are blacks and Hispanics" (Harris and Associates, 1986, p. 114). The same survey revealed shocking evidence of the isolation of individuals with disabilities. Whereas 78% of all adults had attended a film at least once in the past year, only 36% of their disabled counterparts had gone to a movie theater in the same time. Similarly, 58% of nondisabled persons, but only 34% of disabled respondents, typically ate at a restaurant once a week or more. The comparable figures for supermarket visits were: 87% of nondisabled persons versus 62% of disabled persons; significantly, 13% of disabled adults had never been to a supermarket (Harris and Associates, 1986). These percentages may reflect the mixed effects of functional issues, architectural barriers, and social aversion, but the combination of these factors undoubtedly has left millions of disabled men and women with a profound sense of personal and sociocultural aloneness.

Furthermore, unlike many minorities, persons with disabilities lack a feeling of generational continuity. If they acquire their disabilities as children, they are usually raised by nondisabled parents who might not be adequately prepared to provide a source of solace and understanding when their children encounter the animosity and aversion of the outside world. If they become disabled later in life, they may have even fewer resources to cope with the discriminatory attitudes that they confront. Like other disadvantaged groups, such as women, blacks, Hispanic Americans, Asian Americans, and aging citizens, people with disabilities must refute accusations that their subordinate status in society results from biological inferiority rather than from prejudice. Perhaps the principal distinction between these other segments of society and the disabled minority, however, is that most of the former groups have been at least partially successful in rebutting charges of biological inferiority. In contrast, vestiges of this notion continue to be used to explain the social inequality of persons with disabilities.

Disabled children and adults also share many experiences that may eventually become the basis of a distinctive subculture. While the complete range of these common incidents have not been extensively studied or enumerated as yet, at least a few of them that have important implications for education deserve mention. As a result of their almost universal exposure to the medical model, for example, a disproportionate number of individuals with disabilities become involved in a problematic relationship with physicians and professional authorities who seem to exercise undue influence over their personal activities. This fact may explain the misunderstandings that frequently permeate the subsequent interactions between disabled students and teachers, rehabilitation personnel, and others who attempt to assert what they consider their professional responsibilities. In addition, persons with disabilities are aware of the need for detailed planning to meet the routine demands of everyday life. As Gliedman and Roth (1980) have documented extensively, the achievements of disabled children may not fit developmental theories that have been prepared to chart the progress of their nondisabled counterparts. Consequently, there is a serious danger that teachers might fail to recognize both the abilities and the significant contributions that students with disabilities can make to the educational process.

Perhaps most importantly, there is a pressing need for educators to understand the nature of the discrimination directed against the disabled minority. A recent analysis has contended that this prejudice can be attributed either to "existential" anxiety, the worry that "there but by the grace of . . . go I," or to "aesthetic" anxiety, the fearful response to others whose appearance is perceived as unpleasant or upsetting (Hahn, 1988a). While "existential" concerns seem to be most closely aligned with the cognitive orientation of the functional limitations approach and special education, "aesthetic" reactions reflect powerful visceral and even unconscious feelings that are often manifested by aversion. In most studies of prejudice against people with disabilities or other disadvantaged groups, comparatively little attention has been devoted to the aesthetic dimension of such attitudes. For some observers, this factor may even be perceived as a relatively trivial source of discrimination and segregation. And yet, the accusation that someone is unappealing or even repugnant seems to be one of the most damaging insults that can be hurled at another human being. To a far greater extent than many might be prepared to admit, pervasive notions of attractiveness or unattractiveness could have a determinative effect on the sense of self-esteem that is crucial to educational success and to social and political advancement.

In fact, aversion to persons with disabilities could be a principal explanation for the failure of the disabled minority to develop a positive sense of personal and political identity. The development of such an identity is an essential foundation of the movement to improve the status of persons with disabilities in society. Many men and women with disabilities are affected by the stigma that is also the major source of their oppression. To be disabled not only involves functioning in an environment replete with obstacles that eventually may be circumvented or surmounted, but it also means living with a prominent physical characteristic that is generally considered unattractive. Often, disabled individuals would prefer to identify socially and politically with other personal attributes, such as their age, gender, ethnicity, occupation, or socioeconomic status, rather than with a disability that might constitute the most salient and significant aspect of their lives. As a result, even though disabled citizens form one of the largest minorities in the United States, they have never been able to organize a powerful political constituency capable of exerting a strong impact on educational reform and other relevant policy issues.

The most debilitating effects of prejudice based on aesthetic considerations undoubtedly have been imposed upon children and adults with visible disabilities. The realization that this form of aversion has affected interactions between nondisabled persons and persons with a wide range of sensory and mobility impairments, therefore could provide a means of developing a sense of organizational cohesion to transcend the etiologically based diagnostic classifications that have previously fragmented and divided the disabled minority. In addition, people with so-called "hidden" disabilities have been subjected to similar discrimination through the process of labeling (e.g., Mercer, 1973). And there is even strong evidence that the treatment of students with learning disabilities is significantly influenced by responses to their physical appearance and behavior (Bryan, 1976; Bryan & Bryan, 1978; Bryan & Sherman, 1980; Schumaker, Wildgen, & Sherman, 1982; Shepard, Smith, & Vojir, 1983). Hence, there is a pressing need for educators as well as other nondisabled professionals to become involved in the struggle to redefine the personal and political identities of citizens with disabilities in a manner that might allow them to combat the aesthetic aversion and discrimination that has been a major source of their oppression.

THE PRINCIPLES OF EDUCATIONAL
POLICY FOR STUDENTS WITH DISABILITIES

From a minority group perspective, the principal change to be sought in education policy is the "mainstreaming," or integration, of disabled students into regular classrooms. The foundations for this effort were laid in the historic 1954 United States Supreme Court decision in *Brown v. Board of Education* (345 U.S. 483, 98 L. Ed. 873, 74 S. Ct. 686). In arguing that education is indispensable to success in life, this opinion concentrated on the debilitating effects of the simple separation of students into distinct groups by generating "a feeling of inferiority as to their status in the community that may affect their hearts and minds in a way unlikely ever to be undone." Moreover, in one of the most widely criticized portions of the decision, the Court cited the research of Clark and Clark (1952), which indicated that preference for a white appearance represented a learned value promoted by separate schools for black and white children. The 1886

Plessy doctrine allegedly supporting "separate but equal" educational facilities was founded on sociological theories that assumed there was a natural aversion to "commingling" of the races. Yet, the 1954 Supreme Court justices wanted to emphasize modern studies revealing that attitudes toward physical differences such as skin color reflected socialization perpetuated by segregation rather than innate feelings. Thus, the *Brown* decision turned on the adverse educational impact of separation rather than on the quality of the instruction offered in these schools. The Supreme Court concluded that, "in the field of public education the doctrine of 'separate but equal' has no place. Separate educational facilities are inherently unequal."

Mainstreaming: The Integration of Disabled Students into Regular Classrooms

The principle of mainstreaming seems especially applicable to the education of disabled students. The badge of inferiority inflicted upon them by separation on the basis of aesthetic as well as other considerations has left deep psychological scars that often appear to overshadow any instructional benefits that may be derived from their placement in distinct programs. Informal discussions with disabled adults who attended special schools, for example, have elicited vivid memories of being lifted from a wheelchair and placed on a bus (lacking an appropriate lift) and transported across a city to similarly inaccessible classrooms, while nondisabled students spat on the windows of the bus as it stopped at street corners along the way. Another quadriplegic man, who was fortunate enough to have a highly qualified home tutor, passed the rigorous examinations qualifying him for a full scholarship to his state university. But the university denied him admission because of his disability. This took place in the same year that black students first entered the leading universities of several Southern states. The importance of encouraging increased interaction between disabled and nondisabled children as a means of redressing a sense of inferiority is underscored by the research of Richardson and Royce (1968). Their study indicated that nondisabled children, regardless of their racial or ethnic characteristics, are more liked by other students than their disabled counterparts, and that "physical handicap is such a powerful cue in establishing preference that it largely masks preference based on skin color." The need for desegregated or mainstreamed education is reinforced by the general finding that prejudice may be reduced by frequent contacts between members of the dominant majority and minority groups at equivalent levels of social status (Allport, 1954). Furthermore, there is a great deal of accumulated wisdom suggesting that the most significant educational experiences of students, including those in higher education, result from having increased opportunities to transcend the parochial limits of their own cultural values by frequent exchanges with persons from different backgrounds. Hence, there appear to be persuasive reasons to shift the burden of proof in the education of disabled students to those who would want to attach major qualifications to the principle that "separate educational facilities are inherently unequal."

Perhaps equally pertinent to the development of special education was the second opinion in 1955 of the Supreme Court in *Brown v. Board of Education* (349 U.S. 294, 99 L. Ed. 1083, 755S. Ct. 753), which proposed school desegregation with "all deliberate speed." Such provisions permitted opponents of integration to organize resistance to this policy in the same way that the implementation of subsequent laws to provide equal rights for students with disabilities has been frustrated and delayed. In the controversy surrounding the Coleman Report (1966) more than a decade later, educators debated the failure of desegregation to produce the equivalency between white and black scholastic attainment that many of them had anticipated. What was often ignored in these arguments, however, was acknowledgment of the possibility that academic achievements may be virtually determined by the teacher's early subjective impressions of students on the first day of school. Conveyed by subtle cues, recorded in dossiers, and supposedly validated by later tests, such impressions create expectations and self-fulfilling prophecies that may follow them through the rest of their educational careers (Musick, 1975). In the case of children with sensory, mobility, chronic, or learning disabilities, the probability that this type of instinctive judgment might exert an undue influence on assessments of the intellectual limitations of these individuals seems exceptionally high. In a society that places inordinate emphasis on beauty and attractiveness, unusual care must be taken to ensure that programs designed for such students do not reflect impressionistic bias based on a failure to conform to prevalent standards of physical appearance or behavior.

The Elementary and Secondary Education Act of 1965

One of the most crucial influences affecting the development of public policy for children with disabilities, however, arose from issues that were somewhat unrelated to discrimination or to special education. In the 1960s, the federal government sought to find a way of providing aid to local schools that would circumvent the bitter debates over "states' rights" in education and the "separation of church and state," which raised serious questions about the right of parochial institutions to receive government support. In 1965, these legislative logjams were dislodged by a compromise that permitted the passage of the Elementary and Secondary Education Act. This provided funds for libraries, instructional materials, and educational innovations for schools in districts containing a disproportionate number of low-income students. In some respects, this position appeared to mark a move away from the earlier argument that educational disadvantages could be destroyed by the removal of separate classifications toward the belief, perhaps inspired in part by politicians' reactions to the controversy over the Coleman report, that this objective might be achieved through compensatory efforts. Similar provisions were contained in amendments adopted the following year to support the teaching of disabled young people. As a result, these principles seemed to imply that the instruction of deprived students required unusual concessions to their academic deficits rather than the creation of educational settings based on the concept of equality. In a society that seems to abhor the principle of quotas and the equitable distribution of resources for public schools, there has been a widespread opinion that the basic conditions of equality could be satisfied by the concept of equal educational opportunities. Equal educational opportunity implies the provision of compensatory instruction to ensure that contestants would occupy equivalent positions at the starting line of a race that would ultimately be decided by individual merit, even though some of the lanes on the track may be littered with obstacles that impose undue burdens on disabled persons and other competitors.

The Education for All Handicapped Children Act of 1975

PL 94-142, the Education for All Handicapped Children Act of 1975, included many elements that represented significant departures from the principle that shaped the *Brown* decision. In particular, the formula reflecting the political compromise that allowed the passage of the Elementary and Secondary Education Act became an important precedent for the reform of education for students with disabilities. By treating such support as a special concession to the peculiar needs of disadvantaged youth, this approach reinforced the assumption that they already possessed educational deficiencies that would undermine their academic status and eclipse other talents. It also implied that these programs represented a privilege rather than a resource to which they were entitled as a legal right. This orientation was compatible, however, with the views of many of the principal supporters of PL 94-142, such as the Association for Retarded Citizens (ARC-US) and the Council for Exceptional Children (Levine & Wexler, 1981). Conspicuous by its absence was the disability rights movement, which had not been able to overcome the lack of generational continuity and the disunity imposed by diagnostic categories to play a significant role in the formulation of educational policy. Instead, the movement was focused on the elimination of prejudice against disabled persons in many areas of life. Since both parent and professional organizations have tended to concentrate on the nature of the instruction provided by special education, this concern has tended to overshadow the debilitating effects of stigma resulting from the separation of disabled and nondisabled students in public schools.

Many of the provisions of PL 94-142 seem to reflect the agenda of interest groups representing parents and professionals rather than the interests of the disability rights movement. Instead of basing their legislative and judicial strategies on the struggle of other minorities for equal rights, these groups, perhaps naturally influenced by the legacy of residential institutions in the education of disabled students, developed principles derived from litigation concerning the rights of persons subjected to incarceration (e.g., Rothman & Rothman, 1984). Thus, the somewhat negative concept of a "least restrictive environment" was developed as a standard for evaluating the equality of the school milieu, rather than the distinctly positive goal of creating an environment adapted to the needs of everyone. Integration, or mainstreaming, appeared to become a secondary or distant purpose instead of an urgent or primary objective. And, in the individualization and expansion of services, and in the design of an elaborate system of appeals, the organizations that authored this legislation displayed a strong faith in the efficacy of professional intervention in protecting the interests of a powerless group such as children with disabilities. But, in a pattern reflecting the paternalism that has often characterized the formulation of public policy about disability, Congress adopted the lofty aims of educational reform, perhaps fearing the electoral retribution that might result from a refusal to support the aspirations of disabled citizens, while neglecting to appropriate the funds necessary to implement them (Hahn, 1983; Levine & Wexler, 1981). Moreover, there is significant evidence that the key principles incorporated in PL 94-142 have failed to produce desired results in large measure because the parents of disabled children often feel intimidated by professional expertise (Weatherly, 1979; see also Chapter 9 of this volume).

ALTERNATIVE EDUCATIONAL PROGRAMS

There is a pressing need for a new approach to the education of students with disabilities. Instead of concentrating on the provision of the professional assistance that has long been prescribed by the functional limitations paradigm, teachers might appropriately devote increased attention to the design of programs that would contribute to positive feelings of dignity and pride among disabled youth, especially about those characteristics that have previously caused them to be stigmatized and devalued (see Chapter 14). As the experiences of other minority groups have indicated, such efforts may be essential for the development of a favorable self-image which is crucial to the pursuit of other educational ambitions.[2] What is needed in elementary, secondary, and higher education is a

---

[2]The author's own experience may provide amusing testimony about the importance of self-concepts in determining academic success, and the extent to which testing can either support or undermine this factor. Because I had polio at the age of 6, one week before I was scheduled to begin school, I missed several years of early class work which I never made up when I finally left the hospitals. Since I was raised in a rural area where the nearest special school was more than 30 miles away, I returned to regular classes. At the age of 13, however, I broke my hip; this required me to be in a full body cast for more than 6 months. Because an economic rationale was needed to justify the expense of installing a telephone line that would enable me to keep up with my classes during this period, the state vocational rehabilitation agency sent a specialist to administer an IQ test verbally. What this man did not know, however, was that he arrived on a day of the World Series and that I was listening to the baseball game on a radio under my pillow throughout the exam. For some reason, which I can only attribute to fortuitous luck that altered the course of my life, I gave a series of random answers to his questions that fit the profile of academic ability. The befuddled man left convinced that I was a genius; since the test seemed to support this erroneous impression, I never questioned his judgment, even though I secretly knew that the results were spurious. Thus, I acquired what I consider the most crucial determinant of educational success: confidence in one's own capabilities, and I never had any serious difficulties in my subsequent academic career. If my random answers had fit a less favorable profile, the outcome could have been decisively negative.

disability equivalent to the "black is beautiful" movement of the 1960s that would focus on the potential abilities of disabled young people, rather than on their supposed functional deficiencies. Although the full scope of this approach has not been developed as yet, an increased appreciation of the history of a minority, especially one that lacks generational continuity, and an enhanced awareness of alternative aesthetic values are two critical components of educational activities that could promote a growing sense of dignity and pride.

The largely unexamined recorded history of persons with disabilities dates back to accounts of the Neanderthal, Shanidar I, named for the cave in Iraq where his skeleton was discovered, whose "remains . . . show that even in death his person was an object of some esteem" (Solecki, 1971, p. 196). There is evidence that disabled slaves performed during the Roman Saturnalia, and that they worked as entertainers at royal courts and medieval festivals. It has been suggested that the appearance of women and men with disabilities was commonly associated with a heightened atmosphere of sensuality and the relaxation of ordinary inhibitions on social, political, and sexual behavior. However, this legacy was gradually eclipsed by changing concepts of work that eventually reduced disabled persons to the status of pitiful beggars or objects of charity whose survival depended upon the benevolence of the nondisabled majority (Hahn, 1988a). Considerable care, therefore, must be exercised in the interpretation of the history of persons with disabilities, which seems to raise basic epistemological as well as pedagogical issues. The few historical accounts of the role of disabled entertainers in ancient and medieval times, for example, are replete with terms implying that these practices were "barbaric" or "uncivilized" in comparison with the more "benign" and "enlightened" attitudes of the modern era. In many respects, these activities undoubtedly were crude, and the humor was often at the expense of performers as well as audiences. And yet, for disabled individuals who have been influenced by their milieu to believe that their disabilities can only be viewed as a source of stigma and shame, the realization that physical differences historically evoked sensuous and even bawdy feelings may represent an important new insight. The study and teaching of any subject, and especially such a provocative phenomenon as disability, is strongly affected by the temporal and cultural constraints of the theoretical framework through which it is examined. The need for a history of disabled people might be appropriately coupled with the need to develop a revisionist history based on the experience and perspectives of this minority.

As another crucial aspect of this endeavor, increased attention could be devoted to exploring the historical sources of the disability rights movement. In the United States, for example, important precursors of these trends may be traced to the writings of Helen Keller (Foner, 1967), who derived many of her socialist beliefs directly from her disability experience. Another early advocate was Paul Strachan, leader of the American Federation of the Physically Handicapped. In the 1940s, Strachan advocated for the establishment of a quota for the employment of disabled workers and for an early form of "disability allowance" to offset the additional costs that must be borne by individuals with disabilities (Berkowitz, 1980). Although the ideas promulgated in the nineteenth century by major thinkers such as Charles Darwin, Karl Marx, and Sigmund Freud did not provide the basis for a favorable assessment of disability (Hahn, 1987a), there appears to be ample evidence to permit the preparation of a new history of disabled people that could be introduced into the curricula of elementary, secondary, and higher education.

A second important innovation that might be readily incorporated in school classes involves the aesthetic aversion that is often a major source of prejudice against students with disabilities. In an era when young people are exposed to millions of hours of visual messages, through television and film, about a relatively restricted range of bodily images, it would seem appropriate for schools to devote at least some attention to the issue of physical appearance. Students may need to learn that preferences about this matter are molded primarily by the process of socialization, and that all human beings have the capacity to appreciate a broader range of aesthetic values than the idealized standards of physical beauty presented in the mass media. A candid discussion of these topics could help disabled children cope with the rejection that they encounter from their nondisabled peers. Such coping skills become increasingly important with the burgeoning sexuality of adolescence which, as Elkind and Weiner (1978, p. 550) note, is also the age when "previously happy, cheerful, and 'gutty' handicapped and crippled (sic) children often experience their first real depression." This sort of instruction could also be of major benefit in freeing nondisabled youth from the psychological pressures of the conformist notions of appearance and attractiveness exerted by the media.

The logical implications of the minority group model of disability denote a different agenda from the principles inferred by the functional limitations approach. From the former perspective, perhaps the most important task is the development of a positive sense of identity among disabled children and adults that will sustain their strivings to achieve educational and other major objectives in life. In the immediate aftermath of the onset of disability, people of all ages are required to solve two of the most difficult metaphysical questions that can be posed to any human being, namely: "Why?" and "Why me?" Answers obviously vary, but one experience seems almost universal. Having a disability gives a person a different view of the world; that difference can become a valuable source of personal insight and creativity. Educators may need to learn to encourage disabled students to use these original perspectives as an asset to further their academic ambitions. Participation in the disability rights movement may furnish a sense of meaning and purpose in life that can also support the pursuit of high scholastic aspirations. In all of these endeavors, educators can emphasize the benefits of self-help rather than professional intervention as a means of instilling a sense of empowerment that may permit disabled persons to fulfill their potential.

Finally, the educational implications of the minority group model point toward the creation of a new set of countercultural values. In a fundamental sense, aversion toward persons with disabilities signifies the superficiality of physical standards in the modern age. For thousands of years, disabled people have survived and made valuable contributions to their communities even in the face of overwhelming stress on their supposed defects and deficiencies. In a society that seems obsessed with competing to attain bodily perfection in appearance and functional skills, disabled men and women may have much to teach their nondisabled counterparts about the value of cooperation based on the creativity of alternative perspectives.

REFERENCES

Allport, G.W. (1954). *The nature of prejudice*. Garden City, NY: Doubleday.

Berkowitz, E.D. (1980). Strachan and the limits of the federal government. *International Review of History and Political Science, 42,* 65–81.

Berkowitz, E.D. (1987). *Disabled policy: America's programs for the handicapped.* New York: Cambridge University Press.

Berkowitz, M., Johnson, W.G., & Murphy, E.H. (1976). *Public policy toward disability*. New York: Praeger.

Bowe, F. (1978). *Handicapping America: Barriers to disabled people*. New York: Harper & Row.

Bowe, F. (1980). *Rehabilitating America: Toward independence for disabled and elderly people*. New York: Harper & Row.

Bryan, J.H., & Sherman, R. (1980). Immediate impressions of nonverbal ingratiation attempts by learning disabled boys. *Learning Disability Quarterly, 3,* 19–28.

Bryan, T.H. (1976). Peer popularity of learning disabled children: A replication. *Journal of Learning Disabilities, 9,* 307–311.

Bryan, T.H., & Bryan, J.H. (1978). Social interactions of learning disabled children. *Learning Disability Quarterly, 1,* 33–38.

Burgdorf, R.L., Jr. (Ed.). (1980). *The legal rights of handicapped persons: Cases, materials, and text*. Baltimore: Paul H. Brookes Publishing Co.

Clark, K.B., & Clark, M.P. (1952). Racial identification and preference in Negro children. In G.E. Swanson, T.M. Newcomb, & E.L. Hartley (Eds.), *Reading in social psychology* (pp. 551–560). New York: Holt.

Elkind, D., & Weiner, I.B. (1978). *Development of the Child*. New York: John Wiley & Sons.

Foner, P.S. (Ed.). (1967). *Helen Keller: Her socialist years*. New York: International Publishers.

Gliedman, J., & Roth, W. (1980). *The unexpected minority: Handicapped children in America*. New York: Harcourt Brace Jovanovich.

Hahn, H. (1982). Disability and rehabilitation policy: Is paternalistic neglect really benign? *Public Administration Review, 42,* 385–389.

Hahn, H. (1983). Paternalism and public policy. *Transaction/SOCIETY, 20,* 36–46.

Hahn, H. (1985a). Changing perceptions of disability and the future of rehabilitation. In L.G. Perlman & G.F. Sustin (Eds.), *Societal influences in rehabilitation planning: A blueprint for the 21st century* (pp. 53–64). Alexandria, VA: National Rehabilitation Association.

Hahn, H. (1985b). Toward a politics of disability: Definitions, disciplines, and policies. *The Social Science Journal, 22,* 87–105.

Hahn, H. (1986). Disability and the urban environment: A perspective on Los Angeles. *Society and Space, 4*, 273–288.

Hahn, H. (1987a). Adapting the environment to disability: Paradigms, people, places, and things. In W.G. Emener (Ed.), *Public policy issues impacting the future of rehabilitation in America* (pp. 58–86). Stillwater, OK: National Clearing House of Rehabilitation Training Materials.

Hahn, H. (1987b). Advertising the acceptably employable image: Disability and capitalism. *Policy Studies Journal, 15*, 551–570.

Hahn, H. (1987c). Civil rights for disabled Americans: The foundation of a political agenda. In A. Gartner & T. Joe (Eds.), *Images of the disabled/Disabling images* (pp. 181–203). New York: Praeger.

Hahn, H. (1988a). Can disability be beautiful? *Social Policy, 18*, 26–32.

Hahn, H. (1988b). The politics of physical differences: Disability and discrimination. *The Journal of Social Issues, 4*, 39–48.

Harris, L., and Associates. (1986). *The ICD survey of disabled Americans: Bringing disabled Americans into the mainstream.* New York: Author.

Howards, I., Brehm, H.P., & Nagi, S.Z. (1980). *Disability: From social problem to federal program.* New York: Praeger.

Jones, R.L. (Ed.) (1984). *Attitudes and attitude change in special education: Theory and practice.* Reston, VA: The Council for Exceptional Children.

Levine, E.L., & Wexler, E.M. (1981). *PL 94-142: An Act of Congress.* New York: Macmillan.

Mercer, J.R. (1973). *Labeling the mentally retarded: Clinical and social system perspectives on mental retardation.* Berkeley: University of California Press.

Musick, D. (1975). A multivariate analysis of academic achievement. Unpublished paper, University of California, Riverside.

Parsons, T. (1951). *The social system.* New York: The Free Press.

Richardson, S.A., & Royce, J. (1968). Race and physical handicap in children's preference for other children. *Child Development, 39*, 467–480.

Rothman, D.J., & Rothman, S.M. (1984). *The Willowbrook wars.* New York: Harper & Row.

Schumaker, J.B.,Wildgen, J.S., & Sherman, J.A. (1982). Social interaction of learning disabled junior high students in their regular classrooms: An observational analysis. *Journal of Learning Disability, 15*, 355–358.

Scotch, R.K. (1984). *From good will to civil rights: Transforming federal disability policy.* Philadelphia: Temple University Press.

Shepard, L.A., Smith, M.L., & Vojir, C.P. (1983). Characteristics of pupils identified as learning disabled. *American Educational Research Journal, 20*, 309–331.

Siegler, M., & Osmond, H. (1974). *Models of madness, models of medicine.* New York: Macmillan.

Solecki, R.S. (1971). *Shanidar: The first flower people.* New York: Alfred A. Knopf.

Stubbins, J. (1982). *The clinical attitude in rehabilitation: A cross-cultural view.* New York: World Rehabilitation Fund.

Weatherly, R.A. (1979). *Reforming special education: Policy implementation from state level to street level.* Cambridge, MA: The MIT Press.

chapter **13**

The Right to an Effective Education
From *Brown* to PL 94-142 and Beyond

Thomas K. Gilhool

Following Thurgood Marshall in the first argument of the *Brown v. Board of Education* (1954) cases before the Supreme Court, John W. Davis, in the opening words of his argument on behalf of the defendant South Carolina school district, anticipated exactly the ultimate reach of the decision:

> May it please the Court, I think if the appellants' construction of the Fourteenth Amendment should prevail here, there is no doubt in my mind that it would catch the Indian within its grasp just as much as the Negro. If it should prevail, I am unable to see why a state would have any further right to segregate . . . on the ground of sex or on the ground of age or on the ground of mental capacity.

Brown's freshly revolutionary contribution to our unfolding constitutional experience is its announcement that we are, in contemplation of the Fourteenth Amendment to the Constitution, one nation and one people, that everyone is included, everyone belongs: the principle of equal citizenship.

It is no accident that this announcement came in the context of public education, for it is with regard to education that this society has paid most tribute to ideas of universality. It was a part of the genius of Charles Houston's strategy, formulated with the National Association for the Advancement of Colored People and culminating in *Brown,* that he chose to make the claim for equal respect and full admission into American society initially in terms of schooling.

Since the 1970s, the claims of disabled people to equal education and citizenship have taken on some reality and constitutional standing. The claims of disabled people share *Brown's* principle of equal citizenship. They derive strength from the movement that led to *Brown* and have grown even stronger since. Their defining strength is in the conception of our constitutional order as established in *Brown.*

The needs of persons with disabilities have still not been met, because they continue to be excluded from many aspects of American society, just as blacks have been excluded and discriminated against throughout American history. When these injustices have been fully realized, they will redress the precisely similar historical wrongs. And, in an example of the just contributions made to each other by each set of people who struggle for justice, when the claims of people who are disabled are honored, disabled people may have helped significantly, in turn, to establish for all people during their childhood not simply the opportunity for equal and integrated access to schools, but a right to *effective* schooling.

THE INTEGRATION IMPERATIVE

PL 94-142 is the fulcrum of the charter of equal citizenship for people with disabilities. The linchpin of every disability enactment is the integration imperative expressly articulated in PL 94-142. Section 1412 (5) (B) requires that all states must establish procedures to ensure:

> that to the maximum extent appropriate, handicapped children, including those children in public or private institutions or other care facilities, are educated with children who are not handicapped, and that special classes, separate schooling, or other removal of handicapped children from the regular educational environment occurs only when the nature or severity of the handicap is such that education in regular classes with the use of supplementary aids and services cannot be achieved satisfactorily.

The legislative history of the integration imperative discloses several Congressional judgments:

1. If children with handicaps are to live a decent independent adult life in the ordinary community, handicapped and nonhandicapped children must come to know each other in the schools.
2. Learning by all children, including those who are severely disabled, proceeds in significant part from other children, from seeing and hearing and modeling from each other.
3. Noting the frequent assignment of schooling for children with handicaps to basement classrooms (e.g., next to the boiler room) and unbalanced distribution of school resources, Congress concluded that if children with handicaps were educated with nonhandicapped children, they would together be protected by the common and joint influence of their parents and the school's community constituency. Congress thus sought to structure the political process of community supervision of the schools to include children with handicaps.

It has long been clear that separate environments are unnecessary and destructive in the education of severely disabled children. If they are useful at all, it is only for a tiny number of children and then only for sharply limited periods (see Chapter 3, this volume).

Four cases establish the meaning of the integration imperative for severely disabled children:

New York State Association for Retarded Children v. Carey (612 F. 2d 644, 2d Cir. 1979)

Roncker v. Walter (700 F. 2d 1058, 6th Cir. 1983)

Campbell v. Talladega County Board of Education (518 F. Supp. 47, 55, N.D. Ala. 1981)

PARC II (C. A. No. 71-42, 3d Cir. June 14, 1983).

In the *N.Y.S.A.R.C.* case, Judge Newman, of the Second Circuit Court of Appeals, affirmed a district court order rejecting a New York City School District's plan to isolate, in nine separate classes, 48 children who had once been residents of the Willowbrook institution and who were carriers of hepatitis B. They had been intentionally infected at Willowbrook in a medical experiment conducted while they were residents. Applying the integration imperative of Section 504 of the Rehabilitation Act of 1973, the Court of Appeals held:

> As is apparent from its language, Section 504 is intended to be part of the general corpus of discrimination law. . . . It is a general princip[le] of discrimination law that once the plaintiff has established a *prima facie* case that he has been discriminated against, the defendant must present evidence to rebut the influence of illegality. (612 F. 2d at 649)

Upholding the children's education in regular schools, the court wrote:

> [T]he formation of special classes for this small group of children will naturally lead to a decrease in the curricular options that are available for each child. . . . Separation of the carrier children will also limit the extent to which they can participate in school wide activities such as meals, recesses, and assemblies, and will reinforce the stigma to which these children have already been subjected. (612 F. 2d. at 650-51)

In *Roncker v. Walter,* decided after the Supreme Court's decisions in *Amy Rowley* (discussed below), the Sixth Circuit gave the first plenary address to the integration requirement of PL 94-142 from a Court of Appeals. In *Roncker,* a parent challenged the placement of her 9-year-old severely retarded son in one of Ohio's "County Board" schools maintained exclusively for retarded children. The parent argued that he would have no contact with nonhandicapped children at the school. Upholding the parent, Judge Contie appraised the weight of the integration requirement:

> The Act does not require mainstreaming in every case but its requirement that mainstreaming be provided to the *maximum* extent appropriate indicates a very strong congressional preference. The proper inquiry is whether a proposed placement is appropriate under the Act. In some cases, a placement which may be considered better for academic reasons may not be appropriate because of the failure

to provide for mainstreaming. The perception that a segregated institution is academically superior for a handicapped child may reflect no more than a basic disagreement with the mainstreaming concept. Such a disagreement is not, of course, any basis for not following the Act's mandate. (700 F. 2d at 1063; Court's emphasis)

The judgment and action required of school districts and courts by the integration imperative was clearly delineated:

In a case where the segregated facility is considered superior, the court should determine whether the services which make that placement superior could feasibly be provided in a non-segregated setting. *If they can, the placement in the segregated school would be inappropriate under the Act.* (700 F. 2d at 1063; emphasis supplied)

The *Roncker* decision puts two matters into focus. First, the Education for All Handicapped Children Act (1975) clearly contemplates that common and customary, and even well-rationalized arrangements concerning disabled people, will *change,* and it *requires* they change. Creating new arrangements is precisely the injunction of the act. If the act is respected, executive and judicial enforcement will often be necessary.

The second matter was addressed by the *Roncker* Court:

In these cases, the question is not one of [mere educational] methodology but rather involves a determination of whether the school district satisfied the Act's requirement. . . .

We recognize that the mainstreaming issue imposes a difficult burden on the district court. Since Congress has chosen to impose that burden, however, the courts must do their best to fulfill their duty.

A basic disagreement with [the Act's requirement] is not, of course, any basis for not following the Act's mandate. (700 F. 2d at 1062 and 1063)

Congress makes the choice. Congress makes policy. Where Congress has done so, the job of the courts is to defer and to enforce.

The integration imperative speaks also to the education of mildly disabled or "minimally" disabled students. For example, the problem of overrepresentation of racial and national origin minorities in EMR (educable mentally retarded) classes has been addressed thus far almost entirely in terms of the act's requirement that

testing and evaluation materials and procedures utilized for purposes of evaluation and placement of handicapped children will be selected and administered so as not to be racially or culturally discriminating . . . and no single procedure will be the sole criterion for determining an appropriate educational program for a child. (20 U.S.C.A. 1412 [5] [c])

Yet, that problem might just as well be analyzed, and perhaps more effectively remedied, in terms of the integration requirement. And it may be important both to integration and to effective state-of-the-art schooling for all students, including those who are minimally disabled, that it be analyzed and addressed in those terms.

One may conclude that both the legal wrong underlying overrepresentation of EMR in such classes and the remedy to it are in the integration imperative. It may be argued that *everybody* is overrepresented, and the crucial problem is that there are separate "special" classes for *any* child said to be disabled. There is no reason to believe that effective schooling of disabled children—whether retarded, learning disabled, or emotionally disturbed—requires separate educational settings, "special" classes, or any other pull-out programs. Nor is there reason to believe that such special classes are more effective than regular classes. The evidence is to the contrary (see Chapter 1, this volume). If that is so, the act's integration imperative requires the abolition of separate, special classes for disabled children and calls for the education of these children in regular educational environments.

Recognition that effective schooling for disabled children is not to be found in separation would intensify attention to determining what is effective education for disabled and nondisabled children. The requirements of the Education for All Handicapped Children Act for "appropriate . . . education," "individualized education," and for parental direction would be found by all disabled children in their regular education environments.

THE STATE-OF-THE-ART REQUIREMENT

Section 1413 (a) (3) of the act, what my former colleagues and I at the Public Interest Law Center of Philadelphia have called "the state-of-the-art requirement," is probably the most important provision of the act.

Congress knew in directing that all children with handicaps be educated that it was possible. Congress knew that there were known procedures for effectively educating disabled children, particularly those most severely disabled. Congress knew also that the knowledge of how to do so was not widely distributed.

The Congress, therefore, imposed two duties on every local and state education authority:

(A) the development and implementation of a comprehensive system of personnel development which shall include the in-service training of *general* and *special* educational *instructional and support personnel*, detailed procedures to assure that all personnel necessary to carry out the purposes of this chapter are appropriately and adequately trained, and effective procedures for *acquiring* and *disseminating* to teachers and administrators of programs for handicapped children *significant information derived from educational research, demonstration, and similar projects*, and (B) *adopting*, where appropriate, *promising educational practices and materials*. (U.S.C.A. 1412 [3]; emphasis supplied)

In *Campbell v. Talladega County Board of Education* (1981) questions of the content, design, and quality of schooling were raised. Fifth Circuit Judge Vance, sitting by designation, addressed the claims of an 18-year-old severely retarded student (518 F. Supp. 47, N.D. Ala. 1981).

Judge Vance' summary of the *Campbell* case summarizes what the act is about, what education for all handicapped children is about, and what the education of every child and citizen, handicapped or not, is ultimately about:

> [D]efendants have acted from the conviction that Joseph Campbell was capable of little progress toward self-sufficiency. This conviction may have resulted from the failure to offer Joseph a full range of appropriate tests [to identify his strengths and capabilities] or it may have stemmed in part from widely held social stereotypes concerning the abilities of retarded citizens. Consequently, a program was developed, the chief function of which was to occupy Joseph's time in as pleasant a manner as possible. Rather than deal with the difficulties which must necessarily accompany any challenge, the school effectively isolated him. . . . While we sympathize with the problems that the Talladega school system faces, its assumptions about Joseph's ability are inconsistent with the evidence presented at trial and its actions [and inactions] are in clear violation of the law. (518 F. Supp. at 55)

PARC II (1983) speaks similarly. The plaintiffs demanded injunctive action seeking schooling of effective design, content, and quality from the state and the school district for the full class of Philadelphia school children assigned to programs for the "severely and profoundly impaired."

The plaintiffs, aided by 14 educators steeped in the schooling of severely disabled children from school districts and universities across the country, arrayed from the literature and experience the elements of the state of the art in educating severely disabled children. They also systematically compared the practice in a representative sample of the district's 82 programs for the "severely and profoundly impaired" with the state-of-the-art programs. The school district, by its own distinguished expert, sorted the same literature and experience, developed its own instruments, and took its own measure of its practice. The dual identification of the elements of the state of the art and the measure of the shortfall in practice coincided exactly.

The crucial ruling came when state counsel sought to demonstrate that the practice in Philadelphia was no worse than the practice in other large urban districts. Judge Becker ruled that the standard under Section 1413 (a) (3) and the "appropriate education" requirement of the act was not the state of practice but the state of the art.

Thereupon, *PARC II* settled, and a decree was entered requiring the following of the state and school district:

Integrated programs for severely disabled students located in age-appropriate regular elementary, junior, senior, and vocational high schools

Schooling in functional life skills including teaching in community environments where skills are ordinarily practiced

Job-directed vocational training for all children from the age of 14

Closed loops to ensure parental direction and common-home-school approaches to learning and mastery

Training for teachers and parents alike in the state of the art in effectively educating severely disabled students

The burden of implementation rests chiefly on what the decree calls "clinical in-service training." With respect to inservice training, there is also a state of the art: not Saturday lectures, or "cook books," but in-classroom work by each teacher with another professional who has command of the state of the art until each teacher has a working mastery. The necessity is teacher command of the state of the art, not just intellectually knowing what it is, but such a mastery in concept and in operation that the state of the art flows from the fingertips.

AMY ROWLEY'S CASE AND ITS IMPLICATIONS FOR ALL OF EDUCATION

The Education for All Handicapped Children Act received its first plenary consideration by the Supreme Court in *Board of Education of the Hendrick Hudson Central School District v. Amy Rowley* (1982). Amy Rowley's case speaks volumes to the appropriate education of disabled children and of all children.

Amy Rowley, a deaf child of deaf parents, who has minimal residual hearing, attended regular kindergarten and first grade at the Furnace Woods School. The district provided her with an FM hearing aid which amplified words spoken into a wireless receiver by the teacher or fellow students. As framed, the question in the case was whether the act required that Amy Rowley be provided a sign language interpretation for all of her academic classes. The district court found that with the hearing aid, and making use of what the Supreme Court called her "excellent" lip-reading skills, Amy Rowley was able to identify only 59% of the words that were spoken to her. In first and second grade, to which she had advanced when the case was before the district court, she was performing well above the median for her class. In fact, she was near the top in first and second grade; by the time of the Supreme Court consideration, she was, in the fourth grade, in the middle of her class.

The Supreme Court reversed the lower courts and held that the school district did not have to supply sign language interpretation. Thus, for Amy Rowley, the case was a loss (and the loss may be all of society's, for the life prospects suggested by Amy Rowley's considerable intellectual talents, marked on the record of the case, had caused it to be known in the disability movement as the "deaf Madame Curie" case). For many other children, however, Amy Rowley's case may be a victory.

The case raised for resolution by the Court the question of what the word "appropriate" in the Act's requirement of "a free appropriate public education" means. The *Rowley* majority held that "appropriate education" requires education *"reasonably calculated to enable the child . . . to receive [real] educational benefits"* (102 S. Ct. 3034). The question to be answered in suits under the act is twofold:

> [H]as the [district and] the State complied with the procedures under the Act? [A]nd . . . is the individualized educational program . . . reasonably calculated to enable the child to receive [real] educational benefits. (102 S. Ct. at 3051)

The standard must turn on "real" educational benefits, engaging both design *and* results, and *real, not merely formal, results,* since the Court was at pains expressly to say three times:

> The achievement of passing marks and advancement from grade to grade will be *one* important factor in determining educational benefit. (102 S. Ct. at 3051; emphasis supplied)
>
> We do *not* attempt today to establish any *one* test for determining the *adequacy* of the educational benefits. (102 S. Ct. at 3051, note 28; emphasis supplied)
>
> We do *not* hold that every . . . child who is advancing from grade to grade . . . is *automatically* receiving 'a free appropriate public education.' In this case. . . we find Amy's academic *progress,* when considered with the special services and professional consideration accorded by the Furnace Woods school administrators, to be dispositive. (102 S. Ct. at 3049; emphasis supplied)

Immediately upon establishing the meaning of "appropriate" and the standard required by the act in the education of each student, Justice Rehnquist's opinion for the Court notices the state-of-the-art provision of the act, Section 1413 (a) (3), and calls it "a clear statutory directive." He writes:

> The Act expressly charges States with the responsibility of "acquiring and disseminating to teachers and administrators of programs for handicapped children significant information derived from educational research, demonstration, and similar projects, and [of] adopting, where appropriate, promising educational practices and materials." (102 S. Ct. at 3050)

The standard for appropriate education, reasonably calculated to provide real educational benefit to the child, may arise from a "parsimonious reading" of the act and the intentions of Congress. Certainly, it is a mean standard as thus far applied for Amy Rowley, although, should she now not "perform above average," even if passing from grade to grade, the standard may yet avail her further. Indeed, an important decision by the Third Circuit Court, filed July 26, 1988, holds that the real educational benefits required by *Rowley* must promise and supply more than "trivial educational advancement" (*Polk v. Central Susquehanna Intermediate Unit 16,* C.A. No. 87-5585).

Nonetheless, for others, even such a parsimonious standard for public education to meet may open worlds if the schools must, with respect to every child, proceed in ways that are reasonably calculated to yield real education benefits.

STATE SCHOOL CODES: A GENERAL DUTY TO PROVIDE APPROPRIATE SCHOOLING TO ALL CHILDREN

The duty to provide appropriate schooling to all children rests with the schools as a matter of common state law across the country. The school laws of at least 18 states carry provisions setting forth the duties of the schools exactly in terms of "appropriate," "suitable," "proper," or "fit" education. For example, the Pennsylvania School Code provides:

The board of directors in every school district . . . shall arrange a course or courses of study adapted to the age, development and needs of the pupils. (Pa. Stats. Ann. Tit. 24, 15-1512)

The Oregon School Code requires: "sound, comprehensive curriculum best suited to the needs of the students" (Oregon Rev. Stats., 326.011). California requires: "any course of study adopted . . . shall be designed to fit the needs of the pupils for which the course of study is prescribed" (Ann. Calif. Educ. Code, 1204). Florida requires: "a system of schools, courses, classes, . . . and services adequate to meet the educational needs of all citizens of the state" (Fla. Stats. Ann., 228.01).

If state statutory words like: "adapted to," "suited to," "designed to fit," and "adequate to meet," are to be given the meaning for all students that Amy Rowley's case gave the federal statutory word "appropriate"—as at minimum, they likely must—then as a matter of state law, in providing for the education of each of its pupils, schools must teach in ways reasonably calculated to yield real educational benefits.

Why might this be significant? First, in earlier cases, lawyers for ill-schooled children sought to parse education as if it were a science with strict relationships of causation between particular inputs and particular outcomes. We could not satisfactorily do so, particularly in outlining the relationship between dollars and outcomes. The standard calculated to yield real educational benefits sets a much less heavy burden. It recognizes education as an art. Choosing and using the state of the art, or more accurately, choosing from among *states* of the art, is a much easier, more readily reviewable matter, which would be nonetheless stark in its effect upon the state of the practice, and the accomplishments of children, in many urban and other schools.

Second, much more is known now about what works and what does not. The present author is among those persons (a latent popular majority perhaps, but there are fewer believers among leaders of public discourse) who believe that the Great Society worked. As to schooling, for example, between 1965 and 1975 there was a marked decrease in dropouts, and an increase in school finishing, and in admissions of racial and national origin minority students to colleges. More important, and indisputable, as a result of the Elementary and Secondary Education Act of 1965, there have been 2 decades of extraordinarily introspective and systematic scrutiny of what works in education and what does not.

The net result of this scrutiny is a rich array of demonstrably effective approaches to teaching and learning, or, to understate: of "promising practices and materials." They include:

Effective Schooling: the elements of principal leadership and teacher, parent, and student organization that evoke and sustain high morale, consistently high expectations for achievement by all students, and effective concentration on the tasks of teaching and learning

Effective Teaching: some six identified elements that are present in the teaching
of any subject that yield a high degree of mastery by each child: review,
presentation, guided practice, feedback and corrections, independent practice, and periodic review

Cooperative, rather than competitive or individualistic, styles of teaching and
structuring learning tasks yield markedly better results in achievement and
self-confidence

Classes sized under 20 (*if* teachers are schooled to adjust their teaching styles as
classes under 20 allow) yield radically better results

There are enough demonstrably effective approaches to teaching reading to say
there is no reason, so long as one or a successive combination is tried, for
any child who is not severely disabled not to master reading.

(Chapters 2 through 7, and Chapters 8 and 14, this volume, detail many of these
effective practices.)

Thus, there are now identified *states* of the art, and, given a duty upon the
schools to use them, not to merely play school, every child may have a right to an
effective education. What such an eventuality might mean is suggested, but not
exhausted, by the decisions of the West Virginia State Circuit Court Judge and
the West Virginia Supreme Court in *Pauley v. Bailey* (No. 74-1268, W. Va. Cir.
Court). The case addressed a conventional school finance case as an action to
evoke and enforce state-of-the-art undertakings upon the schools under requirements of "a thorough and efficient system of free common schools" in the state
constitution. The adumbration now of a legal duty to provide effective schooling
would coincide with the renewed national scrutiny of the efficacy of the schools.
It would also coincide with the insistence by educators and administrators themselves that education is a profession, with all that means for the standards to
which their performance and their service to school children should be held.

THE EFFECTIVE EDUCATION ACT OF 1990

The next general education statute of Congress should articulate for each child a
right to effective education, and for each state and district, each school and
teacher, the duty to supply it. The Education for All Handicapped Children Act
of 1975 undertook to require for each disabled child "an education reasonably
calculated to yield real educational benefits," and "the adoption of promising
practices and materials." These provisions, plus the insistent use of the *states* of
the art, should be extended to all children, in the service of making equal
citizenship real for each.

REFERENCES

Board of Education of the Hendrick Hudson Central School District v. Amy Rowley, 102
S.Ct. 3034 (1982).

Campbell v. Talladega County Board of Education, 518 F. Supp. 47 (N.D. Ala. 1981).

Education Code, Ann. Calif. Educ. Code, § 1204.

Education for All Handicapped Children Act of 1975, 20 U.S.C. § 1401.

The Elementary and Secondary Education Act of 1965.

Fla. Stats. Ann., §228.01.

Friedman, L. (Ed.). (1968). *Argument: The oral argument before the Supreme Court in Brown v. Board of Education of Topeka, 1952–55*. New York: Walker.

New York State Association for Retarded Children v. Carey, 612 F.2d 644 (2d Cir. 1979).

Oregon Rev. Stats., §326.011.

PARC II, C.A. No. 71–42, (3d Cir. June 14, 1983).

Pauley v. Bailey, No. 74–1268 (W. Va. Cir. Court).

Pennsylvania Stats. Ann. Tit. 24, §§ 15-1512.

Polk v. Central Susquehanna Intermediate Unit 16, C.A. No. 87–5585.

Roncker v. Walter, 700 F.2d 1058 (6th Cir. 1983), *cert. denied,* 104 S.Ct. 196 (1983).

chapter **14**

Building the Future

Dorothy Kerzner Lipsky and Alan Gartner

There is mounting concern about the future of education. The basic issue is how to create and sustain effective programs for all students, including those now labeled as handicapped. While educators are seeking improvements in specific practices, including school organization, assessment, teacher roles, and curriculum, the issue has increasingly come to be seen in a larger frame; in Kuhn's (1962) formulation, it is a time of paradigm shift. A recent report by the Office of Technology Assessment (U.S. Congress, 1988) offers stark expression of the alternatives facing American public education:

> The system could change in a way that makes learning more productive and fun while allowing teachers more time to spend with individuals as coaches or tutors. It could put more power in the hands of the learner, tailor instruction to each person's level of understanding and learning speed and technique, and make it easier for an individual to learn when instruction is most needed.
>
> Or, the system could create rigid centralization of course design, mechanical and impersonal instruction, national regulations, and a contraction of choice for both students and instructors. (p. 48)

While the needed reforms affect the education of all children, particular attention should be given to the needs of students now placed in separate programs (e.g., special education, remedial programs, and bilingual education). For each of these groups of students, there are high dropout rates, low graduation rates, limited learning for those who complete school, and poor preparation for subsequent education or employment. Among a growing group of advocates and researchers, there is agreement on the points made by a National Academy of Sciences report a decade ago that there are no sound educational bases either to distinguish among these groups of students or to fashion different instructional strategies (Heller, Holtzman, & Messick, 1982). If the mounting research findings are correct, as we believe they are, then the effort required of educators, parents, the government, and citizens at large, is to fashion educational programs to achieve excellence and equity for all students. The task is to develop educational services for all students and to assume the responsibility of student success in learning and in personal development.

Educational restructuring begins with the way children are viewed. It is a question of how they are valued and what is expected of them. The current literature on school effectiveness adopts Edmonds's (1979) findings as to the importance of high expectations for achievement for all students. The Congress, in the title given to PL 94-142, the Education for All Handicapped Children Act (1975), declared its intent to see that all children were educated. Too often, however, public policies and human services practices (particularly education) incorporate "disabling images" (Gartner & Joe, 1987), which lead to the denial of choice-making and autonomy for persons with disabilities, premised on the belief that they are incapable of managing their lives independently. The bedrock of educational initiatives requires the repudiation of such beliefs. Instead, there must be acceptance that all children, including those with impairments, can learn, and that their learning is of importance.

THE WORLD OF DISABILITY

It is not solely about the education of children with disabilities that a new set of attitudes needs to be developed. Attitude change must encompass persons with disabilities of all ages and levels of severity.

A World of Disabling Attitudes

The National Council on the Handicapped, appointed by President Reagan, has reiterated what people with disabilities have been saying for years: their major obstacles arise from external rather than internal barriers. The Council cites with approval the statement of an expert United Nations panel:

> Despite everything we can do, or hope to do, to assist each physically or mentally disabled person achieve his or her maximum potential in life, our efforts will not succeed until we have found the way to remove the obstacles to this goal directed by human society—the physical barriers we have created in public buildings, housing, transportation, houses of worship, centers of social life and other community facilities—the social barriers we have evolved and accepted against those who vary more than a certain degree from what we have been conditioned to regard as normal. More people are forced into limited lives and made to suffer by these man-made [sic] obstacles than by any specific physical or mental disability. (*Report,* 1975, p. 3)

Individuals with disabilities make the point even more directly:

> In his classic article entitled 'What does it mean when a retarded person says, "I'm not retarded"?' Bogdan tells of people labeled retarded who say, "I have never really thought of myself as retarded. I never really had that ugly feeling deep down," and another who says, "The worst word I have been called is retarded." The single largest self advocacy organization of people labeled retarded calls itself

"People First." Marsha Saxton, a person with Spina Bifida, reports, "As I see it, I'm not lucky or unlucky. I'm just the way I am. But I'm not disabled, I always thought. Or handicapped." Denise Karuth, who also has a physical disability, . . . writes, "Put your handkerchiefs away. I'm a lot more like you than you probably imagine." The message in each of these instances . . . is that a disability is only one dimension of a person, not all-defining and not inherently a barrier to being recognized as fully human. (Biklen, in press)

More than 25 years ago, Erving Goffman (1963) addressed this issue. He wrote: "By definition, of course, we believe the person with a stigma is not quite human." The point has been made more recently by Ved Mehta (1985): "You see, we are confronted with a vast ignorance in the world about the handicapped [so that] they would not understand if we acted like normal people" (p. 61).

In a variety of ways, persons with disabilities are neither treated nor viewed as "normal people." More often, they are treated "specially," either for their own good or for someone else's, but always according to an externally imposed standard.

Given public attitudes and policies such as these, persons with disabilities have increasingly developed a new perspective. This has been reflected recently in writings by disability rights activists and others in the independent-living movement (see Chapter 10 and Chapter 12, this volume; Fine & Asch, 1988; Funk, 1987; Gliedman & Roth, 1980; Scotch, 1988). For them, "the problem of disability is not only of physical impairment but also of unnecessary dependence on relatives and professionals, of architectural barriers and of unprotected rights" (DeJong & Lifchez, 1983, p. 48). This formulation is echoed in the report of the first national survey of self-perceptions of Americans with disabilities (Louis Harris & Associates, 1986):

An overwhelming majority, 74%, say they feel at least some sense of common identity with other people with disabilities (p. 110)

Nearly half, 45%, feel that disabled persons are a minority group in the same sense as blacks and Hispanics. Fifty-six percent of those disabled between birth and adolescence, and 53% of those 44 years of age and younger, share this view (p. 113).

The emerging and growing involvement of adults with disabilities can have a positive impact in the field of special education, for such individuals will be less likely to tolerate an educational system that does not recognize the capabilities of students with impairments and that fails to prepare them to deal with the realities of the outside world.

It is the force of a mobilized community of persons with disabilities that has been missing in the struggle for quality integrated education. Their involvement is essential (see Chapter 12, this volume). For unlike minority group students and others ill-served by the school, most students with disabilities are not born into a community of shared experiences. They need to partake of the strength that comes from those who are "ready with the armor and anger to fight to preserve their sense of themselves that the [larger] world [tries] to shatter" (Asch, 1984, p. 551).

The involvement of the community of adults with disabilities goes beyond the standard call for role models:

> It goes to the power of mutual support, the understanding of shared experiences and shared strength, the anger at oppression which powers advocacy and social action. Individuals with disabilities are less likely to tolerate a system which is disdainful of the capability of students with handicapping conditions; a system which fails to prepare them well for the larger world; a system which in the name of compassion and understanding gives caring and love but fails to provide education; a system which is special in its resources, but not its results; a system which sees the problem located solely in the biology of the individual; and ultimately a system which fails to prepare students to recognize and then to confront and change a disabling environment. (Lipsky & Gartner, 1987, pp. 72–73)

Beyond the advocacy that can come from seeing the education of those labeled as handicapped as part of the broad disability rights struggle, and as a struggle to ensure dignity and respect (Scotch, 1988), there is also a direct pedagogic consequence. In education, the students are both consumers and producers. That is, the student is not only the beneficiary of the learning activity, he or she does the work of learning, too. To put it another way, while teaching can take place without learning, learning cannot take place without the learner's efforts. The key to the achievement of learning becomes the effective engagement of the student. To do so, respect for the student is essential. Such respect will come about only when there is an end to the disabling attitudes that confront people, including students, with disabilities.

Special Education: Disabling Attitudes in Practice

It is the attitudinal milieu more than the individual's physical condition that influences society's response to persons with disabilities. An all-or-nothing concept of disability requires proof of total incapacity in order to gain entitlement to various benefit programs (National Council, 1986). Further, the media portray persons with disabilities as either heroic individuals or pathetic cripples, rather than as human beings with a multiplicity of qualities (Gartner & Joe, 1987). Such images of disability burden policy, including the education of students with disabilities.

Society's attitudes toward disability are deeply ingrained in professional practice. This is particularly evident in the social-psychological literature, where disability is based on the following assumptions:

1. Disability is biologically based.
2. Disabled persons face endless problems that are caused by the impairment.
3. Disabled persons are "victims."
4. Disability is central to the disabled person's self-concept and self-definition.

5. Disability is synonymous with a need for help and social support (Fine & Asch, 1988).

Similar assumptions hold true in special education. The child is considered impaired, instruction is disability-focused, professional personnel are often trained and certified to work only with specific disabilities, and attention to societal issues is often considered too political and not the business of educational institutions. Additionally, the child's parents are often treated as disabled (see Chapter 9, this volume. See also Ferguson & Asch, in press; Ferguson & Ferguson, in press; Lipsky, 1985; Sarason & Doris, 1979; Turnbull & Turnbull, 1985).

The assumptions underlying such beliefs can be tersely summarized: "(1) disability is a condition that individuals have, (2) disabled/typical is a useful and objective distinction, and (3) special education is a rationally conceived and coordinated system of services that help children labeled disabled" (Bogdan & Kugelmass, 1984, p. 173). This view of students labeled as handicapped adversely affects expectations regarding their academic achievement. It causes them to be separated from other students, to be exposed to a watered-down curriculum, to be excused from standards and tests routinely applied to other students, to be allowed grades that they have not earned, and, in some states, to be awarded special diplomas.

The rationale given for such watered-down expectations is that they are in the best interest of the child. Professionals often suggest that a child be placed in an environment where he or she will be "safe . . . because he would never be asked to do things there 'we know he cannot do' " (Granger & Granger, 1986, p. 26).

A report in the journal of the professional organization of special education administrators demonstrates this rationale. In a survey as to the desired basis for grading special education students when attending mainstreamed classes, among special and regular educators, school administrators, and parents, none favored having the regular classroom teacher use the same grading procedures that are used for the rest of the class (Mishal & Trippi, 1987). This is in contrast to findings based upon interviews with young adults with disabilities about their elementary and secondary education. Those special education students said that teachers should have high expectations of their disabled pupils. As one student labeled as learning disabled put it, "They'd give me the answer and let me get by. Teachers have to be flexible but tough" (Disabled students, 1988, p. 5; see also Chapter 10, this volume).

Not only do "small expectations" excuse students from academic performance, but they have also led state education departments, school systems, and the courts to excuse such students from the social and behavioral expectations and standards set for other students.

The medical or clinical model that undergirds special education inextricably leads to the belief that persons with handicaps, especially the severely disabled, are not capable of making choices or decisions. This conceptualization diminishes

> our ability to see them as individuals capable of ever making a choice, let alone the right choice. Seldom, if ever, is the person with the handicapping condition involved in the process of determining how their behavior, or the behavior of those around them, will be modified. The end result is more control for the caregivers and less control for the person being cared for. (Guess, Benson, & Siegal-Causey, 1985, p. 83)

Having denied individuals with disabilities autonomy and decision-making authority—in effect, denying them the respect given to people whom society respects—we then excuse their behavior, ascribing it to the disability.

Alternative Visions

Autonomy, that is, self-determination or control over decision-making, is something granted to persons who are valued. For individuals to be autonomous, or to have decision-making authority, reflects acceptance of three interrelated beliefs. They are:

1. A statement as to the *right* to control one's own life
2. An expression of belief in the individual's *capacity* to do so
3. A recognition of the *benefits* to the individual of doing so

For persons with disabilities, autonomy is limited by at least three factors. These include:

1. The limitations consequent upon *the impairment*
2. Broad *societal attitudes* toward persons with disabilities
3. The nature of current *human services practice*

Currently, it is the first of these that has most effect. Specifically, it is assumed that having a disability in itself precludes (or at least substantially limits) being autonomous. While the impairment itself may warrant some limitations on autonomy, such limits should come only after the limits caused by factors 2 and 3, above, are removed. Even then, great care must be exercised in coming to a priori assumptions as to the extent of such limitations. Until an accommodating society is established, the full range of an individual's capacity, and the extent to which apparent limitations are inherent or are a function of externally imposed barriers, will be unknown.

Earlier in this chapter, we discussed the societal attitudes that handicap persons with impairments. In a recent Supreme Court case, *School Board of Nassau County v. Arline,* Justice Brennan captured the point, writing: "Congress acknowledged that society's accumulated myths and fears about disability and disease are as handicapping as are the physical limitations that flow from actual impairment" ("On cases of contagion," 1987, p. A21). Despite changes in the recent past, too often it remains true that to have an impairment is to be seen as invalid.

Human service practice, in general, operates from a deficit model. That is, the consumer (student, patient, client) is seen as having some inadequacy, shortcoming, failure, or disease. The provider (teacher, doctor, therapist) is seen as knowing something, doing something, or having something that will overcome the deficit, fix the problem, or cure the disease. Central to this formulation is the assumption that in exchange for accepting and not challenging the expertise of the provider, the consumer is excused from normal obligations. That is, the consumer is allowed to be dependent, and thus, not autonomous. Such a deficit-based model stands at odds with the beliefs that undergird autonomy. Table 1 (see p. 262) compares autonomy-limiting with autonomy-enhancing approaches. Several general categories are described. Then autonomy-limiting and autonomy-enhancing formulations are identified.

Taylor (1988) addresses autonomy-enhancing issues and offers a radical challenge to the long-accepted principle of the least restrictive environment (LRE). While they were progressive when they were developed, LRE, the concepts of a "continuum of placements" (Reynolds, 1962) and a "cascade" of services (Deno, 1970), today do not promote the full inclusion of persons with disabilities in all aspects of societal life nor do they serve as guiding principles for the education that is the necessary means toward the goals' achievement. Taylor identifies seven conceptual and philosophic flaws in the acceptance of the LRE principle.

The LRE Principle Legitimates Restrictive Environments   While the LRE principle incorporates a presumption favoring less restriction, it also implies a more restricted and segregated environment is appropriate for at least some students. And as noted in Chapter 1, a significant percentage of students labeled as handicapped are placed in separate and segregated settings.

The LRE Principle Confuses Segregation and Integration on the One Hand with Intensity of Services on the Other   Intensity of services has traditionally been correlated with the extent of restrictiveness. That is, the more intensive the service need, the greater the segregation of the setting. This need not be the case. As Brown et al. (1983) state: "Any developmentally meaningful skill, attitude, or experience that can be developed or offered in a segregated school can also be developed or offered in a chronological age appropriate regular school" (p. 17). (See the following section for specific examples.)

The LRE Principle is Based on a "Readiness Model"   Rather than starting from the premise that the integrated setting is best, the LRE concept requires persons to earn the right to be in such a setting, to prove they are "ready" for a less restrictive setting. As we point out in Chapter 1, few students move through the continuum, whether in "mainstreaming" or to decertification. Not only is this morally unacceptable, the evidence is that more restrictive placements do not prepare people for less restrictive ones. Institutions do not prepare people for community living, segregated day programs do not prepare people for competitive work, and segregated schooling does not prepare students for integrated education.

Table 1.   Definitions

Autonomy-Limiting	*Autonomy-Enhancing*
Medical model; disability inherent in the adoption of "sick role" (tradeoff of dependency for care); the impairment is viewed as the central feature of the individual (language used, "the deaf boy").	Ecological or minority model; handicap a consequence of societal response to impairment; the individual with a disability (and his/her family) shares most characteristics with "normal" persons; disability is not the central variable defining the individual.

Decision making: LOCUS

Autonomy-Limiting	*Autonomy-Enhancing*
Professionals as decision-makers, viewed as both more knowledgeable and dispassionate.	Individual as key decision-maker, viewed as both more knowledgeable and interested.

Decision making: INSTRUMENT (e.g., IEP:)

Autonomy-Limiting	*Autonomy-Enhancing*
Prepared by school personnel, reviewed and "signed off" by parents.	Developed jointly by school personnel and parents, with input from both. Role for older students.

Environment

Autonomy-Limiting	*Autonomy-Enhancing*
Physical barriers, or limited accessibility (e.g., one ramp or restrooms on selected floors or a few accessible apartments).	Barrier-free environment, "open society."
All communication done assuming sighted and hearing recipients.	Availability of Braille or taped material, signing or closed-captioning.
Paratransit or special system.	Accessible regular transportation.

Autonomy-limiting and autonomy-enhancing practices may be found in the following specific areas:

Education

Autonomy-Limiting	*Autonomy-Enhancing*
Separate system with its own norms, limited standards, lowered expectations, special rules, separate diplomas.	Integrated system, with high expectations for all students.
Always the object of help (i.e., tutee).	Seen as able to give help (i.e., tutor).
Planning done for and decisions made for student in his or her best interest. Curriculum emphasizing rote learning and forced answer (multiple choice) responses.	Participant in planning and opportunities to make appropriate decisions. Higher order learning and open response opportunities.
Separate curriculum.	Adapted curriculum.
Structured classroom, teacher-centered organization.	Learner-centered, opportunities for and training in self-scheduling.
A continuum of placements, with students required to prove capacity to move to less restrictive settings(s).	Assumption that integrated setting is appropriate, levels of support provided on an individual basis.

(*continued*)

Table 1. (*continued*)

Media:

Autonomy-Limiting	*Autonomy-Enhancing*
Presentation of persons with disability as invalid, always in need of help, with impairment as only or central characteristic.	Presentations in full range of human activity, subject and object, help-giver and help-receiver, with disability highlighted only when appropriate.

Community living:

Autonomy-Limiting	*Autonomy-Enhancing*
Need to "prove" capacity to live in a community setting.	Presumption of capacity to live in normal setting. Provision of accommodations to make this possible.
Attendant care provided by attendants selected, hired, trained, supervised by agency.	Attendant services made available with selection and supervision by the individual.
Predesigned family support services provided by agencies.	Individuals/families able to select from a "cafeteria" of services and/or funds provided to purchase services.
Respite care arrangements designed solely to relieve families.	Respite arrangements made to offer new opportunities for individual.

Employment:

Autonomy-Limiting	*Autonomy-Enhancing*
"Sheltered" or other separate settings, on a permanent basis or until the individual "proves" capacity.	Supported employment bringing resources to "normal" workplace, increasing or fading them, as appropriate.
Special job finding and referral systems.	Use of regular systems, adapted as appropriate.
Presumptions as to appropriate employment areas (e.g., watch repair by the blind, repetitive work by the retarded).	Full range of opportunities, with initial selection based upon individual's interests, and then exploration of capacity, training needed, and reasonable accommodations.

The LRE Principle Supports the Primacy of Professional Decision-Making Rather than seeing integration as something that the individual wants or desires, professional judgment is invoked in striking the balance between LRE and "appropriateness."

The LRE Principle Sanctions Infringements on People's Rights Drawn from constitutional principles of due process, equal protection, and liberty, LRE formulates the issue not as whether persons with disabilities may on that basis be restricted, but the acceptable extent of the restriction (Turnbull, 1981, p. 17).

The LRE Principle Implies that People Must Move as They Develop and Change As persons with disabilities show they are "ready" for less restrictive settings, in communities or in schools, they are transferred to those settings, blunting the opportunity to sustain friendships or to build a community.

Table 2. Comparison of the LRE model and the Integration model

	LRE model	
Degree of impairment	Intensity of service	Location of service
Mild or moderate	Low	In or near the mainstream
Profound or severe	High	Separate or distant from mainstream
	Integration model	
Degree of impairment	Intensity of service	Location of service
Mild or moderate	Low	Fully integrated
Profound or severe	High	Fully integrated

The LRE Principle Directs Attention to Physical Settings Rather than to the Services and Supports People Need to be Integrated into the Community The issue becomes, for example, the size of the institutions, rather than the intensity of supports needed (Taylor, 1988).

The contrast between adherence to the LRE principle and a design that starts with integration and then varies the nature and intensity of services to support it in an educational setting can be seen in Table 2. This table portrays the relationship between the individual's degree of impairment, the intensity of service, and the location of the service.

EDUCATIONAL REFORM

As indicated in the first pages of this book, the educational reforms needed encompass the whole of the educational system, not only that part called special. Indeed, the origin, growth, and shape of special education have in many ways been defined by general education and the attitudes and behavior of mainstream educators toward students declared to be disabled. There has been a narrowing definition of what is considered normal, accompanied by the growth of ever more expanded programs for special populations. While their professional organization promotes alternative approaches (Canter, Dawson, Silverstein, Hale, & Zins, 1987), the role of school psychologists, given the present educational philosophy and their current training (*School Psychology*, 1984), often gives professional rationale for the increasing identification of deviant, or to use the current phrase, "at-risk" students. In the obverse, there is consequence for those students who remain in general education classrooms:

> Every time a child is called mentally defective and sent off to the special education class for some trivial defect, the children who are left in the regular classroom receive a message: no one is above suspicion; everyone is being watched by the authorities; nonconformity is dangerous. (Granger & Granger, 1986, p. xii)

The problem is not special education or general education alone. "In a sense, regular and special education teachers have colluded to relieve regular teachers of responsibilities for teaching children functioning at the bottom of their class" (Shepard, 1987, p. 328). The pressure to "succeed" with high test scores, and with the very large class sizes that make individual attention extremely difficult, makes it more likely that teachers will seek uniformity of students rather than diversity. To put it more sharply, there is, in effect, a "deal" between special and general education. The former asserts a particular body of expertise and a unique understanding of "special" students, thus laying claim both to professional obligation and student benefit. The latter, because of the lack of skills and resources, or because of prejudice, is often happy to hand over these students to a welcoming special education system. The

> deal is sanctioned, on one hand, by the clinicians who provide an intrapsychic justification for the referral, and, on the other hand, by those in the role of advocacy who see increasing numbers of students in special education as providing evidence of their effectiveness. (Lipsky & Gartner, 1987, p. 59)

And, as Lilly points out in Chapter 8, this volume, a similar situation exists in professional preparation programs, separating regular and special education teacher training.

A part of the separation between general and special education is revealed in special educators' decrying the absence of attention to special education in the numerous national reports about education. Indeed, nearly an entire issue of *Exceptional Children* addressed this topic. The inattention to special education is described and the alleged tradeoff between excellence and equity deplored (Pugach & Sapon-Shevin, 1987; Sapon-Shevin, 1987). However, Stephen Lilly (1987) suggests that the reason special education is ignored is that "current special education policies and practices for students labeled mildly handicapped are neither conceptually sound nor of sufficient quality to be included in the 'ideal' educational system described by these authors" (p. 326). Thus, rather than deploring the inattention, he applauds it, saying that

> Until we are willing to examine our flawed assumptions about children and teachers and become integral members of the general education community, we cannot expect either to be featured in reform reports or to be involved in construction of the next era of public education in the United States. (Lilly, 1987, p. 326)

Broad national educational reforms that, for the most part, ignore students labeled as handicapped, are presented here. Following this discussion, the chapter focuses on change affecting all students.

Reforms in General

School reform, while sometimes a slogan without substance, has become a prominent activity throughout the nation. Since the publication in 1983 of *A Nation at Risk*, there have been hundreds of reports, increasing almost daily, from special commissions, educational, professional and business groups, governors, and other public officials. The first round of reforms focused upon externals, largely from the state level, such as raising standards and addressing the imposition of new requirements on students, as well as increasing teacher salaries, and developing of career ladder programs. This was followed by a "second wave" of reforms that gave increased attention to school level concerns, for example, their organization, governance, staffing, teacher roles, and the relationships to parents and community. More recently, in what some have called a "third wave" of reform, there has been attention to "at-risk" students, a euphemism for students of color, those living in poverty, and residents of inner cities, but not (generally) including those labeled as handicapped.

The focus of the current efforts is captured in a set of recommendations for reform of high schools developed by the Coalition of Essential Schools, by Theodore R. Sizer (Wiggins, 1988):

1. Do not waste class time on "teaching." Class time can be better spent with students working collaboratively, practicing or performing, sharing knowledge or experience.
2. Focus on helping students learn how to learn, not on course "coverage" of material which is soon forgotten.
3. Stop thinking about education in terms of "content" and start thinking of it in terms of "intellectual habits."
4. Insist that all major decisions about curriculum, discipline, and school standards be made by consensus among school staff.
5. Recognize that good teaching is personalized and requires a sharply reduced teacher-to-student ratio.
6. Do not "plan" for change; rather, get change underway and institutionalize the making of intelligent adjustments.
7. Conceive of all academic courses as if they were to be taught to the top-track students.
8. Adopt a grading system that creates stronger incentives for all students.
9. Develop in each school a pretest and a posttest to measure, to the school's own satisfaction, its effect upon student performance.
10. Make schools, not universities, the primary home of researchers. (pp. 28–30)

The new attention to the "at-risk" student is in part a return to the work of Ron Edmonds (1979), who challenged the belief that schools could not make a difference for poor and minority students. The recommendations of the two major recent reports are similar. The Committee for Economic Development (*Children in Need*, 1987) calls for prevention through early (preschool) intervention, restructuring the schools (new roles for teachers, bottom up management, collaboration with the home, employability skills, ease of reentry for dropouts), and partnerships among schools, business, and the community. The Carnegie Commission (*An Imperiled Generation*, 1988) also calls for priority to be given to the early years, and advocates smaller schools where students have a sense of belonging, as well as a coherent curriculum, more flexibility in calendar and access, better facilities, and collaboration among schools, parents, colleges, and corporations. While including proposals similar to the national studies, such as parental choice and school-based management, the California Business Roundtable, declaring that "small improvements are no longer acceptable," proposes reducing the time students spend in comprehensive public schools from 13 to 9 years. Children between the ages of 4 and 6 would attend primary schools run by public or private organizations that would compete for state contracts, those between the ages of 7 and 16 would attend comprehensive schools that teach core competencies to all students in heterogeneous ability groupings, and those who master the core competencies by age 16 would be entitled to 2 additional years of specialized training at the high school or postsecondary institution of their choice (Snider, 1988b).

Unlike the earlier round of school reform, which seemed more interested in selecting "winners," these newer reforms address a wider audience. A report assessing the nation's success in teaching reading, for example, calls for the use with all students of the same thought-stretching activities as used with the better readers (*Who Reads Best?*, 1988).

Challenging the notion that individual learning differences require radically different curriculums, Goodlad and Oakes (1988) cite misconceptions about learning, individual differences, and the organization of opportunity. They declare that the consequent tracking of students and the establishment of rigid ability groups, as well as separate programs, "are generally ineffective means for addressing individual differences, and for many children, harmful" (p. 19).

Alternative Programs

In a report by the National Academy of Sciences (Heller et al., 1982), the authors emphasize that the "main purpose of assessment in education is to improve instruction and learning . . . [and] a significant portion of children who experience difficulties in the classroom can be treated effectively through improved instruction [in the regular classroom]" (p. 72). They go on to point out that "in planning instruction for the special child, primary attention should be directed to the specific features of the instructional treatments identified as fostering academic progress in children with initial poor performance" (p. 88).

The importance of effective instructional practices in the context of setting and placement is emphasized by Lloyd (1984), who argues that it makes more sense to organize instruction on the basis of "skills students need to be taught" than on categorical labels (p. 13–14).

Cooperative learning programs have demonstrated success in accommodating student diversity in instruction. Here, students of differing ability levels work together in small groups with individual success dependent upon collaboration and group learning. Developed initially to bring together white and nonwhite students, they have proven successful in educating students in heterogeneous classes, including those incorporating mainstreamed special education and remedial reading students (Slavin, 1987; Slavin, Stevens, & Madden, 1988). Research on both the cooperative learning model developed at the Johns Hopkins University and that on the cooperation education model developed at the University of Minnesota indicate success in learning for a diverse student population.

While cooperative learning programs involve students learning together, peer learning programs involve one student as tutor and the other as tutee. And in cross-aged tutoring programs, "the achievement gains for the tutor are often as great or greater than those for the tutees" (Slavin, 1986, p. 13). A study for the Carnegie Commission (Hedin, 1986) recommends involvement in tutoring for all students. The U.S. Department of Education (1986) includes tutoring as a practice that "works," and Levin (1984), in a study comparing the cost-effectiveness of various remedial programs, found tutoring as the most cost effective. For tutees, benefits come about through the individualization and additional time in instructional activities provided. Tutoring can provide the "scaffold" some students need to provide support as they learn new material (Brown & Campione, 1986). For tutors, there is the opportunity to practice activities for which learning has occurred, but mastery has not yet been attained, or for which learning in one setting has been achieved but not yet generalized to other settings.

Jenkins and Jenkins (1981) report on programs where students labeled as handicapped benefit as tutees and tutors, in both academic skills and social behavior. Strain (1981) describes particular benefits for behaviorally disturbed students. And a unique program in Utah used students labeled as handicapped as cross-aged tutors of nonhandicapped students, to their mutual benefit (Osguthorpe & Scruggs, 1986).

Slavin (1987) proposes that the success of cooperative learning programs, including peer learning, offers the basis for more fundamental school reorganization. This would include cooperative learning in the classroom, integration of special education and remedial services with the regular program, peer coaching, cooperative activities among teachers, collaborative school governance, and cooperation with parents and community members.

While cooperative schools represent a potential, school improvement projects building upon the effectiveness research (Edmonds, 1979, 1982) are a present reality. This research identified five key characteristics of effective schools: 1) educational leadership, 2) orderly school climate, 3) high achievement expectations for all students, 4) systematic monitoring of student performance, and 5) emphasis on basic skills. Following Edmonds's work in the New York City Public Schools, most states have initiated school improvement programs explicitly structured upon the characteristics of the effective schools research (see Chapter 2, this volume).

Bickel and Bickel (1986) have assessed the school effectiveness and effective classroom instruction research for their implications for special education. Their major finding is that

> more integrated planning is likely to be far more productive than continuing the historical separateness [between general and special education]. The same school environment that can affect regular classroom instruction will also impact on special classrooms in the same building. . . . A recognition of the importance of the vested relationship of classroom instruction to the larger school environment is a fundamental message of the effective schools research. (p. 497)

Reforms of Special Education

The research data clearly show that the paradigm that undergirds the current organization and conduct of special education is defective:

> [It] operates to identify among persons with disabilities areas of deficits and 'deviancies,' as determined by the consensus of those persons who assume responsibility (and control) over their behavior, and buttressed by an array of diagnostic instruments and surveys that depict either expected 'normal' development or assumed community standards for behavior and conduct. The assumption is, of course, that once having identified the problems associated with the disability, the environment can be arranged, controlled, or otherwise manipulated to bring about the desired change in the student. This organization, variously referred to as 'prescriptive-teaching,' 'remedial,' 'let's fix it,' and so on, always carried with it the (at least) implicit assumption that persons with disabilities are somehow less than normal or, at its worst, 'deviant.' (Guess & Thompson, in press)

Skrtic (1986) argues that these assumptions are challenged by different understandings of disability, ones that are less rooted in biology and psychology, "and derive more from sociological, political, and cultural theories of deviance, and which provide many different perspectives on virtually every aspect of special education and 'disability'" (p. 6). Skrtic (1987) argues that

> current school organization creates—and can do nothing but create—students with mild disabilities as artifacts of the system, and, furthermore, [current] efforts to reform the system—without replacing it with an entirely different configuration—do little to eliminate mild disabilities or their effects, produce even more students with mild disabilities, and create a new and largely hidden class of student casualties. (p. 3)

While much of the criticism of the current organization of special education comes from actual practice, increasingly, there are more fundamental challenges to its basic conceptualization (Berres & Knoblock, 1987; Biklen, 1985, 1987; Biklen, Lehr, Searl, & Taylor, 1987; Bogdan & Kugelmass, 1984; Gartner & Lipsky, 1987; Lipsky & Gartner, 1987; Stainback & Stainback, 1984; Skrtic, 1986, 1987). Some of these formulations focus on the nature of students, while others emphasize the conceptualization of special education.

Stainback and Stainback (1984) emphasize the shared characteristics of students. They argue, first, that there are not two distinct groups of students, regular or normal students and others who deviate from the norm, but rather that all students vary across a range of physical, intellectual, psychological, and social characteristics. Second, they suggest that it is not only special education students who can benefit from (or indeed need) individualized services, but that all students can benefit.

Given the variety of criticisms of the current organization of special education services, it is not surprising that current reform activities range across a broad spectrum. Some proposals seek to bridge the gap between the two parallel systems, others attempt to blend aspects of each together, and yet others call for an end to dual systems.

Bridging Parallel Systems

The current organization of special education has developed an elaborate system to assess and classify students for the purpose of placing them in appropriate programs, broadly organized in a bimodal design of special and general education systems. Within this basic dual system approach, there have been various efforts to bridge the gap between them.

One set of activities might be described as strengthening the holding power of the general education system. This includes the development of prereferral alternatives, including providing assistance to general education teachers to strengthen and expand their skills. The most prominent of these is the "consulting teacher" model (Huefner, 1988). Discussed prior to the passage of PL 94-142, it has gained increasing attention in the past several years, for example, in a special issue of *Teacher Education and Special Education* (Blankenship & Jordan, 1985), and in the report of the National Task Force on School Consultation (Idol, 1986). This model is being used statewide in Idaho, Massachusetts, and Vermont, as well as in districts in many other states.

The "ultimate goal of the consulting teacher model is to enable the regular education teacher to successfully instruct children with special needs" (Huefner, 1988, p. 404). Advocates of this approach claim an array of potential benefits, including "decreasing special education enrollment, allowing more handicapped learners to compete in the mainstream, perhaps reducing special education costs. . . ." Additional benefits include the reduction of stigma, the production of greater understanding across disciplines, the provision of on-the-job training for regular educators in special education skills, the reduction of mislabeled non-handicapped students, and the availability of spill-over benefits to regular students (Huefner, 1988). An interesting design with significant potential, there is not yet a sufficient body of data to warrant wholesale adoption, and its advocates are careful to warn of inappropriate or premature implementation (Huefner, 1988). Furthermore, in the context of our argument, as presently conducted this design continues the dual system. However, its underlying principle, that of bringing assistance to general education teachers to enhance their ability to educate students in a mainstream setting, is a necessary part of the larger reforms.

"Mainstreaming" is a term used extensively, although it does not appear in PL 94-142. It slides together two concepts worth keeping separate: 1) the general stricture for placement in the least restrictive environment (LRE), and 2) activities involving a student whose basic placement is in a special education setting, and who spends a portion of the day in a general education ("mainstream") setting. In this latter regard, a recent ERIC search identified over 120 studies. The data assessing effectiveness of this type of mainstreaming are mixed: some show positive social benefits, other reveal both social and academic benefits, and still others show no benefits (*Research on the Effectiveness of Mainstreaming*, 1987). Basically, the studies identify two sets of factors that determine the effectiveness of "mainstreaming": 1) the adequacy of the preparation and the appropriateness of the identification of the students to be mainstreamed, and 2) the activities in the mainstreamed class, including organization of the environment, adaptation of the curriculum, and teaching strategies.

The limits in the quality of the instruction students receive in separate special education programs are noted throughout this book. In Chapter 1, a study in Pittsburgh (Sansone & Zigmond, 1986) is discussed that identifies the limited amount of mainstreaming taking place in the city's elementary schools. Fewer than 10% of the mild to moderately handicapped students participated, and for those few who did, opportunities were sharply limited. In four studies involving the mainstreaming of students labeled as learning disabled in 12 high schools, Zigmond, Levin, and Laurie (1985) found very little that was different instructionally when these students were mainstreamed. The major adjustment that they found was the lowering of grading standards so that the students had a better opportunity to pass the course. Given the inadequacies of the adjustments made, it is not surprising that only 1.4% of the special education students in Pittsburgh returned to general education classrooms (*Special Education*, 1986).

Blending at the Margin

Increasingly, there are efforts underway to break down the wall between the special and regular or general education systems. That is, there are educational programs designed to serve students now in special education, those variously called mild or moderately handicapped, in a common setting with other students with learning problems, or those "at risk." Among the various efforts are those under the rubric of the "general education initiative" launched by U.S. Department of Education Assistant Secretary Madeleine Will.

Called "the hottest debate in special education" (Viadero, 1988, p. 1), the "general education initiative" has sparked attention throughout the field. It has been the subject of numerous conferences, hundreds of professional presentations, and of the most comprehensive survey of special education research thus far (Wang, Reynolds, & Walberg, 1987a). It was also the subject of a petulant attack in a special issue of the *Journal of Learning Disabilities* (Kauffman, Lloyd, & McKinney, 1988) and of an extensive response (Wang & Walberg, 1988). For some, it is a "promising approach,"(Wang, 1988), while for others, a "slippery slope" (Gerber, 1988). In Chapter 3 of this volume, Stainback and Stainback describe both the rationale and the substance of the initiative, and present a critique of its limits. For our purposes, it is enough to note the main direction of the approach. In a report to the Secretary of the U.S. Department of Education, Assistant Secretary Will pointed to current practices that suffer from fragmented approaches, a dual system, stigmatization of students, and battles between parents and school people about placement decisions (*Educating Students with Learning Problems,* 1986). Few would argue the accuracy of this analysis; the conflict has been about how to change the system. In its report to the Secretary, the Office of Special Education and Rehabilitative Services stated the challenge was to "search for ways to serve as many children as possible in the regular classroom by encouraging special education . . . to form partnership with regular education" (*Educating Students,* 1986, p. 20). Among the components of the initiative are increased instructional time, support systems for teachers, empowerment of principals to control all programs and resources at the building level, and new instructional approaches that involve "shared responsibility" between general and special education (*Educating Students,* 1986).

One approach proposed by general education initiative advocates involves a "waiver" of existing federal and state regulations to allow for needed changes (Viadero, 1988). According to Reynolds and Lakin (1987), a more proactive approach is to emulate the Food and Drug Administration's role rather than, as at present, a federal role that is

> largely limited to the disbursement of funds. In the FDA approach, the federal Department of Education would have a clearly defined obligation and commitment to use its vested authority (and budget) to promote demonstrably effective approaches to educating mildly handicapped students and to support research dedicated to that same purpose. (Reynolds & Lakin, 1987, p. 348)

One "regular education initiative" is the Adaptive Learning Environment Model (ALEM) developed by Margaret Wang (Epps & Tindal, 1987; Wang & Reynolds, 1985; Wang, Reynolds, & Walberg, 1987a; Wang & Walberg, 1988). According to Wang, ALEM programs are in effect in scores of schools across the country. The fullest expression of the model is at the Verner School, Riverview School District, Pennsylvania. All 50 students labeled as handicapped are in integrated classes full-time. Classes are taught by a general education teacher, with two special education teachers circulating to provide assistance to teachers and direct services to students. Rather than presenting ALEM as a single teaching technique, in their most recent iteration, its designers (Wang & Walberg, 1988) describe it as "a comprehensive, multi-faceted education system that provides a built-in mechanism to incorporate on an ongoing basis the best practices that have a strong research base for improving instruction and learning on a year-round basis" (p. 132).

Another approach, the Integrated Classroom Model (ICM) was developed at the University of Washington, and has been in operation since 1980. Since that time, participants have been working with local school systems to develop programs to educate students with mild handicaps in integrated classrooms. A study of one integrated classroom model program in the Issaquah school district involved 13 classrooms in three buildings, grades 1 through 6, with approximately one-third of the students in each class labeled mildly handicapped (learning disabled, mildly mentally retarded, and behaviorally disabled). Comparing the results in academic achievement for special education students in the ICM program versus those served in a pull-out resource room program, the project found: "the integrated classroom model [was] a viable alternative service delivery model for students with learning disabilities, as the results are virtually indistinguishable from those of the resource room program. Any significant differences found supported the integrated model" (Affleck, Madge, Adams, & Lowenbraum, 1988, pages 345–346). As for the general education students, "There were no distinguishable differences in achievement between these students in an ICM classroom and those in a classroom with no handicapped peers" (p. 346). Furthermore, the staffing of the ICM program produces a significant cost savings (about $50,000 a year in an elementary school). Thus, according to the research, the ICM is a program that costs less, that fully integrates students it serves, and that produces equal learning, as in segregated programs.

In a project called Maximizing Educational Remediation within General Education (MERGE), in Olympia, Washington, students with mild handicaps are served in an integrated setting with low-achieving, nonhandicapped students. While the ICM program serves students in an integrated setting with a single teacher, Project MERGE brings support staff into integrated classrooms, both to assist the regular education teacher and to work directly with students. As with the ICM program, the evaluation of Project MERGE indicates achievement benefits for students, as well as greater integration and cost savings. Of particular note is the inclusion of behaviorally disabled students: those students generally regarded as the most difficult to integrate. And, promising for the future, the support given in these integrated general education classes has reduced the number of students labeled as handicapped. Indeed, the program is designed to provide assistance to all students without the requirement that they first be labeled as handicapped (Wood, MacDonald, & Siegelman, 1987).

At the same time as there are increasing questions about services for those labeled as mild or moderately handicapped, concerns are being expressed about other students in pull-out programs, such as Chapter I and other remedial efforts. Indeed, some of the same researchers are involved in what has been termed "repairing the second system" (Wang, Reynolds, & Walberg, 1987b). In this formulation, the unmet needs of a broader group of students are addressed. The basis of these efforts is the recognition that a variety of school programs have been created to provide special, compensatory, and/or remedial education services for students not well served in the general education system. Whatever the improvements of such efforts, they nonetheless have created large, separate, costly, and overall ineffective systems. Furthermore, they have left the mainstream largely unaffected. Unaffected, that is, except for having those extruded as students who do not fit an ever narrowing standard of normalcy.

Redesigning Education Programs

Redesign efforts are taking several different forms. Some are being put forward by state education departments, such as those in Washington, Connecticut, Vermont, and Pennsylvania. Other efforts are being made by individual school systems, such as Johnson City and Syracuse, New York. Still others are being initiated by foundations. In Minneapolis, with support from the General Mills Foundation, there is a plan to establish an academy that will eliminate pull-out programs and will serve a full cross section of the city's pupils, K–6 (Gold, 1988). And in five cities across the country, the Annie E. Casey Foundation "New Futures" program is supporting efforts fundamentally to redesign education for those students traditionally served in pull-out programs.

Some researchers, coming at these issues from the perspective of remedial education programs, have called for the redesign of both remedial and special education to serve what are viewed as students with common needs (See Chapter 5). Other educators have identified specific instructional strategies, such as cooperative learning, for integrating special education and remedial services within the regular program (see earlier section of this chapter). The Council of Chief State School Officers has proposed to "guarantee" to students least likely to graduate from school access to quality education programs (*Elements of a Model State Statute to Provide Educational Entitlements for At-Risk Students*, 1987). Unlike previous efforts by governors (Honetschlager & Cohen, 1988) and the business community (*Children in Need*, 1987), the "Chiefs" proposal explicitly includes students now labeled as handicapped.

Before turning to regular education initiatives, three additional special education developments are worth noting. The first is an issue likely to come to a head in the near future: the role of intermediate units. The pattern of bringing groups of students together in separate settings seems to favor administrative efficiency over pupil entitlement to education in the least restrictive environment. For example, in Nassau County, New York, where the Board of Cooperative Education Services (BOCES) is the intermediate unit, "out of 230 special education classes, 208 are in segregated facilities" ("Special Ed Students," 1986). And the balance of responsibility between such intermediate units and local districts for the education of students with handicaps is at the core of a dispute in Pennsylvania ("Renewed Debate: Which Pennsylvania Agencies are Responsible for EHA, 504?" 1988).

A second development concerns noncategorical organization of special education programs. Instead of organizing classes based upon specific handicapping conditions, this approach organizes classes based upon learning needs. A recent study (Alberg et al., 1988) compared this approach as carried out in Massachusetts and South Dakota to the categorical organization of classes in New Jersey and North Dakota. The two approaches were compared in terms of three broad sets of implementation patterns: 1) student assignment (including referral, assessment, eligibility, IEPs, placement); 2) organization of the education process (including student integration and grouping, instruction and evaluation, curriculum and instructional materials, exit criteria, and teacher preparation); 3) administration (including staff organization and staff attitudes).

> Despite the fact that this study was designed to identify differences between the implementation of categorical and noncategorical approaches, the overwhelming result was that these states' service programs were more alike than different. The noncategorical and categorical states served relatively the same percentages of students in their special education programs. No consistent differences were found in the way in which students were grouped or in the type of instructional programs employed. Other than the fact that in the categorical approach the students were initially labeled and placed according to handicapping conditions, few differences were found in the implementation of the two approaches. (Alberg et al., 1988, p. 10)

The third development is beyond the scope of our work here. It is worth noting, however, that in a number of foreign countries, Australia, Canada, Denmark, Sweden, and the United Kingdom, for example, there are major efforts toward full integration of students labeled as handicapped. Given similarities with the United States, the work in Canada, especially in the Woodstock District in New Brunswick and in several Ontario districts, warrants further analysis.

A Single System

There is an alternative to separate systems: a merged or unitary system. The conception of a unitary system requires a fundamental change in the way differences among people are perceived, in the ways the educational programs in schools are organized, and in how the purpose of that education is viewed. This alternative system rejects the bimodal division of handicapped and nonhandicapped students, and recognizes that individuals vary, and that single-characteristic definitions fail to capture the complexity of people. Moreover, it rejects the medical or deviancy model, and the notion that the problem lies in the individual and the resolution lies in one or another treatment modality. The unitary system, in contrast, requires adaptations in society and in education, not solely in the individual:

> No longer would there be a need to approach differences in human capabilities or characteristics as disabilities on which to base categorical groupings. In a merged system, an individual difference in visual ability, for example, could be viewed as only one of numerous characteristics of a student, rather than the over-riding educa-

tional focus of a student's life. . . . It would not dictate differential placement and treatment according to a categorical affiliation which is often inherent in the disabilities approach to education. (Stainback & Stainback, 1984, p. 109)

In a merged or unitary system, effective practices in classrooms and schools would characterize education for all students. No longer would there be an education system that focuses on the limitations of "handicapped" students, a teacher's incapacity to teach students because of a lack of special credentials, or instruction that is determined by the label attached to students. Nor would blame be placed on students or on family characteristics. Rather, the focus would be on effective instruction for all students based on the belief that "substantial student improvements occur when teachers accept the responsibility for the performance of all their students and when they structure their classrooms so that student success is a primary product of the interaction that takes place there" (Algozzine & Maheady, 1985, p. 498).

While not quite fully giving up a dual system approach, the "rights without labels" concept put forward by the National Coalition of Advocates for Students, National Association of School Psychologists, and the National Association of School Social Workers moves in that direction. While affirming that access to special education must be ensured for all significantly handicapped children who need and can benefit from it, they point out that it is not a benign act to label as "handicapped" a child who is not. They state that

1. Such labels are often irrelevant to instructional needs.
2. Such labels lead to reduced expectations for children so labeled.
3. The process of assessment to assign such labels depletes scarce resources.
4. This all leads to a decreased willingness on the part of general education to meet the diverse needs of all students.

The groups' support for alternatives is conditioned upon assurances that: 1) targeted funds will not be diverted from students in need, 2) that the full panoply of PL 94-142 due process rights be maintained, and, 3) that parents be afforded the opportunity to select a traditional categorical approach for their child(ren). (While this may be appropriate during an interim stage, this last assurance should not be necessary when there is a unitary system.) Perhaps most interestingly, going beyond PL 94-142 and offering guidance for the future, they propose standards for both program design and assessment. As to program design, they state that any noncategorical program or system shall:

1. Employ prereferral screening/intervention measures and utilize evaluation procedures that include curriculum-based assessments.
2. Employ methodology known to be associated with effective teaching/learning (e.g., provide students with orderly and productive environments, ample learning/teaching time, systematic and objective feedback on performance, well sequenced curricula).

3. Focus attention on basic skills as priority areas for instruction (e.g., language, self-dependence, reasonable social behavior, mathematics, health and safety).
4. Provide procedures to identify and respond to the individual needs of all students, and in particular, those who may need modifications in their school programs.
5. Provide for special education aids, services, and resources to be delivered in regular education settings.

Concerning assessment of outcomes, any proposed noncategorical program shall:

1. Have an objective methodology for assessing the educational progress of students in major curriculum domains (including academic, social, motivational and attitudinal variables) and for comparing such progress with results in traditional programs.
2. Contain and utilize a cost-benefit analysis to compare costs with traditional programs.

The above standards far exceed those required of present programs.

There is a growing body of practice that builds upon these new conceptualizations. In part, they borrow from the school effectiveness work in general education (Edmonds, 1979), and its adaptation to special education (Bickel & Bickel, 1986; Goodman, 1985; Jewell, 1985; Peterson, Albert, Foxworth, Cox, & Tilley, 1985). Knoll and Meyer (n.d.) summarize these principles as follows:

Principals in effective schools are instructional leaders, who pose high expectations for students and teachers.

The climate in an effective school is orderly, disciplined, and comfortable. A commitment to excellence is evident and there are high expectations for student achievement.

Students' goals and objectives are meaningful, clearly written, sequenced, and reviewed and updated periodically based on student progress data that are collected on a regular basis.

Student achievement is recognized and rewarded frequently. Student progress is monitored using a criterion-reference approach: the measures used are directly related to the instructional objectives.

Within effective classrooms, "down time" is kept to a minimum. Students spend a high percentage of their time actively engaged in learning tasks.

Effective teachers spend a high percentage of their time involved in active instruction.

Effective teachers adapt, modify, and create curricular units for their own class that are sequenced and integrated into the long range educational goals of the school.

Effective schools tend to have a low teacher/student ratio.

Administrators, teachers, support personnel, students, and parents in effective schools describe an atmosphere of cooperation and open communication.

Parents support and are actively involved in effective schools. (p. 2–3)

Knoll and Meyer (n.d.) conclude "that these same principles are outlined in virtually every special education text as the hallmarks of a good 'special' education program" (p. 3).

Integrated Programs

Programs of full integration (or nearly so) are being carried out in a few states, such as Vermont and Washington, and in individual schools within some school districts, such as Johnson City and Syracuse, in New York, and in the Riverview School District, in Pennsylvania. In Vermont, for example, the "Homecoming Model" brings students from regional special education centers to their local school, and in individual districts, such as Winooski, there are no full-time self-contained classes. Key in achieving success is the integration of support services for all students in a single unit.

In Washington, as noted in the previous section, the focus has been on integrating students with mild handicaps, as well as sustaining youngsters in general education; a state education department official describes the program as "replacing a failure-response system with a success maintenance one."

In Johnson City, New York, mastery learning principles have long been a critical feature of district activities, and more recently, an outcomes-based model has been adopted (Vickery, 1988; for a broader discussion of outcomes-based models, cf. Glatthorn, 1987). Except for a few older students whose parents wanted them to stay in out-of-district schools, all students are served in the district, and all those with mild and moderate handicapping conditions are in integrated classes. The use of teacher teams, specialists coming into the classroom, and teacher control over time and pace of learning are key features.

In Syracuse, New York, at the Ed Smith Elementary School (and to a lesser extent at the Levy Middle School), a full range of students labeled as handicapped are integrated, including several autistic children. Team teaching is a key resource. (Chapter 11 is based upon experiences at the Ed Smith School.)

While there are limits to the evaluation data (for example, random assignments of pupils to control groups would likely violate PL 94-142), in each of these programs, research indicates that student learning is enhanced. Additionally, after initial start-up costs, the programs operate at costs equal to, or less than, the previous segregated models.

In summarizing the steps necessary to achieve an integrated school, Knoll and Meyer (n.d.) identify three elements: 1) commitment, 2) planning, and 3) staff involvement, preparation, and training. The first element is the key. "What distinguishes the programs [that work] is a strong belief in the value of educating children with severe disabilities alongside typical peers and preparing them to participate fully in community life. Integration works when people are committed to it" (Taylor, 1988, p. 48). Initial commitment may come from diverse sources: parents, administrators, and teachers. Several of the recent "bottom-up" innovations launched by teachers and principals have included students labeled as handicapped. Among these are the Key School in Indianapolis (Fiske, 1988, A16), where teachers are using Howard Gardner's ideas (see Chapter 7, this volume), and at the Montlake Elementary School in Seattle. At the Montlake School, the principal has structured the school so that there are no "pull-out" programs, and, as a result, has been able both to redefine and redeploy staff (Olson, 1988, 1, 22). Regardless of its initial source, the commitment to educate all students in a unitary system must ultimately be shared by all the "stakeholders."

A common feature of each of these programs is that while they provide integrated settings, they do not ignore the individual needs of students, whether or not they are labeled as handicapped. Features of these programs may include: use of aides and support staff in the classroom, teaming between general and special education teachers, consultation and technical assistance to teachers, adaptation of curricula, and the use of specific learning strategies, such as cooperative learning designs and peer instruction, and outcome-based approaches. By providing for the individual needs of each student, a unitary system is not a "dumping" ground. Rather, it is a refashioned mainstream.

Central to the new design for students are new roles for teachers. While varying from district to district, they include such factors as:

1. Delabeling of teachers, that is, eliminating narrow categorical responsibilities in favor of broader responsibilities
2. Collaboration and consultation among teachers
3. Greater teacher control over their own time, and variation in the use of students' time: not everything is organized in lock step periods
4. Greater variety in teacher-student interactions, including whole class instruction, small group work, individual tutoring, managing of peer learning groups, monitoring of student self-scheduled activities
5. Broader teacher involvement with other adults, including support staff, out-of-school learning resources, and parents

Summarizing the look of a system that educates all of its students together, Stainback, Stainback, and Forest (in press) compare dual and unitary systems (see Table 3, p. 278).

The characteristics of a unitary system square with a consensus as to Program Quality Indicators. In a survey (Meyer, Eichenger, & Park-Lee, 1987) of behavior therapy experts, experts in severe disabilities, experts in programs for the deaf and blind, directors of special education, and parents involved in advocacy efforts, the highest rated included:

Whether the program philosophy emphasizes preparation for living in the least restrictive environment, professional staff talk with students in a manner that communicates respect, alternative communication modes and adaptive equipment are used to meet individual needs, instructional strategies are individualized, the program philosophy emphasizes both educability and program accountability for stu-

Table 3.   Comparison of dual and unified systems

Concern	Dual system	Unified system
Student characteristics	Dichotomizes students into special and regular	Recognizes continuum among all students of intellectual, physical, and psychological characteristics
Individualization	Stresses individualization for students labeled special	Stresses individualization for all students
Instructional strategies	Seeks to use special strategies for special students	Selects from range of available strategies according to each student's learning needs
Type of educational services	Eligibility generally based on category affiliation	Eligibility based on each student's individual learning needs
Diagnostics	Large expenditures on identification of categorical affiliation	Emphasis on identifying the specific instructional needs of all students
Professional relationships	Establishes artificial barriers among educators that promote competition and alienation	Promotes cooperation through sharing resources, expertise, and advocacy responsibilities
Curriculum	Options available to each student are limited by categorical affiliation	All options available to every student as needed
Focus	Student must fit regular education program or be referred to special education	Regular education program is adjusted to meet all students' needs
The "real" world	Some students educated in an artificial special world	All students educated in mainstream of regular education
Attitude	Some students given an education as a special or charity-like favor	All students given an education as a regular and normal practice

Adapted from Stainback, S., Stainback, W., & Forrest, M. (in press). *Educating All Students in the Mainstream of Regular Education*. Baltimore: Paul H. Brookes Publishing Co.

dent gain, training is provided in actual situations and environments where skills will be used, and caregiving interactions are used for instruction. (p. 260)

The examples cited here, while not the only ones, do represent some of the major efforts currently available. It is not dissimilar from the work in the reform of general education a few years ago. As in that effort, when the late Ron Edmonds argued that if some schools could be effective in the education of low-income and minority students, then others—with commitment—could do so

(Edmonds, 1979), the education of students labeled as handicapped can be made effective.

Summary

What is known about the education of students labeled as handicapped? We know that separate special education does not work. It does not function along any of the axes of appropriate assessment, such as pupil learning or development of self-confidence and social skills, preparation for the future as student, worker, or citizen. And its failure is costly in several currencies, in dollars, in public confidence, and, most importantly, in students' lives.

We know enough to go forward as has been described in earlier pages of this and previous chapters. We know that integrated programs work. We know that preparation for full lives can only occur in integrated settings.

Drawing upon his extensive study of factors affecting student achievement, Brophy (1986) states:

> [T]he settings in which compensatory education take place are not nearly as impor-
> tant determinants of outcomes as the amount and nature of the instruction that occurs
> within those settings. . . . [R]esearch has turned up very little evidence suggesting
> the need for qualitatively different forms of instruction for students who differ in
> aptitude, achievement level, socioeconomic status, ethnicity, or learning style. (pp.
> IV–122)

Succinctly, Hilliard (n.d.) says, "There is no special pedagogy for 'at-risk' students. The pedagogy that works for them is good for all students. Further, it is due to the fact that appropriate regular pedagogy was not provided to 'at-risk' students that they fail to achieve" (p. 4).

PUBLIC POLICY INITIATIVES

As we have noted earlier, the achievements of PL 94-142 have been consider-able. In barely a dozen years, major changes have occurred in the education of students labeled as handicapped. Their education is now seen as the appropriate responsibility of public education. Increasingly, they are being served in the public schools, the due process rights of parents are honored in most schools, and there has been little in the way of "backlash" as to the costs of such services. To argue for new legislation, built upon a new paradigm, is not to gainsay these achievements.

The present period is one of heightened scrutiny and concern about special education. While not often included in the debate about educational reform, the education of students labeled as handicapped is likely to be a major agenda item in the coming years. What follows are some proposals for inclusion in that forthcoming debate.

First, the interests of students labeled as handicapped must be incorporated into the broad debate on educational reform. A part of this is to examine the extent to which the labeling and consequent separation of these students is warranted. More broadly, it is to challenge the premise of much of that debate: that the purpose of school reform is to pick and promote "winners" rather than to nurture and educate all students.

Second, the quality of education provided to students in current special education programs must be scrutinized with greater care. And the focus of the scrutiny must be on outcomes for students. This must be done despite the fears of some that the findings will be dismal and may threaten hard won current programs. Indeed, the presence of this fear is all the more reason to undertake such scrutiny. The scarce resources of public funds and trust, and most importantly student needs, demand no less.

Third, building upon the "rights without labels" formulation described earlier, the yoking of funding and program services to the categorization of students serves no educational function. Similarly, the debate needs to be shifted from concerns about placement to a concern for quality in academic and social learning, preparation for work, and participation in community life and citizenship. This involves identifying and promoting effective practices. Given the knowledge base being developed, there is little continuing justification for the perpetuation of practices that are not effective, especially those that offer limited opportunities based upon pernicious notions of the limited capacities of students labeled as handicapped.

Fourth, given the development of successful educational models of effective unitary designs, serious consideration must be given to a new formulation of what a "free appropriate public education" means. Thomas Gilhool, then a lawyer at the Public Interest Law Center of Philadelphia (and now Secretary of Education, Commonwealth of Pennsylvania), put forward what he called the "developmental twin" argument. "If a child with a particular type of disability can be successfully integrated, with special services in a regular class or school, then why can't all children with the same type and level of disability also be integrated?" (Gilhool, 1976, p. 13). There are now, more than 10 years after Gilhool posed this question, enough examples of quality and integration for all students for his challenge to be answered with commitment and action.

Finally, it is now time to reshape PL 94-142 into a "new" appropriate vehicle for the future: one that focuses less on procedures and more on outcomes, one that challenges and rejects the dual system approach, and one that requires a unitary system, that is "special" for all students. It is time to shape its successor into an effective schools act for all students.

FORCES FOR CHANGE

In *Board of Education v. Rowley* (1982), the Supreme Court held that a school district satisfied its Education for the Handicapped Act mandate to provide a free appropriate public education:

if it provided personalized instruction and services that were reasonably calculated to bring about educational benefit and if all the [Act's] procedural provisions were adhered to in formulating the child's Individualized Education Program (IEP). The Court further stated that the service provided . . . must meet the state's educational standards. Additionally, for those students who received the majority of instruction in the regular classroom, the instruction provided was to be sufficient to allow the students to earn passing grades and be promoted annually. (Osborne, 1988, p. 22)

While this ruling was a victory in upholding the law in general, the Supreme Court overturned the lower court's ruling that the schools were required to maximize the potential of each child with a handicap commensurate with the opportunity provided to nonhandicapped students. The decision itself offers guidance in the effort to challenge this circumscription of opportunity. The reference to state educational standards, as Thomas Gilhool points out (see Chapter 13, this volume), is an avenue toward higher standards. The reference to a higher standard for those students in regular classes—passing grades and annual promotion—is a mixed matter. It is an opportunity in general but tricky in reality given the grading practices used for students labeled as handicapped in mainstreamed classes (see earlier discussion).

The larger question, however, is not the court's reading of PL 94-142. Assuming it is correct, if the results are not what is desired, then the *Rowley* decision need not be the last word. A new law, with new standards, can be proposed and enacted. Indeed, there is a recent, if small, example of this. In *Smith v. Robinson*, 104 S. Ct. 3457 (1984), the Supreme Court ruled that the Education of the Handicapped Act (ECHA) was the sole source of attorney's fees for parents who had prevailed in a special education suit. Disagreeing with this outcome, the Congress in 1986 passed the Handicapped Children's Protection Act (HCPA), PL 99-372, "which had the effect of reversing the Supreme Court's *Smith* decision, the HCPA amended the ECHA to indicate that nothing within the Act was to be used to limit a handicapped student's right to seek redress under other federal statutes or the U.S. Constitution" (Osborne, 1988, p. 24).

The systems established in compliance with PL 94-142 have not succeeded. In a series of essays concerning the use of the then new IQ tests to measure officer candidates for World War I, Walter Lippman wrote of his fear that these tests would be used to label children as inferior, and, thus, to consign them to a second-class life. In comments almost prescient in terms of what has occurred under PL 94-142, he said:

It is not possible, I think, to imagine a more contemptible proceeding than to confront a child with a set of puzzles, and after an hour's monkeying with them, proclaim to the child, or to his parents, that here is a C-minus individual. It would not only be a contemptible thing to do. It would be a crazy thing to do. . . . (Granger & Granger, 1986, p. v.)

But, of course, this is what we now do, and, per *Rowley,* "a C-minus" is a passing grade.

Speaking of the turmoil created in a high school characterized by "the wrongs of racial discrimination and segregation and the treatment of the handicapped" and its efforts to reform, Albert Shanker (1988) points out that "a school is . . . a moral community . . . [which cannot] be 'good' for only a small, privileged handful at the expense of discriminating against or excluding many others" (p. E7).

A community, indeed a "moral community," is the result of human choice. Persons with disabilities can be full participants in a community, as friends, neighbors, workers, citizens, and family members. Based upon the experience on Martha's Vineyard in the eighteenth and nineteenth centuries, when it was the home of the highest concentration in the United States of people who were deaf, Groce (1985) wrote:

> The fact that a society could adjust to disabled individuals, rather than requiring them to do all the adjusting, as in the case in American society as a whole, raises important questions about the rights of the disabled and the responsibilities of those who are not. The Martha's Vineyard experience suggests strongly that the concept of a handicap is an arbitrary social category. And if it is a question of definition, rather than a universal given, perhaps it can be redefined, and many of the cultural preconceptions summarized in the term 'handicapped,' as it is now used, eliminated.
>
> The most important lesson to be learned from Martha's Vineyard is that disabled people can be full and useful members of a community if the community makes an effort to include them. (p. 27)

What can be done to shape an educational system that includes all students, including those with disabilities, and is both consonant with and builds toward an inclusive society? Clearly, it is not done by taking students from the regular education setting, labeling them as "deficient," and offering them a separate, second-class program. Rather than becoming dead ends where goals have been dropped altogether, special programs—for those labeled as handicapped, and increasing numbers of others—school organizations can be developed to adapt "instruction to individual differences to maximize common goal attainment" (Snow, 1984, p. 13).

At least four sets of interrelated factors conduce toward the achievement of this goal: broad social and economic factors, the disability rights struggle, parents' involvement, and the school reform movement. While each of these are topics that have been discussed earlier, they are summarized below.

The American economy needs a well-educated work force, and the demographics of the future make it clear that this cannot be achieved if large portions of our population are discarded.

Persons with disabilities are increasingly asserting their entitlement to a full place in society.

Growing numbers of advocates and parents with children labeled as handicapped are recognizing that the PL 94-142 achievement of access to a separate system is not an adequate preparation for a full life.

The most recent school reform efforts manifest concern for the full range of students and demonstrate the capacity to effectively educate all students together.

The ultimate rationale for quality education of students in an integrated setting is based not only on economics, law, or pedagogy, but also on values. What values do we honor? What kind of people are we? What kind of society do we wish to build, for ourselves and for all of our children? The current failure to provide quality education to all students, and the perpetuation of segregated settings is morally unsound and educationally unnecessary. We can do things differently, in Ron Edmonds's (1979) words, depending "on how we feel about the fact that we haven't done it so far" (p. 29).

REFERENCES

Affleck, J.Q., Madge, S., Adams, A., & Lowenbraum, S. (1988). Integrated classrooms versus resource model: Academic viability and effectiveness. *Exceptional Children, 54* (4), 339–348.

Alberg, J.Y., Pyecha, J.N., Schulte, S.T., Hocutt, A.M., Yin, R.K., & Scott, A. (1988). *A case study of the application of noncategorical special education in two states.* Research Triangle Park, NC: Research Triangle Institute.

Algozzine, B., & Mahcady, L. (1985). When all else fails, teach! *Exceptional Children, 52,* 16–22.

An imperiled generation: Saving urban schools. (1988). Princeton, NJ: The Carnegie Foundation for the Advancement of Teaching.

Asch, A. (1984). Personal reflections. *American Psychologist, 39,* 551–552.

Baker, M.J., & Salon, R.S. (1986). Setting free the captives: The power of community integration in liberating institutionalized adults from the bonds of their past. *Journal of The Association for Persons with Severe Handicaps, 11*(3), 176–181.

Berres, M.S., & Knoblock, P. (Eds.). (1987). *Program models for mainstreaming: Integrating students with moderate to severe disabilities.* Rockville, MD: Aspen Publishers.

Bickel, W.E., & Bickel, D.D. (1986). Effective schools, classrooms, and instruction: Implications for special education. *Exceptional Children, 52*(6), 489–500.

Biklen, D. (1985). *Achieving the complete school: Strategies for effective mainstreaming.* New York: Teachers College Press.

Biklen, D. (1987). In pursuit of integration. In M.S. Berres & P. Knoblock (Eds.), *Program models for mainstreaming: Integrating students with moderate to severe disabilities* (pp. 19–39). Rockville, MD: Aspen Publishers.

Biklen, D. (in press). The culture of poverty: Disabling images in literature and their analogies in public policy. *Public Policy Journal.*

Biklen, D., Lehr, S., Searl, S.J., & Taylor, S.J. (1987). *Purposeful integration . . . Inherently equal.* Boston: Technical Assistance for Parent Programs.

Blankenship, C.S., & Jordan, L. (Eds.). (1985). [Special Issue]. *Teacher education and special education, 8*(3).

Board of Education v. Rowley, 102 S. Ct. 3034. (1982).

Bogdan, R., & Kugelmass, J. (1984). Case studies of mainstreaming: A symbolic interactionist approach to special schooling. In L. Barton & S. Tomlinson (Eds.), *Special education and social interests* (pp. 83–97). London: Croom-Helm.

Brophy, J.B. (1986). Research linking teacher behavior to student achievement. In B.I. Williams, P. A. Richmond, & B.J. Mason (Eds.), *Designs for compensatory education: Conference proceedings and papers* (IV, pp. 121–179). Washington, DC: Research and Evaluation Associates.

Brown, A.L., & Campione, J.C. (1986). Psychological theory and the study of learning disabilities. *American Psychologist, 41*(10), 1059–1068.

Brown, L., Ford, A., Nisbet, J., Sweet, M., Donnilhan, A., & Gruenewald, L. (1983). Opportunities available when severely handicapped students attend age appropriate regular schools. *Journal of The Association for the Severely Handicapped, 8*(1), 16–24.

Canter, A., Dawson, P., Silverstein, J., Hale, L., & Zins, J. (1987). *NASP directory of alternative service delivery models*. Washington, DC: National Association of School Psychologists.

Children in need: Investment strategies for the educationally disadvantaged. (1987). New York: Committee for Economic Development.

DeJong, G., & Lifchez, R. (1983). Physical disability and public policy. *Scientific American, 248*, 40–49.

Deno, E. (1970). Special education as developmental capital. *Exceptional Children, 37*, 229–237.

Disabled students call for "flexible but tough" teachers. (1988, May 6). *Education Daily*, p. 5.

Edmonds, R. (1979). Some schools work and more can. *Social Policy, 9*(5), 26–31.

Edmonds, R. (1982). Programs of school improvement: An overview. *Educational Leadership, 40*(3), 4–11.

Educating students with learning problems. (1986). Washington, DC: Office of Special Education and Rehabilitative Services, U.S. Department of Education.

Elements of a model state statute to provide educational entitlements for at-risk students. (1987). Washington, DC: Council of Chief State School Officers.

Epps, S., & Tindal, G. (1987). The effectiveness of differential programming in serving students with mild handicaps: Placement options and instructional programming. In M.C. Wang, M.C. Reynolds, & H.J. Walberg (Eds.), *Handbook of special education research and practice: Vol. 1, Learner Characteristics and Adaptive Education* (pp. 213–248). New York: Pergamon Press.

Ferguson, P.M., & Asch, A. (in press). What we want for children: Perspectives of parents and adults with disabilities. In D. Biklen, P.M. Ferguson, & A. Ford (Eds.), *Schooling and disability*. Chicago: National Society for the Study of Education.

Ferguson, P.M., & Ferguson, D.C. (in press). Parents and professionals. In P. Knoblock (Ed.), *Introduction to special education*. Boston: Little, Brown.

Fine, M., & Asch, A. (1988). Disability beyond stigma: Social interaction, discrimination, and activism. *Journal of Social Issues, 44*(1), 3–22.

Fiske, E.B. (1988, May 24). In Indiana, public school makes "frills" standard. *New York Times*, p. A16.

Funk, R. (1987). Disability rights: From caste to class in the context of civil rights. In A. Gartner & T. Joe (Eds.), *Images of the disabled/disabling images* (pp. 7–30). New York: Praeger.

Gartner, A. (1988, April). *Tutoring, what works: Why and how*. A paper presented at the Council for Exceptional Children, Washington, DC.

Gartner, A., & Joe, T. (Eds.). (1987). *Images of the disabled/disabling images*. New York: Praeger.

Gartner, A., & Lipsky, D.K. (1987). Beyond special education: Toward a quality system for all students. *Harvard Educational Review, 57*(4), 367–395.

Gerber, M.M. (1988). Weighing the "Regular-Education Initiative." *Education Week, 7* (32), 28, 36.

Gilhool, T.K. (1976). Changing public policies: Roots and forces. In M.C. Reynolds (Ed.), *Mainstreaming: Origins and implications* (pp. 8–13). Reston, VA: Council for Exceptional Children.

Glatthorn, A. (1987). How do you adapt the curriculum to respond to individual differences? In A. Glatthorn (Ed.), *Curriculum renewal* (pp. 99–109). Alexandria, VA: Association for Supervision and Curriculum Development.

Gliedman, W., & Roth, W. (1980). *The unexpected minority: Handicapped children in America.* New York: Harcourt Brace Jovanovich.

Goffman, E. (1963). *Stigma: Notes on management of spoiled identities.* Englewood Cliffs, NJ: Prentice-Hall.

Gold, D.L. (1988). Firm to fund model school in Minneapolis. *Education Week, 7*(24), 8.

Goodlad, J.I., & Oakes, J. (1988). We must offer equal access to knowledge. *Educational Leadership, 45*(5), 16–22.

Goodman, L. (1985). The effective schools movement and special education. *Teaching Exceptional Children, 17,* 102–105.

Granger, L., & Granger, B. (1986). *The Magic Feather.* New York: E.P. Dutton.

Groce, N.E. (1985). *Everyone here spoke sign language: Hereditary deafness on Martha's Vineyard.* Cambridge, MA: Harvard University Press.

Guess, D., Benson, H.A., & Siegel-Causey, E. (1985). Concepts and issues related to choice-making and autonomy among persons with severe disabilities. *Journal of The Association for Persons with Severe Handicaps, 10*(2), 79–86.

Guess, D., & Thompson, B. (in press). Preparation of personnel to educate students with severe and multiple disabilities: A time for change? In L. Meyer, C. Peck, & L. Brown (Eds.), *Critical issues in the lives of people with severe disabilities.*

Hedin, D. (1986). *Students as teachers: A tool for improving school climate and productivity.* A paper prepared for the Task Force on Teaching as a Profession, Carnegie Forum on Education and the Economy.

Heller, K.A., Holtzman, W.H., & Messick, S. (Eds.). (1982). *Placing children in special education: A strategy for equity.* Washington, DC: National Academy Press.

Hilliard, A.G. (n.d.). *Public support for successful instructional practices for "at risk" students.* Unpublished manuscript.

Honetschlager, D., & Cohen, M. (1988). The governors restructure schools. *Educational Leadership, 45*(5), 42–43.

Huefner, D.S. (1988). The counseling teacher model: Risks and opportunities. *Exceptional Children, 54*(5), 403–414.

Idol, L. (1986). *Collaborative school consultation.* Reston, VA: The Council for Exceptional Children.

Jenkins, J.R., & Jenkins, L.M. (1981). *Cross-Age and peer tutoring: Help for children with learning problems.* Reston, VA: The Council for Exceptional Children.

Jernigan, K. (1988). Handicapped parking permits for the blind. *The Braille Monitor,* 12–14.

Jewell, J. (1985). One school's search for excellence. *Teaching Exceptional Children, 17,* 140–144.

Kauffman, J.M., Lloyd, J.W., & McKinney, J.D. (Eds.). (1988). [Special Issue]. *Journal of Learning Disabilities, 21*(1).

Knoll, J., & Meyer, L. (n.d.). *Principles and practices for school integration of students with severe disabilities: An overview of the literature.* Syracuse, NY: Center on Human Policy.

Kuhn, T.S. (Ed.). (1962). *The structure of scientific revolutions.* Chicago: University of Chicago Press.

Levin, H.M. (1984). *Costs and cost-effectiveness of computer-assisted instruction.* Stanford, CA: California Institute for Research on Educational Finance and Governance.

Lilly, M.S. (1987). Lack of focus on special education in literature on school reform. *Exceptional Children, 53*(4), 325–326.

Lipsky, D.K. (1985). A parental perspective on stress and coping. *American Journal of Orthopsychiatry, 55*(4), 614–617.

Lipsky, D.K., & Gartner, A. (1987). Capable of achievement and worthy of respect: Education for the handicapped as if they were full-fledged human beings. *Exceptional Children, 54*(1), 69–74.

Lloyd, J.W. (1984). How shall we individualize instruction—or should we? *Remedial and Special Education, 5*(1), 7–15.

Louis Harris & Associates. (1986). *Disabled Americans' self-perceptions: Bringing disabled Americans into the mainstream.* New York: Author.

Mehta, V. (1985). Personal history. *New Yorker,* p. 60.

Meyer, L.H., Eichenger, J., & Park-Lee, S. (1987). A validation of program quality indicators in educational services for students with severe disabilities. *Journal of The Association for Persons with Severe Handicaps, 12*(4), 251–263.

Mishal, R.J., & Trippi, J.A. (1987, Fall). Grading mainstreamed handicapped pupils: Parental and educators' views. *CASE Newsletter,* p. 4.

National Council on the Handicapped. (1986). *Toward Independence: A Report to the President and to the Congress.* Washington, DC: The National Council on the Handicapped.

Olson, L. (1988). A Seattle principal defies the conventional wisdom. *Education Week, 7* (29), 1, 22.

On cases of contagion. (1987, March 4). *New York Times,* p. A21.

Osborne, A.G., Jr. (1988). The Supreme Court's interpretation of the education for all handicapped children act. *Remedial and Special Education, 9*(3), 21–25.

Osguthorpe, R.T., & Scruggs, T.E. (1986). Special education students as tutors: A review and analysis. *Remedial and Special Education, 7*(4), 15–26.

Peterson, D., Albert, S.S., Foxworth, A.M., Cox, L.S., & Tilley, B.K. (1985). Effective schools for all students: Current efforts and future directions. *Teaching Exceptional Children, 17,* 106–110.

PL 94-142, *the Education for All Handicapped Children Act,* 1975.

PL 99-372, *the Handicapped Children's Protection Act,* 1986.

Poll results: Interest high, vote total low. (1988). *New York State Advocate, 11*(4), pp. 1, 7.

Pugach, M., & Sapon-Shevin, M. (1987). New agendas for special education policy: What the national reports haven't said. *Exceptional Children, 53*(4), 295–299.

Renewed debate: Which Pennsylvania agencies are responsible for EHA, 504? (1988, February 18). *Education Daily,* pp. 3–4.

Report of the United Nations Expert Group meeting on barrier-free design. (1975). *Rehabilitation Review, 26.*

Research on the effectiveness of mainstreaming. (1987). Reston, VA: ERIC Clearinghouse on Handicapped and Gifted Children.

Reynolds, M.C. (1962). A framework for considering some issues in special education. *Exceptional Children, 28,* 367–370.

Reynolds, M.C., & Lakin, K.C. (1987). Noncategorical special education: Models for research and practice. In M.C. Wang, M.C. Reynolds, & H.J. Walberg (Eds.),

Handbook of special education research and practice: Vol. 1, Learner Characteristics and Adaptive Education (pp. 331–356). New York: Pergamon Press.

Ringlaben, R.P., & Weller, C. (1981). Mainstreaming the special educator. *Education Unlimited, 3*(4), 19–21.

Rosenberg, M.S., & Jackson, L. (1988). Theoretical models and special education: The impact of varying world views on service delivery and research. *Remedial and Special Education, 9*(3), 26–34.

Sansone, J., & Zigmond, N. (1986). Evaluating mainstreaming through an evaluation of students' schedules. *Exceptional Children, 52*(5), 452–458.

Sapon-Shevin, M. (1987). The national excellence reports and special education: Implication for students. *Exceptional Children, 53*(4), 300–307.

Sarason, S.B. (1982). *The Culture of the School and the problem of change.* Boston: Allyn & Bacon.

Sarason, S.B., & Doris, J. (1979). *Educational handicap, public policy, and social history.* New York: Free Press.

School psychology: A blueprint for training and practice. (1984). Minneapolis, MN: National School Psychology Inservice Training Network.

Scotch, R.K. (1988). Disability as the basis for a social movement: Advocacy and the politics of definition. *Journal of Social Issues, 44*(1), 159–172.

Shanker, A. (1988, June 11). Doing right wrong: The lesson of Hamilton High. *New York Times,* p. E7.

Shepard, L.A. (1987). The new push for excellence: Widening the schism between regular and general education. *Exceptional Children, 53*(4), 327–329.

Skrtic, T. (1986). The crisis in special education knowledge: A perspective on perspective. *Focus on Exceptional Children, 18*(7), 1–16.

Skrtic, T. (1987). *Prenuptual agreements necessary for wedding special education and general education.* Paper presented to the American Education and Research Association, Washington, DC.

Slavin, R.E. (1986). Learning together. *American Educator,* 6–13.

Slavin, R.E. (1987). Cooperative learning and the cooperative schools. *Educational Leadership, 45*(3), 7–13.

Slavin, R.E., Stevens, R.J., & Madden, N.A. (1988). Accommodating student diversity in reading and writing instruction: A cooperative learning approach. *Remedial and Special Education, 9*(1), 60–66.

Smith v. Robinson, 104 S. Ct. 3457 (1984).

Snider, W. (1988a). New technology seen as charting 2 U.S. "Futures." *Education Week, 7*(34), 1, 16.

Snider, W. (1988b). "Small changes" won't do, says California panel. *Education Week, 7*(37), 1, 12.

Snow, R.E. (1984). Placing children in special education: Some comments. *Educational Researcher, 13,* 12–15.

Special ed students kept in restrictive environments, disability groups say. (1986, October 29). *Education of the Handicapped,* pp. 5–6.

Special education: Views from America's cities. (1986). Washington, DC: The Council of Great City Schools.

Stainback, W., & Stainback, S. (1984). A rationale for the merger of special and regular education. *Exceptional Children, 51*(2), 102–111.

Stainback, S., Stainback, W., & Forest, M. (Eds.). (in press). *Educating All Students in the Mainstream of Regular Education.* Baltimore: Paul H. Brookes Publishing Co.

Stevens, R.J., Madden, N.A., Slavin, R.E., & Farnish, A.M. (1987). Cooperative integrated reading and comprehension. *Reading Research Quarterly, 22*(4), 433–453.

Strain, P. (Ed.). (1981). *The utilization of classroom peers as behavior change agents.* New York: Plenum.

Taylor, S.J. (1988). Caught in the continuum: A critical analysis of the principle of least restrictive environment. *Journal of The Association for Persons with Severe Handicaps, 13*(1), 41–53.

Turnbull, H.R. III. (1981). *Least restrictive alternatives: Principles and practices.* Washington, DC: American Association on Mental Deficiency.

Turnbull, H.R. III, & Turnbull, A.P. (Eds.). (1985). *Parents speak out: Then and now* (2nd ed.). Springfield, OH: Charles C. Merrill.

U.S. Congress, Office of Technology Assessment. (1988). *Technology and the American economic transition: Choices for the future.* Washington, DC: U.S. Government Printing Office.

U.S. Department of Education. (1986). *What works: Research about teaching and learning.* Washington, DC: Author.

Viadero, D. (1988). Researchers' critique escalates the debate over "Regular Education" for all students. *Education Week, 7*(28), 20.

Vickery, T.R. (1988). Learning from an outcomes-driven district. *Educational Leadership, 45*(5), 52–56.

Wang, M.C. (1988). Weighing the "Regular-Education Initiative." *Education Week, 7* (32), 28, 36.

Wang, M.C., & Reynolds, M.C. (1985). Avoiding the "Catch 22" in special education reform. *Exceptional Children, 51,* 497–502.

Wang, M.C., Reynolds, M.C., & Walberg, H.J. (1987a). *Repairing the second system for students with special needs.* Paper presented at the 1987 Wingspread Conference on the Education of Children with Special Needs.

Wang, M.C., Reynolds, M.C., & Walberg, H.J. (Eds.). (1987b). *Handbook of special education research and practice: Vol. 1, Learning Characteristics and Adaptive Education.* New York: Pergamon Press.

Wang, M.C., & Walberg, H.J. (1988). Four fallacies of segregationism. *Exceptional Children, 55*(2), 128–137.

Who Reads Best? (1988). Princeton, NJ: Educational Testing Service.

Wiggins, G. (1988). Ten "radical" suggestions for school reform. *Education Week, 7* (24), 28, 20.

Wood, S., MacDonald, M., & Siegelman, L. (1987). Seriously behaviorally disabled children in the mainstream. In M.S. Berres & P. Knoblock (Eds.), *Program models for mainstreaming: Integrating students with moderate to severe disabilities.* Rockville, MD: Aspen Publishers.

Zigmond, N., Levin, E., & Laurie, T.E. (1985). Managing the mainstream: An analysis of teacher attitudes and student performance in mainstream high school programs. Unpublished manuscript.

Index

Academic life, students' comments on, 183–190
  see also Student reports of experience
Access
  right of, to public education programs, 4
  see also Programs for educational accessibility (PEAs)
Accommodation to disability, *see* Adaptation(s)
Accountability model, 93–94
Accreditation agencies, regional, 35
Achievement
  reporting of, 46
  statewide testing of, handicapped students' exclusion from, 87–88
  see also Student outcomes
Activities, after-school, 191–193
Adaptation(s)
  inclusion and, 203
  patronization versus, 184–187, 203
  unobtrusive implementation of, 219–220
Adaptive instruction, 45, 99–114
  description of, 100–102
  effective, characteristics of, 108–109, 112–113
  research base on, 102–107
  see also Educational reform
Adaptive instruction cycle, 109, 112–113
Adaptive Learning Environment Model (ALEM), 272–273
Adolescent children, parents of, 168
Age-appropriate environments, 59, 69
Agencies, and local school development, 34–35
Aides, one-to-one, 187

ALEM (Adaptive Learning Environment Model), 272–273
Alternative programs, 237–240, 267–269
American Federation of the Physically Handicapped, 238
Amy Rowley, court case of, 249–250, 282–283
Appropriate education
  Amy Rowley case and, 249–250
  state school codes and, 250–252
ARC-US (Association for Retarded Citizens), 236
Assertiveness, and friendships with nondisabled classmates, 198–199
Assessment, 12–13
  adaptations in, integration and, 45–47
  in adaptive instruction cycle, 112–113
  classification systems and, inadequacy of, 123
  multiple intelligence theory and, 127–128
  in Project Spectrum, 129–130
  special education implications of, 131–133
  for students with physical or sensory disabilities, 186–187
Association for Retarded Citizens (ARC-US), 236
Assumption(s)
  about disability, individualization of services and, 5
  that separation is not needed, 5
  see also Attitudes
"At-risk" students, 266
Attitudes
  disabling, 256–258, 260
  special education and, 258–260

291

in transition phase, 69
see also Parent(s)
Family life, changing patterns of,
162–164
Family member training, 171
Family support systems, 170–173
Father(s)
involvement of, 164
see also Parent(s)
Federal aid, *see* Funding
Federal influences, on instructional
support program design, 85–86
Financial assistance, 171
see also Funding
Florida School Code, 251
Foreign countries, integration efforts in,
275
Friends, special, 66
Friendships
among people with disabilities, 200–
201
formation of, disabled students'
comments on, 193–195
with nondisabled classmates, 195–200
among students in integrated classes,
216–217
see also Relationships
Functional limitations model, 225
minority group paradigm versus,
228–230
Funding
and "overclassification" of students as
handicapped, 88
problems related to, 10
transition phase and, 69
Future considerations, 255–285
autonomy enhancement, 260–264
disabling attitudes and, 256–258
special education and, 258–260
for educational reform, 264–281
see also Educational reform
forces for change and, 282–285
public policy initiatives and, 281–282

General education initiative, 271–272
see also Regular education initiative
Generalization
community intensive instruction and,
67
social interaction and, 58

for students with severe disabilities,
56, 58
Graded structure, of regular education
programs, 47–48
Great Britain's Family Fund, 172–173
Group planning, integration and, 220
Guilt, in family response, 165

Handicap(s), *see* Disability; Mild
handicaps, persons with; Moderate
handicaps, persons with; Severe
handicaps, persons with
Handicapped Children's Early Education
Projects, 170
Hearing impairments, students with,
185–186
preferences of, mainstreaming and, 189
High school, and transition phase of CLS
model, 68–70
"Homecoming Model," 276
Horizontal interactions, 65–66
House of Representatives Select
Committee on Children, Youth,
and Families, 163
Housing assistance services, 171
Human service practice, deficit model in,
261

ICM (Integrated Classroom Model), 273
ICSC (International Congress on School
Effectiveness), 36
Identity, self-concept and, 237–238, 239
IEP, *see* Individualized education
program
IFSP (Individualized Family Service
Plan), 170
Individualization of services, 5
Individualized education program (IEP),
86, 189–190, 203
parents and, 166–168
student participation and, 189
Individualized Family Service Plan
(IFSP), 170
Individualized programming, 45
see also Adaptive instruction; MI-
theory (of multiple intelligence)
Individualized school, role of teacher in,
135–137
Individualized transition plan (ITP), 67